# Red-Tape

AND

# PIGEON-HOLE GENERALS

★ ★ ★

# Andrew A. Humphreys

IN THE

# ARMY OF THE POTOMAC

COMMENTARY
BY
FREDERICK B. ARNER

Rockbridge Publishing
an imprint of
HOWELL PRESS, INC.
Charlottesville, Virginia

Published by
Rockbridge Publishing
*an imprint of*
HOWELL PRESS, INC.
1713-2D Allied Lane • Charlottesville, VA 22903
Telephone: 804-977-4006 • http://www.howellpress.com
*A Katherine Tennery Book*

**Photographic credits:** Fred Arner: 5, 10, 127, 357; Historical Society of Pennsylvania: 133; John Jay Library, Brown University: dust jacket, from a drawing by J. G. Keyser; Library of Congress: 4, 15, 23, 24, 57, 152, 182, 183, 196, 197, 264, 265, 324, 354; National Archives: 12, 18, 51, 88, 185; USAMHI: 13, 33, 45; USAMHI (MOLLUS): xxii; USAMHI (Ronn Palm Collection): xv, 16, 104

**Publishing History:** *Red-Tape and Pigeon-Hole Generals: As Seen from the Ranks During a Campaign in the Army of the Potomac* was published anonymously by Carleton of New York in 1864.

**Library of Congress Cataloging-in-Publication Data**
Armstrong, William H. (William Henry), 1833-1896.
    Red-tape and pigeon-hole generals : Andrew A. Humphreys in the Army of the
  Potomac / by a citizen-soldier : commentary by Frederick B. Arner. — 1st ed.
        p.        cm.
    Originally published : New York : Carleton, 1864.
    Includes bibliographical references (p.    ) and index.
    ISBN 1-883522-15-3
     1. Humphreys, A. A. (Andrew Atkinson), 1810-1883—Military leadership.
  2. Humphreys, A. A. (Andrew Atkinson), 1810-1883—Ethics. 3. United States.
  Army of the Potomac—Management. 4. United States. Army of the Potomac—
  Military life. 5. United States. Army of the Potomac—Biography. 6. Military
  ethics—United States—History—19th century. 7. United States. Army.
  Pennsylvania Infantry Regiment, 129th (1862-1863) 8. United States—
  History—Civil War, 1861-1865—Regimental histories. 9. Pennsylvania—
  History—Civil War, 1861-1865—Regimental histories. I. Arner, Frederick B.
  II. Title. III. Title: Red-tape.
  E467.1.H885A74  1998
  973.7'448—dc21

                                                    97-47436
                                                      CIP

10  9  8  7  6  5  4  3  2  1
First edition
Printed in Canada

# Table of Contents

## RED-TAPE AND PIGEON–HOLE GENERALS

### CHAPTER I.

### CHAPTER II.

### CHAPTER III.

### CHAPTER IV.

CHAPTER X.

CHAPTER XI.

CHAPTER XII.

CHAPTER XIII.

CHAPTER XIV.

## CHAPTER XXI.

## COMMENTARY

## MAPS

# Foreword

For the better part of the last 133 years the book you are about to read lay on the library shelves mislabeled as fiction, wrongly attributed to a hack nineteenth-century novelist, and largely ignored or overlooked by historians. Rescued from obscurity by the persistence of Fred Arner, *Red-Tape and Pigeon-Hole Generals*, written by Lt. Col. William H. Armstrong, presents a fresh, from-the-ranks regimental history of men and boys who volunteered to fight for the Union when the war was growing increasingly unpopular in the North. It offers a lively, biting commentary on the consequences of the unlikely pairing of these 'citizen soldiers' with their division commander, Andrew Atkinson Humphreys, a regular army officer who had never before held combat command and whose capricious penchant for strangling the requests and requisitions of his men in endless tangles of red tape earned him the epithet "pigeon-hole general." *Red-Tape* paints a vivid portrait, by turns comic and heartrending, of the trials and horrors these men faced in the nine short yet brutal months of their enlistment.

Primarily, *Red-Tape* is the story of the 129th Pennsylvania Volunteer Infantry. Formed in response to Lincoln's call for fresh volunteers in the summer of 1862, the 129th was recruited in the hard coal regions of northeastern Pennsylvania and in small towns and rural areas outside Philadelphia; the recruits were mine laborers and merchants, store clerks and farmhands. By late summer the easy enthusiasm that had fired Northern enlistments after Fort Sumter had dimmed nearly to the point of extinguishment. Numbed by the long casualty lists from McClellan's failed Peninsula Campaign, few Federals continued to harbor illusions that the war would be short, glorious, and relatively bloodless. Pennsylvania's mining communities had already sent a fair share of their men to bleed on the eastern battlefields and were increasingly uncomfortable about making additional sacrifices for a struggle that seemed to be losing its central conservative focus on preserving the Union and expanding its efforts to encompass a radical aim of dubious value to these largely Democratic strongholds—the eradication of Negro slavery.

It took courage, therefore, for the volunteers of the 129th to buck the conventions of their community and shoulder arms in the Union army. The company and field grade officers of the regiment were for the most part Republicans, believers in a hard war against the South and unopposed in principle to the idea of emancipation as a measure to speed the end of the war. As Mr. Arner notes in his perceptive commentary, such views put the leadership of the 129th at odds with much of the professional military that dominated the upper ranks of the Army of the Potomac and contributed to the almost immediate friction that developed between the officers of the regiment and its division commander, a tension that permeates the pages of *Red-Tape*.

Andrew Humphreys has come down to us as an almost mythical figure, a real 'fighting general' of the Army of the Potomac. The *Civil War Book of Lists* grades him as among the "ten best Union officers," and a recent ruminative book on Gettysburg lauds the man as "courageous, skillful, intelligent . . . a man to depend on with your life, or to go fishing with." A measure of Humphreys's military esteem—something he and his intimates calculatingly cultivated after and even during the war—can be found in the number of monuments to him that dot the battlefield parks. At Fredericksburg, his statue stands solemnly atop Marye's Heights at the center of the National Cemetery; at Gettysburg he poses confidently in bronze astride the Emmitsburg Road. William Armstrong's *Red-Tape* and Fred Arner's essay on "The Many Faces of Andrew A. Humphreys" together supply a healthy corrective to the hagiographic treatment the general has received from generations of historians. Although undeniably brave in battle, Humphreys is shown to be the worst sort of martinet and brutishly mean to his new troops, who fairly come to hate him. The men accord him precious little respect, which enrages the general all the more. And, as *Red-Tape* makes painfully clear, Humphreys's problems with the bottle apparently crossed into the realm of bona fide alcoholism.

With all of these impediments, it is a wonder that the regiment made it into battle at all, which makes its record of service all the more remarkable. Although its men were in uniform just nine months, the 129th packed a whole war's worth of experience into fewer than three awful and unforgettable hours of fighting at Fredericksburg. In the gloaming of a December day the regiment led a final, forlorn bayonet charge against the stone wall "with a spirit and determination," wrote Fighting Joe Hooker, "seldom, if ever, equaled in war." The 129th lost a full third of its number in little more than ten minutes' time.

At Chancellorsville the following May, just two weeks shy of its muster-out date, the regiment found itself trapped in a smoky wood, out of ammunition, outnumbered, and locked in bitter hand-to-hand fighting with swarming Confederate infantry. In two hours of struggle the 129th's colors were twice taken and retaken, and it suffered an additional forty-two casualties. Commenting on the Pennsylvanians' courage under fire, the regiment's brigade commander, Erastus Tyler, enthused, "No man ever saw cooler work on *field drill* than was done by this regiment."

While Armstrong's tale and Arner's carefully researched commentary bring alive these horrific moments in battle, the real value of this combined work lies in its illumination of the everyday struggles of the men of the 129th. It shows us the sad fate of 2d Lt. Edward Wertley, who takes his "everlasting furlough," slowly choking to death of typhoid fever in a squalid camp outside Falmouth, Virginia, the paperwork for his pass home hopelessly tied up in red tape. We see Capt. George Lawrence of Company A shot in the back at Fredericksburg while turning to exhort his men toward the stone wall; paralyzed and left to lie facedown in the cold mud, he was eventually dragged from the field and shipped to Washington, only to die in a hospital a few days into the new year. In contrast to the personal sacrifices of the troops, we are shown the petty bickering and feuding of the officers, the charges and courts-martial that arose from Humphreys's imperious order demanding dress coats for the soldiers, and we marvel that the officers and men of the 129th maintained the resolve to see their service through.

At a time when popular Civil War fiction masquerades as 'history,' it is fitting that *Red-Tape*, long miscast as fiction, has been resurrected to reveal hard and moving truths about the trials of one Union regiment.

Charles T. Joyce
Ardmore, Pennsylvania

# RED-TAPE

### AND

# PIGEON-HOLE GENERALS:

### AS SEEN FROM THE RANKS
#### DURING A

## Campaign in the Army of the Potomac.

#### BY

## A CITIZEN-SOLDIER.

"We must be brief when Traitors brave the Field."

### NEW YORK:

## Carleton, Publisher, 413 Broadway.

#### M DCCC LXIV.

*Facsimile of the original title page of* Red-Tape and Pigeon-Hole Generals.

## Introduction

*Red-Tape and Pigeon-Hole Generals* was written by Lt. Col. William H. Armstrong of the 129th Pennsylvania Volunteer Infantry to address some deficiencies he recognized in the operation of the Army of the Potomac. The young whistle-blower was just out of the service in 1864 when he published *Red-Tape* under the pseudonym 'A Citizen-Soldier.' He knowingly risked a libel action for his message, yet he also recognized that abuses within the system could not be addressed and corrected without first being exposed. "If [these words] lighten the toil of the humblest of our soldiers, or nerve anew the resolves of loyalty tempted to despair, the writer will have no reason to complain of labor lost," he tells us in his preface to the work (page xx). Unfortunately, the publication of *Red-Tape* does not seem to have triggered any significant outcry among the populace at the time.

An informal poll of about a dozen Civil War historians taken at the outset of this project revealed an almost universal lack of familiarity with the book. Frank O'Reilly, staff historian at the Fredericksburg-Spotsylvania National Battlefield Park, and Dr. Richard Sommers of the U.S. Army Military History Institute were exceptions. Author Bruce Catton referred to it in describing the battle of Fredericksburg in *Glory Road,* and Richard Sauers drew from it for his capsule history of the 129th in his book *Advance the Colors: Pennsylvania Civil War Battle Flags.*

That the book should have languished unrecognized for its insightful commentary is not surprising considering its mode of presentation.

Because its author and major characters were deliberately disguised, it has often been miscataloged. Allen Nivens, James I. Robertson Jr., and Bell Irvin Wiley in their *Civil War Books: A Critical Bibliography* declare it to be the work of Henry Morford, a novelist who wrote of the Civil War. They describe it as a "delightful denunciation of Federal commanders by a Federal private in the East; much of the book borders on satire." Armstrong would be chagrined to know that the Pennsylvania State Library at Harrisburg still catalogs his book under Morford's name.

Col. John Page Nicolson, who after the war collected an outstanding library of Civil War materials that now resides in the Huntington Library in California, understood the significance of the book. His catalog notes: "Autograph of Col. Armstrong reflects upon Gen. A. A. Humphreys and relates the service of the 129th Regt. Pa. Vols." Nicolson's collection contains an 1878 letter from Col. Jacob G. Frick referring Nicolson to *Red-Tape*, "which illustrates the eccentricities and habits of Gen. Humphreys which you can see by calling upon him." Frick was the commander of the 129th Pennsylvania Volunteer Infantry and as such was Armstrong's superior officer. An examination of the courts-martial records indicates that there was no love lost between Frick and Humphreys.

*Red-Tape* contains far more than merely a scathing attack on Humphreys's character and military ability. Included is a vivid, firsthand description of the violent history of the 129th and the Tyler brigade; the roles of the commanders of those units, Frick and Erastus B. Tyler, respectively; and their strange collision with Andrew Humphreys. Research materials on these effective and brave Union officers is scant; thus *Red-Tape* fills a long-standing void.

Armstrong's tale offers interesting vignettes about the camp life of a short-term Union regiment that present both civilian characters (the baker and the sutler) and military characters (the little Dutch doctor, the unhappy chaplain, and the little Irish Corporal; the latter offers his account of events involving the three-month First Pennsylvania Regiment). Interspersed throughout the book are poignant stories, such as those of the lieutenant "who took the everlasting furlough" and the fighting chaplain who prayed and bushwhacked with Gen. William Rosecrans in West Virginia. There is humor to be found in the description of the West Virginia captain "on a whiskey scent," the inebriated headquarters on the Mud March, the apple brandy caper, the impersonation of Gen. William Franklin at Snickers's Gap, and the explosive farewell to General Humphreys from the volunteers.

Armstrong characterizes Humphreys as a hyperactive, profane, and whiskey-loving martinet who "has no judgment"—far from the high view of him held by most Civil War historians and buffs today but supported to a substantial degree by other regimental historians, diarists, and letter writers. In *Three Years in the Army of the Potomac,* Capt. Henry Blake

*Lt. Col. William H. Armstrong, 129th Pennsylvania Volunteer Infantry.*

of the Eleventh Massachusetts Infantry includes Humphreys in a list of generals under whom he was "compelled" to serve. Blake's list of defective generals also includes Irvin McDowell, William B. Franklin, William H. French, and Joseph B. Carr.

Blake and Armstrong were idealistic young officers, each one a lawyer and stalwart Republican supporter of Abraham Lincoln; each responded to Lincoln's first call for volunteers in April 1861 and served with distinction as a line officer. Both men knew army justice well from having performed extensively as judge advocates as well as sitting as defendants in their own courts-martial. In the latter role each was convicted of purported crimes of a noncombatant and trivial nature. In

Blake's case the charges were brought in the context of an alleged mutiny described in detail in my earlier book, *The Mutiny at Brandy Station*. In Armstrong's case the charges were even more petty, as *Red-Tape* makes clear. Finally, each author, under a very thin veil of anonymity, had the courage to risk public censure and litigation by criticizing General Humphreys, a powerful and combative figure in the military establishment, at the height of the war.

The Armstrong and Blake books stand in stark contrast to the standard text on Humphreys, a flattering report published by his son and aide Henry H. Humphreys. The writings of another aide, Carswell McClellan, and those of the flamboyant historian and militia general J. Watts DePeyster are even more extravagant in their praise. During the war and afterward Humphreys fought with some success to have official reports changed if they presented him as a less-than-sterling character. Modern historians have tended to rely on these rather one-sided views of Humphreys; even today works that lionize him are being published.

An exception to the current writings favorable to Humphreys is *Rising Tide: The Great Mississippi Flood of 1927 and How It Changed America* by John M. Barry, published in 1997. Barry deals with Humphreys's role as an engineer in that catastrophe at considerable length. Although Barry appears not to have been acquainted with *Red-Tape* and the stormy relationship Humphreys had with his troops, *Rising Tide* supports Armstrong's description of some of the negative characteristics that Armstrong ascribes to the general.

Perhaps most historians have accepted the favorable portrayals of Andrew Humphreys and ignored the caustic commentaries of Blake and Armstrong because of some skepticism as to the objectivity and accuracy of a work the author of which is anonymous and in which units and personae are incorrect on their face. But, when the fictional wrapper is removed and *Red-Tape* is examined in depth, much insight is gained into the 129th, Humphreys, and the tension that existed between the officers of the volunteer regiments and the officers of the regular army in the Fifth Corps of the Army of the Potomac.

Charges of mutiny and treason were thrown about indiscriminately during the period that Humphreys headed the Third Division of the Fifth Corps, and the bruised egos and stubbornness of Humphreys and his detractors played an important role in the confrontations. Divergent political ideologies, views on slavery and the use of black troops, and opinions regarding the discipline and command of volunteer soldiers — very real issues, all of which contributed to tension between Humphreys and his soldiers—are revealed in *Red-Tape*.

Many of the characters in the book—Humphreys's staff, many officers and men of the 129th, and members of other Pennsylvania regiments—have been identified by researching official military records and other archives. The identities of some characters have not been ascertained; they may be fictional devices used to carry the narrative forward. Their stories, however, are consistent with those found in official records and a multitude of courts-martial transcripts. They have a ring of authenticity about them.

*Red-Tape*, then, offers a look at the Army of the Potomac from the point of view of a colonel who recognized deficiencies in its leadership and effectiveness and attempted to call attention to them in the only way available to him at the time. His observations do not carry the patina of time that softens the mettle of so many reminiscences but present a sometimes rollicking view of the way it was—and who made it that way.

## The Major Characters & Their Real-Life Counterparts

**The Division General, also called Old Pigey**—Brig. Gen. Andrew A. Humphreys, Commander, Third Division, Fifth Corps

**Division Adjutant General, also the sucker-mouthed aide**—Capt. Carswell McClellan

**Our Brigadier**—Brig. Gen. Erastus B. Tyler, Commander, First Brigade, Humphreys Division

**Colonel of the 210th**—Col. Jacob G. Frick, Commander, 129th Pennsylvania Volunteer Infantry

**Lieutenant Colonel of the 210th**—Lt. Col. William H. Armstrong of the 129th Pennsylvania Volunteer Infantry

**Major of the 210th**—Maj. Joseph Anthony of the 129th Pennsylvania Volunteer Infantry

**West Virginia Captain of the 210th**—Capt. David Eckar, Company F, 129th Pennsylvania Volunteer Infantry

**Little Dutch Doctor**—Otto Schittler, Asst. Surgeon of the 129th Pennsylvania Volunteer Infantry

**The Chaplain**—Chaplain William H. Rice of the 129th Pennsylvania Volunteer Infantry

**Squab**—Col. Peter Allabach, Commander, Second Brigade, Humphreys Division

**The Exhorting Colonel, also Pap**—Col. Edgar M. Gregory, Ninety-first Pennsylvania Infantry

**The Wharf-Rat of an Adjutant**—1st Lt. Benjamin J. Tayman, adjutant to Col. Gregory of the Ninety-first Pennsylvania Infantry

# PREFACE.

"GREEK-FIRE has shivered the statue of John C. Calhoun in the streets of the City of Charleston,"—so the papers say. Whether true or not, the Greek-fire of the righteous indignation of a loyal people is fast shattering the offspring of his infamous teachings,—the armed treason of the South, and its more cowardly ally in the insidious treachery that lurks under doubtful cover in the loyal States. In thunder tones do the masses declare, that now and for ever, they repudiate the Treason and despise the Traitor. Nobly are the hands of our Honest President sustained in prosecuting this most righteous war.

In a day like this, the least that can be expected of any citizen is— duty. We are all co-partners in our beneficent government. We should be co-laborers for her defense. Jealous of the interests of her brave soldiery; for they are our own. Proud of their noble deeds; they constitute our National Heritage.

If these campaign sketches, gathered in actual service during 1862-3, and grouped during the spare hours of convalescence from a camp fever, correct one of the least of the abuses in our military machinery— if they lighten the toil of the humblest of our soldiers, or nerve anew the resolves of loyalty tempted to despair, the writer will have no reason to complain of labor lost. Great latitude of excuse for the existence of abuses must be allowed, when we consider the suddenness with which our volunteers sprang into ranks at the outset of the Rebellion. Now that the warfare is a system, there is less reason for their continuance. Reformers must, however, remember, that to keep our citizen-soldiery effective, they must not make too much of the citizen and too little of the soldier. Abuses must be corrected under the laws; but to be corrected at all they must first be exposed.

Drunkenness, half-heartedness, and senseless routine, have done much to cripple the patriotic efforts of our people. The patriotism of the man who at this day doubts the policy of their open reproof can well be questioned. West Point has, in too many instances, nursed imbecility and treason; but in our honest contempt for the small men of whom, in common with other institutions, she has had her share,—we must not ignore those bright pages of our history adorned with the skill and heroism of her nobler sons. McClellanism did not follow its chief from Warrenton; or Burnside's earnestness, Hooker's dash, and Meade's soldierly stand at Gettysburg, backed as they were by the heroic fighting of the Army of the Potomac, would have had, as they deserved, more decisive results.

The Young Men of the Land would the writer address in the following pages—"because they are strong," and in their strength is the nation's hope. In certain prospect of victory over the greatest enemy we have yet had as a nation—the present infamous rebellion—we can well await patiently the correction of minor evils.

> "Meanwhile we'll sacrifice to liberty,
> Remember, O my friends! the laws, the rights,
> The generous plan of power delivered down
> From age to age by your renowned forefathers,
> (So dearly bought, the price of so much blood;)
> Oh, let it never perish in your hands!
> But piously transmit it to your children.
> Do thou, great liberty! inspire our souls,
> And make our lives in thy possession happy
> Or our deaths glorious in thy just defense."

February, 1864.

*Brig. Gen. Andrew A. Humphreys, chief topographical engineer
on General McClellan's staff in the Army of the Potomac
during the Peninsula Campaign, June 1862.*

# CHAPTER I.

*The Advent of our General of Division—Camp near Frederick City, Maryland —The Old Revolutionary Barracks at Frederick—An Irish Corporal's Recollections of the First Regiment of Volunteers from Pennsylvania— Punishment in the Old First.*[1]

"OUR new Division General, boys!" exclaimed a sergeant of the 210th Pennsylvania Volunteers[2] whose attention and head were turned at the clatter of horses' hoofs to the rear. "I heard an officer say that he would be along today, and I recognize his description."

The men, although weary and route-worn, straightened up, dressed their ranks, and as the General and Staff rode past, some enthusiastic soldier proposed cheers for our new Commander. They started with a will, but the General's doubtful look, as interpreted by the men, gave little or no encouragement, and the effort ended in a few ragged discordant yells.

"He is a strange-looking old covey anyhow," said one of the boys in an undertone. "Did you notice that red muffler about his neck, and how

---

(1)    The text of *Red-Tape* is verbatim; illustrations and footnotes have been added.

(2)    In reality this was the 129th Pennsylvania Volunteers; the 210th designation is fictitious, although later in the war a real 210th Pennsylvania did form. The "new Division General" was Andrew A. Humphreys.

pinched up and crooked his hat is, and that odd-looking moustache, and how savagely he cocks his eyes through his spectacles?"

"They say," replied the sergeant, "that we are the first troops that he has commanded. He was a staff officer before in the Topographical Corps. Didn't you notice the T.C. on his coat buttons?"

"And is he going to practise upon us?" blurts out a bustling red-faced little Irish corporal. "Be Jabers, that accounts for the crooked cow road we have marched through the last day—miles out of the way, and niver a chance for coffee."

"You are too fast, Terence," said the sergeant; "if he belongs to the Topographical Corps, he ought at least to know the roads."

"And didn't you say not two hours ago that we were entirely out of the way, and that we had been wandering as crooked as the creek that flows back of the old town we are from, and nearly runs through itself in a dozen places?"

The sergeant admitted that he had said so, but stated that perhaps the General was not to blame, and added somewhat jocosely: "At any rate the winding of the creek makes those beautiful walks we have so much enjoyed in summer evenings."

"Beautiful winding walks! is it, sergeant! Shure and whin you have your forty pound wait upon your back, forty rounds of lead and powdher in your cartridge-box, and twenty more in your pocket, three days' rations in your haversack, a musket on your shoulder, and army brogans on your throtters, you are just about the first man that I know of to take straight cuts."     *     *     *     *     *

It was a close warm day near the middle of September. The roads were dusty and the troops exhausted. Two days previously the brigade to which they belonged had left the pleasantest of camps, called "Camp Whipple" in honor of their former and favorite Division Commander. Situated in an orchard on the level brow of a hill that overlooked Washington, the imposing Capitol, the broad expanse of the Potomac dotted with frequent craft, the many national buildings, and scenery of historic interest, the men left it with regret, but carried with them recollections that often in times of future depression revived their patriotic ardor.

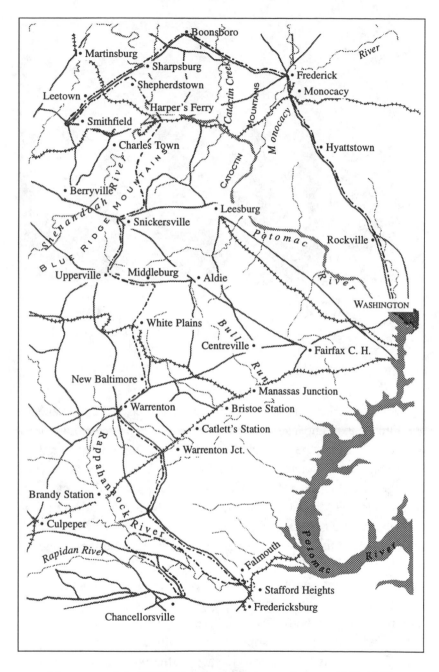

*Movements of the 129th Pennsylvania Volunteer Infantry 1862-1863.*

*The 129th marched from Camp Whipple, on the hills in the right foreground, to*
*Georgetown and Washington City over the Aqueduct Bridge.*

Over dusty roads, through the muddy aqueduct of the Chesapeake
and Ohio Canal, hurried on over the roughly paved streets of Georgetown, and through the suburbs of Washington, they finally halted for
the night, and, as it chanced through lack of orders, for the succeeding
day also, near Meridian Hill. Under orders to join the Fifth Army Corps
commanded by Major-General Fitz John Porter, to which the Division
had been previously assigned, the march was resumed on the succeeding day, which happened to be Sunday, and in the afternoon of which
our chapter opens.

A march of another day brought the Brigade to a recent Rebel camp
ground. Traces of their occupancy were found not only in their depre-
dations in the neighborhood destructive of railroad bridges, but also in
letters and wall-paper envelopes adorned with the lantern-jawed phiz
of Jefferson Davis. The latter were sought after with avidity as soon as
ranks were broken and tents pitched; the more eagerly perhaps for the
reason that during the greater part of their previous month of service

*The Revolutionary Barracks, which held captured Hessians during the Revolution, housed the First Pennsylvania in June 1861.*

they had been frequently within sound of rebel cannon, although but once under their fire. During the previous day, in fact, they had marched to the music of the artillery of South Mountain.

That night awakened lively recollections in the mind of Terence McCarty, our lively little Irish corporal. His duty for the time as corporal of a relief gave him ample opportunity to indulge them. He had belonged to the old First Pennsylvania Regiment of three months men, that a little over a year before, when Maryland was halting between loyalty and disloyalty, had spent its happiest week of service in the yard of the revolutionary barracks in the city of Frederick. Terence was but two short miles from the spot. Brimfull of the memories, he turned to a comrade, who had also belonged to the First, and who with others chanced to stand near.

"I say, Jack! Do you recollect the ould First and Frederick, and do you know that we are but two miles and short ones at that from the blissed ould white-washed barracks, full of all kind of quare guns and canteens looking like barrels cut down; and the Parade Ground where our ould Colonel[3] used to come his 'Briskly, men! Briskly,' when he'd put us through the manual, and where so many ladies would come to see our ivolutions, and where they set the big table for us on the Fourth, and where—

"Hold on, corporal! you can't give that week's history tonight."

"I was only going to obsarve, Jack, that I feel like a badly used man."

"How so, Terence?"

"Why you see nearly ivery officer, commissioned and non-commissioned, of the ould First has been promoted. The Colonel was too ould for service, or my head on it, he would have had a star. Just look at the captains by the way of sample—Company A, a Lieutenant-Colonel, expecting and desarving an eagle ivery day; Company B, a Lieutenant-Colonel; Company C, our own Lieutenant-Colonel;[4] Company D, a Brigadier for soldierly looks, daring, and dash; Company E, a Captain in an aisy berth in the regular service; Company F, a Colonel; Company G, a Major; Company H, a Lieutenant-Colonel; Company I, I have lost sight of, and the lion-hearted captain of Company K, doing a lion's share of work at the head of a regiment in Tennessee. Now, Jack, the under officers and many privates run pretty much the same way, but not quite as high. Bad luck to me, I was fifth corporal thin and am eight now—promoted crab-fashion. Fortune's wheel gives me many a turn, Jack! but always stops with me on the lower side."

"I saw you on the upper side once," retorted Jack roguishly.

"And whin? may I ask."

"When, do you say? why, when you took about half a canteen too much, and that same old colonel had you tied on the upper side of a barrel on the green in front of the barracks."

"Bad luck to an ill-natured memory, Jack, for stirring that up," replied the corporal, breaking in upon the laughter that followed, "but I now

---

(3)    The old colonel was Samuel Yohe, a judge from Easton, Pennsylvania.

(4)    The captain of Company C of the First Pennsylvania was William H.
       Armstrong, who had risen to lieutenant colonel of the 129th and is the author
       of *Red-Tape*.

recollect, it was the day before you slipped the guard whin the colonel gave you a barrel uniform with your head through the end, and kept me for two mortal long hours in the hot sun, a tickling of you under the nose with a straw, and daubing molasses on your chaps to plaze the flies, to the great admiration of a big crowd of ladies and gentlemen."

Jack subsided, and the hearty laughter at the corporal's ready retort was broken a few minutes later by a loud call for the corporal of the guard, which hurried Terence away, dispersed the crowd, and might as well end this chapter.

## CHAPTER II.

*The Treason at Harper's Ferry—Rebel Occupation of Frederick—Patriotism of the Ladies of Frederick—A Rebel Guard nonplussed by a Lady—The Approach to Antietam—Our Brigadier cuts Red Tape—The Blunder of the day after Antietam—The little Irish Corporal's idea of Strategy.*

THE Brigade did not rest long in its new camp. The day and a half, however, passed there had many incidents to be remembered by. Fish were caught in abundance from the beautiful Monocacy. But the most impressive scene was the long procession of disarmed, dejected men, who had been basely surrendered at Harper's Ferry, and were now on their way homeward, on parole. Many and deep were the curses they uttered against their late commanders. "Boys, *we've* been sold! Look out," cried a comely bright-eyed young officer of eighteen or there-abouts. "That we have," added a chaplain, who literally bore the cross upon his shoulders in a pair of elegant straps. When will earnest men cease to be foiled in this war by treacherous commanders? was an inquiry that pressed itself anxiously home.

But the thunders of Antietam were reverberating through that mountainous region, distinctly heard in all their many echoes, and of course the all-absorbing topic. At 3 P.M. orders came to move a short distance beyond Frederick. The division was rapidly formed, and the men marched joyously along through the streets of Frederick, already crowded with our own and Rebel wounded, to the sound of lively martial music; but none more joyously than the members of the old

First, whose recollections were brisk of good living as they recognized in many a lady a former benefactress. Bradley T. Johnson's[1] race, that commenced with his infamously prepared and lying handbills, was soon run in Frederick. No one of the border cities has been more undoubtedly or devotedly patriotic. Its prominent ministers at an early day took bold positions. The ladies were not behind, and many a sick and wounded soldier will bless them to his latest hour. The world has heard of the well deserved fame of Florence Nightingale. History will hold up to a nation's gratitude thousands of such ministering angels, who, moving in humbler circles, perhaps, are none the less entitled to a nation's praise. "Great will be their reward."

To show the spirit that emboldened the ladies of Frederick, a notable instance is related as having occurred during the Rebel occupation of the city under General Stuart. Many Union ladies had left the place. Not so, however, with Mrs. D., the lively, witty, and accomplished wife of a prominent Lutheran minister. The Union sick and wounded that remained demanded attention, and for their sake, as well as from her own high spirit, she resolved to stay. Miss Annie C., the beautiful and talented daughter of Ex-U.S. Senator C., an intimate friend of Mrs. D., through like devotion, also remained. Rebel officers, gorgeous in grey and gilt lace, many of them old residents of the place, strutted about the streets. The ragged privates begged from door to door. Mrs. D., and her friend had been separated several days—a long period considering their close intimacy and their present surroundings. Mrs. D. resolved to visit her, and with her to resolve was to execute. Threading her way through the crowded streets, heeding not the jeers or insults of the rebel soldiery, she soon came in front of the Cooper Mansion, to find a rebel flag floating from an upper window, and a well dressed soldierly looking greyback, with bayonet fixed, pacing his beat in front. Nothing daunted, Mrs. D. approached. "Halt," was the short sharp hail of the sentinel, as he brought his bayonet to the charge. "Who is quartered here?" asked

---

(1)    Bradley T. Johnson, an attorney, led a group of the Frederick Mounted
       Guards who joined the Confederates. Johnson commanded a brigade of
       cavalry at the battle of Monocacy in June 1864.

*The Cooper Mansion, where Kate D. Diehl confronted General J. E. B. Stuart while visiting her friend, Miss Anne C. Cooper.*

Mrs. D., gradually nearing the sentry. "Maj.-Gen.-Stuart," was the brief reply, "I want to visit a lady acquaintance in the house." "My orders are strict, madam, that no one can cross my beat without a pass." "*Pass or no pass, I must and will go into that house,*" and quick as thought this frail lady dashed aside the bayonet, sprang across the beat, and entered the hall, while the sentry confused, uncertain whether he should follow or not, stood a minute or two before resuming his step. From an upper window Gen. Stuart laughed heartily at the scene, and was loud in praise of her tact and pluck.

But all this time our division has been moving through the streets of Frederick, in fact has reached what was to have been its camping ground for the night. The reader will excuse me; older heads and more exact pens have frequently, when ladies intervened, made much longer digressions.

The halt was but for a moment. An aide-de-camp, weary-looking, on a horse covered with foam, dashed up to the division commander, bearing an order from the commander-in-chief that the division must join its corps at Antietam without delay. The fight might be renewed in the morning, and if so, fresh troops were needed. The order was communicated through the brigade commanders to commanders of regiments, while the subordinate field officers went from company to company encouraging the men, telling them that a glorious victory had been gained, that the rebels were hemmed in by the river on three sides, and our army in front; that there was but one ford, and that a poor one, and that the rebels must either take to the river indiscriminately, be cut to pieces, or surrender. In short, that we had them.

These statements were received with the most enthusiastic applause. As the Division proceeded on its march, they were confirmed by reports of spectators and wounded men in ambulances. What was the most significant fact to the men who had seen the thousands of stragglers and skulkers from the second battle of Bull Run, was the entire absence of straggling or demoralization of any kind. Our troops must have been victorious, was the ready and natural suggestion. The thought nerved them, and pushing up their knapsacks, and hitching up their pantaloons, they trudged with a will up the mountain slope.

That mountain slope!—it would well repay a visit from one of our large cities, to descend that mountain a bright summer afternoon. A sudden turn in the road brings to view the sun-gilded spires of the city of Frederick, rising as if by enchantment from one of the loveliest of valleys. Many of the descriptions of foreign scenery pale before the realities of this view. When will our Hawthornes and our Taylors be just to the land of their birth?

Scenery on that misty night could not delay the troops. The mountain-top was gained. About half way down the northern slope of the mountain the Division halted to obtain the benefits of a spring fifty yards from the road. A steep path led to it, and one by one the men filed down to fill their canteens. The delay was terribly tedious, and entirely unnecessary, as five minutes' inquiry among the men, many of whom were familiar with the road, would have informed the Commanding General of abundance of excellent water, a short mile beyond, and close by the wayside. Pride, which prevails to an unwarranted extent among too many regular officers, is frequently the cause of much vexation. Inquiry and exertion to lighten the labors of our brave volunteers would, with every earnest officer, be unceasing. A short distance further a halt

*"Our brigadier" is Gen. Erastus B. Tyler, an Ohio fur trader who led the Seventh Ohio in West Virginia in 1861 and whose earlier brigade had inflicted heavy losses on the Stonewall Brigade at Kernstown and Port Republic in the Valley Campaign of 1862.*

was ordered for coffee, that "sublime beverage of Mocha," indispensable in camp or in the field. Strange to say, our brigadier, who habitually confined himself closely to cold water, was one of the most particular of officers in ordering halts for coffee.

South Mountain was crossed, but in the dusky light little could be seen of the devastation caused by the late battle. "Yonder," said a wounded man who chanced to be passing, "our gallant General lost his life." The brave, accomplished Reno! How dearly our national integrity is maintained! Brave spirit, in your life you thought it well worth the cost; your death can never be considered a vain sacrifice!

Boonsboro' was entered about daybreak. The road to Sharpsburg was here taken, and at 7½ A.M., having marched during that night twenty-eight miles, the Division stood at arms near the battle-ground along a road crowded with ammunition trains. Inquiry was made as to the ammunition, and the number of rounds for each man ordered to be increased immediately from forty to sixty.

"Pioneer! hand me that axe," said our brigadier, dismounting. "Sergeant," addressing the sergeant of the ammunition guard, "hand out those boxes." "The Division General has given strict orders, if you please, General, that the boxes must pass regularly through the hands of the ordnance officer," said the sergeant, saluting. "I am *acting* ordnance officer; hand out the boxes!" was the command, that from its tone and manner brooked no delay. A box was at his feet. In an instant a clever blow from the muscular arm of the hero of Winchester laid it open. Another and another, until the orderly sergeant had given the required number of rounds to every man in the brigade. "Attention! Column! Shoulder Arms! Right Face! Right Shoulder Shift Arms!" and at a quick step the brigade moved towards the field.

After passing long trains of ambulances and ammunition wagons, the boys were saluted as they passed through the little

*"The Colonel" is Jacob G. Frick, a businessman from Pottsville, Pennsylvania. He served in the Mexican War and led the Ninety-sixth Pennsylvania in the Peninsula Campaign. He was awarded the Medal of Honor for his efforts at the battles of Fredericksburg and Chancellorsville.*

town of Keetysville by exhortations from the wounded, who crowded every house, and forgot their wounds in their enthusiasm. "Fellows, you've got 'em! Give 'em h—l!" yelled an artillery sergeant, for whom a flesh wound in the arm was being dressed at the window by a kind-hearted looking country woman. "Give it to 'em!" "They're fast!" "This good lady knows every foot of the ground, and says so." The good lady smiled assent, and was saluted with cheer upon cheer. Dead horses, a few unburied men, marks of shot in the buildings, now told of immediate proximity to the field. A short distance further, and the Division was drawn up in line of battle, behind one of the singular ridges that mark this memorable ground. Fragments of shells, haversacks, knapsacks, and the like, told how hotly the ground had been contested on the previous day. The order to load was quickly obeyed, and the troops, with the remainder of the Fifth Corps in their immediate neighborhood, stood to arms.

A large number of officers lined the crest of the ridge, and thither, with leave, the Colonel and Lieut.-Colonel of the 210th repaired. The scene that met their view was grand beyond description. Another somewhat higher and more uniform ridge, running almost parallel to the ridge or rather connected series of ridges on one of which the officers stood, was the strong position held by the rebels on the previous day. Between the ridges flowed the sluggish Antietam, dammed up for milling purposes. Beyond, on the crest of the hill, gradually giving way, were the rebel skirmishers; our own were as gradually creeping up the slope. The skirmishers were well deployed upon both sides; and the parallel flashes and continuous rattle of their rifles gave an interest to the scene, ineffaceable in the minds of spectators.

"Do you hear that shell, you can see the smoke just this side of Sharpsburg on your left," said the Colonel, addressing his companion. "There it bursts," and a puff of white smoke expanded itself in the air fifty yards above one of our batteries posted on a ridge on the left. Two pieces gave quick reply. "Officers, to your posts," shouted an aide-de-camp, and forthwith the officers galloped to their respective commands.

"Boys, the ball is about to open, put your best foot foremost," said the Colonel to his regiment. The men, excited, supposing themselves about to pass their first ordeal of battle, straightened up, held their pieces with tightened grips, and nervously awaited the "forward." Beyond the sharp crack of the rifles, however, no further sound was heard. Hour after hour passed. At length an aide from the staff of the Division General cantered to where the Brigadier, conversing with several of his field officers, stood, and informed him that it was the pleasure of the Division General that the men should be made comfortable, *as no immediate attack was apprehended.* "No immediate attack apprehended!" echoed the Colonel. "Of course not. Why don't we attack them?"

The aide flushed, said somewhat excitedly: "That was the order I received, sir."

*Coffee break. (Edwin Forbes drawing)*

"Boys, cook your coffee," said our Brigadier, somewhat mechanically—a brown study pictured in his face.

The field officers scattered to relieve their hunger, or rather their anxiety as to the programme of the day.

"Charlie," said the Lieut.-Col., addressing a good-humored looking Contraband, "get our coffee ready."

The Colonel, with the other field and staff officers, seated themselves upon knapsacks unslung for their accommodation, silently, each apparently waiting upon the other to open the conversation. In the meantime several company officers who had heard of the order gathered about them.

"I don't understand this move at all," at length said the Colonel nervously. "Here we are, with a reserve of thirty thousand men who have not been in the fight at all, with ammunition untouched, perfectly fresh and eager for the move. The troops that were engaged yesterday have for the most part had a good night's rest and are ready and anxious for a brush today. The rebels, hemmed in on three sides by the river—with a miserable ford, and that only in one place, as every body

*"The Major" was Joseph Anthony, an Irish-born innkeeper from Pottsville, Pennsylvania, who had served with Frick as captain in the Ninety-sixth Pennsylvania.*

knows, and as there is no earthly excuse for our generals not knowing, as this ground was canvassed often enough in the three months' service. Why don't we advance?" continued the Colonel, rising. "Their sharpshooters are near the woods now, and when they reach it, they'll run like Devils. Why don't we advance? We can drive them into the river, if they like that better than being shelled; or they can surrender, which they would prefer to either. And as to force, I'll bet we have one third more."

The Colonel, an impressive, fine-looking man, six feet clear in his socks, of thirty-eight or thereabouts, delivered the above with more than his usual earnestness.

The Adjutant,[2] of old Berks by birth, rather short in stature, thick-set, with a mathematically developed head, was the first to rejoin.

"It can't be for want of ammunition, Colonel! This corps has plenty. An officer in a corps engaged yesterday told me that they had enough, and you all saw the hundreds of loaded ammunition wagons that we passed in the road close at hand—and besides, what excuse can there be? The Rebs I understand did not get much available ammunition at

---

(2)    The Adjutant was Lt. David B. Green, a Yale graduate and an attorney in Pottsville.

the ferry. They are far from their base of supplies, while we are scant fifteen miles from one railroad, and twenty-eight from another, and good roads to both."

"Be easy," said the Major, a fine specimen of manhood, six feet two and a half clear of his boots, an Irishman by birth, the brogue, however, if he ever had any, lost by an early residence in this country. "Be easy. Little Mac is a safe commander. We tried him, Colonel, in the Peninsula, and I'll wager my pay and allowances, and God knows I need them, that he'll have his army safe."

"Yes, and the Rebel army too," snappishly interrupted the Colonel.

"I have always thought," said the Lieut.-Col., "that the test of a great commander was his ability to follow up and take advantage of a victory. One thousand men from the ranks would bear that test triumphantly today. It is a wonder that our Union men stiffened in yesterday's fight, whose blue jackets we can see from yonder summit in the rear of our sharpshooters, do not rise from the dead, and curse the halting imbecility that is making their heroic struggles, and glorious deaths, seemingly vain sacrifices."

"Too hard, Colonel, too hard," says the Major.

"Too hard! when results are developing before our eyes, so that every servant, even, in the regiment can read them. Mark my word for it, Major; Lee commenced crossing last evening, and by the time we creep to the river at five hundred yards a day, if at all, indeed, he will have his army over, horse, foot, and dragoons, and leave us the muskets on the field, the dead to bury, farm-houses full of Rebel wounded to take care of, and the battle-ground to encamp upon—a victory barely worth the cost. Why not advance, as the Col. says. The worst they can do in any event is to put us upon the defensive, and they can't drive us from this ground."

"If old Rosecranz was only here," sang out a Captain,[3] who had been itching for his say, and who had seen service in Western Virginia, "he

---

(3)     The Captain was David Eckar of Company F. He served as an enlisted man in the First U.S. Artillery in the Mexican War and was a first lieutenant in the Second (West) Virginia Infantry from 1861-62.

*Gen. William Rosecrans served in West Virginia in 1861-1862; he transferred to higher command in the West but was relieved after Chickamauga.*

wouldn't let them pull their pantaloons and shirts off and swim across, or wade it as if they were going out a bobbing for eels. When I was in Western Virginia—"

"If fighting old Joe Hooker[4] could only take his saddle today," chimed in an enthusiastic company officer, completely cutting off the Captain, "he'd go in on his own hook."

"And it would be," sang out a beardless and thoughtless Lieutenant—

"Old Joe, kicking up ahind and afore And the Butternuts a caving in, around old Joe."

The apt old song might have given the Lieutenant a little credit at any other time, but the matter in hand was too provokingly serious. Coffee and crackers were announced, the field officers commenced their meal in silence, and the company officers returned to their respective quarters.

The troops rested on their arms all that afternoon, at times lounging close to the stacks. Upon the face of every reflecting officer and private,

---

(4)     Maj. Gen. Joseph Hooker commanded the First Corps at Antietam.

deep mortification was depicted. It did not compare, however, with the chagrin manifested by the Volunteer Regiments who had been engaged in the fight, and whose thinned ranks and comrades lost made them closely calculate consequences. Not last among the reflecting class was our little Irish corporal.

"Gineral," said he, advancing cap in hand, to our always accessible Brigadier, as he sat leisurely upon his bay—"Gineral! will you permit a corporal, and an Irishman at that, to spake a word to ye?"

"Certainly, corporal!" the fine open countenance of the General relaxing into a smile.

"Gineral! didn't we beat the Rebs yesterday?"

"So they say, corporal."

"Don't the river surround them, and can they cross at more than one place, and that a bad one, as an ould woman whose pig I saved today tould me?"

"The river is on their three sides, and they have only one ford, and that a bad one, corporal."

"Thin why the Divil don't we charge?"

"Corporal!" said the General, laughing, "I am not in command of the army, and can't say."

"Bad luck to our stars that ye aren't, Gineral! there would be somebody hurt today thin, and it would be the bluidy Butthernuts, I'm thinking." The corporal gave this ready compliment as only an Irishman can, and withdrew.

At dusk orders were received for the men to sleep by their arms. But there was no sleep to many an eye until a late hour that night. Never while life lasts will survivors forget the exciting conversations of that day and night. "Tired nature," however, claimed her dues, and one by one, officers and privates at late hours betook themselves to their blankets. The stars, undisturbed by struggles on this little planet, were gazed at by many a wakeful eye. Those same stars will look down as placidly upon the future faithful historian, whose duty it will be to place first in the list of cold, costly military mistakes, the blunder of the day after the battle of Antietam.

# CHAPTER III.

*The March to the River—Our Citizen Soldiery—Popularity of Commanders how Lost and how Won—The Rebel Dead—How the Rebels repay Courtesy.*

A N early call to arms was sounded upon the succeeding morning, and the Division rapidly formed. The batteries that had been posted at commanding points upon the series of ridges during the previous day and night were withdrawn, and the whole Corps moved along a narrow road, that wound beautifully among the ridges.

The Volunteer Regiments were unusually quiet; the thoughts of the night previous evidently lingered with them. The American Volunteer is no mere machine. Rigorous discipline will give him soldierly characteristics—teach him that unity of action with his comrades and implicit obedience of orders are essential to success. But his independence of thought remains; he never forgets that he is a citizen soldier; he reads and reflects for himself. Few observant officers of volunteers but have noticed that affairs of national polity, movements of military commanders, are not infrequently discussed by men in blouses, about camp fires and picket stations, with as much practical ability and certainly quite as courteously, as in halls where legislators canvass them at a nation's cost. It has been justly remarked that in no army in the world is the average standard of intelligence so high, as in the American volunteer force. The same observation might be extended to earnestness of purpose and honesty of intention. The doctrine has long since been exploded that scoundrels make the best soldiers. Men of no character under discipline will fight, but they fight mechanically. The determination so necessary to success is wanting. European serfs trained with the precision of puppets, and like puppets unthinking, are wanting in the dash that characterizes our volunteers. That creature of impulse the Frenchman, under all that is left of the first Napoleon, the shadow of a mighty name, will charge with desperation, but fails in the cool and quiet courage so essential in seeming forlorn resistance. In what other nation can you combine the elements of the American volunteer? It may be said that the British Volunteer Rifle Corps would prove a force of similar character. In many respects undoubtedly they would; as yet there is no basis of comparison. Their soldierly attainments have not been tested by the realities of war.

There was ample food for reflection. On the neighboring hills heavy details of soldiers were gathering the rebel dead in piles preparatory to committing them to the trenches, at which details equally heavy, vigorously plied the pick and spade. Our own dead, with few exceptions, had already been buried; and the long rows of graves marked by head and foot boards, placed by the kind hands of comrades, attested but too sadly how heavily we had peopled the ridges.

While the troops were *en route*, the Commander-in-Chief in his hack and four, followed by a staff imposing in numbers, passed. The Regulars cheered vociferously. The applause from the Volunteers was brief, faint, and a most uncertain sound, and yet many of these same Volunteer Regiments were rapturous in applause, previous to and during the battle. Attachment to Commanders so customary among old troops—so desirable in strengthening the morale of the army—cannot blind the intelligent soldier to a grave mistake—a mistake that makes individual effort contemptible. True, a great European Commander has said that soldiers will become attached to any General; a remark true of the times perhaps—true of the troops of that day,—but far from being true of volunteers, who are in the field from what they consider the necessity of the country, and whose souls are bent upon a speedy, honorable, and victorious termination of the war.

A glance at the manner in which our Volunteer Regiments are most frequently formed, will, perhaps, best illustrate this. A town meeting is called, speeches made appealing to the patriotic, to respond to the necessities of the country; lists opened and the names of mechanics, young attorneys, clerks, merchants, farmers' sons, dry-goods-men and their clerks, and others of different pursuits, follow each other in strange succession, but with like earnestness of purpose. An intelligent soldiery gathered in this way, will not let attachments to men blind them as to the effects of measures.

About 10 A.M., our brigade was drawn up in line of battle on a ridge overlooking the well riddled little town of Sharpsburg. Arms were stacked, and privilege given many officers and men to examine the adjacent ground. A cornfield upon our right, along which upon the north side ran a narrow farm road, that long use had sunk to a level of two and in most places three feet, below the surface of the fields, had been contested with unusual fierceness. Blue and grey lay literally with arms entwined as they fell in hand to hand contest. The fence rails had been piled upon the north side of the road, and in the rifle pit formed to their hand with this additional bulwark, they poured the most galling of fires with comparative impunity upon our troops advancing to the charge. A Union battery, however, came to the rescue, and an enfilading fire of but a few moments made havoc unparalleled. Along the whole line of rebel occupation, their bodies could have been walked upon, so closely did they lie. Pale-faced, finely featured boys of sixteen, their delicate hands showing no signs of toil, hurried by a misguided enthusiasm from fond friends and luxurious family firesides, contrasted strangely with the long black hair, lank looks of the Louisiana Tiger, or the rough, bloated, and bearded face of the Backwoodsman of Texas. A Brigadier, who looked like an honest, substantial planter, lay half over the rails, upon which he had doubtless stood encouraging his men, while lying half upon his body were two beardless boys, members of his staff, and not unlikely of his family. Perhaps all the male members of that family had been hurried at once from life by that single shell. The sight was sickening. Who, if privileged, would be willing to fix a limit to God's retributive justice upon the heads of the infamous, and in many instances cowardly originators of this Rebellion!

Cavalry scouting parties brought back the word that the country to the river was clear of the rebels, and in accordance with what seemed to be the prevailing policy of the master-mind of the campaign, imme-

*Lincoln meets McClellan at Porter's Fifth Corps headquarters at Antietam.*
*(1) Gen. George Morell; (2) Lt. Col. Alexander Webb;*
*(3) Maj. Gen. George McClellan; (4) Gen. Fitz-John Porter;*
*(5) Gen. Andrew Humphreys; (6) Capt. George Custer.*

diate orders to move were then issued. The troops marched through that
village of hospitals,—Sharpsburg—and halted within a mile and a half
of the river, in the rear of a brick dwelling, which was then taken and
subsequently used as the Head-Quarters of Major-General Fitz John
Porter. A line of battle was again formed, arms stacked, and an order
issued that the ground would be occupied during the night.

In the morning the march was again resumed by a road which wound
around the horseshoe-shaped bend in the river. When approaching the
river, firing was heard, apparently as if from the other side, and a short
distance further details were observed carrying wounded men and
ranging them comfortably around the many hay and straw stacks of the
neighborhood. Inquiry revealed that a reconnoitering party, misled by
the apparent quiet of the other side, had crossed, fallen into an ambus-
cade, and under the most galling of fires, artillery and musketry, kept
up most unmercifully by the advancing rebels, who thus ungraciously
repaid the courtesy shown them the day after Antietam—had been

*The 118th Pennsylvania, recruited by the Corn Exchange of Philadelphia, the "new and most promising regiment," is seen here fording the Potomac near Shepherdstown. (A. R. Waud drawing)*

compelled to recross that difficult ford. Our loss was frightful—one new and most promising regiment was almost entirely destroyed.

The men thought of the dead earnestness of the rebels, and as they moved forward around the winding Potomac—deep, full of shelving, sunken rocks, from the dam a short distance above the ford, that formerly fed the mill owned by a once favorably known Congressman, A. R. Boteler, to where it was touched by our line— they reviewed with redoubled force, the helplessness of the rebels a few days previously, and to say the least, the carelessness of the leader of the Union army.

The regimental camp was selected in a fine little valley that narrowed into a gap between the bluffs, bordering upon the canal, sheltered by wood, and having every convenience of water. The rebels had used it but a few days previously, and the necessity was immediate for heavy details for police duty. And here we passed quite unexpectedly six weeks of days more pleasant to the men than profitable to the country, and of which something may be said in our two succeeding chapters.

# CHAPTER IV.

*A Regimental Baker—Hot Pies—Position of the Baker in line of Battle— Troubles of the Baker—A Western Virginia Captain on a Whiskey Scent—The Baker's Story—How to obtain Political Influence—Dancing Attendance at Washington—What Simon says—Confiscation of Whiskey.*

BESIDES the indispensables of quartermaster and sutler the 210th had what might be considered a luxury in the shape of a baker, who had volunteered to accompany the regiment, and furnish hot cakes, bread, and pies. Tom Hudson was an original in his way, rather short of stature, far plumper and more savory-looking than one of his pies, with a pleasing countenance and twinkling black eye, that meant humor or roguishness as circumstances might demand, and a never-ending supply of what is always popular, dry humor. He was just the man to manage the thousand caprices of appetite of a thousand different men. While in camps accessible to the cities of Washington and Alexandria, matters moved smoothly enough. His zinc-plated bakery was always kept fired up, and a constant supply of hot pies dealt out to the long strings of men, who would stand for hours anxiously awaiting their turn. A movement of the baker's interpreted differently by himself and the men, at one time created considerable talk and no little feeling. On several occasions the trays were lifted out of the oven, and the pies dashed upon the outspread expectant hands, with such force as to break the too often half-baked undercrust. In consequence the juices would ooze out, trickle scalding hot between the fingers, and compel the helpless man to drop the pie. One unfortunate fellow lost four pies in succession. As they cost fifteen cents apiece, the pocket was too much interested to let the matter escape notice. A non-commissioned officer, who had lost a pie, savagely returned to the stand, and demanded another pie or his money. The baker was much too shrewd for that. The precedent, if set, would well nigh exhaust his stock of pies, and impoverish his cash drawer.

"I say," said the officer, turning to the men, "it is a trick. He wants to sell as many pies as he can. He knows well enough that when one falls in this mud fifteen cents are gone slap."

"Now, boys," said the baker blandly, "you know me better than that. I'd scorn to do an act of that kind for fifteen cents. You know how it is —what a rush there always is here. You want the pies as soon as baked, and baking makes them hot. Now I want to accommodate you all as soon as possible, and of course I serve them out as soon as baked. You had better all get tin-plates or boards."

"That won't go down, old fellow," retorted the officer. "You know that there is hardly a tin-plate in camp, and boards are not to be had."

A wink from the baker took the officer to the private passage in the rear of his tent. What happened there is known but to the two, but ever after the officer held his peace. Not so with the men. However, as the pies were not dealt out as hot in future, the matter gradually passed from their minds.

To make himself popular with the men, Tom resorted to a variety of expedients, one of which was to assure them that in case of an enterprise that promised danger, he would be with them. He was taken up quite unexpectedly. An ammunition train on the morning of the second battle of Bull Run, bound to the field, required a convoy. The regiment was detailed. Tom's assertions had come to the ears of the regimental officers, and without being consulted, he was provided with a horse, and told to keep near the Adjutant. There was a drizzling rain all day long, but through it came continually the booming of heavy ordnance.

"Colonel! how far do you suppose that firing is?" "And are they Rebel cannon?" were frequent inquiries made by Tom during the day. About noon he asserted that he could positively ride no further. But ride he must and ride he did. The Regiment halted near Centreville, having passed Porter's Corps on the way and convoyed the Train to the required point. After a short halt the homeward route was taken and Tom placed in the rear. By some accident, frequent when trains take up the road, he became separated from the Regiment and lost among the teams. The Regiment moved on, and as it was now growing dark, turned into a wood about half a mile distant, for the night. Tom had just learned his route, when "ping!" came a shell from a Rebel battery on a hill to the left, exploded among some team horses, and created awful confusion. He suddenly forgot his soreness, and putting spurs to his horse at a John Gilpin speed, rode by, through and over, as he afterwards said, the teams. The shells flew rapidly. Tom dodged as if every one was scorching his hair, at the same time giving a vigorous kick to the rear with both heels. At his speed he was soon by the teams; in fact did not stop until he was ten Virginia miles from that scene of terror. But we will meet him again in the morning.

The Regiment was soon shelled out of the wood, and compelled to continue its march. Three miles further they encamped in a meadow, passed a wet night without shelter, and early next morning were again upon the road. Thousands of stragglers lined the way, living upon rations plundered from broken-down baggage wagons—lounging lazily around fires that were kept in good glow by rails from the nearby fences. The preceding day these stragglers and skulkers were met in squads at every step of the road. At a point sufficiently remote from danger, their camps commenced. In one of these camps, situated in a fence corner, the baker was espied, stretched at full length and fast asleep, upon two rails placed at a gentle slope at right angles to the fence. Surrounding him were filthy, mean-looking representatives of half-a-dozen various regiments—the Zouave more gay than gallant in flaming red breeches—blouses, dress coats, and even a pair of shoulder straps, assisted to complete the crowd. Nearby was tied his jaded horse.

The baker was awakened. To his surprise, as he said, he saw the regiment, as he had supposed them to be much nearer home than himself. One of his graceless comrades, however, bluntly contradicted this, and accused him of being mortally frightened when he halted the night before, as although they assured him that he was full ten miles from danger, he insisted that these rifled guns had terribly long range. The baker quietly resumed his place by the Adjutant and Colonel.

"I have been thinking, Colonel," said he, in the course of a half hour, riding alongside of the Colonel, and speaking in an undertone, "that I ran a great risk unnecessarily."

"Why?" asked the Colonel.

"You see my exhortations are worth far more to the men than my example. When they crowd my quarters, as they do every morning, I never fail to deal out patriotic precepts with my pies."

"But particularly the pies," retorted the Colonel.

"That is another branch of my case," slyly continued the baker. "Suppose, if such a calamity can be dwelt upon, that I had been killed, and there was only one mule between me and death, who would have run my bakery? who," elevating his voice, "would have furnished hot rolls for the officers, and warm bread cakes and pies for the men? Riding along last night, these matters were all duly reflected upon, and I wound up, by deciding that the regiment could not afford to lose me."

"But you managed to lose the regiment," replied the Colonel.

"Pure accident that, I assure you, upon honor. Now in line of battle I have taken pains to ascertain my true position, but this confounded marching by the flank puts me out of sorts. In line of battle the quartermaster says he is four miles in the rear—the sutler says that he is four miles behind the quartermaster, and as it would look singular upon paper to shorten the distance for the baker, besides other good reasons, I suppose I am four miles behind the sutler."

"Completely out of range for all purposes," observed the Adjutant, who had slyly listened with interest.

"There is a good reason for that position, it is well chosen, and shows foresight," continued the baker, dropping his rein, and enforcing his remarks by apt gestures. "Suppose we are in line of battle, and the Rebels in line facing us at easy rifle range. Their prisoners say that they have lived for a month past on roasted corn and green apples. Now what will equal the daring of a hungry man! These Rebel Commanders are shrewd in keeping their men hungry; our men have heart for the fight, it is true, but the rebels have a stomach for it—they hunger for a chance at the spoils. The quartermaster then with his crackers must be kept out of sight—the sutler, too, with his stores, must be kept shady—but above all the baker. Suppose the baker to be nearer," said he, with increased earnestness, "and a breeze should spring up towards their lines bearing with it the smell of warm bread, the rebels would rise instanter on tiptoe, snuff a minute—concentrate on the bakery, and no two ranks or columns doubled on the center, could keep the hungry devils back. Our line pierced, we might lose the day—lose the day, sir."

"And the baker," said the Major, joining in the laugh.

Shortly after that march, matters went indifferently with the baker. Camp was changed frequently, and over the rough roads he kept up with difficulty.

A week after the battle of Antietam, after satisfying himself fully of the departure of the Rebels, he arrived in camp. He had picked up by the way an ill-favored assistant, whose tent stood on the hill side some little distance from the right flank of the regiment.

Two nights after his arrival there was a commotion in camp. A tonguey corporal, slightly under regulation size, in an exuberance of spirits, had mounted a cracker-box almost immediately in front of the sutler's tent, and commenced a lively harangue. He told how he had left a profitable grocery business to serve his country—his pecuniary sacrifices—but above all, the family he had left behind.

"And you've blissed them by taking your character with you," chimed in the little Irish corporal.

"Where did you steal your whiskey?" demanded a second.

The confusion increased, the crowd was dispersed by the guard, all at the expense of the sutler's credit, as it was rumored that he had furnished the stimulant.

The sutler indignantly demanded an investigation, and three officers, presumed to possess a scent for whiskey above their fellows, were detailed for the duty. One of these was our friend the Virginia captain.

Under penalty of losing his stripes, the corporal confessed that he had obtained the liquor at the baker's. Thither the following evening the detail repaired. The assistant denied all knowledge of the liquor. He was confronted with the corporal, and admitted the charge, and that but three bottles remained.

"By —," said our Western Virginia captain, hands in pocket, "I smell ten more. There are just thirteen bottles or I'll lose my straps."

The confidence of the captain impressed the detail, and they went to work with a will—emptying barrels of crackers, probing with a bayonet sacks of flour, etc. A short search, to the pretended amazement of the assistant, proved the correctness of the captain's scent. The baker was sent for, and with indignant manner and hands lifted in holy horror, he poured volley after volley of invective at the confounded assistant.

"But, gentlemen," said the baker, dropping his tone, "I've known worse things than this to happen. I've known even bakers to get tight."

"And your bacon would have stood a better chance of being saved if you had got tight, instead of putting a non-commissioned officer in that condition," said one of the detail. "The Colonel, I am afraid, Tom, will clear you out."

"Well," sighed the baker, after a pause of a moment, "talk about Job and all the other unfortunates since his day, why not one of them had my variety of suffering. Did you ever hear any of my misfortunes?"

"We see one."

"My life has been a series of mishaps. I prosper occasionally in small things, but totals knock me. God help me if I hadn't a sure port in a storm—a self-supporting wife. For instance—but I can't commence that story without relieving my thirst." A bottle was opened, drinks had all around, and the baker continued—

"You see, gentlemen, when Simon was in political power, I waggled successfully and extensively among the coal mines in Central Pennsylvania. In those localities voters are kept underground until election day, and they then appear above often in such unexpected force as to knock the speculations of unsophisticated politicians. But Simon was not one of that stripe. He knew his men—the real men of influence; not men that have big reputations created by active but less widely known under-workers, but the under-workers themselves. Simon dealt with these, and he rarely mistook his men. Now I was well known in those parts—kept on the right side of the boys, and the boys tried to keep on the right side of me, and Simon knew it. No red tape fettered Simon, as the boys say it tied our generals the other side of Sharpsburg in order to let the Rebs have time to cross. If the measures that his shrewd foresight saw were necessary for the suppression of this Rebellion, at its outbreak, had been adopted, we would be encamped somewhat lower down in Dixie than the Upper Potomac—if indeed there would be any necessity for our being in service at all.

"He was not a man of old tracks, like a ground mole; indeed like some military commanders who seem lost outside of them; but of ready resources and direct routes, gathering influence now by one means and then by another, and perhaps both novel. Now Simon set me at work in this wise.

" 'Tom,' one morning, says an old and respected citizen of our place, who knew my father and my father's father, and me as an unlucky dog from my cradle, 'Tom, did ever any idea of getting a permanent and profitable position—say, as you are an excellent penman—as clerk in one of the departments at Harrisburg or Washington, enter your head?'

"At this I straightened up, drew up my shirt collar, pulled down my vest, and said with a sort of hopeful inquiry, 'Why should there?'

" 'Tom, you are wasting your most available talent. Do you know that you have influence—and political influence at that?'

"Another hitch at my shirt collar and pull at my vest, as visions of the Brick Capitol at Harrisburg and the White one at Washington danced before my eyes.

" 'Did you ever reflect, Tom, upon the source of political power?' continued the old gentleman, and without waiting for an answer, fortunately, as I was fast becoming dumbfounded, 'the people, Tom, the people; not you and I, so much as that miner,' said he, pointing to a rough ugly-looking fellow that I had kicked out of my wife's bar-room—or, rather, got my ostler to do it—two nights before, 'That man, Tom, is a representative of thousands; we may represent but ourselves. Now these people are controlled. They neither think nor act for them-selves, as a general rule; somebody does that for them. Now,' as he spoke, trying to take me by a pulled-out button-hole, 'you might as well be that somebody as any man I know.'

" 'Why, Lord bless you, Mr. Simpson, I can't do my own thinking, and as to acting, my wife says I am acting the fool all day long.'

" 'Tom, you don't comprehend me, you know our county sends three members to the State Legislature, and that they elect a United States Senator.'

" 'Yes.'

" 'Well, now, our county can send Simon C— to the United States Senate.'

" 'But our county oughtn't to do it,'—my whig prejudices that I had imbibed with my mother's milk coming up strong.

" 'Tut, tut, Tom, didn't I stand shoulder to shoulder with your father in the old Clay Legion? Whiggery has had its day, and Henry Clay would stand with us now.'

" 'But with Simon's?'

" 'Yes, Simon's principles have undergone a wholesome change.'

"I couldn't see it, but didn't like to contradict the old man, and he continued.

" 'Now, Thomas, be a man; you have influence. I know you have it.' Here I straightened up again. 'Just look at the miners who frequent your hotel, each of them has influence, and don't you think that you could control their votes? Should you succeed, Simon's Scotch blood will never let him forget a friend.'

" 'Or forgive an enemy,' I added.

" 'Tom, don't let your foolish prejudices stand in the way of your success. Your father would advise as I do.'

" 'Mr. S., I'll try.'

" 'That's the word, Tom,' said the old man, patting me on the shoulder. 'It runs our steam-engines, builds our factories, in short, has made our country what it is.'

"I took Mr. S.'s hand, thanked him for his suggestions, with an effort swallowed my prejudices against the old Chieftain, and resolved to work as became my new idea of my position.

"By the way, the recollection of that effort to swallow makes my throat dry, and it's a long time between drinks."

Another round at the bottle, and Tom resumed.

" 'Well, work I did, like a beaver; there wasn't a miner in my neighborhood that I didn't treat, and a miner's baby that I didn't kiss, and often their wives, as some unprincipled scoundrel one day told Mrs. Hudson, to the great injury of my ears and shins for almost a week, and the upshot of the business was, that my township turned a political somerset. Friends of Simon's, in disguise, went to Harrisburg, were successful, and I was not among the last to congratulate him.

" 'Mr. Hudson,' said the Prince of politicians, 'how can I repay you for your services?'

"Like a fool, as my wife always told me I was, I made no suggestion, but let the remark pass with the tameness of a sheep—merely muttering that it was a pleasure to serve him. Simon went to Washington—made no striking hits on the floor, but was great on committees.

"Another idea entered my noddle, this clip without the aid of Mr. S. My penmanship came into play. Days and nights of most laborious work pro-

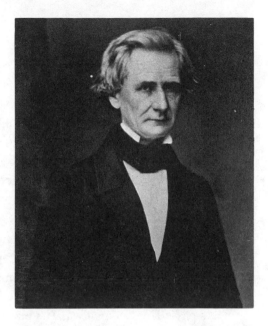

*Simon "The Chieftain" Cameron, secretary of war and longtime U.S. senator, was a power player in Pennsylvania politics.*

duced a full length portrait of Simon, that at the distance of ten feet could not be distinguished from a fine engraving. I seized my opportunity, found Simon in cozy quarters opposite Willard's, and presented it in person. He was delighted—his daughter was delighted—a full-faced heavily bearded Congressman present was delighted, and after repeated assurances of 'thine to serve,' on the part of the Senator,' I crossed to my hotel—not Willard's—hadn't as yet sufficient elevation of person and depth of purse for that,—but an humbler one in a back street. Next day I saw my handiwork in the Rotunda—the admiration of all but a black long-haired puppy, an M.C.[1] and F. F.V., as I afterwards learned, who said to a lady at his elbow who had admired it, "Practice makes

(1)    Member of Congress (M.C.) who belonged to a First Family of Virginia (F.F.V.).

some of the poor clerks at the North tolerably good pensmen." I could have kicked him, but thought it might interfere with the little matter in hand.

" 'Tom,' said the senatorial star of my hopes one day, when my purse had become as lean as a June shad, 'Tom, there is a place of $800 a year, I have in view. A Senator is interfering, but I think it can be managed. You must have patience, these things take time. I will write to you as early as any definite result is attained.'

"Relying on Simon's management, which in his own case had never failed, next morning saw me in the cars with light heart and lighter purse, bound for home and Mrs. H., who I am proud to think regretted my absence more than my presence, although she would not admit it.

"Days passed; months passed; my wife reproached me with lost time —my picture was gone; I had not heard from Simon; I ventured to write; next mail brought a letter rich in indefinite promises.

"Years passed, and Simon was Secretary of War at a time when the office had influence, position, and patronage, unequalled in its previous history. 'Now is your time, Tom,' something within whispered—not conscience—for that did not seem to favor my connection with Simon.

"I wrote again. Quartermasters, Clerks by the thousands, Paymasters —I was always remarkably ready in disposing of funds—and Heaven only knows what not were wanted in alarming numbers. Active service was proposed by Simon; but you know, gentlemen, I am constitutionally disqualified for that. And after tediously waiting months longer, I succeeded without Simon's aid in obtaining my present honorable but unfortunate position.

"And that reminds me of the whiskey, another round, men." It was taken; Tom's idea was to drink the detail into forgetfulness of their errand. But he missed his men. He might as well have tried to lessen a sponge by soaking it. The Virginia Captain announced that the Colonel had ordered them to confiscate the whiskey for the use of the Hospital, and to the Surgeon's quarters the detail must next proceed. The Captain gathered up the bottles. The detail bowed themselves out of the tent, and poor Tom thought his misfortunes crowned, as he saw them leave laboring under a load of liquor inside and out. At the Surgeon's tent we will again see them.

# CHAPTER V.

*The Scene at the Surgeon's Quarters—Our Little Dutch Doctor—Incidents of his Practice—His Messmate the Chaplain—The Western Virginia Captain's account of a Western Virginia Chaplain—His Solitary oath—How he preached, how he prayed, and how he Bush-whacked—His revenge of Snowden's death—How the little Dutch Doctor applied the Captain's Story.*

TAPS had already been sounded before the detail arrived at the Surgeon's tent. The only Surgeon present had retired to his blankets. Aroused by the blustering, he soon lit a candle, and sticking the camp candlestick into the ground, invited them in.

And here we must introduce the Assistant-Surgeon, or rather the little Dutch Doctor as he was familiarly called by the men.[1] Considering his character and early connection with the regiment, we are at fault in not giving him an earlier place in these pages.

The Doctor was about five feet two in height, hardly less in circumference about the waist, of an active habit of body and turn of mind, eyes that winked rapidly when he was excited, and a movable scalp which threw his forehead into multiform wrinkles as cogitations beneath it might demand. A Tyrolese by birth, he was fond of his Fatherland, its mountain songs, and the customs of its people. Topics kindred

---

(1)    Otto Schittler was a physician from Philadelphia.

to these were an unfailing fund of conversation with him. Thoroughly educated, his conversation in badly broken English, for he made little progress in acquiring the language, at once amused and instructed. Among his fellow surgeons and officers of his acquaintance, he ranked high as a skilful surgeon on account of superior attainments, acquired partly through the German Universities and partly in the Austrian service, during the campaign of Magenta, Solferino, and the siege of Mantua. With a German's fondness for music, he beguiled the tedium of many a long winter evening. With his German education he had imbibed radicalism to its full extent. Thoroughly conversant with the Sacred Scriptures he was a doubter, if not a positive unbeliever, from the Pentateuch to Revelation. In addition to this, his flings at the Chaplain,[2] his messmate, made him unpopular with the religiously inclined of the regiment. He had besides, the stolidity of the German, and their cool calculating practicalism. This did not always please the men. They thought him unfeeling.

"What for you shrug your shoulders?" said he on one occasion to a man from whose shoulders he was removing a large fly blister.

"It hurts."

"Bah, wait till I cuts your leg off—and you know what hurts."

"Here, you sick man, here goot place," said he, addressing a man just taken to the hospital with fever, in charge of an orderly sergeant, at surgeon's call, "goot place, nice, warm, dead man shust left." Remarks such as these did not, of course, tend to increase the comfort of the men; they soon circulated among the regiment, were discussed in quarters, and as may be supposed greatly exaggerated, and all at the Doctor's cost. But the Doctor pursued the even tenor of his way, entirely unmindful of them.

About the time of which we write, a clever, honest man died of a disease always sudden in its termination, rheumatic attack upon the heart. The Doctor had informed him fully of his disease, and that but

---

(2)     William H. Rice of Bethlehem, Pennsylvania, was a pastor in the Moravian Church.

little could be done for it. The poor man, however, was punctual in attendance at Surgeon's Call, and insisted upon some kind of medicine. Bread pills were furnished. One morning, after great complaint of pain about the heart, and a few spasms, he died. His comrades, shocked, thought his death the effect of improper medicine. The Doctor's pride was touched. He insisted upon calling in other surgeons; the pills found in his pocket were analyzed, and discovered to be only bread. The corpse was opened, and the cause of death fully revealed. As the Doctor walked away in stately triumph, some of the men who had been boisterous against him, approached by way of excusing their conduct, and said that now they were perfectly satisfied. "What you know!" was his gruff reply, "you not know a man's heart from a pig's."

Many like incidents might be told—but we must not leave these Captains standing too long at the door of the tent; with the production of the light in they came, with the remark that they had brought hospital supplies. In the meantime several officers, field and company, attracted by the noise and whiskey, came in from regimental headquarters.

"Must see if goot," and the Doctor applied the bottle to his lips; it was not a favorite drink of his, and tasted badly in lieu of Rhine wine or lager.

"May be goot whiskey."

"Let practical whiskey drinkers have a chance," said two or three at once, and the bottle went its round.

The test was not considered satisfactory until another and another had been emptied.

The increasing confusion aroused the Chaplain, who hitherto had been snugly ensconced beneath his blankets in the corner opposite the Doctor.

"Here, Chaplain, your opinion, and don't let us hear anything about putting the bottle to your neighbor's lips," said a rough voice in the crowd. The Chaplain politely declined, with the remark that they appeared too anxious to put the bottle to their own lips to require any assistance from their neighbors.

"Chaplain not spiritually minded," muttered the Doctor, "so far but three preaches, and every preach cost government much as sixty tollar."

The calculation at the Chaplain's expense, amused the crowd, and annoyed the Chaplain, who resumed his blankets.

"When I was in Western Virginny, under Rosecrans,"—

"The old start and good for a yarn," said an officer.

"Good for facts," replied the Chief of the Detail.

"Never mind, Captain, we'll take it as fact," said the Adjutant.

"We had a chaplain that was a chaplain in every sense of the word."

"Did he drink and swear?" inquired a member of the Detail.

"On long marches and in fights he had a canteen filled with what he called chaplain's cordial, about one part whiskey and three water. I tasted it, but with little comfort. One day, a member of Rosy's staff seeing him pulling at it, asked for it, and after a strong pull, told the chaplain that he was weak in spiritual things. 'Blessed are the poor in spirit,' was the quick answer of the chaplain. As to swearing, he was never known to swear but once.

"I heard an officer tell the Adjutant a day or two ago, that what was considered the prettiest sentence in the English language, had been written by a smutty preacher. I don't recollect the words as he repeated it, but it was about an old officer, who nursed a young one, and some one told him the young one would die. The old officer excited, said, 'By G—d, he shan't die.' It goes on to say then that an Angel flew up to heaven, to enter it in the great Book of Accounts, and that the Angel who made the charge cried over it and blotted it out. That is the substance anyhow. Well, sir, if the Third Virginny's Chaplain's oath was ever recorded it is in the same fix."

"Well, tell us about it, how it happened," exclaimed several.

"Why you see, Rosy sent over one day for a Major who had lately come into the Division, and told him that 300 rebels were about six miles to our left, in the bushes along a creek, and that he should take 300 men, and kill, capture, or drive them off. The Major was about to make a statement. 'That's all, Major,' with a wave of his hand for him to leave, 'I expect a good account.'

"That was Rosy's style: he told an officer what he wanted, and he supposed the officer had gumption enough to do it, without bothering him, as some of our red-tape or pigeon-hole Generals, as the boys call them, do with long written statements that a memory like a tarred stick couldn't remember—telling where these ten men must be posted, those twenty-five, and another thirty, etc. I wonder what such office Generals think—that the Rebels will be fools enough to attack us when we want them to, or take ground that we would like to have them make a stand on."

"Captain, we talk enough ourselves about that; on with the story."

"Well, four companies, seventy-five strong each, were detailed to go with him, and mine among the number, from our regiment. The chaplain got wind of it, and go he would. By the time the detail was ready, he had his bullets run, his powder-horn and fixin's on, and long Tom, as he called his Kentucky rifle, slung across his shoulder."

"His canteen?" inquired an officer disposed to be a little troublesome.

"Don't recollect about that," said the Captain, somewhat curtly.

"On the march he mixed with the men, talked with them about all kinds of useful matters, and gave them a world of information.

"We had got about a mile from where we supposed the Rebels were; my company, in advance as skirmishers, had just cleared a wood, and were ten yards in the open, when the Butternuts opened fire from a wood ahead at long rifle range. One man was slightly wounded. We placed him against a tree with his back to the Rebels, and under cover of the woods were deciding upon a plan of attack, when up gallops our fat Major with just breath enough to say, 'My God, what's to be done?'

"I'll never forget the chaplain's look at that. He had unslung long Tom; holding it up in his right hand, he fairly yelled out, 'Fight, by G—d! Boys, follow me.' And we did follow him. Skirting around through underbrush to our left, concealed from the Rebs, we came to an open again of about thirty yards. The Rebs had retired about eighty yards in the wood to where it was thicker.

"Out sprang the Chaplain, making a worm fence, Indian fashion, for a big chestnut. We followed in same style. My orderly was behind another chestnut about ten feet to the Chaplain's left, and slightly to his rear. There was for a spell considerable random firing, but no one hurt, and the Rebs again retired a little. We soon saw what the Chaplain was after. About eighty-five yards in his front was another big chestnut, and behind it a Rebel officer. They blazed away at each other in fine style— both good shots, as you could tell by the bark being chipped, now just where the Chaplain's head was, and now just where the officer's was. The officer was left-handed. The Chaplain could fire right or left equally well. By a kind of instinct for fair play and no gouging that even the Rebs feel at times, the rest on both sides looked at that fight, and wouldn't mix. My orderly had several chances to bring the Rebel. Their rifles cracked in quick succession for quite a spell. The Chaplain, at last, not wanting an all-day affair of it, carefully again drew a bead on a level with the chip marks on the left of the Rebel tree. He had barely time to turn his head without deranging the aim, when a ball passed through the rim of his hat. As he turned his head, he gave a wink to the orderly, who was quick as lightning in taking a hint. A pause for nearly a minute. By and by the Rebel pokes his head out to see what was the matter. Seeing the gun only, and thinking the Chaplain would give him a chance when he'd take aim, he did not pull it in as quick as usual. My orderly winked,—a sharp crack, and the Rebel officer threw up his hands, dropped his rifle, and fell backward, with well nigh an ounce ball right over his left eye, through and through his head. Our men cheered for the Chaplain. The Rebs fired in reply, and rushed to secure the body. That cost them three more men, but they got their bodies, and fast as legs could carry them, cut to their fort about three miles to their rear. We of course couldn't attack the fort, and returned to camp. The boys were loud in praise of the Chaplain. Their chin music, as they called camp rumors, had it that the officer killed was a Rebel chaplain. Old Rosy, when he heard of it, laughed, and swore like a trooper. I hear he has got over swearing now—but it couldn't have been until after he left Western Virginny. I heard our Chaplain say that he heard a brother chaplain say, and he believed him to be a Christian,—that he believed that the Apostle Paul himself would learn to swear inside of six months, if he entered the service in Western Virginny. Washington prayed at Trenton, and swore at Monmouth, and I don't believe that the War Department requires Chaplains to be better Christians than Washington. Our old Chaplain used to say that there were many things worse than swearing, and that he didn't believe that men often swore away their chances of heaven."

"Comforting gospel for you, captain," said that troublesome officer.

"He was a bully chaplain," continued the captain, becoming more animated, probably because the regimental chaplain, turtle-like, had again protruded his head from between the blankets. "He had no long tailed words or doctrines that nobody understood, that tire soldiers, because they don't understand them, and make them think that the chaplain is talking only to a few officers. That's what so often keeps men away from religious services. Our chaplain used to say that you could tell who Paul was talking to by his style of talk. I can't say how that is from my own reading; but I always heard that Paul was a sensible man, and if so he certainly would suit himself to the understanding of his crowd.

"Our old chaplain talked right at you. No mistake he meant you—downright, plain, practical, and earnest. He'd tell his crowd of back-woodsmen, flatboatmen and deck hands—the hardest customers that the gospel was ever preached to,—'That the war carried on by the Government was the most righteous of wars; they were doing God's service by fighting in it. On the part of the rebels it was the most unnatural and wicked of wars. They called it a second Revolutionary War, the scoundrels! when my father and your father, Tom Hulzman,' said he, addressing one of his hearers, 'fought in the Revolution, they fought against a tyrannical monarchy that was founded upon a landed aristocracy—that is, rich big feeling people, that owned very big farms. The Government stands in this war, if any thing, better than our fathers stood. We fight against what is far worse than a landed aristocracy, meaner in the sight of God and more hated by honest men, this accursed slave aristocracy, that will, if they whip us—(Can't do that, yell the crowd.) No, they can't. If they should, we would be no better than the poor whites that are permitted to live a dog's life on some worn-out corner of a nigger-owner's plantation. Would you have your children, Joe Dixon, insulted, made do the bidding of some long-haired lank mulatto nabob? (Never, says Joe.) Then, boys, look to your arms, fire low, and don't hang on the aim. We must fight this good fight out, and thank God we can do it. If we die, blessed will be our memory in the hearts of our children. If we live and go to our firesides battle-scarred, our boys can say, "See how dad fought, and every scar in front," and we'll be honored by a grateful people.' And he'd tell of the sufferings of their parents, wives, and children, if we didn't succeed, till the water courses on the dirty faces of his crowd would be as plain as his preaching.

"And pray! he'd pray with hands and eyes both open, in such a way that every one believed it would have immediate attention; that God would damn the Rebellion; and may be next day he'd have Long Tom doing its full share in hurrying the rebels themselves to damnation.

"And kind hearted! why old Tim Larkins, who had a wound on the shin that wouldn't heal, told me with tears in his eyes that he had been mother, wife, and child to him. He went about doing good.

"And now I recollect," and the Captain's eye glistened as he spoke, "how he acted when young Snowden was wounded. Snowden was a slender, pale-faced stripling of sixteen, beloved by everybody that knew him, and if ever a perfect Christian walked this earth, he was one, even if he was in service in Western Virginny. The chaplain was fond of company, and, as was his duty, mixed with the men. Snowden was reserved, much by himself, and had little or no chance to learn bad habits; that is the only way I can account for his goodness. I often heard the chaplain tell the boys to imitate Snowden, and not himself; 'you'll find a pure mouth there, boys, because the heart is pure; you'll see no letters of introduction to the devil,' as the chaplain called cards, 'in his knapsack.' By the way, he was so hard on cards, that even the boatmen, who knew them better than their A B C's, were ashamed to play them. He would say, 'Snowden is brave as man can be; he has a right to be, he is prepared for every fate. A Christian, boys, makes all the better soldier for his being a Christian,' and he would tell us of Washington, Col. Gardner, that preacher that suffered, fought and died near Elizabeth, in the Jerseys, and others.

"In bravery, none excelled Snowden. We were lying down once, but about sixty yards from a wood chuck full of rebels, when word was sent that our troops on the left must be signalled, to charge in a certain way. Several understood the signs, but Snowden first rose, mounted a stump, and did not get off although receiving flesh wounds in half-a-dozen different places, and his clothing cut to ribands, until he saw the troops moving as directed. How we gritted our teeth as we heard the bullets whiz by that brave boy. I have the feeling yet. We thought his goodness saved him. His was goodness! Not that kind that will stare a preacher full in the face from a cushioned pew on Sunday, and gouge you over the counter on Monday, but the genuine article. His time was yet to come.

"One day we had driven the rebels through a rough country some miles, skirmishing with their rear-guard; the Chaplain and Snowden with my company foremost. We neared a small but deep creek the rebels had crossed, and trying to get across, we were scattered along the bank. I heard a shot, and as I turned I saw poor Snowden fall, first on his knee and then on his elbow. I called the Chaplain. They were messmates—he loved Snowden as his own child, and always called him 'my boy.' He rushed to him, 'My boy, who fired that shot?' The lad turned to a clump of bushes about 80 yards distant on the other side of the creek. Long Tom was in hand, but the rebel was first, and a ball cut the Chaplain's coat collar. The flash revealed him; in an instant long Tom was in range, and another instant saw a Butternut belly face the sun. Dropping his piece, falling upon his knee, he raised Snowden gently up with his left hand. 'I am dying,' whispered the boy, 'tell my mother I'll meet her in heaven.' The Chaplain raised his right hand, his eyes swimming in tears, and in tones that I'll never forget, and that make me a better man every time I think of them, he said, 'O God, the pure in heart is before thee, redeem thy promise, and reveal thyself.' A slight gurgle, and with a pleasant smile playing upon his countenance, the soul of John Snowden, if there be justice in heaven, went straight up to the God who gave it." Tears had come to the Captain's eyes, and were glistening in the eyes of most of the crowd.

The Dutch doctor alone was unmoved. Stoically he remarked, "Very goot story, Captain, goot story, do our Chaplain much goot."

The crowd left quietly—all but the Captain, who, never forgetting business in the hurry of the moment, drew a receipt for the transfer of thirteen bottles of whiskey to the hospital department, which the doctor signed without reading.

## CHAPTER VI.

*A Day at Division Head-Quarters—The Judge Advocate—The tweedle-dum and tweedle-dee of Red-Tape as understood by Pigeon-hole Generals—Red-Tape Reveries—French Authorities on Pigeon-hole Investigations—An Obstreperous Court and Pigeon-hole Strictures—Disgusting Head-Quarter Profanity.*

THE General commanding Division desires to see Lieutenant Colonel ——, 210th Regiment, P. V., Judge Advocate,[1] immediately," were words that met the eye of the latter officer, as he unfolded a note handed him by an orderly. It was about nine in the forenoon of a fine day in October. Buckling on his sword, and ordering his horse, he rode at a lively canter to the General's Head-Quarters.

"Colonel," said the General, pulling vigorously at the same time at the left side of his moustache, as if anxious that his teeth should take hold of it, "I have sent for you in regard to this Record. Do you know, sir, that this Record has given me a d—d sight of trouble; why, sir, I consulted authorities the greater part of last night, French and American."

"In regard to what point, General?"

---

(1)    Armstrong appears to have been General Humphreys's favorite judge
         advocate in the fall of 1862.

*General Humphreys's staff. The adjutant, second from the right, is Capt. Carswell McClellan. Had he known it, Armstrong might have mentioned that McClellan had a brother on Confederate general Jeb Stuart's staff.*

"In regard to what point? In regard to all the points, sir. There, sir, is the copy made of that order detailing the Court. It reads, 'Detailed for the Court,' whereas it should be 'Detail for the Court.' My mind is not made up fully as to whether the variance vitiates the Record or not. The authorities appear to be silent upon that point. To say the least, it is d—d awkward."

"General, the copy is a faithful one of the order issued from your Head-Quarters."

"From my Head-Quarters, sir? By G—d, Colonel, that can't be. If I have been particular, and have prided myself upon any one thing, it has been upon having papers drawn strictly according to the Regulations. And I have tried to impress it upon my clerks. That infernal blunder made at my Head-Quarters! I'll soon see how that is." And the General, Record in hand, took long strides, for a little man, towards the Adjutant's tent.

"Captain," said he, addressing an officer who was best known in the Division as a relative of a leading commander, and whose only claim to merit—in fact, it had to counterbalance many habits positively bad—

consisted of his reposing under the shadow of a mighty name, "where is the original order detailing this Court?" "Here, General," said a clerk, producing the paper. The General's eye rested for a moment upon it, then throwing it upon the table, he burst out passionately: "Captain, this is too G— — bad after all my care and trouble in giving you full instructions. Is it possible that the simplest order can't be made out without my supervision, as if, by G—d, it was my business to stand over your desks all day long, see every paper folded, endorsement made, and the right pigeon-hole selected? This won't do. I give full instructions, and expect them carried out. By G—d," continued the General, striding vehemently across to his marquee, "they must be carried out.

"Colonel, I see that you are not accountable for this. If the d—d fool had only made it 'Detail of the Court,' it might have passed unnoticed."

"General," suggested the Colonel, "would not that have been improper? Would it not have implied an already existing organization of the court? whereas the phrase in the order is intended merely to indicate who shall compose the court."

"It would have looked better, sir," said the General, somewhat sharply. "Colonel, you are not to blame for this; you can return to quarters, sir."

The Colonel bowed himself out, remounted his black horse, and while riding at a slow walk, could not but wonder if the Government would not have been the gainer if it had made it the business of the General to fold and endorse papers, and dust pigeon-holes. It was generally understood that this occupation had been, previous to his being placed in command of the division, the sum-total of the General's military experience. And how high above him did this red-tapism extend? The General had been on McClellan's staff, and through his influence, doubtless, acquired his present position. Were its trifling details detaining the grand army of the Potomac from an onward movement in this most favorable weather, to the great detriment of national finances, the encouragement of the Rebellion, and the depression of patriots everywhere? Must the earnestness of the patriotic, self-sacrificing thousands in the field, be fettered by these cobwebs, constructed by men interested in pay and position? If so, then in its widest sense, is the utterance of an intelligent Sergeant, made a few days previous, true, that red-tape was a greater curse to the country than the rebellion. The loyal earnest masses would soon, if unfettered, have found leaders equally loyal and earnest—Joshuas born in the crisis of a righteous cause, whose unceasing blows would not have allowed the rebels breathing spells. It is not too late; but how much time, blood, to say nothing of money, have been expended in ascertaining that a great Union military leader thought the war in its best phase a mere contest for boundaries.

The black halted at the tent door, was turned over to his attendant, and the Lieut.-Colonel joined his tent companion the Colonel.

His stay was brief. In the course of a few minutes an orderly in great haste handed him the following note:

"The General commanding Division desires to see Lieut.-Colonel —— without delay."

The saddle, not yet off the black, was readjusted, and again the Judge-Advocate cantered over the gentle bluffs to Division Head-Quarters.

"Colonel," said the General, hardly waiting for his entrance, "these mistakes multiply so as I proceed in my duty as Reviewing Officer, that I am utterly confounded as to what course to pursue."

"Will you please point them out, General?"

"Point out the Devil!—will you point to something that is strictly in accordance with the regulations? Here you have 'Private John W. Holman, Co. I, 212th Regt. P. V.,' and then not two lines below, it is, John W. Holman, Private, Co. I, 212th Reg. P. V.' Now, by G— Colonel, one is certainly wrong, and *that* blunder did not come from Division Head-Quarters."

"Will the General please indicate which is correct?"

"Indicate! that's the d—l of it, that is the perplexing question; my French authorities are silent on the subject, and yet, sir, you must see that one must be wrong."

"That does not follow, General; it would be considered a mere clerical error. Records that I have seen have titles preceding and following both."

"There is no such thing in military law as a mere clerical error. Every thing is squared here by the regulations and military law. The General or Colonel who is unfortunate in consequence of strictly following these, will not, by military men, regular officers at least, be held accountable. Do not understand me as combating your knowledge of the law, Colonel; you may have excused, in your practice, bad records successfully on the ground of 'clerical errors,' but it will not do in the army. There's where volunteer officers make their mistakes; they don't think and act concertedly as regulars do. Individual judgment steps in too often, and officers' judgments play the D—l in the army. Now, in France, their rules in regard to this, are unusually strict."

"They order this matter better in France then," observed the Colonel, mechanically making use of the hackneyed opening sentence of "The Sentimental Journey." "And they manage them better, Sir;—Another thing, Colonel," quickly added the General, "t's must be crossed and i's carefully dotted. There are several omissions of this kind that might have sent the Record back. By the way, whose handwriting is this copy in?" said the General, looking earnestly at the Colonel. "A clerk's, sir." "A clerk! Another d—d pretty piece of business," continued the General, rising. "Colonel, that record is not worth a G—— not a G——, Sir! Who ever heard of a clerk being employed? no clerk has a right to know any thing of the proceedings."

"I have been informed, General, and have observed from published reports of proceedings of courts-martial, that clerks are in general use."

"Can't be! Colonel, can't be! By G—d, there is another perplexing matter for my already over-taxed time, and yet the senseless people expect Generals to move large armies, and plan big battles, when their hands are full of these d—d business details that cannot be neglected or delayed."

The General resumed his seat, ran his fingers through his hair with frightful rapidity, as if gathering disconcerted and scattered ideas, for a moment or two, and then looking up dismissed the Colonel.

The black was again in requisition; and again the Colonel's thoughts, with increased feelings of disgust, were directed to what he could not but think the trifling details that, as the General admitted, delay the movements of great armies, and the striking of heavy blows. T's must be crossed when they ought to be crossing the Potomac; i's dotted when we ought to be dotting Virginia fields with our tents. And war so proverbially, so historically uncertain, has its rules, which, if adhered to, will save commanders from censure—judgment not allowed to interfere. It would appear so from many movements in the history of the Army of the Potomac. What would that despiser of senseless details, defier of rules laid down by inferior men, and cutter of red tape, as well as master-genius in the art of war, the Great, the First Napoleon, have said to all this. Shades of Washington, Marion, Morgan, all the Revolutionary worthies, Jackson, all our Volunteer Officers, of whose military records we are justly proud—

> "Of the mighty can it be
> That this is all remains of thee!"

Generals leading armies such as the world never before saw, fettering movements on the field by the movements of trifling office details at the desk, which viewed in the best light are the most contemptible of excuses for delay.

This time the old black was not unsaddled;—a fortunate thought, as another request for the immediate presence of the Judge Advocate compelled him to take his dinner of boiled beans hasty and hot.

Whatever the reader may think of the General's condition of mind during the preceding interviews, it was to reach its fever heat in this. The Colonel saw, as he entered the marquee, that his forced calmness of demeanor portended a storm. Whether the Colonel thought that a half-emptied good-sized tumbler of what looked like clear brandy which stood on the table before him, had anything to do with it, the reader must judge for himself.

"Colonel, I had made up my mind to forward that Record with the mistakes I have already indicated to you, but after all I am pained to state that the total disregard of duty by the Court, and perhaps by yourself, in trifling—yes, by G—d —" here the General could keep in no longer, and rising with hand clinching the Record firmly, continued,— "trifling with a soldier's duty, the regulations, and the safety of the army will not allow it. Colonel, you are a lawyer, and is it possible that you can't see what that d—d Court has done?"

"I would be happy to be informed in what respect they have erred, General."

"Happy to be informed! how they have erred! By G—d, Colonel, you take this outrageous matter cool. That Record," said the General, holding it up, and waving it about his head,—the red tape with which the Judge Advocate had adorned it plentifully, if for no other purpose than to cover a multitude of mistakes, all the while streaming in the air, —"that Record is a disgrace to the Division. What does that Record show?" At this he threw it violently into a corner of the tent. "It shows, by G—d, that here was an enlisted soldier in the United States Army, found sleeping on his post in the dead hour of night, in the presence of the enemy, and yet—" said the General, lifting both hands clenched, "a pack of d—d volunteer-officers detailed as a court let him off.[2] Yes, I'll be G——," and his arms came down slapping against his hips, "let him off, with what? why a reprimand at dress parade, that isn't worth a d—n as a punishment. Here was a chance to benefit the Division; yes, sir, a military execution would do this Division good. It needs it; we'll have a d—d sight now to be court-martialed. What will General McClellan say with that record before him? Think of that, Colonel."

"I would be much more interested in what Judge Advocate Holt would say, General, on account of his vastly superior ability in that department; and as to the death penalty, General, I conscientiously think it would be little short of, if not quite, murder." The General had resumed his seat, but now arose as if about to interrupt;—but the Colonel continued:—

"General, that boy is but seventeen, with a look that indicates unmistakably that he is half an idiot. He has an incurable disease that tends to increase his imbecility. His memory, if he ever had any, is completely gone. The Articles of War, or instructions of officers as to picket duty, would not be remembered by him a minute after utterance, and not understood when uttered. I have thought since that I should have entered a plea of insanity for him. He had not previously been upon duty for a

---

(2)     The court-martialed private was Robert Stevens, 155th Pennsylvania.

month, and was that day placed on by mistake. The Court, if it had had the power, would have punished the officer that recruited him severely. He ought to be discharged; and the Court was informed that his application for discharge, based upon an all-sufficient surgeon's certificate, was forwarded to your headquarters a month ago, and has not since been heard from. Besides, this was not a picket station, but a mere inside regimental camp guard."

The Colonel spoke rapidly, but with coolness;—

*Joseph Holt, judge advocate general of the army, a War Democrat from Kentucky, was President Buchanan's last secretary of war.*

all the while the General's eyes, fairly glowing, were gazing down intently upon him.

"Colonel, if your manner was not respectful, I would think that you intended insulting me by your d—d provoking coolness. Conscience!" said the General, sneeringly, "conscience or no conscience, that man must be duly sentenced. By G—d, I order it. You must reconvene the Court without delay. It is well seen it is not a detail of Regulars. Conscience wouldn't trouble them when a d—d miscreant was upon trial. A boy of seventeen! Seventeen or thirty-seven! By G—d! he is a soldier in the Army of the United States, and must be tried and punished as a soldier. An idiot! What need you care about the brains of a soldier? If he has the army cap on his head, that's all you need require. Plea of insanity, indeed! We want no lawyer's tricks here. And as to that discharge, if it is detained at my head-quarters, it is because it was not properly folded or endorsed—may be will not fit neatly in the pigeon-hole. Colonel," continued the General, moderating his tone somewhat, "I must animadvert—by G—d, I must animadvert severely upon that Record."

"General," quietly interrupted the Colonel, "you will publish your animadversion, I trust, so that it can be read at dress parades, and the Division have the benefit of it."

"There, Colonel," said the General, twitching his moustache violently, "there it is again. You appear perfectly courteous—but that remark is cool contempt. I want you to understand," his tones louder, and gesticulations violent, "that you must take my strictures, tell the court that they must impose the sentence I direct, and leave conscience to me, and no d—d plea of insanity about it."

"General," observed the Colonel, rising, "I am the counsel of the prisoner as well as of the United States. I cannot and will not injure my own conscience, wrong the prisoner, or humiliate the Government by insisting upon a death penalty."

"Read my strictures to the court, and do your duty, sir, or I'll court-martial the whole d—d establishment. Go and re-assemble your court forthwith."

As he said this he handed a couple of closely written sheets of large sized letter-paper, tied with the inevitable red-tape, to the Colonel. The Colonel bowed himself out, and the chair in front of the pigeon-holes of the camp desk was again occupied by a living embodiment of red-tape.

The court was forthwith notified. It immediately met. The strictures were read, and in case of many sentences, especially towards the close, from necessity re-read by the Judge Advocate. After considerable laughter over the document, and some little indignation at the unwarranted dictation of "their commanding General," of which title the General had taken especial pains to remind them at least every third sentence, the court decided not to change the sentence, and directed the Judge Advocate to embody their reasons for the character of the sentence in his report. The reasons, much the same as those stated to the General by the Judge Advocate, were reduced to writing, and duly forwarded, with the record signed and attested, to their "commanding General." That record, like some other court-martial records of the

Division, has not since been heard of as far as the Judge Advocate or any member of the court is informed. The poor boy a few days afterwards entered a hospital, not again to rejoin his regiment. His application for discharge has not been heard of. With no prospect of being fit for active service—dying by inches in fact,—he is compelled at Government expense to follow the regiment in an ambulance from camp to camp, and on all its tedious marches.

The profanity in the foregoing chapter has doubtless disgusted the reader quite as much as its utterance did the Judge Advocate. And yet hundreds of the Division who have heard the General on hundreds of other occasions, the writer feels confident will certify that it is rather a mild mood of the General's that has been described. The habit is disgusting at all times. Many able Generals are addicted to the habit; but they are able in spite of it. That their influence would be increased without it, cannot be denied. It has been well said to be "neither brave, polite, nor wise." But now when the hopes of the nation center in the righteousness of their cause, and thousands of prayers continually ascend for its furtherance from Christians in and out of uniform, how utterly contemptible! how outrageously wicked! for an officer of elevated position, to profane the Name under which those prayers are uttered, and upon which the nation relies as its "bulwark," "its tower of strength," a very "present help in this its time of trouble."

# CHAPTER VII.

*A Picket-Station on the Upper Potomac—Fitz John's Rail Order—Rails for Corps Head-Quarters* versus *Rails for Hospitals—The Western Virginia Captain—Old Rosy, and How to Silence Secesh Women—The Old Woman's Fixin's—The Captain's Orderly.*

PICKET duty, while in this camp, was light. Even the little tediousness connected with it was relieved by the beautifully romantic character of the scenery. Confined entirely to the river front, the companies detailed were posted upon the three bluffs that extended the length of that front, and on the tow-path of the canal below.

The duty, we have said, was light. It could hardly be considered necessary, in fact, were it not to discipline the troops. The bluffs were almost perpendicular, varying between seventy-five and one hundred feet in height. Immediately at their base was the Chesapeake and Ohio canal, averaging six feet in depth. A narrow towing-path separated it from the Potomac, which, in a broad, placid, but deep stream, broken occasionally by the sharp points of shelving rocks, mostly sunken, that ran in ridges parallel with the river course, flowed languidly; the water being dammed below as before mentioned.

On one of the most inclement nights of the season, the Company commanded by our Western Virginia captain had been assigned the towing-path as its station. No enemy was in front, nor likely to be, from the manner in which that bank of the river was commanded by our batteries. In consequence, a few fires, screened by the bushes along the river bank, were allowed. Around these, the reserve and officers not on duty gathered.

In a group standing around a smoky fire that struggled for existence with the steadily falling rain, stood our captain. His unusual silence attracted the attention of the crowd, and its cause was inquired into.

"Boys, I'm disgusted; for the first time in my life since I have been in service; teetotally disgusted with the way things are carried on. I'm no greenhorn at this business either," continued the captain, assuming, as he spoke, the position of a soldier, and although somewhat ungainly when off duty, no man in the corps could take that position more correctly, or appear to better advantage. "I served five years as an enlisted man in an artillery regiment in the United States army, and left home in the night when I wasn't over sixteen, to do it; part of that time was in the Mexican war. Yes, sir, I saw nearly the whole of that. Since then, I've been in service nearly ever since this Rebellion broke out, and the hardest kind of service, and under nearly all kinds of officers, and by all that's holy, I never saw anything so mean nor was as much disgusted as I was today. Boys! when shoulder-straps with stars on begin to think that we are not human beings, of flesh and blood, liable to get sick, and when sick, needing attention like themselves, it's high time those straps change shoulders. These damp days we, and especially our sick, ought to be made comfortable. One great and good soldier that I've often heard tell of, wounded, of high rank, and who lived a long time ago, across the ocean, refused, although dying for want of drink, to touch water, until a wounded private near him first had drunk. That's the spirit. A man that'll do that, is right, one hundred chances to one in other respects. We have had such Generals, we have them now, and some may be in this corps, but it don't look like it."

"Well, Captain, what did you see?"

"Well, I had sent my Sergeant to get a few rails to keep a poor boy comfortable who had a high fever, and who could not get into the hospital for want of room. The wood that was cut from the hill was green, and the poor fellow had been nearly smoked to death. The Sergeant went with a couple of men, and was coming back, the men having two rails apiece, when just as they got the other side of the Toll-gate on the hill, the Provost-Guard stopped them, told them there was an order against their using rails, and they must drop them. It did no good to say that they were for a sick man, that was no go. They thought they had to do it, and did it. They hadn't come fifty yards toward camp, before one of those big six-mule corps-teams that have been hauling rails for the last four days, came along, and the rails were pitched into the wagon. When I heard of it I was wrothy. I cut a bee-line for the Adjutant and got the Order, and there it was in black and white, that no more fences— rebel fences—should be destroyed, and no more rails used. Now, I knew well that these corps-teams had hauled and hauled until the whole estab- lishment, from General Porter down to his Darkies, were in rails up to their eyes, and then, when they had their own fill, this order comes, and we, poor devils, might whistle. Here were our hospitals like smoke- houses, not fit for human beings, and especially the sick. It was a little too d—d mean. I couldn't stand it. The more I thought of it the madder I got, and I got fighting mad, when I thought how often that same Gener- al in his kid gloves, fancy rig, and cloak thrown back from his shoulders to show all the buttons and stars, had passed me without noticing my salute. He never got a second chance, and never will. I started off, took three more men than the Sergeant had; went to the first fence I could find, and that was about two miles—for the corps-teams had made clean work—loaded my men and myself, and started back. The Provost- Guard was at the old place; I was bound to pass them squarely.

" 'Captain,' said the Sergeant, 'we have orders to stop all parties carrying rails.'

" 'By whose orders?'

" 'General Porter's.'

" 'I am one of General Porter's men. I have authority for this, sir,' said I, looking him full in the eye.

" 'Boys, move on!' and on we did move. When the Lieut. saw us fil- ing left over the hill towards camp, he sent a squad after us. But it was too late. The Devil himself couldn't have had the rails in sight of my company quarters, and I told him so.

" 'I'll report you to the Division General, and have you court-mar- tialled, sir.'

*A. R. Waud's sketch of troops stripping fence rails for firewood.*

" 'Very well,' although I knew the General had a mania for courts-martial. 'I have been court-martialled four times, and cleared every clip.'

" 'Now let that court-martial come; somebody's meanness will see the light' thought I.

"Old Rosy, boys, was the man. I said I was disgusted, but we mustn't get discouraged. We have some earnest men—yes, I believe, plenty of them; but they're not given a fair show. It'll all come right, though, I believe. Men with hearts in them; and Rosy, let me tell you, is no runt in that litter.

" 'Captain,' said he to me one day when I had gone to his head-quarters according to orders, 'I have something that must be done without delay, and from what I've seen of you, you are just the man for the work. I passed our hospital a few minutes ago, and I thought it was about to blaze; the smoke came out of the windows, chimney, doors, and every little crack so damnably. I turned around and went in, and found that the smoke had filled it, and that the poor fellows were suffering terribly. Now, Captain, they have no dry wood, and they must have some forthwith, and I'll tell you where to get it.

" 'The other day I rode by a nest of she-rebels, and found that they had cord upon cord of the best hickory piled up in the yard, as if cut by their husbands, before leaving, for use this winter. They have made provision enough for our hospital too. Now take three army wagons, as many men as you need, and go about three miles out the Little Gap Road till you come to a new weather-boarded house at the Forks. Make quick work, Captain.'

"I did make quick work in getting there, for that was about ten, and about half-past eleven the government wagons were in the yard of the house and my company in front.

" 'We have no chickens,' squalled an old woman from a second-story window, 'nor pigs, nor anything—all gone. We are lone women.'

" 'Only in the day-time, I reckon,' said my orderly; the same fellow that winked at the chaplain. He was one of the roughest fellows that ever kept his breath over night. Long, lank, ill-favored, a white scrawny beard, stained from the corners of his mouth with tobacco juice; but for all, I'd pick him out of a thousand for an orderly. He was always there, and his rifle—he always carried his own—a small bore, heavy barrel, rough-looking piece, never missed.

"As the old woman was talking from the window, a troop of women, from eighteen to forty years old—but I am a better judge of horses' ages than women's; they slip us up on that point too often—came rushing out of the door. They made all kinds of inquiries, but I set my men quietly to work loading the wood.

" 'Now, Captain, you shan't take that wood,' said a well-developed little, rather pretty, black-haired woman, but with those peculiar black eyes, full of the devil, that you only see among the Rebels, and that the Almighty seems to have set in like lanterns in lighthouses to show that their bearers are not to be trusted. 'You shan't take that wood!' raising her voice to a scream. The men worked on quietly, and I overlooked the work.

" 'You dirty, greasy-looking Yankee,' said another, 'born in some northern poor-house.'

" 'And both parents died in jail, I'll bet.'

" 'If our Jim was only here, he'd handle the cowardly set in less time than one of them could pick up that limb.'

" 'You chicken thief, you come by it honestly. Your father was a thief before you, and your mother—'

"This last roused me. I could hear nothing bad of her from man or woman.

" 'You she-devil,' said I, turning to her, 'not one word more.' She turned toward the house.

"But they annoyed the men, and I concluded to keep them still.

" 'Sergeant,' said I, addressing the orderly, and nearing the house, the women close at my heels. 'Sergeant, as our regiment will camp near here tomorrow, we might as well look out for a company hospital. How big is that house?'

" 'Large enough, Captain; thirty by fifty at least.'

" 'How many rooms?'

" 'About three, I reckon, on first floor, and I guess the upper story is all in one, from its looks through the window. Plenty of room. Bully place, and what is more, plenty of ladies to nurse the poor boys.'

"The noses of the women not naturally cocked, became upturned at this last remark of the sergeant's. But they had become silent, and looked anxious.

" 'Sergeant, here's paper and pencil, just note down the names of the sick, and the rooms we'll put them in, so as to avoid confusion.'

"The sergeant ran the sharp end of the pencil half an inch in his mouth, and on the palm of his horny hand commenced the list, talking all the while aloud—slowly, just as if writing—'Let me see. My mem'y isn't more than an inch long, and there's a blasted lot of 'em.

" 'Jim Smith, Bob Riley, Larry Clark, got small-pox; Larry all broke out big as old quarters, put 'em in back room down stairs.' The women got pale, but small-pox had been common in those parts. 'George Johnson, Bill Davis, got the mumps.' 'The mumps, Sally, the mumps, them's

what killed George, and they're so catchin'—whispered one of the
women—and continued the sergeant, 'Bill Thatcher, George Clifton
the chicken-pox.' 'O Lord, the chicken-pox,' said another woman, 'it
killed my two cousins before they were in the army a week.'—'Put
them four,' said the sergeant, 'in the middle room down stairs. Save the
kitchen for cookin', and up stairs put Jim Williams, Spooky Johnson,
Tom Hardy, Dick Cramer, and the little cook boy; all got the measles.'
'The measles!' screamed out half-a-dozen together; 'Good-Lord, we'll
be killed in a week.' 'They say,' said another black eye, 'that that crack
Mississippi Brigade took the measles at Harper's Ferry, and died like flies.
They had to gather them from the bushes, and all over. Brother Tom told
me. He said our boys were worked nearly to death digging graves.'

" 'That was a good thing,' observed the sergeant.

" 'You beast!' said the little old woman advancing towards him, and
shaking her fist in his face.

" 'And what will become of us women?' screamed she.

" 'A pretty question for an old lady; we calculate that you ladies will
wait on the sick,' drily remarked the sergeant.

"At this the women, thinking their case hopeless, with downcast
looks quietly filed into the house.

"The boys by this time had about done loading the teams. All the
while I had watched the manners of the women closely and the house,
and I came to the conclusion that it would pay to make a visit inside.

"A guard was placed on the outside, and telling the sergeant and two
men to follow, I entered. It was all quiet below, but we found when we
had reached the top of the steps, and stood in the middle of the big room
up stairs, the women in great confusion, some in a corner of the room,
and a few sitting on the beds. Among the latter, sitting as we boys used
to say on her hunkers, with hands clasped about her knees, was the old
woman. Besides the beds the only furniture in the room was a large,
roughly made, double-doored wardrobe that stood in one corner.

"We hadn't time to look around before the old woman screeched
out—

" 'You won't disturb my private fixin's, will you?'

" 'I rather think not,' slowly said the sergeant, giving her at the same
time a comical look.

"Notwithstanding repeated and tearful assurances that there was nothing there, that the men had taken off all the arms, hadn't left lead enough to mend a hole in the bottom of the coffee-pot, etc., etc., we began to search the beds, commencing at one corner. There were two beds between us and the old woman's, and although we shook ticks and bolsters, and made otherwise close examination, we discovered nothing beyond the population usually found in such localities in Western Virginia.

"The old woman was fidgety. Her face, that at two reflections would have changed muscatel into crab apple vinegar, was more than usually wrinkled. 'O Lord, nothing here,' groaned she, as she sat with her back to the head-board. She did not budge an inch as we commenced at her bed.

"The sergeant had gone to the head-board, I to the foot. I saw a twinkle in his eye as he turned over the rough comfort, his hand reached down—he drew it up gradually, and the old woman slid as gradually from the lock to the muzzle of a long Kentucky rifle. 'O Lord,' groaned she, as she keeled over on her right side at the foot of the bed.

"A glow of admiration overspread the Sergeant's face as he looked at that rifle.

" 'Well, I swow, old woman, is that what you call a private fixin'?' said the Sergeant. 'A queer bed-fellow you've got; and just look, Captain,' said he, trying the ramrod, 'loaded, capped, and half cocked.'

"The heavy manner in which the old lady fell over satisfied me that we hadn't all the armory, and I directed her to leave the bed and stand on the floor.

" 'Can't, can I, Ann?' addressing one of the women.

" 'No, marm can't, she is helpless.'

" 'Got the rheumatics, had 'em a year and better,' groaned the old woman.

" 'Hadn't 'em when you shook your fist under my nose in the yard,' said the Sergeant. 'Get off the bed;' catching the old woman by the arm, he helped her off. She straightened up with difficulty, holding her clothes at the hips with both hands. 'Hold up your hands,' said the Sergeant. He was about to assist her, when not relishing that, she lifted them up; as she did so, there was a heavy rattling sound on the floor.

The old woman jumped about a foot from the floor clear out of a well filled pillow cushion, dancing and yelling like an Indian. Some hardware must have struck her toe and made her forget her rheumatism.

"That bag had two Colt's navy size, two pistols English make, with all the trappings for both kinds, and two dozen boxes of best make English water proof caps.

" 'Old woman,' said the Sergeant with a chuckle, 'your private fixin's as you call 'em, are worth hunting for.'

"But the old woman had reached the side of a bed, and was too much engaged in holding her toe, to notice the remark.

"The other beds were searched, but with no success. I had noticed while the old woman was hopping about a short fat woman getting behind some taller ones in the corner and arranging her clothing. The old woman's contrivance made me think the corner worth looking at.

"The women sulkily and slowly gave way, and another pillow-case was found on the floor, from which a brace of pistols, one pair of long cowhide riding boots, three heavy-bladed bowie knives, and some smaller matters, were obtained.

"The wardrobe was the only remaining thing, and on it as a center the women had doubled their columns.

" 'Oh, Captain, don't,' said several at once beseechingly, 'we're all single women, and that has our frocks and fixin's in it,' as I touched the wardrobe.

" 'As far as I've seed there is not much difference between married women's fixin's and single ones,' coolly said the Sergeant.

" 'There is not one of us married, Captain.'

" 'Sorry for that,' said the Sergeant, leisurely eyeing the women. 'If you'd take advice from a Yankee, some of you had better hurry up.'

"The women were indignant, but smothered it, having ascertained that a passionate policy would not avail.

"By this time one of the men had succeeded with his bayonet in forcing a door. The Sergeant had laid his hand on the door, when a pretty face, lit up with those same devilish black eyes, was looking into his half winningly, and a pair of small hands were clasping his arm. The Sergeant's head gradually fell as if to hear what she had to say, when magnetism, a desire to try experiments, or call it what you will, as 'love,' although said to 'rule the camp,' has little really to do with the monotony of actual camp scenes, or the horrors of the field itself,—at any rate the Sergeant's head dropped suddenly,—a loud smack, followed instantly by the dull sound of a blow,—and the Sergeant gently rubbed an already blackening eye, while the woman was engaged in drawing her sleeve across her mouth. Like enough some tobacco juice went with the sleeve, for the corners of the Sergeant's mouth were regular sluices for that article.

"The Sergeant's eye did not prevent him from opening the door, however.

" 'Well, I declare, brother Jim's forgot his clothes and sword,' said one of the women, manifesting much surprise.

" 'Do you call that brother Jim's clothes?' said the Sergeant, grasping a petticoat, above which appeared the guard of a cavalry sabre, and holding both up to view. 'I tell you it's no use goin' on,' said the Sergeant, somewhat more earnestly, his eye may be smarting a little, 'we're bound to go through it if it takes the hair off.' The women squatted about on the beds, down-hearted enough.

"And through it we went, getting five more sabres and belts, and two Sharp's rifles complete in that side, and a cavalry saddle, holsters with army pistols, bridles, and a rifled musket, in the other side; all brand new. There was nothing in the lower story or cellar.

"When I showed Rosy our plunder—and it hadn't to be taken to his tent either—when he heard of it, he came out as anxious and pleased as any of the boys,—he was a General interested in our luck more than his own pay,—he clapped me on the shoulder right before my men, and all the officers and men looking on, and said: 'Captain, you're a regular trump. Three cheers, boys, for the Captain and company.' And as he started them himself, the boys did give 'em, too. 'Captain, you'll not be forgotten—be easy on that point.' And I was easy, until a fit of sickness that I got put my fortune for the time out of Rosy's hands. The men never forgot that trip. The Sergeant often said though, it was the only trip he wasn't altogether pleased with, because, I suppose, his black eye was a standing joke."

Just then, a sentinel's hail and the reply, "Grand Rounds," "Field Officer of the day," hurried the Captain off, and the crowd to their posts.

## CHAPTER VIII.

*The Reconnoissance—Shepherdstown—Punch and Patriotism—Private Tom on West Point and Southern Sympathy—The Little Irish Corporal on John Mitchel—A Skirmish—Hurried Dismounting of the Dutch Doctor and Chaplain—Battle of Falling Waters not intended—Story of the Little Irish Corporal—Patterson's Folly, or Treason.*

AN old German writer has said that "six months are sufficient to accustom an individual to any change in life." As he might fairly be supposed to have penned this for German readers and with the fixed habits and feelings of a German, if true at all, it ought to hold good the world over. As we are more particularly interested in camps at present, we venture the assertion that six weeks will make a soldier weary of any camp. With our Sharpsburg camp, however, perhaps this feeling was assisted by the consciousness so frequently manifested in the conversation of the men that the army should be on the move.

Hundreds of relatives and friends had taken advantage of the proximity of the camp to a railroad station to pay us a visit, and with them of course came eatables—not in the army rations—and delicacies of all kinds prepared by thoughtful heads and willing hands at home. Not unfrequently the marquees of the officers were occupied by their families, who, in their enjoyment of the novelties of camp life, the drills, and dress parades of the regiment, treasured up for home consumption, brilliant recollections of the sunny side of war. All this, to say nothing of the scenery, the shade of the wood, that from the peculiar position of the camp, so gratefully from early noon extended itself, until at the hour for dress parade the regiment could come to the usual "parade rest" entirely in the shade. But the roads were good, the weather favorable, the troops effective, and the inactivity was a "ghost that would not down" in the sight of men daily making sacrifices for the speedy suppression of the Rebellion. The matter was constantly recurring for discussion in the shelter tent as well as in the marquees, in all its various forms. A great nation playing at war when its capital was threatened, and its existence endangered. A struggle in which inert power was upon one side, and all the earnestness of deadly hatred and blind fanaticism upon the other. An enemy vulnerable in many ways, and no matter how many loyal lives were lost, money expended by the protraction of the war, but to be assailed in one. But why multiply? Ten thousand reasons might be assigned why a military leader, without an aggressive policy of warfare, unwilling to employ fully the resources committed to him, should not succeed in the suppression of a Rebellion. The nation suffered much in the treason that used its high position to cloak the early rebel movement to arms, and delayed our own preparations; but more in the incapacity or half-heartedness that made miserable use of the rich materials so spontaneously furnished.

In the improvement of the Regiment the delay at the Sharpsburg camp was not lost. The limited ground was well used, and Company and Battalion drills steadily persevered in, brought the Regiment to a proficiency rarely noticed in regiments much longer in the field.

"Three days' cooked rations, sixty rounds of ammunition, and under arms at four in the morning. How do you like the smack of that, Tom?"

"It smacks of war," says Tom, "and it's high time." The first speaker had doffed the gown of the student in his senior year, greatly against the wishes of parents and friends, to don the livery of Uncle Sam. One would scarcely have recognized in the rough sunburned countenance, surmounted by a closely fitting cap, once blue but now almost red, and not from the blood of any battle-field—in the course slovenly worn blue blouse pantaloons, unevenly suspended, and wide unblacked army shoes, the well dressed, graceful, accomplished student that commended himself to almost universal admiration among the young ladies of his acquaintance. The second speaker, thinking that a more opportune war had never occurred to demand the silence of the law amid resounding arms, had left his desk in an attorney's office, shelved his Blackstone, and with a courage that never flinched in the field of strife or in toilsome marches where it can perhaps be subjected to a severer test, had thoroughly shown that the resolution with which he committed himself to the war was one upon which no backward step would be taken. They were old friends, and fast messmates. Their little dog-tent, as the shelter tents were called, had heard from each many an earnest wish that their letters might smell of powder.

The feeling then with which George uttered this piece of news, and the joy of Tom as he heard it, can be appreciated.

"What authority have you, George?"

"Old Pigeon-hole's. I heard him, while on duty about his Headquarters today, tell a Colonel, that the move had been ordered; that the War Department had been getting uncommonly anxious, and that it interfered with certain examinations he was making into very important papers."

"I'll warrant it. I would like to see any move in a forward direction that would not interfere with some arrangement of his. His moves are on paper, and a paper General is just about as valuable to the country as a paper blockade."

"Is the movement general?"

"I think it is."

"Of course then it interferes. George, did you ever hear any patriotism about those Headquarters? You have been a great deal about them."

"No, but I have seen a good deal of punch in that neighborhood."

"I'll warrant it—more punch than patriotism. A great state of affairs this. There are too many of these half-hearted Headquarters in the army. They ought to be cleaned out, and I believe that before this campaign is through it will be done. If it is not done, the country is lost."

"Country lost! why of course; that is almost admitted about that establishment. They say we may be able to pen them up, and as they don't say any more they must think that is about all. I heard a young officer—a Regular—who seems to be intimate up there say: that there was no use talking—that men that fought the way the Southerners— he didn't use the word Rebels—did, could not be conquered,—that they were too much for our men, etc., etc. I could have kicked the shoulder-strapped coward or traitor, maybe both, but if I had, old Pigeon-hole would have had a military execution for the benefit of the Volunteers in short order. And then he strutted, talking treason and squirting tobacco juice—and all the while our Government supporting the scoundrel. West Point was on his outside, but his conversation and vacant look told me plainly enough that outside of a Government position the squirt had not brains enough to gain a day's subsistence. But he's one of Pigey's 'my Regulars,' and to us Volunteers he can put himself on his dignity with a '*Procul, Procul, este Profani.*' "

"George, don't stir me up on that subject any more. I get half mad when I think that Uncle Sam's worst enemies are those of his own household. We had better anticipate the Captain's order about this in our preparations, and not be up half the night."

"Even so, Tom."

George was correct; as to a move at least, for early dawn saw the Division and a detachment from another Division, en route to the river. There was the usual quiet in the camps along which they passed, showing that George was mistaken as to the move being general. The troops marching through a winding and wooded defile, passed the deservedly well known Brigade of General Meagher. "Here's Ould Ireland Boys," said the little Irish Corporal, pointing, as his face glowed with pride, to the flag adorned with "The Harp of Ould Ireland, and the Shamrock so green," the emblems of the Emerald Isle.

"Their General is an Irishman thrue to the sod, none of your rinegade spalpeens like John Mitchel—fighting for slave-holders in Ameriky, and against the Lords and Dukes in Ould Ireland, and the slave-holders as Father Mahan tould me the worst of the two, more aristocratic, big-feeling, and tyrannical than the English nobility. He said, too, that the blackguard could never visit the ould sod again unless he landed in the night-time, and hid himself by day in a bog up to his eyes, and even then the Father said he believed the blissed mimory of St. Patrick,

> 'Who drove the Frogs into the Bogs,
> And banished all the Varmint,'

would clean him out after the rist of the varmin."[1]

"Three cheers for the Irish Brigade" greeted the Corporal's remarks.

The troops crossed with difficulty and delay at the only ford—and wondered with reason at the activity of the Rebels in having transported across not only their army and baggage, but hundreds if not thousands of their dead and wounded. The road winding around the high rocks on the Virginia side, must have been in more peaceful times a favorite drive for the gentry of the neighborhood. Shepherdstown itself adorns a most commanding position. On the occasion of this Union visit its inhabitants appeared intensely Secesh. Not so in the early history of the rebellion; when Patterson's column "dragged its slow length along" through the valley of the Shenandoah. Scouting parties then saw Union flags from many a window. True, they streamed from dwellings owned by the merchants, mechanics, and laborers, the real muscle of the country; but this was true of most of the towns of the Border States, and more early energetic action in affording these classes protection would have secured us the aid of their strong hands. As it was, these resources were in great measure frittered away—gradually drawn by what appeared an irresistible influence into the vortex of the Rebellion—or scattered wanderingly through the Loyal States, and worn down and exhausted in the support of dependent and outcast families.

Sharpsburg was greatly altered. The yellow Rebel Flag designated almost every other building as a Hospital. Their surgeons in grey pompously paraded the streets. As the troops marched through, they were subjected to almost every description of insult. One interesting group of Rebel petticoated humanity standing in front of premises that would not have passed inspection by one of our Pennsylvania Dutch housewives, held their noses by way of showing contempt.

---

(1)     John Mitchel and Thomas Francis Meagher had been exiled to Australia as a
        result of the Irish Uprising in 1848. They escaped and made their way to New
        York, where they worked for Irish freedom. Mitchel found the South more
        compatible and during the war was a newspaper editor in Richmond. Despite
        the Corporal's prediction, a tumultuous welcome greeted him when he finally
        returned to Ireland in 1874, and he was elected to Parliament.

"Guess you have to do that, about them diggins. When did you scrub last?" said a bright-eyed officer's servant, whom a few years' service as a newsboy had taught considerable shrewdness.

To annoy others "My Maryland" and "John Brown" were sung by the men. Around a toll-house at the west end of town, occupied by an old lady whose husband had been expelled with a large number of other patriotic residents, had congregated some wives of exiled loyal husbands, who were not afraid to avow their attachment for the old Union, by words of encouragement and waving of handkerchiefs. They were backed by a reserve force of negroes of both sexes, whose generous exhibition of polished ivories, to say the least, did not represent any great displeasure at the appearance of the troops.

"There are the Reserves," said one of the boys, pointing to where the negroes stood.

"Yes, and if they were called in the issue of this Rebellion would be speedy and favorable," said a Captain in musical tones, "and I can't think but that this costly child's play will drive the nation into their use much sooner than many expect. Let them understand that they are the real beneficiaries of this war, and they will not stay their hands. And why shouldn't we use them? 'They are one of the means that God and nature have placed in our hands,' and old Virginia can't object to that doctrine."

"But, Captain," said his First Lieutenant, "would you fight alongside of a darkie?"

"Would you drive a darkie away if he came to assist you in a struggle for life?"

"Yes, but we have men enough without their aid."

"You forget, Lieutenant, that, as matters now are, we have them fighting against us."

"How so?"

"They raise the crops that feed the Rebel army. They are just as much, perhaps not as directly, but just as really fighting against us as the founders who cast their cannon. And as to fighting alongside of them, they may have quite as many prejudices against fighting alongside of us. There is no necessity of interfering with either. Organize colored regiments; appoint colored line officers if efficient, and white field and staff officers, until they attain sufficient proficiency for command. As to their fighting qualities, military records attest them abundantly. The shrewd 'nephew of his uncle' has used them for years."

The earnest argument of the Captain made a deep impression upon the men. The desperation of our case, depressed finances, heavy hospital lists, and many other causes, independently of abstract justice, are fast removing that question beyond the pale of prejudice.

A halt was ordered, and the men rested on the sward that bordered the hard pike, and in the immediate neighborhood of the village cemetery. It was literally crowded with graves, many of them fresh. Large additions had been made from surrounding fields, and they too were closely taken up by ridges covering the dead of Antietam.

The surrounding country had suffered little from the ravages of war. Visited occasionally by scouting parties—principally cavalry—of both sides, there had been none of the occupation by large bodies of troops, which levels fences, destroys crops, and speedily gives the most fertile of countries the seeming barrenness of the desert. The valley had a reputation that ran back to an ante-Revolutionary date for magnificence of scenery and fertility of soil. Washington, with all the enthusiasm of ardent youth, paid it glowing encomiums in his field-notes of the Fairfax surveys. In later times, when the destinies of our struggling colonies rested upon his ample shoulders, the leaders of the faction opposed to him—for great and good as he was, he had jealous, bitter, and malignant enemies—settled a few miles beyond Shepherdstown, at what has since been known as Leetown. The farms, with few exceptions, had nothing of the slovenly air, dilapidated, worn-out appearance, that characterized other parts of Virginia. Upon inquiry we found that the large landowners were in the habit of procuring tenants from the lower counties of Pennsylvania, and that the thrift and close cultivation were really imported. In the course of time these tenants, with their customary acquisitiveness, became landowners themselves, and their farms were readily distinguishable by the farm buildings, and particularly by the large substantial red bank barns.

The troops moved on to a wood, skirting either side of the road, and were thrown into line of battle. The country was gently rolling, and the woods in front that crowned the summit of the low ridges were shelled before advancing. Occasionally Rebel horsemen could be seen rapidly riding from one wood to another, making observations from some commanding point.

In the line of battle by Brigade, flanked by skirmishers, the advance was made. To the troops this, although toilsome, was unusually exciting. Through woods, fields of corn whose tall tops concealed even the mounted officers, and made the men, like quails in standing grain, be guided by the direction of the sound of the command, rather than by the touch of elbows to the center,—over the frequent croppings out of ledges of rock, through the little streams of this plentifully watered country, the movement slowly progressed. They had not advanced far when a shell screamed over their heads, uncomfortably close to the Surgeon and Chaplain, some fifty yards in the rear, and mangled awfully a straggler at least half a mile further back. As may be supposed, his fate was a standing warning against straggling for the balance of the campaign.

Notwithstanding further compliments from the rebels, who appeared to have our range, a roar of laughter greeted the dexterity with which the Chaplain and Surgeon ducked and dismounted at the sound of the first shell. Of about a size, and both small men, they fairly rolled from their horses. The boys had it that the little Dutch Doctor grabbed at his horse's ear, or rather where it ought to have been; as the horse was formerly in the Rebel service, and was picked up by the Doctor after the battle of Antietam, minus an ear, lost perhaps through a cut from an awkward sabre, and missing it fell upon his hands and knees in front of the horse's feet.

As the shells grew more frequent and direct in range, the men were ordered to halt and lie down. The field officers dismounted, and were joined by the Chaplain and Doctor leading their horses.

"Colonel, I no ride that horse," said the Doctor, sputtering and brushing the dust off his clothes.

"Why not, Doctor?"

"Too high—very big—" touching the top of the shoulder of the bony beast, and almost on tip-toe to do it, "had much fall, ground struck me hard," continued he, his eyes snapping all the while.

"Well, Doctor," remarked one of the other field officers, "we have told you all along that if you ever got in range with that horse, your life would hardly be worth talking about."

"They not know him," anxiously said the Doctor.

"Of course they know him. He has the best and plainest ear-mark in the world."

"Pretty close shoot that, anyhow."

The result of this conversation was, that in the further movement the Doctor led his horse during the day.

The firing ceased with no damage, save the bruises of the Doctor, and those received by our tonguey little Corporal, who asserted that the windage of a shell knocked him off a fence. As he fell into a stone heap, it is more than probable that he had some good reason for the movement —besides, why cannot Corporals suffer from wounds of that kind, frequently so fashionable among officers of higher grade?

The onward movement was resumed. In the course of half an hour the cannonading again opened, interspersed with occasional volleys of musketry. The rattling of musketry became incessant. Advancing under cover of rocky bluffs, the shells passed harmlessly over the Brigade. We soon ascertained that the Rebels had made a stand at a point where our advance, from the character of the country, necessarily narrowed into the compass of a strip of meadow-land. Here a brigade of Rebel infantry were drawn up in line of battle. Their batteries posted on a neighboring height, were guided by signals, the country not admitting of extended observation. The contest was brief. The gleam of the bayonets as they fell for the charge, broke the Rebel line, and they retired in considerable confusion to the wood in their rear. Our batteries soon shelled them from those quarters, and the advance continued—the skirmishers of both sides keeping up a rattling fire. Some Rebel earthworks were passed, and late in the afternoon the track of the Baltimore and Ohio railroad was crossed. The Rebels, before leaving, had done their utmost to complete the destruction of that much abused road. At intervals of every one hundred yards, piles of ties surmounted by rails were upon fire. These were thrown down by our men. About half a mile beyond the road, in a finely sodded valley, the troops were halted for the night, pickets posted, and the men prepared their meals closely in the rear of their stacks. The night was a pleasant one. An open air encampment upon such a night is one of the finest phases of a soldier's life. Meals over, the events of the day were discussed, or such matters as proved of interest to the different groups.

One group we must not pass unnoticed. The majority lounged lazily upon the grass, some squatted upon their knapsacks, while a large stone was given by common consent to a tall, fine-looking Lieutenant, the principal officer present.

"Corporal," said he, addressing the little Irish Corporal, "do you know how near we are to Martinsburg?"

"Faith I don't, Lieutenant."

"I do not know the exact distance myself, but we are not over three or four miles from the road that we took when we guarded the ammunition train from Martinsburg to Charlestown."

"Oh, it's the ould First ye are spaking about, is it? Ov coorse I ricollect Martinsburg, and the markit-house where I guarded the fifty nagurs that Gineral Patterson had ordered to be arrested for having stripes on their pantaloons, Uncle Sam's buttons on their caps, and belts with these big brass U.S. plates on. Oh, but it was a swate crowd. The poor divils were crowded like cattle on cars, and it was one of the hot smothering nights. I couldn't help thinkin', that by and by, if our armies didn't move faster, the nagurs would have little trouble gettin' into uniforms. They have a nat'ral concate about such things. One poor fellow rolled the whites of his eyes awfully, and almost cried when I ordered him out of his red breeches."

"The day has not come yet, and need not," rejoined the Lieutenant, "if our generals do their duty. Don't you recollect how we were hurried from Frederick, and after marching seven miles out of the way, made good time for all to Williamsport—how bayonets appeared to glisten upon every road leading into the town; and then our crossing the river, the band all the while playing 'The Star-spangled Banner,' and the march we made to Martinsburg, passing over the ground where the battle of Falling Waters had but a few days before been fought? If that battle had been followed up as it should have been, Johnson would never have reached Bull Run."

"Be jabers! do you know, Lieutenant, that that fight was all a mistake upon our part? Shure, our ginerals niver intended it."

A laugh, with the inquiry "how he knew that?" followed.

"Didn't I hear a Big Gineral, that I was acting as orderly for while in Martinsburg—for they made orderlies of corporals thim days—tell a richly-dressed old lady, 'That it was our policy to teach our misguided Southern brethren, by an imposing show of strength, how hopeless it would be to fight against the Government.' The lady said, 'That would save much bloodshed, would become a Christian nation, and would return them as friends to their old way of thinking.' 'Yes, madam!' said the Gineral, 'there is no bitter feeling in our breasts,' clasping his breast. 'The masses south will soon see their country surrounded by volunteers in great numbers, and that the war, if protracted, must involve them all in ruin. When the war is over, madam, fanatics on both sides can be hung.'

" 'That was a dreadful affair at Falling Waters, General,' said the lady, with a strange twinkle in her eyes.

" 'Yes, madam,' replied the General, coloring up to his ears, 'a blunder of some of our volunteer officers. Ordinary military prudence made us send forward some force to reconnoitre before crossing the main army. These troops were to fall back if the enemy appeared in force. Not understanding their orders, or carried away by the excitement of the moment, they engaged the enemy with the unfortunate results to which you allude.'

"Av it would have been proper for a corporal, I would have asked the Gineral what Johnny Reb would do while we were taching him all that. Thim's the Gineral's exact words, for I paid particular attention. I put them tegither with what I had heard from a Wisconsin boy, and I got the whole history of that fight."

"Let's have it," shouted the crowd, now considerably increased, "at once!"

"Well, you see, they were sent forward to reconnoitre, as the Gineral said, and there was a Wisconsin regiment of bear hunters and the like, and a Pennsylvania regiment of deer hunters and Susquehannah rafts-men pretty well forward. These Wisconsin chaps, in dead earnest, brought their rifles along all the way from Wisconsin, and, like the

Susquehannah fellows, they couldn't kape hands off the trigger if there was any game about.

"Well, they got to Falling Waters without stirring up anything; you recollect, Lieutenant, where that rebel officer's house was burned down, and then the battery that was along with them, seeing some suspicious-looking Grey Backs dodging in and out of a wood, let them have a few round of shells just to see whether they were in force or not, according to orders. The Rebs made tracks for a low piece of ground behind a ridge, and then formed line of battle. Our men, with a yell, went forward, and when they saw the Rebs in line, these two Colonels, thinking they had been sent out to fight, and that their men didn't carry guns for nothing, ordered them to fire; and then they ordered them to load again, in order to relave their hips as much as possible from the load of ammunition; and then they fired again; and then, gittin' excited, and thinkin' this work too slow, and that it wouldn't do to take such bright bayonets home, they ordered a charge, and cheering, yelling, and howling, our boys went at the Rebs. The Rebs didn't stand to meet them, but fell back behind a barn. The batteries burned that,—and then they tried to form line again, but no use. As soon as our fellows gave the yell, they were off like all possessed. They had prepared to run by tearing the fences down; and then it was trying to form line, and breaking as soon as our fellows howled a little, all the way for five long miles to Martinsburg; and the last our boys saw of the Rebs was their straight coat-tails at the south end of the town. And that was the whole battle of Falling Waters; and may be Ould Patterson wouldn't have got to Martinsburg if them Colonels had reported the Rebs in force, and not got excited."

"But how did you hear all this? You forget that part of it."

"And couldn't you let that go? I thought I could concale that.

"Well, you know, Lieutenant, our ould Colonel boarded at the Brick Hotel, along the Railroad, above where the long strings of locomotives were burned, as the Gineral says, by our 'misguided southern friends'; and I was about there considerably on duty. One afternoon, a jolly-looking little chap, one of the Wisconsin boys, and one after my own heart— and he proved it, too, by trating me to several drinks—came along with a Rebel Artillery officer's coat under his arm. And we looked at the coat, and talked and drank, and drank and talked, until the Wisconsin chappy put it on, just to show me how the Rebel officer looked in it. It was a fine grey, trimmed with gold lace and scarlet, and the Wisconsin chappy looked gay in it, barring the sleeves were several inches too long, and the waist buttons came down nearly a foot too far, and it was too big round the waist. And he showed me after every drink what he did and what the Officer did,—and, to tell the plain truth, we got a drop too much,—and the Wisconsin chappy got turning back-hand springs against the side of the hotel, and I tried to do the same, to the great sport of the crowd. But it didn't last long. A corporal's guard took—or rather carried—us to the guard-house, and towards morning, when we sobered up, he tould me the whole story."

"Pretty well put together, Terry."

"And the blissed truth, ivery word of it."

The night was wearing away—work before them in the morning—and the group dispersed for their blankets, from which we will not disturb them until the succeeding chapter.

# CHAPTER IX.

*Reconnoissance concluded. What we Saw and What we didn't See, and what the Good Public Read—Pigeon-hole Generalship and the Press—The Preacher Lieutenant and how he Recruited—Comparative Merits of Black Union Men and White Rebels—A Ground Blast, and its effect upon a Pigeon-hole General—Staff Officers Striking a Snag in the Western Virginia Captain—Why the People have a right to expect active Army Movements—Red Tape and the Sick List—Pigeon-holing at Division Headquarters.*

IN the misty morning arms were taken and the forward resumed. Occasional Rebel corpses passed showed the work of our sharpshooters. In a short time the ground again prevented the movement in line of battle, and the troops marched by the flank over a road well wooded on each side, until they reached what proved to be the farthest point made by the reconnoissance—a large open plateau, bounded on the north and west by a wooded ridge to which it gradually rose, and which was said to border the Oppequan. On the south, at an average distance of five hundred yards from the road, was a strip of timber land. Slightly west by south, but upon the north side of the road, was a rise of ground, in the rear of which, but upon the south side of the road, were a farmer's house and out-buildings. The troops pursued their march until the head of the column arrived opposite the house. Suspicious-looking horsemen were discovered on the edge of the woods that crowned the ridge. The order was given that the troops should leave the road and take cover on its south side, a position not commanded by the ridge. The order was not executed before a Rebel officer, on a white-tailed dun horse, the tail particularly conspicuous against the dark background of the wood, was observed signalling to the extreme right of what was now supposed to be the Rebel line. Almost instantly some half a dozen pieces of artillery were placed in position, at various points on the brow of the circular ridge, completely commanding, in fact flanking our position. Our troops, however, were not disturbed, although every instant expecting a salute from the batteries, as the range was easy and direct. While the troops were being placed in position behind the house the batteries were posted on the rise. A few hours passed in this position. The Rebel batteries in plain view, horsemen continually emerging and disappearing in the wood. Was it the force that we had driven before us? or were the Rebels in force upon that ridge, making the Oppequan their line of defense? Better ground upon which to be attacked could not be chosen. The long distance to be traversed under fire of any number of converging batteries, would have slaughtered men by the thousands. But again, if the Rebels were in force, why did they not attack us? Outflanking us was easy. With a superior force our retreat could easily be intercepted, and if we escaped at all, it would be with heavy loss. Their batteries threatened, but no firing. All was quiet, save the noise made by the men in stripping an orchard in their immediate front, and the commands of their officers in ordering them back to the ranks.

The quiet was provoking, and all manner of discussion as to the Rebel force, movements, etc., was indulged in. Many contended that they were but threatening—others, that they were in force, that was their line of defense, and the plateau in front their battle-ground. This decision the General in command seems to have arrived at, as the flaming telegrams in the Dailies, in the course of a day or two, announced that the Rebels were discovered in great force, strongly posted in a most defensible position. After the lapse of an hour or two, the order for the homeward march was given, and strange to say, that although marching by the flank the last man had disappeared from their view, behind the cover of the wood, before they opened fire. They then commenced shelling the woods vigorously, and continued firing at a respectful distance, doing no damage, until night set in. In the course of the afternoon it commenced raining, and continued steadily throughout the night. The troops encamped for the night in Egyptian darkness, and what was worse, in a meadow fairly deluged with water.

"Well, what does all this mean?" inquired one of a crowd, huddled together, hooded by blanket and oil-cloth, protecting themselves as best they could from the falling rain, for sleep was out of question to all but the fortunate few who can slumber in puddles.

"What does it all mean, Charlie? Why it means a blind upon Uncle Abraham and his good people. That's what it means."

"Well, Lieutenant, I am surprised that a man of your usual reserve and correct conversation, should talk in that style about our commander."

"Sergeant, it is high time that not only individuals, whether reserved or not, but the people at large should denounce this delay that is wearing out the life of the nation. Weeks have passed since the battle of Antietam, and after repeated urgings on the part of the President, and repeated promises on the part of our commander, we have this beggarly apology for a movement. Yes, sir, apology for a movement. Tomorrow's Dailies will tell in flaming capitals, how the Rebels were posted in large force in a strong position, and in line of battle upon the Oppequan, intimating thereby that further delay will be unavoidable to make our army equal to a movement. Now this humbugging an earnest people is unfair, unworthy of a great commander, and if he be humbugged himself again as with the Quaker guns at Manassas, the sooner the country knows it the better for its credit and safety. How can any living man tell that the batteries we saw today upon the ridge, are not the batteries we drove before us yesterday? The probability is that they are."

The speaker, as intimated by the Sergeant, was a man of reserve, quiet, and to the last degree inoffensive in his manner. A professing Christian, consistent in, and not ashamed of his profession, he had the respect of his command, and a friend in every acquaintance in the regiment. Educated for the ministry, he threw aside his theological text books on the outbreak of the Rebellion, and bringing into requisition some earlier lessons learned at a Military Academy, he opened a recruiting list with the zeal of a Puritan. It was not circulated, as is customary, in bar-rooms, but taking it to a rural district, he called a meeting in the

Township Church, and in the faith of a Christian and the earnestness of a patriot, he eloquently proclaimed his purpose and the righteousness of the war. Success on a smaller scale, but like that of Peter the Hermit, followed his endeavor, and his quota of the Company was soon made up by the enlistment of nearly every able-bodied young man in the Township. His recruits fairly idolized him, and in their rougher and more unlettered way, were equally earnest advocates of the suppression of the Rebellion by any and every means.

"Your Abolitionism will crop out from time to time, like the ledges of rock in the country we have just been passing through," said a Junior Lieutenant.

"Call it Abolitionism, or what you will," replied his Senior.[1] "I am for the suppression of the Rebellion by the speediest means possible. I am for the abolition of everything in the way of its suppression."

"You would abolish the Constitution, I suppose, if you thought it in the way."

"I would certainly amend the Constitution, had I the power, to suit the exigencies of the times. What is the Constitution worth without a country for it to control?"

"There it comes. Anything to ease the nigger."

"Yes, sir, I thank God that this Rebellion strikes a death-blow at slavery. That wherever a Federal bayonet gleams in a slave State, we can see a gleam of eternal truth lighting up the gloom of slavery. The recent Proclamation of the President was all that was needed to place our cause wholly upon the rock of God's justice, and on that base the gates of the hell of slavery and treason combined, shall not prevail against it."

"Preaching again, Lieutenant," said our Western Virginia Captain, who was the Lieutenant's Senior officer, as he strolled leisurely toward the crowd. "I tell you, Lieutenant, if Old Abe don't make better prepara-

---

(1)　　The "preaching Lieutenant" and the more "abolitionist," skeptical Second Lieutenant were said to be from Company F and thus would have been Philip Reese and Josephus Lynn, respectively.

tions to carry out his Proclamation, he had better turn Chinese General at once."

"Give him time, Captain. January 1 may bring preparations that we little dream of. At any rate, it places us in a proper position before the world. What ground had we to expect sympathy from the anti-slavery people of Europe, when we made no effort to release the millions enslaved in the South from bondage?"

"As far as using the negroes as soldiers is concerned, it seems a day behind the fair. It should have been issued earlier. Why, we could have had them by thousands in Western Virginny, and officers in our regiment, who were with him, tell me that Patterson could have mustered an army of them. Instead of that they were driven from his lines, and when they brought him correct information as to the Rebels at Winchester, it was 'don't believe the d—d nigger,' and all this while he dined and wined with the Rebel nabobs about Charlestown. Boys, we commenced this war wrong. I'm a Democrat, and always have been one; but I'm not afraid to say that we've all along been trying our best to make enemies of the only real friends we have inside of Rebel lines. Now, I don't like the nigger better than some of my neighbors; but in my opinion, a black Union man is better than a white Rebel any day. To say nothing of their fighting, why don't our Generals use them as servants, and why are they not our teamsters and laborers? Look at our able-bodied men detailed for servants about Pigeon-hole's Headquarters."

"Well, Captain," interrupted the Sergeant, "Pigey has a big establishment, and see if the papers don't make him out a big General for this daring reconnoissance."

"This daring tomfoolery! If he'd come back to old Rosecrans with his story about a few pieces of artillery posted on a ridge, Rosy would want to know why the d—l he didn't find out what was behind them."

"He showed great experience a few weeks ago," continued the Sergeant, "when the Western fellows let off one of their ground blasts. 'Where did that shell explode?' inquired Pigey, galloping up with his staff and orderlies to our Regimental Headquarters. 'I heard no shell,' says the Colonel. 'Nor I,' says the Lieut.-Colonel. 'I did hear a ground blast,' said the Lieut.-Colonel, 'such as the boys in the Regiment below occasionally make from the rebel cartridges they find.' 'Ground blast! h—l!' says the General, excitedly, his eyes flashing from under his crooked cocked hat. 'Don't you think that an officer of my experience and observation would be able to distinguish the explosion of a shell from that of a ground blast?' 'No shell exploded, General,' said the Colonel, 'within the limits of my regiment.' 'The d—l it didn't—would you have me disbelieve my own ears? Now, I have issued orders enough about permitting these unexploded shells to lie about, and I propose holding the Colonels responsible for all damage. Suppose that explosion was heard at corps headquarters, as it doubtless was, and the inquiry is made from what quarter the rebels threw the shell, what reply am I, as the commanding General of this division, to make?'

" 'Tell them that it was a ground blast,' said a Second Lieutenant, politely saluting. 'I have just been down and saw the hole it made.'

" 'You saw the hole! and just below here! The d—l you did! D—n the ground blasts!' and the General turned his horse's head and started towards division headquarters at a full gallop, followed by his grinning staff."

"He's not to blame so much, boys," remarked the Captain. "He was a quiet clerk in the Topographical Department when the war broke out, I've been told, and I've no doubt he dusted the pigeon-holes in his charge carefully, and folded the papers neatly. When McClellan looked about for material to fill up his big staff with, who was so well calculated to attend to the topography of his battle-fields, considering that he fought so few, and most of those he had to fight on the Peninsula, the rebels got next day, as our Division General. Now, as Little Mac is not particularly noted for close acquaintance with rebel shells, the General has had small chance of knowing what kind of noise they do make when they burst. His great blunder, or rather, the Government's, is his taking command of a division, if it has but two brigades. I heard a Major say he had greatness thrust upon him. He's a small man in a big place. West Point has turned out some big men, like Rosecrans, Grant, Hooker, and many others that are a credit to the country—men of genuine talent, who have none of those foolish prejudices, that the regulars are the only soldiers, and that volunteers are a mere make-shift, that can't be depended upon. And West Point, like all other institutions, has had its share of small men, that come from it with just brains enough to carry a load of prejudice against volunteers and the volunteer service, and a very little knowledge of the ordinary run of military matters. An officer of real ability will never be a slave to prejudice. These small men are the Red-Tapists of the army—the Pigeon-Hole-Paper Generals, and being often elevated and privileged unduly, because they are from West Point, they play the very devil in their commands. Our corps commander, who was a teacher there, has brought a full share of the last kind into the corps.

"I wander about a good deal among other camps of this corps, pick up information and make myself acquainted without standing on ceremony. I never wait for that. I always had a habit of doing it, and I honestly believe, from what I see and hear, there has been a studied effort, from some high commander, to teach these young regular officers treason,—yes, boys, treason,—because when a man tells me that we can't conquer the Rebels, and that after a while we'll have to make peace, etc., I set him down for a traitor; he is aiding and abetting the enemies of his country. If that ain't treason I'd like to know what is."

"The Captain headed off a lot of young regulars the other evening a little the prettiest," said the Sergeant.

"Let's have it!" said a dozen in the crowd, now considerably increased.

"The Captain," continued the Sergeant, "had asked me to take a walk with him after dress-parade, and we strolled along the Sharpsburg road towards Corps Headquarters. As we got just beyond the house and barn where the Rebel wounded are, we came upon a crowd of officers, commissioned and non-commissioned, and some privates. A quite young officer, with a milk-and-water face and a moustache like mildew on a damp Hardee, was talking very excitedly about the Administration not appreciating General McClellan; that there wasn't intellect enough there to appreciate a really great military genius; that European officers praised him as our greatest General, and that even the Rebel officers said that they feared him more than any of our Commanders; and yet all the while the Abolition Administration tied his hands and fettered his movements, and all because Little Mac wasn't crazy enough to say that the Rebels could be subjugated and their armies exterminated, as some fanatical Regulars and nearly all the Volunteer officers pretend to say. 'Now, I believe,' said the officer, thrusting his thumbs between his armpits and his vest, and puffing out his breast pompously, 'I believe, as Little Mac says, "we can drive them to the wall"; we can lessen the limits of their country; but, gentlemen, after all, there will have to be a peace.'

"I thought," said the Sergeant, "the Captain was going to break in upon him here. He threw back his cap till the rim was on top of his head, rammed his hands into his pockets, and edged his way a little further into the crowd, towards the speaker; but he didn't, and the speaker went on to say:

" 'There are the people, too, crazy about a forward movement. Why don't they come down and shoulder muskets themselves?'

"The Captain could hold in no longer. He drew his hands out of his pockets, straightened them along his side, like a game rooster stretching his wings just before a fight, and sidling up to the officer, looking at him out of the corner of his eye, he burst out—

" 'Why don't they shoulder muskets themselves? I'll tell you why,— because we are here to do it for them. They have sent us, they pay us, and they've a right to talk, and I hope they will talk. Anything like a decent forward movement of this Corps would have saved the disgrace of the second Bull Run battle. We all know how the Corps lagged along the roadside, and the Rebel cannon all the while thundering in the ears of its Commander.'

" 'A Volunteer officer, I suppose,' said the young officer, somewhat sneeringly. 'Where have you ever seen service?'

" 'Yes, sir, a Volunteer officer,' said the Captain straightening up, facing full the officer, and eyeing him until his face grew paler. 'Where have I seen service? In Mexico, as private in the 4th Regular Artillery, while you were eating pap with a spoon, you puppy! You had better have stayed at that business; it was an honest one, at any rate, and Uncle Sam would have been saved some pay that you draw, while, like a dishonest sneak, you preach treason."

" 'How dare you insult a Regular officer?' said a gold-striped, dandified fellow, as he twisted the ends of his moustache into rat-tails.

" 'Who the d—l are you?' said the Captain, turning on him so suddenly that the officer commenced to back; 'with your gold lace on your shoulders that may mean anything or nothing. What are you anyhow? Captain? Lieutenant? Clerk? or Orderly? Those straps are a good come off, boys.' The crowd laughed. 'I suppose he thinks he's a staff officer.'

" 'I am, and a Lieutenant in the Regular army,' said the officer angrily, and giving the word 'Regular' the full benefit of his voice.

" 'Regular and be d—d,' retorted the Captain. 'I want you both to understand that I am a Captain in the Volunteer service of the United States; that that service is by Act of Congress on a footing with the Regular service, and that I'll always talk in this style when I hear treason. I am the superior officer of you both, and have a right to talk to you. I've been in service since the Rebellion broke out, and by the mother of Moses, I never heard treason preached by officers in Uncle Sam's uniform till I got into this Corps. It makes my blood boil, and I won't stand it. Pretty doctrine you are trying to teach these soldiers; but I know by their faces they understand the matter better than you, and you can't do them any damage.' 'That's so,' sang out several of the crowd. 'You fellows all talk alike. I have heard dozens of you talk in the same way, and I believe your ideas are stocked from a higher source. There is something wrong in the head of this Grand Army of the Potomac. The way it's managed, grand only in reviews.'

" 'We shall report you, sir,' said the Rat-tailed Moustache, 'for speaking disrespectfully of your superior officers.'

" 'Report as quick as you please. About that time you'll find another report at the War Department, against two Regular Lieutenants, for speaking discouraging and disloyal sentiments.'

" 'A Volunteer officer would stand a big chance at the Department making a complaint against Regulars,' said the officer, as they both backed out of the crowd, followed by a couple of non-commissioned officers and privates.

" 'You d—d butterflies,' roared the Captain after them. 'I'll bet ten dollars to one that you only stayed in service when the war broke out, because you thought you could trust greenbacks better than Confederate scrip.'

" 'You shall hear from us,' replied Rat-tail, as they walked on.

" 'Am ready to hear from both at once now, you cowardly sneaks,' sang out the Captain. 'Don't believe you ever smelt powder, or ever will, if you can help it,'

" 'Boys,' said the Captain, who had the sympathies of the crowd that remained strongly with him. 'These shallow-brained fellows and some older ones that wear stars, that haven't head enough to cut loose from the Red-tape prejudice against us Volunteers, are a curse to the Army of the Potomac. Is it any wonder that this Grand Army, burdened with squirts of that stripe, is a burlesque and a disgrace to the country for its inefficiency. In the West, where Regular officers, unprejudiced, go hand in hand with Volunteers, we make progress. But what's the use of talking, the body won't move right if the heart's rotten.'

" 'True as preachin',' said one of the men, and the sentiment seemed approved by the crowd, as we gradually took up the homeward step."

"Has the Sergeant told 'the whole truth,' and nothing but the truth?" inquired a Lieutenant, a lawyer at home, of the Captain.

"Yes, sir," replied the Captain firmly, "and I'll stick by the whole of it, and a good deal more."

"Well, I've been slow about believing many statements that I have heard," continued the Lieutenant; "but today I heard some facts from a Colonel in the Second Brigade that fairly staggered me. His Regiment, through some Red-tape informality, has been without tents. In consequence, considerable sickness, principally fever, has prevailed. Some time ago he made a request to Division Head-quarters, for permission to clean out and use the white house that stands near his Regiment, and that, until lately, was full of wounded rebels, as a hospital. Corps Head-quarters must be heard from. After considerable delay, the men in the meanwhile sickening and dying, the request was denied. The sickness, through the rains, increased, and the application was renewed with like success. The owner, who was a Rebel sympathizer, was opposed, and other like excuses, that in the urgency of the case should not have been considered at all, were given. The sickness became alarming in extent. The Regiment was entirely without shelter, save that made from the few pine boughs to be had in the neighborhood. The Colonel took some boards that the rebels had spared from the fence surrounding the house, and with them endeavored to increase the comfort of the men. In the course of a day or two, a bill was sent to him from Head-quarters, with every board charged at its highest value, with the request to pay, and with notice that in failure of immediate payment the amount would be charged upon his pay-roll. This treatment disgusted the Colonel, who is a gentleman of high tone and the kindliest feelings, and angered by the heartlessness that denied him proper shelter for his sick, now increased to a number frightfully large, with a heavy share of mortality, he cut red-tape, sent over a detail to the house, had it cleansed of Rebel filth, and filled it with the sick. The poor fellows were hardly comfortable in their new quarters, before an order came from Division Head-quarters for their immediate removal.

" 'I have no place to take them to; they are sick, and must be under shelter,' was the Colonel's reply.

" 'The Commanding General of the Division orders their instant removal,' was the order that followed.

" 'The Commanding General of Division must take the responsibility of their removal on his own head,' was the spirited reply of the Colonel.

"That evening towards sunset, the second edition of Old Pigeon, 'Squab,' as the boys called him, rode up with the air of 'one having authority,' and in a conceited manner informed the Colonel that the General commanding the Division had directed him to place him under arrest. Now these things I know to be facts. I took pains to inform myself."

The Lieutenant's story elicited many ejaculations of contempt for the heartlessness of some in high places; but they were cut short by the Captain's stating that he knew the circumstances to be true, and that Old Pigeon stated the Colonel should wait for his hospital tents, the requisition for which had been sent up months before. It was shelved in some pigeon-hole, and the Colonel was to stand by and see his men sicken and die, while a rebel farmer's house near by would have saved many of them.

"But we're in for it, boys. No use of talking. Obedience is lesson No. 1 of the soldier, and you know that we must not 'mutter or murmur' against our Commanding General, which position Old Pigey so often reminds us he holds. The old fellow half suspects that if he didn't, we'd

*Col. Peter Allabach, commander of
the Second Brigade in Humphreys's division,
was dubbed "Squab" by Armstrong
in* Red-Tape.

forget it from day to day; for Lord knows there is nothing about the man but his position to make any one remember it. Now I am determined to have some sleep."

"Sleep! such a night as this?" said one of the crowd.

"Of course; we'll need it tomorrow, and an old soldier ought to be able to sleep anywhere, in any kind of weather."

The Captain left. There was a partial dispersing of the crowd, but many a poor fellow shivered in that pelting rain the night long.

The morning found the enemy at a respectful distance, and the homeward route was quietly resumed. Late in the afternoon the advance entered Shepherdstown. At this time the rear was shelled vigorously, and as the troops continued their passage through the town cavalry charges were made upon both sides. That only ford was again crossed, and the evening was well advanced ere the troops regained their camps.

A day later, and the Dailies, through their respective reporters, told an astonished public how the brilliant and daring reconnoissance had discovered qualities of great generalship in a man who but a short time before had figured as a quiet literary man in the seclusion of an office.

"And, be jabers," said our little Irish Corporal, on hearing it read, "Uncle Sam would have gained by paying him to stay in that office."

# CHAPTER X.

*Departure from Sharpsburg Camp—The Old Woman of Sandy Hook— Harper's Ferry—South sewing Dragon's Teeth by shedding Old John's Blood —The Dutch Doctor and the Boar—Beauties of Tobacco—Camp Life on the Character—Patrick, Brother to the Little Corporal—General Patterson no Irishman—Guarding a Potatoe Patch in Dixie—The Preacher Lieutenant on Emancipation—Inspection and the Exhorting Colonel—The Scotch Tailor on Military Matters.*

OCTOBER was drawing to a close rapidly, when, at last, after repeated false alarms, the actual movement of the army commenced. No one, unless himself an old campaigner, can appreciate the feelings of the soldier at the breaking up of camp. Anxious for a change of scenery as he may be, the eye will linger upon each familiar spot, the quarters, the parade ground, and rocky bluff and wooded knoll, until memory's impress bears the lasting distinctness of a lifetime. Those leaving could not banish from their minds, even if disposed, the thought that, although but a temporary sojourn for them, it had proved to be the last resting-place of many of their comrades. The hospital, more dreaded than the field, had contributed its share to the mounds that dotted the hills from the strife of Antietam.

> "There is not an atom of this earth
> But once was living man—"

was a day dream, doubtless, of the poetic boy of eighteen; but how suggestive it becomes, when we consider how many thousands and hundreds of thousands of mounds rising upon every hill in the border States, attest devotion to the cause of the Union, or treason, in this foulest of Rebellions.

The route lay, after passing the village of Sharpsburg, through a narrow valley, lying cozily between the spurs of two ridges that appeared to terminate at the Ferry. On either hand the evidences of the occupation of the country by a large army were abundant. Fences torn down, ground trampled, and fields destitute of herbage. The road bordering the canal, along which is built the straggling village of Sandy Hook, was crowded with the long wagon trains of the different Corps. A soldier could as readily distinguish the Staff from the Regimental wagons, as the Staff themselves from Regimental officers. The slick, well fed appearance of the horses or mules of Staff teams, usually six in number, owing to abundance of forage and half *loaded* wagons, were in striking contrast with the four half fed, hide-bound beasts usually attached to the overloaded Regimental wagons. Order after order for the reduction of baggage, that would reduce field officers to a small valise apiece, while many line officers would be compelled to march without a change of clothing, did not appear to lessen the length of Staff trains. That the transportation was unnecessarily extensive, cannot be doubted. That the heaviest reduction could have been made with Head-quarter trains, is equally true.

"Grey coats one day and blue coats the next," said an old woman clad in homespun grey, who came out of a low frame house as the troops slowly made their way past the teams through the village of Sandy Hook.

"Right on this rock is where General Jackson rested hisself," continued the old woman.

"Were there many Rebs about?" inquired one of the men.

"Right smart of them, I reckon;" replied the old woman; "but Lord! what a lookin' set of critters. Elbows and knees out; many of them hadn't shoes, and half of them that had had their toes out. You boys are dandies to them. And tired too, and hungry. Gracious! the poor fellows, when their officers weren't about, would beg for anything almost to eat.

Why, my daughter Sal saw them at the soap-fat barrel! They said they were nearly marched and starved to death. And their officers didn't look much better. Lord! it looks like a picnic party to see you blue coats, with your long strings of wagons, and all your other fixins. You take good care of your bellies, the way you haul the crackers and bacon. Old Jackson never waits for wagons. That's the way he gets around you so often."

"Look here, old woman," roared out one of the men, "you had better dry up."

"Yes, and he'll get around you again," continued the old woman in a louder key. "You think you're going to bag him, do you. You're some on baggin'; but he'll give you three days' start and beat you down the valley. They acted like gentlemen, too, didn't touch a thing without leave, and you fellows have robbed me of all I have."

"They were in 'My Maryland,' and wanted to get the people all straight," suggested one of the boys.

The old lady did not take the hint, but kept on berating the fresh men as they passed—taunting them by disparaging comparison with the Rebel troops. A neighbor, by informing them of the fact of her having two sons in the Rebel service, imparted the secret of her interest.    *   *   *   *   *   *   *   *

And there is the Ferry, so often pictured, or attempted to be, by pen and pencil. Either art has failed, and will fail, to do justice to that sublimely grand mountain scenery. Not quite three years ago, an iron old man, who perished with the heroism of a Spartan, or rather, to be just, the faith of a Christian; but little more than a year in advance of the dawn of the day of his hope, centered upon this spot the eyes of a continent. A crazy fanatic, was the cry, but—

> "Thy scales, Mortality, are just
> To all that pass away."

Time will reveal that it was not the freak of a madman, but rather a step in the grand progress of universal emancipation, and that Old John [Brown] had foundations for his purposed campaign, quite as substantial as those upon which better starred enterprises have succeeded.

"Lor, Massa, if Old John had only had these men," said a wench to one of Patterson's Captains, as he paused for a few moments while drilling his command at Charlestown, during that fruitless campaign, so formidable in preparation, and so much more disgraceful than that of Old John in its termination, for the latter, in his dying heroism, won the admiration of a world.

"Why, what could Old John have done with them?" replied the Captain.

"Golly, Massa," said the wench, with a knowing grin; "he would have walked right through Virginny, and he'd have had plenty of help too. I knows, many a nigger about here that didn't say nuthin', would have jined him."

"Why didn't they join him?"

"Lor, Massa, they didn't know it in time. Hadn't any chance. Massa wanted us to go see him hung; but only the youngsters went. We colored pussons neber forget Old John. No sah!"

The men wound their way as best they could beneath the precipitous and towering rocks of the Maryland Heights, through the teams that blocked up the road, and a short distance above the Railroad Bridge, filed to the left, and crossed upon the pontoons. As they passed the Engine House, the utmost endeavors of the officers could not prevent a bulge to the right, so great was the anxiety to see the scene of Old John's heroic but hopeless contest. Denounced by pro-slavery zealots as a murderer, by the community at large as a fanatic, who fifty years hence will deny him honorable place in the list of martyrs for the cause of eternal truth!

The town itself was almost a mass of ruins; both sides, at various stages of the war, having endeavored to effect its destruction. Another pontoon bridge was crossed, bridging the Shenandoah—sparkling on its rocky bed—the *Dancing Water*, as termed by the Aborigines, with their customary graceful appropriateness. To one fond of mountain scenery, and who is not? the winding road that follows the Shenandoah to its junction, then charmingly bends to the course of the Potomac, is intensely interesting. But why should an humble writer weary the reader's patience by expatiating upon scenery, the sight of which Jefferson declared well worth a visit across the Atlantic, at a day when such visits were tedious three month affairs, and uncertain at that? War now adds a bristling horror to the shaggy mountain tops, and from the hoarse throats of heavy cannon often "leap from rock to rock the beetling crags among" well executed counterfeits of "live thunder."

The Potomac is followed but a short distance, the road winding by an easy ascent up the mountain ridge, and descending as easily into a narrow and fruitful valley. In this valley, four miles from the Ferry, a halt was ordered, and the Division rested for the night and succeeding day, in a large and well sodded field.

"Gentlemen," said our Brigadier, in a sly, good-humored way, as he rode up to the field officers of the Regiment, "the field upon which you are encamped, and all the land, almost as far as you can see, on the left of yon fence, belong to a Rebel now holding the rank of Major in the Rebel service. All I need say, I suppose, gentlemen," and the General left to communicate the important information to the other Regiments of the Brigade. As a fine flock of sheep, some young cattle, a drove of porkers that from a rear view gave promise of prime Virginia hams, and sundry flocks of chickens, had been espied as the men marched into the field, the General's remarks were eminently practical and suggestive.

"Charlie, what's the state of the larder?" said the Major, with his usual thoughtfulness, addressing the cheerful mess cook.

"Some boiled pork and crackers. Poor show, sir!" Such fare, after a hard day's march, in sight of a living paradise of beef, mutton, pork, and poultry, would have been perfectly inexcusable; and forthwith, the Major, "the little Dutch Doctor," and a short, stoutly-built Lieutenant, all armed to the teeth, started off to reconnoitre, and ascertain in what position the Rebel property was posted. As they went they canvassed the respective merits of beef, mutton, pork and poultry, until a short grunt from a porker, as he crossed the Doctor's path, ended the discussion. The Major and Lieutenant cocked their pistols, but withheld firing, as they saw the Doctor prostrate, holding by both hands the hind leg of a patriarch of the flock.

"Oh, Heavens! we don't want that old boar!" cried out at once both the Major and Lieutenant.

"Goot meat, make strong, goot for health, very," said the Doctor, holding on with the grasp of a vice, while the boar fairly dragged him, face to the ground, "after the manner of all creeping things." The Doctor was in a fix. Help his companions would not give. He could not hold the boar by one hand alone. After being considerably bruised, he was compelled to release his hold, to his intense disgust, which he evinced as he raised himself up, puffing like a porpoise, by gesticulating furiously, and muttering a jargon in which the only thing intelligible was the oft-repeated word, "tam." A well-directed shot from the Major, shortly afterwards, brought down a royal "Virginia mutton," as the camp phrase is. Another from the Lieutenant grazed the rear of a fine young porker's ham; but considerable firing, a long chase, and many ludicrous falls occurred, before that pig was tightly gripped between the legs of the Lieutenant.

The expedition was so successful that the aid of some privates was called in to help carry to quarters the rich spoils of the chase. As for the Doctor,—after the refusal of assistance in his struggle, he walked homeward in stately but offended dignity, and shocked the Chaplain, as he was occasionally in the habit of doing, by still muttering "tam."

A person enjoying the comforts of home, testy as to the broiling of a mutton-chop perhaps, for real, unalloyed enjoyment of appetite should form one of a camp circle, toasting, at a blazing fire, as the shades of evening gather round, steaks freshly cut with a camp-knife from flesh that quivered with remaining life but a moment before, assisting its digestion by fried Hardees, and washing both down by coffee innocent of cream. That is a feast, as every old campaigner will testify; but to be properly appreciated a good appetite is all essential. To attain that, should other resources fail, the writer can confidently recommend a march, say of about fifteen miles, over rough or dusty roads.

And then, as the appetites of the men are sated by the hardy provender of Uncle Sam, varied, as in this instance, by Virginia venison, and they respectively fall back and take to

"Sublime Tobacco! glorious in a pipe;"

what more pleasant than the discussion of the doings of the day, or of the times, the recital of oft-repeated and ever-gaining yarns, or the heart-stirring strains of national ballads, while each countenance is lit with the ever-varying glow of the fire.

Upon this evening not only Headquarters but the Regiment was exultant in the feast upon the fat of a rebellious land. To add to their comfort several large stacks of hay and straw had been deprived of their fair proportions, and preparations had been made for the enjoyment of rest upon beds that kings would envy, could they but have the sleepers' sound repose.

The morrow had been set apart as a day of rest—a fact known to the Regiment, and their fireside enjoyment was accordingly prolonged.

The camp, more than any other position in life, develops the greatest inconsistencies in poor human nature. The grumbler of the day's march is very frequently the joker of the bivouac. The worse, at the expense of man's better qualities, are rapidly strengthened, and the least particle of selfishness, however concealed by a generous nature at the period of enlistment, fearfully increases its power with every day of service. The writer remembers well a small, slightly-built, bow-legged fellow, who would murmur without ceasing upon the route, continually torment his officers for privilege to fall out of ranks to adjust his knapsack, fasten a belt, or some such like purpose, who, on the halt, would amuse his comrades for hours in performing gymnastic feats upon out-spread blankets. Another, who at home flourished deservedly under the sobriquet of "Clever Billy," became, in a few brief months of service, the most surly, snappish, and selfish of his mess.

Pipe in mouth, their troubles are puffed away in the gracefully ascending smoke. Many a non-user of the weed envies in moody silence the perfect satisfaction resting upon the features of his comrade thus engaged. Non-users are becoming rare birds in the army. So universal is the habit, that the pipe appears to belong to the equipment, and the tobacco-pouch, suspended from a button-hole of the blouse, is so generally worn that one would suppose it to have been prescribed by the President as part of the uniform.

The crowd gathered about the Headquarters had largely increased, and while luxuriating upon the straw, time passed merrily. The Colonel, who never let an opportunity to improve the discipline of his command pass unimproved, seized the occasion of the presence of a large number

of officers to impress upon them the necessity of greater control of the
men upon the march. The easy, open, but orderly route-step of the Regulars was alluded to—their occupying the road alone, and not spread out
and straggling like a drove of cattle. A stranger seeing our Volunteers
upon the march would not give them credit for the soldierly qualities
they really possess. Curiosity, so rampant in the Yankee, tempts him
continually to wander from the ranks to one or the other side of the road.

"Well, Colonel," said a tall Lieutenant, "the Regulars look prim and
march well, but they have done little fighting, as yet, in this Army of
the Potomac."

"You forget the Peninsula," replied the Colonel.

"Oh, there they were caught unexpectedly, and forced into it. In this
Corps they are always in reserve; and that's what their officers like,—
everything in reserve but pay and promotion. It is rather doubtful
whether they will fight."

"Ov coorse they'll fight," said the little Irish Corporal, half rising
from his straw on the outskirts of the crowd; "Ov coorse they will.
They're nearly all my own countrymen. I know slathers of them; and
did you iver in your born days know an Irishman that wouldn't fight,
anywhere, any time, and for anything, if he had anybody to fight?"

"And a quart of whiskey in him," interrupts the Adjutant. "As Burns
says of the Scotch—

> 'Wi' Tippeny they fear nae evil,
>   Wi' Usquebagh they'll face the Devil.' "

"Now, don't be comparing an Irishman, if you plaze, Adjutant, to a
scratch-back Scotchman. The raal Irishman has fire enough in his bluid;
but there's no denying a glass of potheen is the stuff to regulate it. Talk
about Rigulars or Volunteers fighting;—it's the officers must do their
duty, and there's no fear thin of the men."

"What did you enlist for, anyway, Terence?" broke in a Second
Lieutenant.

"It's aisy seeing that it wasn't for a Lieutenant's pay," retorted
Terence, to the amusement of the crowd, and then, as earnestness

gathered upon his countenance, he continued: "I enlisted for revinge, and there's little prospect of my seeing a chance for it."

"For revenge?" said several.

"Yis, for revinge. I had worked early and late at a liv'ry stable, like a nagur, to pay the passage money of my only brother to this country. Faith, he was a broth of a boy, the pride of all the McCarthy's,"— tears welled in his eyes as he continued,—"just three years younger than mysilf, a light, ruddy, nately put togither lad as iver left the bogs; and talk about fightin'!—the divil was niver in him but in a fight, and thin you'd think he was all divil. That was Patrick's sport, and fight he would, ivery chance, from the time whin he was a bit of a lad, ten years ould, and bunged the ould school teacher's eyes in the parish school-house. Will, he got a good berth in a saloon in the Bowery, where they used Patrick in claning out the customers whin they got noisy, and he'd do it nately too, to the satisfaction of his employer. He did well till a recruiting Sergeant—bad luck to him—that knew the McCarthys in the ould country, found him out, and they drank and talked about ould times, and the Sergeant tould him that the army was the place for Irish-men,—that there would be lots of fightin'. The chance of a fight took Patrick, and nixt day he left the city in a blouse, as Fourth Corporal in an Irish Rigiment, and a prouder looking chappie, as his own Captain tould me, niver marched down Broadway. And thin to think he was murthered by my own Gineral."

"Who? How was that?" interrupted half a dozen at once.

"Giniral Patterson, you see, to be shure."

"Why, Terence," broke in the Lieutenant, "you shouldn't be so hard upon General Patterson; he's of an Irish family."

"The Giniral an Irishman! Niver! Of an Irish family! must have been hundreds of years back, and the bluid spoiled long before it got into his veins, by bad whiskey or something worse. It takes the raal potheen, that smacks of the smoke of the still, to keep up the bluid of an Irishman. Rot-gut would ruin St. Patrick himself if he were alive and could be got to taste it. Giniral Patterson an Irishman! no, sir; or there would have been bluidy noses at Bunker's Hill or Winchester, and that would have saved some at Bull Run."

"On with your story, Terence," said the crowd.

"Beggin' your pardon, there's no story about it,—the blissid truth, ivery word of it.

"Will, you see, while our ould Colonel, under the Gineral's orders, had me guarding a pratie patch—"

"Set an Irishman to guard a potato patch!" laughed the Second Lieutenant.

"It wasn't much use," said Terence, smiling, "for they disappeared the first night, and the slim college student that was Sergeant of that relief was put under guard for telling the officer of the guard, next morning, that there had been a heavy dew that night, and it evaporated so fast that it took the praties along. We lived on praties next day, but the poor Sergeant had to foot the bill.

"Well, as I was going on to say, while I was helping guard a pratie patch, an ice-house, corn-crib, smoke-house, and other such things that were near our camp ground, and that belonged to a Rebel Colonel under Johnston;—Johnston himself was staling away with all his army to help fight the battle of Bull Run. Patrick—pace to his sowl—was in that battle and fought like a tiger, barrin' that he would have done better, as his Captain tould me, if he hadn't forgot the balls in his cartridge-box, and took to his musket like a shelaleh all day long. Patrick's regiment belonged to a Brigade that was ordered to keep Johnston in check, and there stood Patrick in line, like a true lad as he was, clubbing back the Butternuts, striking them right and left—maybe the fellows belonged to this same Rebel Colonel's regiment—until a round shot struck him full in the breast, knocking the heart out of as true an Irishman as iver lived, and killing dead the flower of the McCarthys.

"I didn't know it till we got to Baltimore, and thin whin I riflicted how the poor boy marched up to fight the bluidy Rebels, and how they killed him, my own brother, while I—I, who would have given my right hand to save him,—yis," said Terence, rising, and tears streaming from his eyes, "would have waded through fire and bluid to help the darlin', the pride of his mother,—I was guarding a Rebel Colonel's property, whin the whole of us, if we had fought Johnston, as we ought to have done, might have kept him back and saved our army, and that would have saved me my brother. And thin whin I remembered how thick the Gineral was with the Rebel gentry, and how fine ladies with the divil in their eyes bowed to him in Charlestown, and spit at and cocked up their noses at us soldiers, while their husbands were off, maybe, mur-thering my brother; and how the Gineral, proud as a paycock on his prancing chestnut sorrel, tould us in the meadow that Johnston was too strong for us to attack, but that if he would come out from behind his big guns the Gineral would lay his body on the sod before he'd lave it, whin he intended his body to lie on a soft bed the rest of his life, and how he said and did all this while our men, and my brother among them, were being murthered by this same Johnston that he was sent to hould back,—I couldn't keep down my Irish bluid. I cursed him and all his tribe by all the Saints from St. Peter to St. Patrick, until good ould Father Mahan told me, whin I confessed, that he was afraid I would swear my own sowl away, and keep Patrick in Purgatory; and the Father told me that I should lave off cursin' Patterson, for the Americans themselves would attend to that, and take to fighting the Rebels for revinge; and he said by way of incouragement that at the same time I'd be sarving God and my adopted country. And here I am, under another safe Com-mander. Four months and no fight,—nearly up to the ould First, that sarved three months without sight of a Rebel, barrin' he was a prisoner, or in citizen dress, like some we have left behind us."

"Boys, Terence tells the truth about Patterson's movements," said the tall Lieutenant. "The day before we left we were ordered to be ready to move in the morning, with three days' cooked rations. We were told that our Regiment was assigned a place in the advance, and it was semi-officially rumored that a flank attack would be made upon Winchester. At this day the whole affair appears ridiculous, as Johnston had at that very time left Winchester, leaving only a trifling show of force, and he never, at his best, had a force equal to Patterson's. Half of his troops were the raw country militia. But we under-officers were none the wiser. It was rumored that Bill McMullen's Rangers[1] had found charts that informed the General of the extent and strength of the Rebel works and muster-rolls, that showed his force to be over 50,000. That those

---

(1)    Capt. William McMullen's Independent Philadelphia Rangers.

works had no existence to the extent alleged, and that the muster-rolls were false, are now well known. But that night it was all dead earnest with us. Rations were cooked and the most thorough preparations made for the expected work of the morrow. Sunrise saw the old First in line, ready for the move. Eight o'clock came; no move, Nine—Ten, and yet no move. Arms had been stacked, and the men lounged lazily about the stacks. Eagle eyes scanned the surrounding country to ascertain what other Brigades were doing. At length troops were seen in motion, but the head of the column was turned towards the Ferry. 'What does this mean?' was the inquiry that hastily ran from man to man; and still they marched towards the Ferry. By and by an aide-de-camp directed our Brigade to fall into the column, and we then discovered that the whole army was in line of march for the Ferry, with a formidable rear-guard to protect it from an enemy then triumphing at Bull Run.

"Well, Patterson's inertness, to speak of it tenderly, cost the country much blood, millions of money, and a record of disgrace; but it gave a Regiment of Massachusetts Yankees opportunity to whittle up for their home cabinets of curiosities a large pile of walnut timber which had formed John Brown's scaffold, and to make extensive inroads in prying with their bayonets from the walls of the jail in which he had been confined pieces of stone and mortar. Guards were put upon the Court House in which old John heard his doom and the dignity of a Cato, at an early date, or it would have been hewn to pieces. A fine crop of corn in full leaf was growing upon the field of execution, and for a space of ten feet from the roadside the leaves had been culled for careful preservation in knapsacks. The boys had the spirit. Their Commander lacked capacity or will to give it effect. A beggarly excuse was set up after the campaign was over,—that the time of service of many of the Regiment was about expiring, and that the men would not reënlist,—not only beggarly, but false. The great mass volunteered to remain as it was, with no prospect of service ahead. All would have stayed had the General shown any disposition for active work, or made them promise of a fight."

"Golly," said a tall, raw-boned Darkie, showing his ivories to a crowd of like color about him, as the fine band of the Fencibles played in front of the General's Head-quarters. "Dese Union boys beat de Mississippi fellurs all hollur playing Dixie."

Hardly a face was to be seen upon the streets, but those of these friendly blacks. They thronged about the camps, to be repulsed by stringent orders at all quarters. Property they were, reasoned the commander, and property must be respected. And it was; even pump handles were tied down and placed under guard. Oh! that a Ben Butler had then been in command, to have pronounced this living property contraband of war, and by that sharp dodge of a pro-slavery Democrat, to have given Uncle Sam the services of this property. Depend upon it, that would have ended campaigning in the valley of the Shenandoah, that store-house of Rebel supplies, as it has turned out to be; supplies too, gathered and kept up by the negroes that Patterson so carefully excluded from his lines.

"And would have saved us this march," says the Colonel, "a goose chase at any rate."

"Yes, and had the policy of using the negro been general at the commencement of this Rebellion, troops would not be in the field at this day," responded the Lieutenant.

"Why do they not now, come boldly out and acknowledge that slavery is a curse to any nation?" said the Preacher Lieutenant. "It caused the Rebellion, and its downfall would be the Rebellion's certain and speedy death. Thousands of years ago, the Almighty cursed with plagues a proud people for refusing to break the bonds of the slave. The day of miracles is past. But war, desolating war, is the scourge with which He punishes our country. The curse of blood is upon the land; by blood must it be expiated. We in the North have been guilty, in common with the whole country, in tolerating, aiding, and abetting the evil. We must have our proportion of punishment. Why cannot the whole country meet the issue boldly as one man, and atone for past offense by unanimity in the abolition of the evil?"

"On the nigger again," said his Junior Lieutenant, assuming, as he spoke, an oratorical attitude. "Why do you not go on and talk about them working out their own salvation, with muskets on their shoulders and bayonets by their sides, and with fear and trembling too, I have no doubt it would be. Carry out your Scripture parallels. Tell how the walls of Jericho fell by horns taken from the woolly heads of rams; but now that miracles are no more, how the walls of this Jericho of Rebeldom are destined to fall before the well-directed butting of the woolly heads themselves. You don't ride your hobby with a stiff rein tonight, Lieutenant."

The taunting air and strained comparison of the Lieutenant enlivened the crowd, but did not in the least affect the Senior, who calmly replied:

"If our Government does not arm the negro on the basis of freedom, the Rebels in their desperation will, and although we have the negro sympathy, we may lose it through delay and inattention, and in that event, prepare for years of conflict. The negroes, at the outset of this Rebellion, were ripe for the contest. Armies of thousands of them might have been in the field today. Now the President's Proclamation finds them removed within interior Rebel lines, and to furnish them arms, will first cost severe contests with the Rebels themselves."

The toil of the day and the drowsiness caused by huge meals, gradually dispersed the crowd; but the discussion was continued in quarters by the various messes, until their actual time of retiring.*       *       *
*       *       *       *       *

"Inspection! inspection!" said the Adjutant, on the succeeding afternoon, to the Lieutenant-Colonel for the time being in command of the Regiment, handing him, at the same time, an order for immediate inspection. "Six inspections in two weeks before marching," continued the Adjutant, "and another after a day's march. I wonder whether this Grand Army of the Potomac wouldn't halt when about going into battle, to see whether the men had their shoe-strings tied?"

The Adjutant had barely ceased, when the Inspecting officer, the ranking Colonel of the Brigade, detailed specially for the duty, made his appearance. He was a stout, full-faced man of fifty or upwards, with an odd mixture in his manner of piety and pretension. Report had it that his previous life had been one of change,—stock-jobber, note-shaver, temperance lecturer, and exhorter—

"All things by turns, and nothing long."

The latter quality remained with him, and it was a rare chance that he could pass a crowd of his men without bringing it into play. His "talks," as the boys called them, were more admired than his tactics, from their tone of friendly familiarity, he was called by the fatherly title of "Pap" by his Regiment, and known by that designation throughout the Brigade.

The Regiment was rapidly formed for inspection, and after passing through the ranks of the first Company, the Colonel pompously presented himself before its center, and with sober tones and solemn look, delivered himself as follows:

"Boys, have your hearts right," the Colonel clapping, at the same time, his right hand over his diaphragm. "If your hearts are right your muskets will be bright." The men stared, the movement not being laid down in the Regulations, and not exactly understanding the connection between the heart and a clean musket; but the Colonel continued, "the heart is like the mainspring of a watch, if it beats right, the whole man and all about him will be right. There is no danger of our failing in this war, boys. We have a good cause to put our hearts in. The Rebels have a bad cause, and their hearts cannot be right in it. Good hearts make brave men, brave men win the battles. That's the reason, boys, why we'll succeed."

"Can't see it!" sang out some irreverent fellow in the rear rank.

The Colonel didn't take the hint; but catching at the remark continued, "You do not need to see it, boys, you can feel whether your heart is right." This provoked a smile on the faces of the more intelligent of the officers and men, which the Colonel noticed. "No laughing matter, boys," he said emphatically, at the same time earnestly gesticulating, "your lives, your country, and your honor depend upon right hearts." And thus the old Colonel exhorted each Company previous to its dismissal, amusing some and mystifying others. The heart was his theme, and time or place, a court-martial or review, did not prevent the introduction of his platitudes.

Said the Major, after inspection, "The Colonel, in the prominence he gives the heart in its control of military affairs, rather reverses a sentiment I once heard advanced by a little Scotch tailor, who had just been elected a militia colonel."

*Col. Edgar Mantlebert Gregory of the Ninety-first Pennsylvania, the "exhorting" colonel, was formerly a lumber merchant and banker.*

"Let's have it, Major," said the Adjutant.

"The little Scotchman," continued the Major, "had been a notorious drunkard and profane swearer. Through the efforts of a travelling Evangelist, he became converted and joined a prominent denomination. His conversion was a remarkable instance, and gave him rapid promotion and a prominent position in the church. While at his height, through some scheme of the devil, I suppose, he was elected colonel of militia. The elevation overcame him. Treat he must and treat he did, and to satisfy the admiring crowd in front of the bar drank himself, until reason left, preceded by piety, and his old vice of profanity returned, with seven-fold virulence. He was discovered by a brother of the church, steadying himself by the railing of the bar, and rehearsing, amid volleys of oaths, the fragments that remained in his memory of an old Fourth of July speech. 'Brother,' said his fellow church-member, as he gently nudged his arm. 'Brother!' in a louder key, and with a more vigorous nudge, 'have you forgotten your sacred obligations to the church, your position as a—'

" 'The church!' echoed the tailor, all the blood of the MacGregor rising in his boots, with an oath that shocked the brother out of all hope—'What's the church to military matters?' "

# CHAPTER XI.

*Snicker's Gap—Private Harry on the "Anaconda"—Not inclined to turn Boot-Black—"Oh! why did you go for a Soldier?"—The ex-News-Boy—Pigeon-Hole Generalship on the March—The Valley of the Shenandoah—A Flesh Carnival—The Dutch Doctor on a Horse-dicker—An Old Rebel, and how he parted with his Apple-Brandy—Toasting the "Union"—Spruce Retreats.*

THE movement down the Valley[1] was one of those at that time popular "bagging" movements, peculiar to the Grand Army of the Potomac, and in their style of execution, or to speak correctly, intended execution—for the absence of that quality has rendered them ridiculous —original with its Commander. Semi-official reports, industriously circulated from the gold-striped Staff to the blue-striped Field Officer, and by the latter whispered in confidence in the anxious ears of officers of the line, and again transferred in increasing volume to the subs, and by them in knowing confidence to curious privates, had it that the principal rebel force would be hemmed in, in the Valley of the Shenandoah, by our obtaining command of the Gaps, and then we would be nearest their Capital in a direct line—we would compel them to fight us, where, when, and how we pleased, or else beat them in a race to Richmond, and then——. The reader must imagine happy results that could not

---

(1)    Their movement was in a southerly direction. To local residents "down the
        Valley" implies northward movement, as the Shenandoah runs south to north.

consistently be expected, while to gain the same destination over equi-distant and equally good roads, Strategy moved by comparatively slow marches and easy halts, while Desperation strained every nerve, with rattling batteries and almost running ranks.

"But, Lieutenant, if that's so," alluding to the purpose of their march, "why are we halting here?"

"Our troops block up the roads, I suppose."

"We could march in the fields," rejoined the anxious private, "by the roadside; they are open and firm."

"We'll see, Harry, in a day or two, what it all amounts to. May be the 'Anaconda' that is to smash out the rebellion, is making another turn, or 'taking in a reef,' as the Colonel says."

"Well," rejoined the Private, "I have endeavored to book myself up, as far as my advantages would allow, in our army movements; and the nearest approach to anything like an anaconda, that I can see or hear of, is that infernal Red-tape worm that is strangling the soul out of the army. What inexcusable nonsense to attempt to apply to an immense army in time of war, such as we have now in the field, the needless, petty pigeon-hole details that regulated ten thousand men on a peace establishment. And to carry them out, look how many valuable officers, or officers who ought to be valuable, from the expense Uncle Sam has been at to give them educational advantages, are doing clerkly duty—that civil-ians, our business men, our accountants, could as well, if not better, attend to—in the offices of the Departments at Washington, in the Com-missary and Quarter-Master's Departments,—handling quills and cheese-knives instead of swords, and never giving 'the villainous smell of saltpeter' the slightest chance 'to come betwixt the wind and their nobility.' "

Harry, at the time of his volunteering was an associate editor of a well established and ably conducted country newspaper. He had thrown himself with successful energy into the formation of the regiment to which he belonged. A prominent position was proffered him, but he sturdily refused any place but the ranks, alleging that he had never drilled a day in his life, and particularly insisting that those who had seen service and were somewhat skilled in the tactics, although many of them were far his inferiors in intelligence, should occupy the offices.

From his gentlemanly deportment and ability he was on familiar terms with the officers, and popular among the men. Withal, he was a finely formed, soldierly-looking man. In the early part of his service he was reserved in his comments upon the conduct of the war, and considered, as he was in fact, conservative,—setting the best possible example of taciturnity, subordinate to the wisdom of his superiors.

"Harry, you have been detailed as a clerk about Brigade Head Quarters," said the Orderly Sergeant of his company, one morning, after he had been in service about two months.

Harry did not like the separation from his Company in the least, but notwithstanding, quietly reported for duty. Several days of desk drudgery, most laborious to one fresh from out-door exercise, had passed, when one morning about eight o'clock, a conceited coxcomb of an aide, in slippers, entered the office-tent, and holding a pair of muddy boots up, with an air of matter-of-course authority—ordered Harry to blacken them, telling him at the same time, in a milder and lower tone, that black Jim the cook had the brush and blackening.

"What, sir?" said Harry, rising like a rocket, his Saxon blood mounting to the very roots of his red hair.

"I order you to black those boots, sir," was the repeated and more insolent command.

"And I'll see you d—d first," retorted Harry, doubling his fist.

The aide not liking the furious flush upon Harry's face, with wise discretion backed out, muttering after he was fairly outside of the tent, something about a report to the Brigadier. Report he did, and very shortly after there was a vacancy in his position upon the Staff of that Officer. Harry, at his own request, was in the course of a week relieved from duty, and restored to his Company. Ever after he had a tongue.

The reply of the Lieutenant to Harry's remarks has all this time been in abeyance, however.

"Harry," said that officer, "we must follow the stars without murmuring or muttering against the judgment of superiors,—but one can't help surmising, and," the Lieutenant had half mechanically added when the Sergeant-Major saluted him.

"Where is the Captain, Lieutenant?"

"Not about, at present."

"Well," continued the Sergeant, "reveille at four, and in line at five in the morning."

Those beds of thickly littered straw were hard to leave in the chill mist of the morning. The warning notes of the reveille trilling in sweetest melody from the fife of the accomplished fife-major, accompanied by the slumber-ending rattle of the drum, admitted of no alternative. Many a brave boy as he stood in line that morning, ready for the march, the first sparkle of sunrise glistening upon his bayonet, wondered whether father or mother, sister or brother, yet in their slumbers, doubtless, in the dear old homestead, knew that the army was on the move, and that the setting sun might gild his breast-plate as in his last sleep he faced the sky.

"Oh! why did you go for a soldier?" sang our little newsboy, tauntingly, as he capered behind a big burly Dutchman in the rear rank, who had encountered all manner of misfortune that morning,—missing his coffee—and what is a man worth on a day's march without coffee—because it was too hot to drink, when the bugle sounded the call to fall in, his meat raw, not even the smell of fire about it, and his crackers half roasted; his clothes, too, half on, belts twisted, knapsack badly made up. As he grumbled over his mishaps, in his peculiar vernacular, laughter commenced with the men, and ended in a roar at the song of the newsboy.

A crowd gathers food for mirth from the most trivial matters. Incidents that would not provoke a smile individually, convulse them collectively. Men under restraint in ranks are particularly infectious from the influence of the passions. With lightning-like rapidity, to misapply a familiar line—

"They pass from grave to gay, from lively to severe."

Snickers' Gap, which drew its euphoneous name from a First Virginia family that flourished in the neighborhood, was one of the coveted points. In the afternoon our advance occupied it, and the neighboring village of Snickersville;[2] fortunately first perhaps, in force, or what is most probable, considering results, amused by a show of resistance to cover the main Rebel movement then rapidly progressing further down the valley. From whatever cause, firing—musketry and artillery—was heard at intervals, all the latter part of the afternoon; and as the troops neared the Gap, they were told that the Rebels had been driven from it across the river, and that it was now in our possession. Night was rapidly setting in as the division formed line of battle on the borders of the village. A halt but for a few moments. Their position was shortly changed to the mountain slope below the village. Down the valley sudden flashes of light and puffs of smoke that gracefully volumed upwards, followed by the sullen roar of artillery, revealed a contest between the advancing and retreating forces. That fire-lit scene must be a life picture to the fortunate beholders. Directly in front and on the left, thousands of camp fires burning in the rear of stacks made from line-of-battle, blazed in parallel rows, regular as the gas-lights of the avenues of a great city, and illumining by strange contrasts of light and shade the animated forms that encircled them. Far down to the right, the vertical flashes from the cannon vents vivid as lightning itself, instantly followed by horizontal lurid flames, belched forth from their dread mouths, lighting for the instant wood and field, formed the grandest of pyrotechnic displays. Rare spectacle—in one magnificent panorama, gleaming through the dark mantle of night, were the steady lights of peaceful camps, and the fitful flashing of the hostile cannon.

"Fall in, fall in!" cried the officers, at the bugle call, and in a few moments the Brigade was in motion. Some in the ranks, with difficulty, at the same time managing their muskets and pails of coffee that had not had time to cool; others munching, as they marched, their half-fried crackers, and cooling with hasty breath smoking pieces of meat, while friendly comrades did double duty in carrying their pieces. The soldier never calculates upon time; the present is his own when off duty, and he is not slow to use it; the next moment may see him started upon a long march, or detailed for fatigue duty, and with a philosophy apt in his position, he lives while he can.

---

(2)     The town name was changed to Bluemont at the turn of the century.

The road through Snickersville, and up the romantic gorge or gap between the mountains, was a good pike, and in the best marching condition. At the crest the Brigade undoubled its files, and entered in double ranks a narrow, tortuous, rocky road, ascending the mountain to the left, leading through woods and over fields so covered with fragments of rock, that a country boy in the ranks, following up a habit, however, not by any means confined to the country, of giving the embodiment of evil the credit of all unpleasant surroundings, remarked that "the Devil's apron-strings must have broke loose here." That night march was a weary addition to the toil of the day. A short cut to the summit, which existed, but a mile in length, and which the Commander of the Force to which the Brigade formed part, could readily have ascertained upon inquiry, would have saved a great amount of grumbling, many hard oaths, for Uncle Toby's army that "swore so terribly in Flanders," could not outdo in that respect our Grand Army of the Potomac,—and no trifling amount of shoe-leather for Uncle Sam. The night was terribly cold, and the wind in gusts swept over the mountain-top with violence sufficient to put the toil-worn man, unsteady under his knapsack, through the facings in short order. Amid stunted pines and sturdy undergrowth, the Regiments in line formed stacks, and the men, debarred fire from the exposed situation, provided what shelter they could, and endeavored to compose themselves for the night. Vain endeavor. So closely was that summit shaved by the pitiless blasts, that a blanket could only be kept over the body by rolling in it, and lying face downwards, holding the ends by the hands, with the forehead resting on the knapsack for a pillow. Some in that way, by occasionally drumming their toes against the rocks managed to pass the night; many others sought warmth or amusement in groups, and others gazed silently on the camp-fires of the enemy, an irregular reflex of those seen on the side they had left—here glimmering faintly at a picket station, and there at a larger encampment, glowing first in a circle of blaze, then of illumined smoke, that in its upward course gradually darkened into the blackness of night. To men of contemplative habits, and many such there were, though clad in blouses, the scene was strongly suggestive. Our states emblemed in the lights of the valleys and the mountain ridge as the much talked of "impassable barrier." But faith in the success of a cause Heaven founded, saw gaps that we could control in that mountain ridge which would ultimately prove avenues of success.

"Captain, where did you make the raise?" inquired a young Lieutenant, on the following day,—one of a group enjoying a blazing fire, for the ban had been removed at early dawn—of a ruddy-faced, sturdy-looking officer, who bore on his shoulder a tempting hind quarter of beef.

"There is a little history connected with this beef," as he lowered his load, "Lieutenant," replied the Captain, interlarding his further statement with oaths, to which justice cannot and ought not to be done in print, and which were excelled in finish only by some choice ones of the Division General. "I went out at sunrise, thinking that by strolling among the rocks I might stir up a rabbit. I saw several, but got a fair shot at one only, and killed it. While going into a fence corner, in which were some thorn bushes, that I thought I could stir another cotton tail from, I saw a young bullock making for me, with lowered horns and short jumps. I couldn't get through the thorn bushes, and the fact is, being an old butcher I didn't care much about it, so I faced about, looked the bullock full in the eyes, and the bullock eyed me, giving at the same time an occasional toss of his short horns. Now I was awful hungry, never was more hollow in my life—the hardees that I swallowed dry in the morning fairly rattled inside of me. By-and-by I smelt the steaks, and a minute more I felt sure that he was a Rebel beast. Our young cattle up North don't corner people in that way. What's the use, thought I, and out came my Colt, and I planted a ball square between his eyes. As I returned the pistol he was on his side kicking and quivering. While looking at him, and rather coming to the conclusion that I had bought an elephant after all, as I had not even a penknife to skin it with, I spied that sucker-mouthed Aide[3] of Old Pigeon-Hole coming from another corner of the field, cantering at full jump. I left, walking towards Camp.

" 'Captain, where was that picket-firing?'

---

(3)    Capt. Carswell McClellan.

"I pointed towards the wood, and told him that I thought it was along the picket-line.

" 'It must have been, I suppose,' said the Aide, in a drawling manner. 'The General was sure it was a rifle. The rest of us thought it a pistol shot,' he said, as he rode off.

"When he got into the wood I returned to the bullock, cursing Old Pigey's ears for want of experience in shots. They made me come mighty close to being arrested for marauding.

" 'Oh! whar did you git the jump-high?' said a darkie, who came up suddenly, pointing to the rabbit which I had put on the fence, with mouth open and a big show of the whites of his eyes. When he saw the carcass he fairly jumped.

" 'Massa has had me shinning it round de rocks all morning. When I'm on de one side de jump-high is on de oder; and if I go back widout one he'll cuss me for a d—d stumbling woolly-head. Dat's his name for me any way.'

"I struck a bargain with the boy; he loaned me his jack-knife, and held the legs, and I had the skin off as soon as a two-inch blade (hacked at that) would allow, and I gave him the jump-high, and told him if he'd watch the beef till I carried this quarter home, I'd give him a fore quarter. I knew his Master was as bad off as myself, and would ask no questions, and then I sneaked up in rear of the General's quarters."

"That's what I'd call Profane History," said the Lieutenant, as the Captain resumed his load.

"Well, boys! Go into the Third Cavalry four months, as I did; and if any of you swear less than I do, I'll treat."

"One fault with the story, Captain," said another Lieutenant, detaining him; "you make no application."

"I didn't intend it as a sermon; what application would you make?"

"A very practical one, Captain. I would apply half a quarter to one man, half a quarter to another. Make a distribution among your friends."

The Captain, somewhat sold, told them to send down a detail, and he would distribute.

The detail returned, well loaded, having performed their duty faithfully, with the exception of trimming Sambo's fore-quarter "mighty close," as he phrased it.

That bullock turned out to be merely the first course of a grand flesh carnival, which lasted the remaining two days of the stay on Snicker's summit. The wood and fields almost swarmed with rabbits and quails; but although furnishing amusement to all, they were but tidbits for the delicate. By some remissness of vigilance under the stringent orders, cattle, sheep, and hogs were slaughtered on all sides. There was an abundance of them; the farmers in the valley having driven them up, as was their custom, for the pasture and mast to be found in the fields and woods. Half wild, the flavor of their flesh was a close approach to that of game. As may be supposed, where license was untrammelled, there was much needless slaughter. Fine carcasses were left as they fell, with the loss only of a few choice cuts. As the beasts, especially the pigs, which looked like our ordinary porkers well stretched, could run with great speed, the chase was amusing as well as exciting. Red breeches and blue fraternized and vied with each other in the sport, to quarrel, perhaps, over the spoils.

Few will fail to carry to their homes recollections of that pleasing episode in the history of the Regiment: the feasts of fat things, the space-built inclosures around the camp-fires that sheltered them from the blast, and were amphitheaters of amusement—recollections that will interest many a future fireside, destined, with the lapse of time, to become sacred as family traditions of the Revolution. And have they not equal claims? The Revolution founded the country; this struggle must save it from the infamous and despotic demands of a most foul and unnatural Rebellion.

"Halloo! Doctor! where did that 'animile' come from," inquired the Major, who formed one of a crowd, on the afternoon of the last day of their stay in the Head Quarters Spruce Retreat, as the little Dutch Doctor strutted alongside of a Corporal of an adjoining regiment, who led by a halter, extemporized from a musket-strap and a cross-belt, a small light dun horse.

"Mine, Major! Pay forty-five tollar—have pay five, only forty yet to get. How you like him? What you tink?"

The "only forty yet to get" amused the crowd, but the Major, with the gravity of a connoisseur, walked around the beast, nipped his legs, and opened his mouth.

"Doctor, it's a pity to use this beast—only two years old, and never shod. Is he broke?"

"No. No broke anywhere. Have look at whole of him."

The crowd laughed, and the Major with them.

"You don't understand me. Can you ride him?"

"Me no ride him, no saddle. Corporal, him ride all round."

The Corporal stated that he was broken in so far as to allow riding, and was very gentle, as indeed was apparent from the looks of the animal.

"When did you get him, Corporal?" was the query of one of the crowd.

"I bought four yesterday for four hundred and seventy-five dollars Confederate scrip."

"Why, where did you get that?"

"Bought it in Washington, when we first went through, of a boy on the Avenue for fifteen cents. I thought there might be a show for it some day or other."

The Corporal was a slender, lantern-jawed, weasel-faced Mononga-hela raftsman, sharp as a steel-trap.

"The old fellow," continued he, "hung on to five hundred dollars for about an hour. He took me into his house, gave me a nip of old apple brandy, and then he'd talk about his horses and then another nip, till we felt it a little, but no go. I had to jew, for it was all I had. I'd just as leave have given him another hundred, but I didn't tell him so. I told him I got it at Antietam.

" 'You d—d rascal,' said he, 'I had a son killed and robbed there, maybe it's his money. It looks as if it had been carried a good while.'

"I had played smart with it, rubbed it, wet it, and in my breast pocket on those long marches it was well sweated.

" 'Suppose it was your son's,' said I, 'all is fair in war.'

" 'That's so,' said the old Rebel. 'I have two other sons there; I would go myself, if I wasn't seventy-eight and upwards.'

" 'Well, looky here,' said I, 'this isn't talking horse; we'll manage your sons, and you, too, if you don't dry up on your treason slang. Now, old covey, four hundred and seventy-five or I'm back to camp without them.'

"I turned and got about ten steps, when he called me back and told me to take them. I got a bully pair of matches, fine blacks, that a Colonel in the Regiment paid me one hundred and twenty-five for at first sight, and a fine pacing bay that our Major gave me seventy-five for, and this one's left.

"Doctor, I'm about tired of trotting around after them other forty. They're givin' out cracker rations, and I don't want to be cheated out of mine, and I must go," said the Corporal, turning quickly to the Doctor.

The latter personage snapped his eyes, and kept his cap bobbing up and down, by wrinkling his forehead, as he somewhat plaintively asked the crowd for the funds.

"Good Lord! Doctor, you might as well try to milk a he-goat with a bramble bush as to get money in camp now," said the Major.

"Corporal," said the Adjutant, a fast friend of the Doctor's, and being of a musical turn, his partner in many a Dutch duet, as a bright idea struck him, "you don't want the money now—there are no sutlers about, suppose the Doctor gives you an order on the Pay-Master."

"Well," said the Corporal, after some little study, and keeping a sharp look-out on the Adjutant, whose features were fixed, "that's a fact, I have no use for the money now. If one of you Head-Quarter officers endorses it, I will. 'Spose it's all straight."

The Adjutant drew the order, and one of the Field-Officers endorsed it, after the manner of documents forwarded through regular military channels:

"Approved and respectfully forwarded."

It was handed to the Corporal, and he turned to go, leaving the horse with the Doctor, and giving the crowd an opportunity for their laugh, so far suppressed with difficulty. He had gone but a few paces when an exclamation from the quondam Third cavalryman called him back, and ended for the moment the laughter.

"Where does the old fellow live, Corporal?"

"Keep out that lane to the left, then across lots by a narrow path. Can't miss it. He has no more horses."

"Don't want horses."

"That apple brandy it's no use trying for."

"Boys," said the Captain, "I'm good for half a dozen canteens of the stuff, I'll bet my boots on it. Who'll go along?"

"I," replied a sturdy brother Captain.

"Recollect now. All here at nine tonight to receive our report. No use to tell you that, though, when whiskey is about," said the first Captain, as the crowd dispersed.

And that report was given by his comrade to the punctual crowd as follows:

"When I came out to the charred pine stumps on the lane, where I was to meet the Captain, it was a little before dusk. I was just about clear of the wood, when the Colonel's big black mare, ridden by the Captain, came bouncing over a scrub pine and lit right in front of me. The d—l himself couldn't have made me feel a colder shudder.

" 'What's the matter? Where's your horse?'

" 'I thought we had better walk,' said I, recovered from the fright; 'it's only a short distance.'

" 'That ain't the thing. There must be some style about this matter.'

"I had noticed that the Captain had on the Colonel's fancy Regulation overcoat, a gilt edged fatigue cap, his over-long jingling Mexican spurs, and the Major's sabre dangling from his side. I came back, got the Adjutant's horse, and rejoined him.

" 'Now, I want you to understand,' said the Captain, putting on his prettiest, as we jogged along the lane, 'that I'm General Burnside. How does that strike you?'

" 'That you don't look a d—n bit like Burney. He is no fancy man. Your style is nearer the Prince's,—Fitz John. All you want are the yellow kids,' rejoined I.

" 'Too near home, that. How will Gen. Franklin[4] do?'

---

(4)     Maj. Gen. William B. Franklin, commander of the Left Grand Division, then
          at Fredericksburg.

"As I knew nothing about Franklin's appearance, I said I supposed that would do. Before respectable people I'd have hated to see any of our Generals wronged by the Captain's looks, but as it was only a Rebel, it didn't make any difference. And then the object overcame all scruples.

" 'Well,' continued the Captain, 'you are to be one of my aides. When we get near the house, just fall back a pace or two.'

"And off he rode, the big mare trotting like an elephant, and keeping my nag up to a gallop. Keeping back a pace or two was a matter of necessity. The Captain was full a hundred yards ahead when he halted near the house to give me time to get in position, his black mare prancing and snorting under the Mexican ticklers in a manner that would have done credit to Bucephalus. He pranced on up towards the house, which was a long weatherboarded structure, a story and a half high, with a porch running its entire length. The building was put up, I should judge, before the war of 1812, and not repaired since. A crabbed old man in a grey coat, with horn buttons, and tan-colored pantaloons, looking as if he didn't know what to make exactly of the character of his visitors, was on the porch. Near him, and somewhat in his rear, was a darkie about as old as himself.

" 'Won't you get off your critters?' at length said the old man, his servant advancing to hold the horses.

"The Captain dismounted, and as his long spurs jingled, and the Major's sabre clattered on the rotten porch floor, the old fellow changed countenance considerably, impressed with the presence of greatness.

" 'I am Major-General Franklin, sir, commander of a Grand Division of the Grand Army of the Potomac,' pompously said the Captain, at the same time introducing me as his Aide, Major Kennedy.

" 'Well, gentlemen officers,' stammers the old man, confusedly, and bowing repeatedly, 'I always liked the old Union. I fit for it in the milish in the last war with the Britishers. Walk in, walk in,' continued he, pointing to the door which the darkie had opened.

"We went into a long room with a low ceiling, dirty floor with no carpet on, a few old chairs, with and without backs, and a walnut table that looked as if it once had leaves. In one corner was a clock, that stopped some time before the war commenced, as the old man afterwards told us, and in the opposite corner stood a dirty pine cupboard. While taking seats, I couldn't help thinking how badly the room would compare with a dining room of one of the neat little farm houses that you can see in any of our mountain gaps, where the land produces nothing but grasshoppers and rocks, and the farmers have to get along by raising chickens to keep down the swarms of grasshoppers, and by peddling huckleberries, and they say, but I never saw them at it, by holding the hind legs of the sheep up to let them get their noses between the rocks for pasture."

This latter assertion was indignantly denied by an officer who had his home in one of the gaps.

"Well," continued the Captain, "I only give it as I heard it. The old man talked Union awhile, said he tried to be all right, but that his sons had run off with the Rebels; and he hemmed and hawed about his being all right until the Captain, who had been spitting fips for a long time, got tired, especially after what the Corporal had said.

" 'Well, my old brother patriot,' said the Captain, bending forward in his chair, and putting on a stern look, 'it don't look exactly right.'

" 'How! What! gentlemen officers,' said the old Rebel, pretending, as he raised his hand to his ear, not to hear the Captain.

"The Captain repeated it louder in his gruff voice, and with a few more airs.

" 'Why, gentlemen officers?' said the old man, rising, half bowing, and looking about, ready to do anything.

" 'You know as well as we do,' said the Captain, 'that you wouldn't let two of your neighbors be this long in the house without offering them something to drink. Now, my old friend, as you say you're all right, we're neighbors in a good cause, and one neighborly act deserves another; you might be wanting to have your property protected, or to go to the Ferry, or to send something, and you could hardly get a pass without a Major-General having something to do with it.'

"At this last the old fellow's face brightened up somewhat.

" 'I'll lose a right smart lot of crops,' said the old man, drawing his chair close to the Captain in a half begging, confidential sort of a way, 'if I don't get to the Ferry this fall. They're stored up there, and I want to go up and show them I am a Union man all right. George,' turning

to the darkie, who, cap in hand, stood at the door, 'strike a light and get
the waiter, and three glasses, and bring up some of the old apple in a
pitcher. Be careful not to spill any. Liquor is mighty scarce,' continued
he, turning to us, 'in these parts since the war. This 'ere I've saved over
by hard squeezin'. It was stilled seven years ago this fall—the fall
apples were so plenty.'

"George had the tallow-dip, a rusty waiter, three small old-fashioned
blue glass tumblers, and a pitcher with the handle knocked off, on the
table in good time. We closed around it with our chairs, and the Captain
filled the glasses, and rising, gave for the first round 'The old Union.'
Our glasses were emptied; the old man had but sipped of his.

" 'My old friend, you fought in 1812, you say, and hardly touch your
tumbler to the old Union. Come, it must have a full glass.' The authority
in the tone of the Captain made the old man swallow it, but as he did
so he muttered something about its being very scarce.

" 'Now,' said the Captain, refilling the glasses, 'Here is The Union
as it is.'

"The old Rebel feeling his first glass a little, and they say anyway
when wine goes in the truth comes out, said in rather a low, trembling
tone,

" 'Now, the fact is, gentlemen officers, some Yankees—not you! not
you! but some Yankees way up North, acted kind of bad.'

" 'That's not the question,' said the Captain, 'there are bad men all
over, and lots of them in Virginia. The toast is before the house,'—the
Captain had already swallowed his—'and it must be drunk'; and the
Major's sabre struck the floor till the table shook.

"With a shudder at the sound the old man gulped it down. The glasses
were refilled and the pitcher emptied.

" 'Here's to The blessed Union as it will be, after all the d—d Rebels
are either under the sod or swinging in hemp neck-ties about ten feet
above it," the Captain shouted, waving at the same time his uplifted
glass in a way that brought a grin on George's face, and made the old
man look pale.

" 'Now! now! now! gentlemen officers,' gasped the old traitor, as if
his breath was coming back by jerks, 'that is pretty hard, considerin'—
considerin' my two sons ran off 'gainst my will—'gainst my will,

gentlemen officers, understand, and jined the Rebels'; and then, as the liquor worked up his pluck and pride, he went on, 'and old Stonewall when he was here last, told me himself at this very table that such soldiers the South could be proud of; and Turner Ashby told me the same thing, and it would be agin all natur for an old man not to feel proud of such boys, after hearing all that from such men, and now you want me to drink such a toast. That—'

" 'Yes, sir,' broke in the Captain, who had emptied his glass, 'and it must be done.'

" 'The fact is, gentlemen officers,' the liquor still working up his pluck, 'we Southerners *had* to fit you. You sent old Brown down to run off our niggers, and then when we hung him, you come yourselves. Every cussed nigger—and I had forty-three in all—has left me and run away but old George and two old wenches that can't run, and are good for nothin' but to chaw corndodgers.' The whiskey now worked fast on the old man, and making half a fist, he said, 'I reckon when hangin' day comes some Blue Bellies will have an airin'.'

" 'You d—d grey-headed old traitor!' roared out the Captain, 'the liquor has let the treason out. Now, by all that's holy, drink that toast standing, head up, as if there was patriotic blood in your veins—as if you lived in the State Washington was born in—or you'll find out what it is to talk treason before a Major-General of the army of the United States.' Another stroke of the sabre on the floor that rattled the broken glass in the windows followed. The old man gave another shudder, straightened up, steadied himself at the table with his left hand, and with a swallow that nearly strangled him, drank off his glass.

" 'Ha! old fellow,' said the Captain, grinning, 'you came near cheating hemp that clip.'

" 'George, show us where the apple brandy is,' he continued, addressing the darkie.

"The darkie bowed, grinned, and pointed to the door leading to the cellar way.

" 'Oh, Lord! my spirits! Don't take it, gentlemen officers, I must have a morning dram, and it's all I've got. Let me keep the spirits.'

" 'You old d—l!' exclaimed the Captain, as he eyed him savagely, 'spirits have made all the trouble in the country. Yes, sir. Bad whiskey and worse preaching of false spiritual doctrines, such as slavery being a Divine institution, and what not, started the Rebellion, and keep it up. Spirits are contraband of war, just as Ben Butler says niggers are, and we'll confiscate it'—here the Captain gave me a sly look—'in the name and by the authority of the President of the United States. Major, where's your canteens?'

"I produced three that had been slung under my cape, and the Captain as many more.

"As the old Rebel saw the preparations he groaned out, 'My God! and only four inches in the barrel George! mind, the barrel in the corner.'

"Knowing the darkie would be all right, we followed under pretty stiff loads, the old man bringing up the rear, staggering to the door and getting down the steps on his hands and knees.

"The Captain tasted both barrels. One in a corner was commissary that the darkie said 'Massa had dickered for just the day afore.' The other was well nigh empty. George, old as he was, had the steadiest hands, and he filled the canteens one by one, closing their mouths on the cedar spigot. As he did it, he whispered, 'Dis'll make de ole nigger feel good. Massa gets flustered on dis and 'buses de ole wimin. De commissary fotches him—can't hurt nuffin wid dat.'

" 'There's devilish little to fluster him now,' said the Captain, as he tipped the barrel to fill the last canteen.

"The old man had stuck at the bottom of the steps. George fairly carried him up, and he lay almost helpless on the floor.

" 'That last toast,' said the Captain, as we left the room, 'will knock any Rebel.'

"George held the horses, and I rather guess steadied our legs as we got on, well loaded with apple juice inside and out. The Captain's spurs sent the black mare off at a gallop, over rocks and bushes, and he left me far behind in a jiffy. But I did in earnest act as an aide before we got to camp. I found him near the place where we turn in, fast between two scrub oaks, swearing like a trooper at the pickets, as he called the bushes, for arresting him, and unable to get backward or forward. His swearing saved him that clip, as it was dark, and I would have gone past if I hadn't heard it."

"I move the adoption of the report, with the thanks of the meeting to Major-General Franklin and his genuine Aide," said the Adjutant, after a stiff drink all around.

"I move that it be referred back for report on the Commissary," said a Lieutenant, after another equally stiff round.

The Adjutant would not withdraw his motion,—no chairman to preserve order,—brandy good,—drinks frequent, and in the confusion that ensued we close the chapter, remarking only that the Commissary was spared to the old Rebel, through an order to march at four next morning, that came to hand near midnight.

# CHAPTER XII.

*The March to Warrenton—Secesh Sympathy and Quarter-Master's Receipts—*
*Middle-Borough—The Venerable Uncle Ned and his Story of the Captain of*
*the Tigers—The Adjutant on Strategy—Red-Tapism and Mac-Napoleonism—*
*Movement Stopped—Division Head-Quarters out of Whiskey—Stragglers and*
*Marauders—A Summary Proceeding—Persimmons and Picket-Duty—A*
*Rebellious Pig—McClellanism.*

THE order to march at four meant moving at six, as was not
unfrequently the case, the men being too often under arms by the
hour shivering for the step, while the Staff Officers who issued the
orders were snoozing in comfortable blankets. Be the cause what it
might that morning, the soldiers probably did not regret it, as it gave
them opportunity to see the lovely valley of the Shenandoah exposed
to their view for the last time, as the fog gradually lifted before the rays
of the rising sun. The Shenandoah, like a silver thread broken by
intervening foliage, lay at their feet. Far to the right, miles distant, was
Charlestown, where old John's soul, appreciative of the beauties of
nature at the dread hour of execution, seeing in them doubtless the
handiwork of nature's God, exclaimed "This is indeed a beautiful
country." In the front, dim in the distance, was Winchester, readily
discovered by the bold mountain spur in its rear. Smaller villages dotted
the valley, variegated by fields and woods—all rebellious cities of the
plain, nests of treason and granaries of food for traitors. A blind mercy

that, on the part of the Administration, that procured its almost total exemption from the despoiling hand of war.

Some in the ranks on Snicker's Summit that fine morning could remember the impudent Billingsgate of look and tongue with which Mrs. Faulkner would fling in their faces a general pass, from a wagon loaded with garden truck for traitors in arms at Bunker Hill—but an instance of long continued good-nature, to use a mild phrase, of the many that have characterized our movements in the field. Well does the great discerner of the desires of men as well as delineator of the movements of their passions, make Crook Richard on his foully usurped and tottering throne exclaim,

"War must be brief when traitors brave the field."

At a later day, in a holier cause, the line remains an axiom. Nor at the time of which we write was the policy much changed. While all admit the necessity, for the preservation of proper discipline, of having Rebel property for the use of the army taken formally under authorities duly constituted for the purpose, and not by indiscriminate license to the troops, none can be so blind as to fail to see the bent of the sympathies controlling the General in command. During the march to Middle-Borough, horses were taken along the route to supply deficiencies in the teams, and forage for their use, but in all cases the women who claimed to represent absent male owners—absent doubtless in arms—and who made no secret of their own Rebel inclinations, received Quarter-Master's receipts for their full value—generally, in fact, their own valuation. These receipts were understood to be presently payable. The interests of justice and our finances would have been much better subserved had their payment been conditioned upon the loyalty of the owner. A different policy would not have comported, however, with that which at an earlier day placed Lee's mansion on the Peninsula under double guard, and when you give it the in that case sorry merit of consistency, its best excuse is given.

Beyond some lives lost by a force of Regulars who ventured too near the river without proper precautions the day after we occupied the Gap, and the loss of a Regimental head-quarters wagon, loaded with the officers' baggage, broken down upon a road on which the exhorting Colonel, after deliberate survey, had set his heart as the safest of roads from the Summit, nothing of note occurred during the stay. Our evacuation of the Gap was almost immediately followed by Rebel occupation.

The statement that nothing of note occurred may, perhaps, be doing injustice to our little Dutch Doctor, who had the best of reasons for remembering the morning of our departure from Snicker's Summit. To the Doctor the mountain, with its rocks, seemed familiar ground. A Tyrolese by birth, he loved to talk of his mountain home and sing its lively airs. But that sweet home had one disadvantage. Their beasts of draught and burden were oxen, and the only horse in the village was a cart-horse owned by the Doctor's father. Of necessity, therefore, his horsemanship was defective, an annoying affair in the army. Many officers and men were desirous of seeing the Doctor mount and ride his newly purchased horse, and the Doctor was quite as anxious to evade observation. His saddle was on and blankets strapped as he surveyed the beast, now passing to this side and now to that, giving wide berth to heels that never kicked, and with his servant at hand, waiting until the last files of the Regiment had disappeared in the woods below. Not unobserved, however, for two of the Field and Staff had selected a clump of scrub pines close at hand for the purpose of witnessing the movement. A rock near by served him as a stand from which to mount. The horse was brought up, and the Doctor, after patting his head and rubbing his neck to assure himself of the good intentions of the animal, cautiously took his place in the saddle and adjusted his feet in the stirrups.

The animal moved off quietly enough, until the Doctor, to increase his speed, touched him in the flank with his spur, when the novel sensation to the beast had the effect of producing a sudden flank movement, which resulted in the instant precipitation of the Doctor upon his back among the rocks and rough undergrowth. The horse stood quietly; there was no movement of the bushes among which the Doctor fell, and the mirth of the observers changed to fear lest an accident of a serious nature had occurred. The officers and servant rushed to the spot. Fortunately the fall had been broken somewhat by the bushes, but nevertheless plainly audible groans in Dutch escaped him, and when aware of the presence of the observers, exclamations in half broken English as to what the result might have been. The actual result was that the horse was forthwith condemned as "no goot" by the Doctor; an ambulance sent for, and necessity for the first time made him take a seat during the march in that vehicle, a practice disgracefully common among army surgeons. The horse in charge of the servant followed, but was ever after used as a pack. No amount of persuasion, even when way-worn and foot-sore from the march, could induce the Doctor to remount his charger.

Middle-Borough, a pretty place near the Bull Run Range of mountains, was reached about ten o'clock in the forenoon of the day after leaving the Gap. After the first Bull Run battle the place was made use of, as indeed were all the towns as far up the country as Martinsburg, as a Rebel hospital. Some of the inmates in butternut and grey, with surgeons and officers on parole in like color, but gorgeous in gilding, were still to be seen about the streets. Grey-headed darkies and picaninnies peered with grinning faces over every fence. The wenches were busily employing the time allowed for the halt in baking hoe-cakes for the men.

In front of the principal mansion of the place, owned by a Major in the Rebel service under Jackson, a small group of officers and men were interesting themselves in the examination of an antique naval sword that had just been purchased by a Sergeant from a venerable Uncle Ned, who stood hat in hand, his bald head exposed to the sun, bowing as each new comer joined the crowd.

"Dat sword, gemmen," said the negro, politely and repeatedly bowing, "belonged to a Captain ob de Louisiana Tigers dat Hannar Amander and me nussed, case he came late and couldn't get into de hospitals or houses, dey was so full right after de fust big Bull Run fight. His thigh was all shot to pieces. He hadn't any money, and didn't seem to hab any friends but Hannar Amander."

"Who is Hannah Amanda?" said one of the crowd.

"My wife, sah," said the old man, crossing his breast slowly with his right hand and profoundly bowing.

"Hannar Amander said de young man must be cared for, dat de good Lor would hold us 'countable if we let him suffer, so we gab him our

*The "principal mansion" was owned by Maj. Arthur Lee Rogers, an aide to Col. Stapleton Crutchfield, Stonewall Jackson's chief of artillery.*

bed, shared our little hoe-cake and rye coffee wid him, and Susan Matildar, my darter, and my wife dressed de wound as how de surgeon would tell us. But after about five days de surgeon shook his head and told de Captain he couldn't lib. De poor young man failed fast arter dat; he would moan and mutter all time ober ladies' names.

" 'Reckon you hab a moder and sisters?' said my wife to him one morning.

" 'Oh, God! yes,' said de fine looking young man, for, as Hannar Amander said, he was purty as a pictur, and she'd often say how much would his moder and sisters gib if dey could only nuss him instead of us poor culled pussons. He said, too, he was no Rebel at heart—dat he was from de Norf, and a clerk in a store at New Orleans, and dey pressed him to go, and den he thought he'd better go as Captain if he had to go, and dey made him Captain. 'And now I must die a traitor! My God! when will my moder and sisters hear of dis, and what will dey say?' and he went on so and moaned; and when we found out he was from up Norf, and sorry at dat for being a Rebel, we felt all de warmer toward

him. He called us bery kind, but moaned and went on so dreadfully dat
my wife and darter didn't know what to do to comfort him. Dey bathed
his head and made him cool drinks, but no use. 'It's not de pain ob de
body,' said Hannar Amander to me, 'it's ob de heart—dat's what's de
matter.'

" 'Hab you made your peace wid God, and are you ready for eber-
lasting rest?' said my wife to him.

" 'My God!' groaned he, 'dere's no peace or rest for me. I'm a sinner
and a Rebel too. Oh, I can't die in such a cause!' and he half raised up,
but soon sunk down again.

" 'We'm all rebels to de bressed God. His Grace alone can sab us,'
said my wife, and she sung from dat good hymn

> " 'Tis God alone can gib
>  De bliss for which we sigh."

" 'Susan Matildar, bring your Bible and read some.' While she said
dis, de poor young man's eyes got full ob tears.

" 'Oh, my poor moder! how she used to read to me from dat book,
and how I've neglected it,' said he.

"Den Susan Matildar—she'd learned to read from her missus' little
girls—read about all de weary laden coming unto de blessed Sabiour.
Wheneber she could she'd read to him, and I went and got good old
Brudder Jones to pray for him. By un by de young man begin to pray
hisself, and den he smiled, and den, oh, I neber can forget how Hannar
Amander clapped her hands and shouted 'Now I know he's numbered
wid de army ob de Lor'! kase he smiles.' Dat was his first smile; but I
can tell you, gemmen, it grew brighter and brighter, and by un by his
face was all smiles, and he died saying he'd meet his moder and all ob
us in Hebben, and praising de bressed Lor'!"

The old man wiped his eyes, and there was a brief pause, none caring
even in that rough, hastily collected crowd to break the silence that
followed his plain and pathetic statement.

"But how did you get the sword?" at last inquired one.

"Before he died he said he was sorry he could not pay us for our kindness," resumed the old man. "Hannar Amander said dat shouldn't trouble him, our pay would be entered up in our 'ternal count.

"And den he gab me dis sword and said I should keep it and sell it, and dat would bring me suffin'. And he gab Susan Matildar his penknife. De Secesh am 'quiring about de sword. I'd like to keep it, to mind de young man by, but we've all got him here," said the old man, pointing to his heart. "I'd sooner gib it to you boys dan sell it to de Rebels, but de Sargeant yer was good enough to pay me suffin for it, and den I can't forget dat good young man, I see his grave every day. We buried him at de foot ob our little lot, and Susan Matildar keeps flowers on his grave all day long. Her missus found out he was from de Norf and was sorry 'fore he died he had been a Rebel, and she told Susan Matildar she wouldn't hab buried him dere. But Hannar Amander said dat if all de Rebels got into glory so nice dey'd do well; and de sooner dey are dere de better for us all, dis ole man say."

This last brought a smile to the crowd, and a collection was taken up for the old man.

"Bress you, gemmen! bress you! Served my Master forty-five years and hab nuffin to show for it. Our little patch Hannar Amander got, but I tries to sarve de Lor at de same time, and dere is a better 'count kept ob dat in a place where old Master dead and gone now pas' twenty years, will nebber hab a chance ob getting at de books."

The old man had greatly won upon his hearers, when the bugle called them to their posts.

Our corps from this place took the road to White Plains, near which little village they encamped in a wood for two nights and a day, while a snow-storm whitened the fields. *   *   *   *   *

"Let the hawk stoop, the bird has flown,"

said a boyish-faced officer who was known in the Regiment as the Poetical Lieutenant, to the Adjutant, as he pushed aside the canvas door of the Office Tent on one of those wintry evenings. The caller had left the studies of the Sophomoric year,—or rather his Scott, Byron, Burns, and the popular novelists of the day,—for the recruiting service in his native county. The day-dreams of the boy as to the gilded glory of the soldier had been roughly broken in upon by severe practical lessons, in tedious out-post duty and wearisome marches. He could remember, as could many others, how he had admired the noble and commanding air with which Washington stands in the bow of the well loaded boat as represented on the historic canvas, and the stern determination depicted upon the countenances of the rest of his Roman-nosed comrades—(why is it that our historic artists make all our Revolutionary Fathers Roman-nosed? If their pictures are faithful, where in the world do our swarms of pugs and aquilines come from worn by those claiming Revolutionary descent? Is it beyond their skill to make a pug or an aquiline an index to nobility of soul or heroic resolve?)—as they keep the frozen masses borne by that angry tide at safe distance from the frail bark—but he then felt nothing of the ice grating the sides of the vessel in which he hoped to make the voyage of life, nor shuddered at the wintry midnight blast that swept down the valley of the Delaware. His dreams had departed, but poetical quotations remained for use at every opportunity.

"What's the matter now?" says the Adjutant.

"One of the Aides just told me," rejoined the Lieutenant, "that the Rebels were in force in our front, and would contest the Rappahannock, while the possession of the Gap we have just left lets them in upon our rear."

"The old game played out again," says the Adjutant. "Another string loose in the bag. Strategy in one respect resembles mesmerism—the object operated upon must remain perfectly quiet. Are we never to suppose that the Rebels have plans, and that their vigilance increases, and will increase, in proportion to the extremity of their case? Our theorists and routine men move armies as a student practices at chess, as if the whole field was under their control, and both armies at their disposal. With our immense resources, vigorous fighting and practical common sense would speedily suppress the Rebellion. Where are our old fighting stock of Generals? our Hookers, Heintzelmans, Hancocks, and men of like kidney? Why must their fiery energies succumb to a cold-blooded strategy, that wastes the material of war, and what is worse, fills our hospitals to no purpose? Those men have learned how to command from actual contact with men. The art of being practical, adapting one's self to emergencies, is not taught in schools. With some it is doubtless innate; with the great mass, it is a matter of education, such as is acquired from moving among men."

> "We have the Pyrrhic dance as yet;
>      Where is our Pyrrhic phalanx gone?
>  Of two such lessons why forget
>      The nobler and the manlier one?"

broke in our Poetical Lieutenant.

"D—n your Pyrrhics," retorted the Adjutant, snappishly. "For the Pyrrhics of past days we have Empirics now. Our phalanxes of old have been led to victory by militia Colonels, who sprang from the thinking head of the people, glowing with the sacred fire of their cause. Do you not believe," continued he enthusiastically, "that the loyal masses who sprang into ranks at the insult upon Sumter would have found a leader long ere this worthy of their cause, whose rapid and decisive blows would have saved us disgraceful campaigns, had the nation been unencumbered by this ruin of a Regular Army, that has given us little else than a tremendous array of officers, many of them of the Pigeon-hole and Paper order,—beggarly list of Privates,—Routine that must be carried out at any cost of success,—and Red Tape that everywhere represses patriotism? And then to think, too, of the half-heartedness and disaffection. How long must these sneaking Catilines in high places abuse our patience? But what can be expected from officers who are not in the service from patriotic motives, but rather from prospects of pay and position? End the war, and you will have men who are now unworthy Major and Brigadier Generals, subsiding into Captains and Lieutenants. Their movements indicate that *they* realize their position fully; but when will the country realize that 'strategy' is played out?"

"The whiskey at Division Head-quarters is played out, any way," said a Sergeant on duty in the Commissary Department, who had entered the tent while the Adjutant was speaking.

>     " 'And not a drop to drink,' "

rejoined the Lieutenant.

"Then, by Heaven, we are lost," continued the Adjutant. "Strategy played out and our General of Division out of whiskey. Yes, sir! those mishaps end all further movement of this Grand Army of the Potomac. But when did you hear that?"

"I was in the marquee of the Brigade Commissary when a Sergeant and a couple of privates on duty about Pigey's Head-quarters came in with a demijohn and a note to the Commissary, presenting the compliments of the General commanding Division, and at the same time the cash for four gallons of whiskey. The Captain read it carefully and told the Sergeant to tell the General that he didn't keep a dram-shop. I expected that this reply would make sport, and I concluded to wait awhile and see the thing out. In a few minutes the Sergeant returned, stating that he had not given that reply to the General, through fear, I suppose, but had stated that the Captain had made some excuse. He said further that Pigey said he was entirely out, and must have some."

" 'Tell him what I told you,' said the Captain, determinedly. Off the Sergeant started. I waited for his return outside, and asked him how Pigey took the answer. 'Took it?' said he, 'I didn't tell him about the dram-shop, but when he found I had none, he raved like mad—swore he was entirely out—had been since morning, and must and would have some. He d—d the Captain for being a temperance fanatic, and for bringing his fanatical notions into the army; and all the while he paced up and down his marquee like a tiger at a menagerie. At last he told me that I must return again and tell the Captain that it was a case of absolute necessity, and that he knew that there was a barrel of it among the Commissary stores, and that he must have his four gallons.'

"I followed the Sergeant in, but he could not make it. The Captain had just turned it over to the Hospital.

"So the Sergeant went back again with the empty demijohn. He told me afterwards that the General was so taken aback by his not getting any, that he sat quietly down on his camp stool, ran his fingers through his hair, pulled at his moustache, 'and then I knew,' said the Sergeant, 'that a storm was brewing, and that the General was studying how to do justice to the subject. At length he rose slowly, kicked his hat that had fallen at his feet to one corner of the marquee, d—g it at the same time; d—d me for not getting it any how, and clenching his fists and

*A Happy Headquarters with a Cooperating Commissary:*
*General Humphreys and aides.*

walking rapidly up and down, d—d the Captain, his Brigadier, and
everything belonging to the Brigade, until I thought it a little too hard
for a man who had had a Sunday School education in his young days
to listen to, and I left him still cursing.' "

"He will court-martial the Captain," said the Colonel, who had
entered the tent, "for signal contempt of the Regular Service. I recollect
a charge of that kind preferred by a Regular Lieutenant against an Adjutant of the —— Maine, down in the Peninsula. In one of our marches
the Adjutant had occasion to ride rapidly by the Regiment to which the
Lieutenant belonged. The Lieutenant hailed him—told him to stop. The
Adjutant knowing his duty, and that he had no authority to halt him,
continued his pace, but found himself for nearly a month afterward in
arrest under a charge of 'Signal contempt for the Regular Service.' "

Sigel's hardy Teutons lined the road in the vicinity of New Baltimore,
through which village the route lay on the following day. Part of his
corps had some days previously occupied the mountain gaps in the Bull
Run range on the left. Other troops, led by a Commander whose strategy

was singularly efficacious to keep him out of fights, were passing to the front, leaving a fighting General of undoubted prowess in European and American history, in the rear. Inefficient himself, and perhaps designedly so, his policy could not, with safety to his own reputation, allow of efficiency elsewhere.

That night our Regiment encamped in one of the old pine fields common in Virginia. The softness of the decaying foliage of the pine which covered the ground as a cushion was admirably adapted to repose, and upon it the men rested, while the gentle evening breeze sighed among the boughs above them, as if in sympathy with disappointed hopes and sacrifices made in vain.

"Stragglers and marauders, sir," said a Sergeant of the Provost Guard, saluting the Colonel, who was one of the circle lying cozily about the fire, pointing as he spoke to a squad of way-worn, woe-begone men under guard in his rear. "Here is a list of their offenses. I was ordered to report them for punishment."

"A new wrinkle, that," said the Colonel, as the Sergeant left. "Our Brigadier must be acting upon his own responsibility. Our General of Division would certainly never have permitted such an opportunity slip for employing the time of officers in Courts-martial. That list would have kept one of our Division Courts in session at least three weeks, and have given the General himself an infinite amount of satisfaction in examining his French authorities, and in strictures upon the Records. What have we here, any how?"

No. 1. "Straggling to a persimmon tree on the road-side."

"That man," said a Lieutenant, "when he saw our Brigadier coming up, presented him with a couple of persimmons very politely. But it was no go; the General ordered him under guard and eat the persimmons as part of the punishment."

"Well," rejoined the Colonel, "we'll let you off with guard duty for the night."

No. 2. "Killing a shoat while the Regiment halted at noon."

The man charged was a fine looking young fellow whose only preparation for the musket, when he enlisted, was previous practice with the yard stick in a dry goods establishment. Intelligent and good-natured, he was popular in the command, and was never known to let his larder suffer.

"Was it a Rebel pig?" inquired a bystander.

"A most rebellious pig," replied he, bowing to the Colonel. "He gave us a great amount of trouble, and rebelled to the last." A laugh followed, interrupted by the Colonel, who desired to hear the circumstances of the case.

"Right after we had halted on the other side of New Baltimore," continued the man, "I saw the pig rooting about a corn shock, and as my haversack was empty, and myself hungry, I thought I could dispose of part of him to advantage, and before I had time to reflect about the order, I commenced running after him. Several others followed, and some officers near by stood looking at us. After skinning my hands and knees in trying to catch him by throwing myself upon him, I finally caught him. When I had him skinned, I gave a piece to all the officers who saw me, saving only a ham for myself, and I was dressing it when up came a Lieutenant of the Provost Guard and demanded it. I debated the matter as well as a keen appetite would allow, and finally coming to the conclusion that I could not serve my country as I should, if half starved, I resolved to keep it, and refused him, and he reported me, and here I am with it at your service," clapping his hand on a well filled haversack.

One-half of the meat was confiscated, but the novelty of the sergeant's patriotic plea saved him further penalty.

No. 3. Caught in a negro shanty, in company with an old wench.

The crowd laughed; while the subject, a tall cadaverous-looking fellow, protested earnestly that he was only waiting while the wench baked him a hoe-cake.

"Guard duty for the night," said the Colonel.

"Poor devil! He will have to keep awake, and can't sing—'Sleeping I dream, love, dream, love, of thee' "—said the poetical Lieutenant, who chanced to be one of the group.

No. 4. Caught by the General Commanding Division, twenty feet high on a persimmon tree, and Nos. 5, 6, 7, 8, 9, and 10 on the ground below; also "Lying."

"Another persimmon crowd. Every night we are troubled with the persimmon business," said the Colonel; "but what does the 'also Lying' mean?"

"Why," said a frank fellow of the crowd, "you see when the old General came up, I said it was a picket station, and that the man up the tree was looking out for the enemy. It was a big thing, I thought, but the General didn't see it, and he swore he would persimmon us."

"Which meant," said the Colonel, "that you would lose your persimmons, and go on extra police duty for forty-eight hours each."

The crowd were lectured upon straggling, that too frequent offense of Volunteers, and after a severe reprimand dismissed.

The country abounded in persimmon trees, and their golden fruit was a sore temptation to teeth sharpened on army crackers. As the season advanced, and persimmons became more palatable, crowds would thus be brought up nightly for punishment. This summary procedure was an innovation by the Brigadier upon the Red-Tape formulary of Courts-martial, so rigidly adhered to, and fondly indulged in, by the General of Division. The Brigadier would frequently himself dispose of delinquencies of the kind, telling the boys in a manner that made them feel that he cared for their welfare, that they had been entrusted to him by the country for its service, and that he considered himself under obligations to their relatives and friends to see that while under his command their characters received no detriment, and while becoming good soldiers they would not grow to be bad citizens. He made them realize, that although soldiers they were still citizens; and many a man has left him all the better for a reprimand which reminded him of duties to relatives and society at large. How much nobility of soul might be spared to the country with care of this kind, on the part of commanders. Punishment is necessary—but how many to whom it is intrusted forget that in giving it a moral effect upon society, care should be taken that it may operate beneficially upon the individual. The General who crushes the soul out of his command by exacting infamous punishments for trivial offenses, is but a short remove from the commander who would basely surrender it to the enemy on the barest pretext. Punishment has too often been connected with prejudice against Volunteers in the Army of the Potomac, controlled as it has been too much by martinets. That a nation of freemen could have endured so long the contumely of a proud military leader when his incapacity was so apparent, will be a matter of wonder for the historian. The inconsistency that would follow the great Napoleon in modelling an army and neglect his example in giving it mobility, with eminent propriety leaves the record of its exploits to depend upon the pen of a scion of the unmilitary House of Orleans.

But the decree "thus far shalt thou come," forced upon an honest but blindly indulgent President by the People, who will not forget that power is derived from them, had already gone forth, although not yet officially announced to the Army; and it was during the week at Warrenton, our halting-place on the morrow, that the army, with the citizens at home, rejoiced that the work of staying the proud waves of imbecility, as well as insult, to our Administration, had commenced. The history of reforms is one of the sacrifice of blood, money, and time. Frightful bills of mortality, shattered finances, nineteen months of valuable time, do not in this case admit of an exception.

## CHAPTER XIII.

*Camp near Warrenton—Stability of the Republic—Measures, not Men, regarded by the Public—Removal of McClellan—Division Head-Quarters a House of Mourning—A Pigeon-Hole General and his West Point Patent-Leather Cartridge-Box—Head-Quarter Murmurings and Mutterings— Departure of Little Mac and the Prince—Cheering by Word of Command— The Southern Saratoga—Rebel Regret at McClellan's Departure.*

WRITERS prone to treat of the instability of Republics, will find serious matter to combat in the array of events that culminated at Warrenton. Without the blood that has usually characterized similar events in the history of Monarchies, in fact with scarcely a ripple upon the surface of our national affairs, a great military chieftain, or to speak truly, a commander who had endeavored, and who had the grandest of opportunities to become such, passed from his proud position as the leader of the chief army of the Republic, to the obscurity of private life. Proffered to a public, pliant, because anxious that its representatives in the field should have a worthy Commander, by an Administration eager to repair the disaster of Bull Run,—puffed into favor by almost the entire press of the country, the day had been when the loyalty of the citizen was measured by his admiration of General McClellan.

Never did a military leader assume command so auspiciously. The resources of a mighty nation were lavishly contributed to the material of his army. Its best blood stood in his ranks. Indulged to an almost criminal extent by an Administration that in accordance with the wishes of the masses it represented, bowed at his beck and was overly solicitous to do his bidding, no wonder that this ordinary mind became unduly inflated. He could model his army upon the precedents set by the great Napoleon; he could surround himself by an immense Staff—the talent of which, however, but poorly represented the vigor of his army,—for nepotism and favoritism interfered to prevent that, as they will with common men; drill and discipline could make his army efficient,—for his subordinates were thorough and competent, and his men were apt pupils; but he himself could not add to all these the crowning glories of the field. Every thing was there but genius, that God-given gift; and that he did not prove to be a Napoleon resulted alone from a lack of brains.

Now that the glare of the rocket has passed from our sky, and its stick has fallen quietly enough among the pines of New Jersey, citizens have opportunity for calm reflection. We are not justified, perhaps, in attributing to McClellan all the evils and errors that disfigure his tenure of office. Intellect equal to the position he could not create for himself, and ninety-nine out of one hundred men of average ability would not have descended from his balloon-like elevation with any better grace. It is in the last degree unjust to brand with disloyalty, conduct that seems to be a result natural enough to incompetency. That upon certain occasions he may have been used for disloyal purposes by designing men, may be the consequence of lack of discrimination rather than of patriotism.

Whatever might have induced his conduct of the war, the nation has learned a lesson for all time. Generals who had grown grey in honorable service were rudely set aside for a Commander whose principal merit consisted in his having published moderately well compiled military books. Their acquiescence redounds to their credit; but their continued and comparatively calm submission in after times, when that General, regardless of soldierly merit, placed in high and honorable positions relatives and intimate friends, who could be but mere place-men, dependent entirely upon him for their honors, and committed to his interests, is strong proof of devoted patriotism. Slight hold had these neophytes upon the stern matter-of-fact fighting Generals, or the equally devoted and patriotic masses in ranks. In their vain glory they murmured and muttered during and subsequent to this week at Warrenton, as they had threatened previously, in regard to the removal of McClellan. They knew not the Power that backed the Bayonet. In the eye of the unreserved and determined loyalty of the masses, success was the test of popularity with any Commander. Not the shadow of an excuse existed for any other issue. Our resources of the material of war were well nigh infinite. Men could be had almost without number, at least equal to the Rebels in courage. There was, then, no excuse for inaction, and none knew it better than our reflecting rank and file.

The effort to inspire popularity for McClellan had been untiring by his devotees in position in the army. In the outset it was successful. Like their friends at home, the men in ranks, during the dark days that succeeded Bull Run, eagerly caught at a name that received such honorable mention. That this flush of popularity did not increase until it became a steady flame like that which burned within the breasts of the veterans of the old French Empire, is because its subject lacked the commanding ability, decision of character, and fiery energy, that made statesmen do reverence, turned the tide of battle to advantage, and swept with resistless force over the plains of Italy and the mountains of Tyrol.

It was with mingled feelings of pleasure and uncertainty, caused by the change, that the Regiment broke to the front in column of company, and encamped on a beautifully wooded ridge about two miles north of Warrenton. Pleasure upon account of the change—as any change must be for the better,—uncertainty, as to its character and extent. In their doubtful future, Generals shifted position, and succeeded each other, very much as dark specks appear and pass before unsteady vision. Who would be the successor? Would the change be radical? were questions that were discussed in all possible bearings around cheerful camp-fires.

Whatever the satisfaction among subordinate officers and the ranks, Division Head-quarters was a house of mourning. To the General removed solely it owed its existence. Connected with his choice Corps, it had basked in the sunshine of his favor. With the removal already ordered, "the dread of something worse"—a removal nearer home was apprehended. As a Field Commander, the officer upon whose shoulders rested the responsibilities of the Division, was entirely unknown previously to his assuming command. His life hitherto had been of such a nature as not to add to his capacity as a Commander. Years of quiet clerkly duty in the Topographical Department may, and doubtless did in his case, make an excellent engineer or draughtsman, but they afford few men opportunities for improvement in generalship. During the Mc-Clellan regime this source furnished a heavy proportion of our superior officers. Why, would be difficult to say on any other hypothesis than that of favoritism. Their educational influences tend to a defensive policy, which history proves Generals of ability to have indulged in only upon the severest necessity. To inability to rise above these strictures of the school, may be traced the policy which has portrayed upon the historic page, to our lasting disgrace as a nation, the humiliating spectacle of a mighty and brave people, with resources almost unlimited, compelled for nearly two years to defend their Capital against armies greatly inferior to their own in men and means.

Independently of these educational defects, as they must be called, there was nothing in either the character or person of the Division Commander to command respect or inspire fear. Eccentric to a most whimsical degree, his oddities were the jest of the Division, while they were not in the least relieved by his extreme nervousness and fidgety habits of body. That there was nothing to inspire fear is, however, subject to exception, as his whims kept subordinates in a continual fever. The art of being practical—adapting himself to circumstances—he had never learned. It belongs to the department of Common Sense, in which, unfortunately, there has never been a professor at West Point. His after life does not seem to have been favorable to its acquirement. Withal, the hauteur characteristic to Cadets clung to him, and on many occasions rendered him unfortunate in his intercourse with volunteer officers. Politeness with him, assumed the airs and grimaces of a French dancing-master, which personage he was not unfrequently and not inaptly said to resemble. Displeasure he would manifest by the oddest of gestures and volleys of the latest oaths, uttered in a nervous, half stuttering manner. Socially, his extensive educational acquirements made him a pleasant companion, and with a friend it was said he would drink as deep and long as any man in the Army of the Potomac. Once crossed, however, his malignity would be manifested by the most intolerable and petty persecution.

"He has no judgment," said a Field-Officer of a Regiment of his command; a remark which, by the way, was a good summary of his character.

"Why?" replied the officer to whom he was speaking.

"I was out on the picket duty," rejoined the other, "yesterday. We had an unnecessarily heavy Reserve, and one half of the men in it were allowed to rest without their belts and boxes. The General in the afternoon paid us a visit, and seeing this found fault, that the men were not kept equipped; observing at the same time that they could rest equally well with their cartridge boxes on; that when he was a Cadet at West Point he had ascertained by actual practice that it could be done."

" 'Do you recollect, General,' I remarked, 'whether you had forty rounds of ball cartridge in your box then?'

"He said he did not know that that made any difference.

"Now considering that the fact of the boxes being filled makes all the difference, I say," continued the officer, "that the man who makes a remark such as the General made, is devoid of judgment."

But he was connected both by ties of friendship and consanguinity with the hitherto Commander of the Army of the Potomac. His Adjutant-General was related to the same personage. The position of the latter, for which he was totally unfitted by his habits, was perhaps a condition precedent to the appointment of the General of Division.

The fifth of November, a day destined to become celebrated hereafter in American as in English history, dawned not less inauspiciously upon the Head-quarters of the Corps. They too could not appreciate the dry humor of the order that commanded Little Mac to report at Trenton. They thought alone of the unwelcome reality—that it was but an American way of sending him to Coventry. The Commander of the Corps had been a great favorite at the Head-quarters of the army—perhaps because in this old West Point instructor the haughty dignity and prejudice against volunteers which characterized too many Regular officers, had its fullest personification. His Corps embraced the largest number of Regular officers. In some Regiments they were ridiculously, and for Uncle Sam expensively, plentiful,—some Companies having two or three Captains, two or three First or Second Lieutenants,—while perhaps the enlisted men in the Regiment did not number two hundred.

But these supernumeraries were Fitz John's favorites, and whether they performed any other labor than sporting shoulder straps, regularly visiting the Paymasters, adjusting paper collars and cultivating moustaches, was a matter of seemingly small consequence, though during depressed national finances.

The little patriotism that animated many of the officers attached to both of these Head-quarters, did not restrain curses deep if not loud. Pay and position kept them in the army at the outbreak of the Rebellion; and pay and position alone prevented their taking the same train from Warrenton that carried away their favorite Commander. A telegram of the Associated Press stated a few days later that a list of eighty had been prepared for dismissal. What evil genius averted this benefit to the country, the War Department best knows. It required no vision of the night, nor gift of soothsaying, to foretell the trouble that would result from allowing officers in important positions to remain in the army, who were under the strongest obligations to the General removed, devotedly attached to him, and completely identified with, and subservient to, his interests. It might at least be supposed that his policy would be persevered in, and that his interests would not suffer. So far the reform was not radical.

"Colonel," said one of these martinets who occupied a prominent position upon the Staff of Prince Fitz John, as with a look of mingled contempt and astonishment he pointed to a Lieutenant who stood a few rods distant engaged in conversation with two privates of his command, "do you allow commissioned officers to converse with privates?"

"Why not, sir? Those three men were intimate acquaintances at home. In fact, the Lieutenant was a clerk in a dry-goods establishment in which one of the privates was a junior partner."

"All wrong, sir," replied the martinet. "They should approach a commissioned officer through a Sergeant. The Inspecting Officer will report you for laxity of discipline in case it continues, and place you under arrest."

The Brigadier, when he heard of this conversation, intimated that should the Inspecting Officer attempt it, he would leave the Brigade limits under guard; and it was not attempted.

Nonsense such as this is not only contemptible but criminal, when contrasted with the kind fellowship of Washington for his men,—his solicitude for their sufferings at Valley Forge,—Putnam sharing his scanty meals with privates of his command,—Napoleon learning the wants of his veterans from their own lips, and tapping a Grenadier familiarly upon the shoulder to ask the favor of a pinch from his snuffbox. Those worthies may rest assured that marquees pitched at Regulation distance, and access through non-commissioned officers, will not, if natural dignity be wanting, create respect. How greatly would the efficiency of the army have been increased, had the true gentility that characterized the noble soul of Colonel Simmons,[1] who fell at Gaines' Mills, and that will always command reverence, been more general among his brother officers of the Regular Army.

These evil results should not, however, lead to a wholesome condemnation of West Point. The advantages of the Institution have been abused, or rather neglected, by the great masses of the Loyal States. In our moral matter-of-fact business communities it has been too generally the case, that cadets have been the appointees of political favoritism, regardless of merit; and that the wild and often worthless son of influential and wealthy parents, who had grown beyond home restraint, and who gave little indication of a life of honor or usefulness, would be turned into the public inclosure at West-Point to square his morals and his toes at the same time at public expense, and the act rejoiced at as a good family riddance. Thus in the Loyal States, the profession of arms had fallen greatly into disrepute previously to the outbreak of the Rebellion, and instead of being known as a respectable vocation, was considered as none at all. Had military training to some extent been connected with the common school education of the land, we would have gained in health, and would have been provided with an able array of officers for our noble army of Volunteers. Among other preparations for their infamous revolt, the Rebels did not fail to give this especial prominence.

---

(1)     Col. Seneca G. Simmons belonged to Gen. George McCall's ill-fated Third
        Division of the Fifth Corps. He was killed at Glendale, not Gaines's Mill, in
        the Seven Days Campaign.

The Northern States have been great in peace; the material is being rapidly educated that will make them correspondingly great in war.

"November's surly blasts" were baring the forests of foliage, when the order for the last Review by McClellan was read to the Troops. Mutinies and rumors of mutinies "from the most reliable sources" had been suspended above the Administration, like the threatening sword of Damocles; but Abraham's foot was down at last, and beyond murmurings and mutterings at disaffected Head-Quarters no unsoldierly conduct marked the reception of the order. So far from the "heavens being hung with black," as a few man-worshippers in their mad devotion would have wished, nature smiled beautifully fair. Such a sight could only be realized in Republican America. A military Commander of the greatest army upon the Continent, elevated in the vain-glory of dependent subordinates into a quasi-Dictatorship, was suddenly lowered from his high position, and his late Troops march to this last Review with the quiet formality of a dress parade. What cared those stern, self-sacrificing men in ranks, from whose bayonets that brilliant sun glistened in diamond splendor, for the magic of a name—the majesty of a Staff, gorgeous, although not clothed in the uniform desired by its late Chief. The measure of payment for toil and sacrifice with them, was progress in the prosecution of their holy cause. The thunders of the artillery that welcomed *him* with the honor due to his rank, reminded *them* to how little purpose, through short-comings upon his part, those same pieces had thundered upon the Peninsula and at Antietam.

Massed in close columns by division along the main road leading to Warrenton, the troops awaited the last of the grand pageants that had made the Army of the Potomac famous for reviews. Its late Commander, as he gracefully sat his bay, had not the nonchalance of manner that he manifested while reading a note and accompanying our earnest President in a former review at Sharpsburg; nor was the quiet dignity that he usually exhibited when at the head of his Staff, apparent. His manner seemed nervous, his look doubly anxious; troubled in the present, and solicitous as to the future. Conscious, too, doubtless, as he faced a nation's Representatives in arms, how he had "kept the word of promise to the ear," and how "he had broken it to the hope;" how while his reviews had revealed a mighty army of undoubted ability and eagerness for the fight, his indecision or proneness to delay had made its campaigns the laughing-stock of the world. His brilliant Staff clattered at his heels; but glittering surroundings were powerless to avert the memories of a winter's inactivity at Manassas, the delay at Yorktown, the blunders on the Chickahominy, or the disgrace of the day after Antietam. How closely such memories thronged upon this thinking soldiery, and how little men who leave families and business for the field, from the necessity of the case, care for men if their measures are unsuccessful, may be imagined, when the fact is known that this same Little Mac, once so great a favorite through efforts of the Press and officers with whom he had peopled the places in his gift, received his last cheers from some Divisions of that same Army by word of command.

"A long farewell to all his greatness."

Imbecile in politics as in war, he cannot retrieve it by cringing to party purposes. The desire that actuates our masses and demands able and earnest leaders has long since dissolved party lines.

This leave-taking was followed a few days later by that of the Corps Commander. Troubled looks, shadows that preceded his dark future, were plainly visible as the Prince passed up and down the lines of his late command.

Another day passed, and with light hearts the men brightened their muskets for a Review by their new Commander, Major-General Burnside, or "Burney," as they popularly called the Hero of Carolina celebrity.

But the day did not seem to be at hand that should have completed the reform by sweeping and garnishing disaffected, not to say disloyal Head-Quarters—removing from command men who were merely martinets, and who were in addition committed body and soul to the interests of their late Commander, and who, had they been in receipt of compensation from Richmond, could not have more completely labored by their half-hearted, inefficient, and tyrannizing course, to crush the spirit of our soldiery.

"What's the matter with Old Pigey?" inquired a Sergeant, detailed on guard duty at Division Head-Quarters, as he saluted his Captain, on one of these evenings at Warrenton.

"Why?" rejoined the Captain.

"The General," continued the Sergeant, "was walking up and down in front of his marquee almost all of last night, talking to himself, muttering, and at almost every other step stamping and swearing. He had a bully old mad on, I tell you, Captain. He went it in something of this style."

And the sergeant himself strode up and down, muttering and stamping and swearing, to the great amusement of the Captain and some bystanders.

The unwillingness to bow to the dictation of the President as Commander-in-Chief in his most righteous removal of their favorite, caused much heart-burning, and gave rise to much disloyal conduct. That it was tolerated at all was owing to the unappreciated indulgence or hesitation of the Administration, lest it should undertake too much. The operation, to have been skilful and complete, required nerve. That article so necessary for this crisis is in the ranks, and let us trust that for the future it will be found in greater abundance at Washington.

The Southern Saratoga, as Warrenton has been styled among the fashionables of the South, has much to commend it in situation and scenery, as a place of residence. The town itself is an odd jumble of old and new buildings, and is badly laid out, or rather not laid out at all, as the streets make all possible angles with each other. Yankee enterprise appears to have had something to do with the erection of the later buildings. Like other towns of that neighborhood its cemetery is heavily peopled with Rebel dead. At the time of our occupancy many of its larger buildings were still occupied as hospitals.

On the day of McClellan's departure the streets were crowded with officers and men, and the sympathies of the Rebel residents seemed strangely in unison with those of the chieftain's favorites. The representatives of the clannish attachments which made McClellanism a species of Masonry in the army, were there in force. In these banded interests brotherly love took the place of patriotism. Little wonder!

looking at the record of the McClellan campaigns, that the Rebels present fraternized with these devotees in their grief.

"You have thrown away your ablest commander," said an elderly man, of intelligent and gentlemanly appearance, clad in the uniform of a surgeon of the Rebel army, who stood conversing with one of our own surgeons, on the sidewalk of the main street of the place, while the crowd gathered to witness the departure of the General.

"Do you really think so?" rejoined the Union Surgeon, as he earnestly eyed the speaker.

"Yes, sir," said the Rebel, emphatically. "It is not only my opinion but the opinion of our Generals of ability, that in parting with McClellan you lose the only General you have who has shown any strategic ability."

"If that be your opinion, sir," was the decided reply, "the sooner we are rid of him the better."

And to this reply the country says, Amen!

"But what a shame it is that military genius is so little appreciated by the Administration, and that he is removed just at this time! Why, I heard our Colonel say that he had heard the General say, that in a few days more, he would have won a decisive victory," remarked a young officer, in a jaunty blue jacket, to a companion, gesticulating as he spoke, with a cigar between the first and second fingers of his right hand.

An older officer, who overheard the remark, observed, dryly:—"He was not removed for what he would do, but for what he had done."

"And for what he had not done," truthfully added another.

Never had a General, burdened with so many sins of omission and commission as the conversation indicated, been so leniently dealt with, now that the Rebels in their favorite, and with him successful game of hide and seek, had again given him the slip, and were only in his front to annoy. As they had it completely in their power to prevent a general engagement at that point, his remark as to what would have been done was a very rotten twig, caught at in the vain hope of breaking his fall.

## CHAPTER XIV.

*A Skulker and the Dutch Doctor—A Review of the Corps by Old Joe—A Change of Base; what it means to the Soldier, and what to the Public—Our Quarter-Master and General Hooker—The Movement by the Left Flank—A Division General and Dog-driving—The Desolation of Virginia—A Rebel Land-Owner and the Quarter-Master—"No Hoss, Sir!"—The Poetical Lieutenant unappreciated—Mutton or Dog?—Desk Drudgery and Senseless Routine.*

IT'S about time, Bill, for you to have another sick on," said a lively lad, somewhat jocosely, as he rubbed away at his musket-barrel, on one of our last mornings at the Camp, near Warrenton. "Fighting old Joe has the Corps now, and he will review us today, the Captain says, and after that look out for a move."

"Don't say," drawled out the man addressed; a big, lubberly fellow, famous in the Regiment for shirking duty—who, when picket details were expected, or a march in prospect, would set a good example of punctuality in promptly reporting at Surgeon's call, or as the Camp phrase had it, "stepping up for his quinine." "Well," continued he, "Lord knows what I'll do. I've had the rheumatics awful bad," clapping at the same time one hand on his hip, and the other on his right shoulder, "the last day or two, and then the chronical diarrhoear."

"You had better go in on rheumatism, Bill," broke in the first speaker, "The Doctor will let you off best on that."

"That's played out, isn't it, Bill," chimed in another; and to Bill's disgust, as he continued, "It don't go with the little Dutch Doctor since

Sharpsburg. Every time his Company's turn would come for picket, while we were at that Camp, Bill would be a front-rank man at the Hospital, with a face as long as a rail, and twisted as if he had just had all his back teeth pulled. The little Dutchman would yell out whenever he would see him—'What for you come? Eh? You tam shneak. Rheumatism, eh? In hip?' And the Doctor would punch his shoulder and hip, and pinch his arms and legs until Bill would squirm like an eel under a gig. 'Here, Shteward,' said the Doctor the last time, as he scribbled a few words on a small piece of paper, 'Take this; make application under left ear, and see if dis tam rheumatism come not out.' Bill followed the Steward, and in a few minutes came back to quarters ornamented with a fly-blister as big as a dollar under his left ear. Next morning Bill didn't report, but he's been going it since on diarrhoea."

"He wasn't smart, there," observed another. "He ought to have done as little Burky of our mess did. He'd hurry to quarters, take the blister off, clap it on again next morning when he'd report, and he'd have the little Dutchman swearing at the blister for not being 'wors a tam.' "

Bill took the sallies of the crowd with the quiet remark that their turn for the sick list would come some day.

The Review on that day was a grand affair. The fine-looking manly form of Old Joe, as, in spite of a bandaged left ankle not yet recovered from the wound at Antietam, and that kept the foot out of the stirrup, he rode down the line at a gait that tested the horsemanship of his followers, was the admiration of the men. In his honest and independent looking countenance they read, or thought they could, character too purely republican to allow of invidious distinctions between men, who, in their country's hour of need, had left civil pursuits at heavy sacrifices, and those who served simply because the service was to them the business of life. With hearts that kept lively beat with the regimental music as they marched past their new Commander, they rejoiced at this mark of attention to the necessities of the country, which removed an Officer, notorious as a leader of reserves, and placed them under the care of a man high on the list of fighting Generals. "Waterloo," says the historic or rather philosophic novelist of France, "was a change of front of the universe." The results of that contest are matter of record, and justify the remark. At Warrenton a great Republic changed front, and henceforth the milk and water policy of conciliating "our Southern Brethren" ranked as they are behind bristling bayonets, or of intimidating them by a mere show of force, must give way to active campaigning and heavy blows.

A rainy, misty morning a day or two after the review, saw the Corps pass through Warrenton, en route for the Railroad Junction, commencing the change of direction by the left flank, ordered by the new Commander of the Army. The halt for the night was made in a low piece of woodland lying south of the railroad. In column of Regiments the Division encamped, and in a space of time incredible to those not familiar with such scenes, knapsacks were unslung and the smoke of a thousand camp-fires slowly struggled upwards through the falling rain. Its pelting was not needed to lull the soldiers, weary from the wet march and slippery roads, to slumber.

At early dawn they left the Junction and its busy scenes—its lengthy freight-trains, and almost acres of baggage-wagons, to the rear, and struck the route assigned the Grand Division, of which they were part, for Fredericksburg. "A change of base" our friends will read in the leaded headings of the dailies, and pass it by as if it were a transfer of an article of furniture from one side of the room to the other. Little know they how much individual suffering from heavy knapsacks and blistered feet, confusion of wagon-trains, wrangling and swearing of teamsters, and vexation in almost infinite variety, are comprised in these few words. It is the army that moves, however, and the host of perplexities move with it, all unknown to the great public, and transient with the actors themselves as bubbles made by falling rain upon the lake. The delays incident to a wagon-train are legion. Occurring among the foremost wagons, they increase so rapidly that notwithstanding proper precaution and slowness in front, a rear-guard will often be kept running. The profanity produced by a single chuck hole in a narrow road appears to increase in arithmetical proportion as the wagons successively approach, and teamsters in the rear find their ingenuity taxed to preserve their reputation for the vice with their fellows.

Why negroes are not more generally employed as teamsters is a mystery. They are proverbially patient and enduring. Both the interests of humanity and horseflesh would be best subserved by such employ-

*Maj. Gen. Joseph Hooker, commander of the Center Grand Division.*

ment, and the ranks would not be reduced by the constant and heavy details of able-bodied men for that duty. Capital and careful horsemen are to be found among the contrabands of Virginia, and many a poor beast, bad in harness because badly treated, would rejoice at the change.

Quarter-masters, Wagon-masters, Commissaries, *et id genus omne*, have their peculiar troubles. Our Regiment was particularly favored in a Quarter-master of accomplished business tact, whose personal supervision over the teams during a march was untiring, and whose tongue was equally tireless in rehearsing to camp crowds, after the march was over, the troubles of the day, and how gloriously he surmounted them. In his department he held no divided command.

"Get out of my train with that ambulance. You can't cut me off in that style," he roared in an authoritative manner to an ambulance driver, who had slipped in between two of his wagons on the second day of our march.

"My ambulance was ordered here, sir! I have General—" The driver's reply was here interrupted by the abrupt exclamation of the Quarter-master[1]—

"I don't care a d—n if you have Old Joe himself inside. I command this train and you must get out." And get out the driver did, at the intimation of his passenger, who, to the surprise of the Quarter-master, notwithstanding his assertion, turned out to be no less a personage than General Hooker himself.

"It is the law of the road," said the General, good-humoredly—candid to his own inconvenience—"and we must obey it."

This ready obedience upon the part of the General was better in effect than any order couched in the strongest terms for the enforcement of discipline. The incident was long a frequent subject of conversation, and added greatly to his popularity as a commander. The men were fond of contrasting it with the conduct of the General of Division, who but a few days later cursed a poor teamster with all manner of profanely qualifying adjectives because he could not give to the General and his Staff the best part of a difficult road.

But perhaps the men held their General of Division to too strict an accountability. He was still laboring under the spell of Warrenton. His nervous system had doubtless been deranged by the removal of his favorite Chief, or rather Dictator, as he had hoped he might be. "No one could command the army but McClellan," the General had said in his disgust—a disgust that would have driven him from the service, but that, fortunately for himself and unfortunately for his country, it was balanced by the pay and emoluments of a Brigadiership. Reluctant to allow Burnside quietly, a Caesar's opportunity to "cover his baldness with laurels," his whimsical movements, now galloping furiously and purposeless from front to rear, and from rear to front of his command, cursing the officers,—and that for fancied neglect of duty,—poorly concealed the workings of his mind.

In one of these rapid rides, his eye caught sight of a brace of young hounds following one of the Sergeants.

"Where did those dogs come from?"

---

(1)    The quartermaster of the 129th was William F. Patterson, a coal merchant from Pottsville.

"They have followed me from the last wood, sir."

"Let them go, sir, this instant. Send them back, sir. D—n you, sir, I'll teach you to respect private property," replied the General, deploying his staff at the same time to assist in driving the dogs back, as notwithstanding the efforts of the Sergeant to send them to the rear, they crouched at a respectful distance and eyed him wistfully. "D—n you, sir, I am the General commanding the Division, sir, and by G—d, sir, I command you, as such, to send those dogs back, sir!" nervously stammered the General as he rode excitedly from one side of the road to the other in front of the Sergeant.

The affair speedily became ridiculous. Driving dogs was evidently with the General a more congenial employment than maneuvering men. But his efforts in the one proved as unsuccessful as in the other, as notwithstanding the aid afforded by his followers, the dogs would turn tail but for a short distance. After swearing most *dogmatically*, as an officer remarked, he turned to resume his ride to the head of the column, but had not gone ten yards before there was a whistle for the dogs. Squab was sent back to ferret out the offender. The whistling increased, and shortly the whole Staff and the Regimental officers were engaged in an attempt at its suppression. But in vain. Whistling in Company A, found echoes in Company B; and after some minutes of fruitless riding hither and thither the General was forced to retire under a storm of all kinds of dog-calls, swelled in volume by the adjacent Regiments.

That authority should be thus abused by the General in endeavoring to enforce his ridiculous order, and set at naught by the men in thus mocking at obedience, is to be deprecated. The men took that method of rebuking the inconsistency, which would permit Regular and many Volunteer Regiments to be followed by all manner of dogs,

> "Both mongrel, puppy, whelp and hound,
>    And cur of low degree,"

and yet refuse them the accidental company of but a brace of canines. A simple report of the offender, supposing the Sergeant to have been one, would have been the proper course, and would have saved a General of Division the disgrace of being made a laughing-stock for his command.

"Talent is something: but tact is everything," said an eminent man, and nowhere has the remark a more truthful application than in the army.

A favorite employment after the evening halt, during this three days' march, was the gathering of mushrooms. The old fields frequent along the route abounded with them, and many a royal meal they furnished. To farmers' sons accustomed to the sight of close cultivation, these old fields, half covered with stunted pines, sassafras, varieties of spice wood, and the never-failing persimmon tree, were objects of curiosity. It was hard to realize that we were marching through a country once considered the Garden of America, whose bountiful supplies and large plantations had become classic through the pen of an Irving and other famous writers. Fields princely in size, but barren as Sahara; buildings, once comfortable residences, but now tottering into ruin, are still there, but "all else how changed." The country is desolation itself. Game abounds, but whatever required the industry of man for its continuance has disappeared.

Civilization, which in younger States has felled forests, erected school-houses, given the fertility of a garden to the barren coast of the northern Atlantic and the wild-wood of the West, could not coalesce with the curse of slavery, and Virginia has been passed by in her onward march. This field of pines that you see on our right, whose tops are so dense and even as to resemble at a distance growing grain, may have been an open spot over which Washington followed his hounds in ante-revolutionary days. The land abounds in memories. The very names of the degenerate families who eke out a scanty subsistence on some corner of what was once an extensive family seat, remind one of the old Colonial aristocracy. Reclamation of the soil, as well as deliverance of the enslaved, must result from this civil war. Both worth fighting for. So "Forward, men," "Guide right," as in very truth we are in Divine Providence guided.

The long-haired, furtive-looking fathers and sons, representatives of all this ancient nobility, after having given over their old homesteads to their female or helpless male slaves, and massed their daughters and wives apparently in every tenth house, were keeping parallel pace with us on the lower bank of the Rappahannock. It was the inevitable logic of the law of human progress, declaring America to be in reality the land of the free, that compelled these misguided, miserable remnants of an aristocracy, to shiver in rags around November camp-fires. "They are joined to their idols"—but now that after years of legislative encroachment upon the rights of suffering humanity, they engage in a rebellious outbreak against a God-given Government, we will not let them alone in an idolatry that desolates the fair face of nature and causes such shameful degeneracy of the human race. Justice! slow, but still sure and retributive justice! How sublimely grand in her manifestations! After years of patient endurance of the proud contumely of South Carolina, New England granite blocks up the harbor of Charleston— Massachusetts volunteers cook their coffee in the fireplaces of the aristocratic homesteads of Beaufort, and negroes rally to a roll-call at Bunker Hill, but as volunteers in a war which insures them liberty, and not as slaves, as was once vainly prophesied.  *     *     *     *     *

"Who commands you?" inquired a long, lean, slightly stooped, sallow-faced man of about fifty, with eyes that rolled in all directions but towards the officer he addressed, and long hair thrown back of his ears in such a way as to make up an appearance that would readily attract the attention of a police officer.

"I command this Regiment, sir," replied the Colonel, who, at the end of the day's march, was busied in directing a detail where to pitch the Head-quarter tents.

"Goin' to stay yer—right in this meadow?" continued the man, in the half negro dialect common with the whites of the South.

"That is what we purpose doing, sir. Are you the owner?"

"Y-a-a-s," drawled out the man, pulling his slouch felt still further over his eyes. "This meadow is the best part of my hull farm."

"Great country, this," broke in the Quarter-master. "Why a kill-deer couldn't fly over it without carrying a knapsack. You don't think that camping upon this meadow will injure it any, do you?"

"Right smart it will, I reckon," rejoined the man, his eyes kindling somewhat, "right smart, it will. $1500 at least."

"What! What did the land cost you?"

"Wall, I paid at the rate of $15 the acre for 118 acres, and the buildings and 12 acres on it are in this meadow, and the best bit of it, too."

"Then you want to make us pay nearly what the whole farm cost you for using the meadow a single night?"

"Wall, I reckon as how the rails will all be gone, and the sod all cut up, and—"

"Well, I reckon," interrupted the Quarter-master, "that you ought to prove your loyalty before you talk about claiming damages from Uncle Sam."

"Oh! I'm on nary side, on nary side;" and he looked half suspiciously about the crowd, now somewhat increased. "I'm too old; besides, my left knee is crippled up bad," limping as he said so, to sustain his assertion.

"Where are your children?"

"My two boys and son-in-law are off with the South, but I'm not 'countable for them."

"Well, sir, you'll have to prove your loyalty before you get a receipt from me for any amount."

"Prove my loyalty?" he muttered, at the same time looking blank. "What sort of swearin' have you for that?"

"Don't swear him at all, at all," broke in the little Irish Corporal. "Swearing is no substitute for swinging. Faith! he's up to that business. It's mate and drink to him. Make him whistle Yankee Doodle or sing Hail Columbia. Be jabbers, it is not in his looks to do it without choking."

Terence's suggestion met with a general laugh of approval. The old fellow, finding himself in a crowd slow to appreciate his claim for damages when his loyalty was at a discount, made off towards his house, a dingy, two-story frame near by, reminded by the Colonel as he left that he would be expected to keep closely within doors while the troops were in that vicinity.

This sovereign of the soil was a fair specimen of the landed gentry of Virginia. "On nary side," as he expressed it, when the Federal troops were in his neighborhood, and yet malignant and dastardly enough to maltreat any sick or wounded Union soldier that chance might throw into his hands. The less reserved tongues of his daughters told plainly enough where the family stood on the great question of the day. But while they recounted to some of the junior officers who were always on the alert in making female acquaintances, their long lists of famous relatives, they had all the eagerness of the Yankee, so much despised in the Richmond prints, in disposing of half-starved chickens and heavy hoe-cakes at extortionate prices. With their dickering propensities there was an amount of dirt on their persons and about the premises, and roughness in their manners, that did great discredit to the memory of Pocahontas.

"You have the old horse tied up close," casually remarked a spruce young Sergeant who, in obedience to orders from Division Head-quarters, had just stationed a guard in the yard of the premises, alluding to an old, worn-out specimen of horseflesh tied up so closely to the house that his head and neck were almost a straight line.

"Yon's no hoss, sir. It's a mare," quickly retorted one of those black-eyed beauties.

The polite Sergeant, who had dressed himself with more than usual care, in the expectation of meeting the ladies, colored somewhat, but the young lady, in a matter-of-course strain, went on to say,

"She's the only one left us, too. Preston and Moncure took the rest with them, and they say they've nearly used 'em up chasing you Yanks."

Her unlady-like demeanor and exulting allusion to the Rebel cavalry tested to the utmost the Sergeant's qualities as a gentleman. A dicker for a pair of chickens, accomplished by his substituting a little ground coffee for a great sum in green-backs, soon brought about a better understanding, however, on the part of the damsel.

A few hours later saw the Adjutant and our poetical Lieutenant snugly seated on split-bottomed chairs in a dirty kitchen. Random conversa-tion, in which the women let slip no opportunity of reminding their visitors of the soldierly qualities of the Rebels, interrupted by the occa-sional bleating of sheep and bawling of calves in the cellar, made the evening's entertainment novel and interesting. So much so that at a late hour the Lieutenant, who had invested closely the younger of the two, said, half sighing, as he gave her a fond look,

> "With thee conversing, I forget all time,
> All——"

"Wall, I reckon I don't," broke in the matter-of-fact young lady. "Sal, just kick yon door around." As Sal did her bidding, and the full moon on the face of an old fashioned corner clock was disclosed, she continued, "It's just ten minutes after eleven, and you Yanks had better be off."

Although the Adjutant was

> "Like steel amid the din of arms;
> Like wax when with the fair,"

this lack of appreciation of poetic sentiment so abruptly shown, brought him out in a roar, and completely disconcerted the Lieutenant. They both retired speedily, and long after, the circumstance was one of the standing jokes of the camp.

One of the most prominent and eagerly wished-for occurrences in camp, is the arrival of the mail. The well filled bag, looking much like one of the bags of documents forwarded by Congressmen for private purposes at Uncle Sam's expense, was emptied out on the sod that evening in front of the Colonel's marquee, and bundles containing boots, tobacco, bread, clothing of all kinds, eatables, and what-not,— for at that time Uncle Sam's army mails did a heavy express business,— were eyed curiously, by the crowd impatient for distribution. Most singular of all in shape and feeling was a package, heavily postmarked, and addressed to the Colonel. It contained what was a God-send to the larder of the mess,—a quarter of fine tender meat. But what kind of animal, was the query. The Major, who was a Nimrod in his own locality, after the most thorough inspection, and the discovery of a short straight hair upon it, pronounced it venison, or young kid, and confirmed the Colonel in the belief that he had been remembered by one of his Western friends. But deer or dog was a matter of indifference to hungry campaigners. A hearty meal was made of it, and speculation continued until the Brigadier, who had perpetrated the joke upon the Colonel, saw fit, long after, to reveal that it was mutton that had been taken from some marauders during the day's march.

During the first and second days of the march, cannonading had been heard at intervals on the right flank. This day, however, the silence was ominous; and now at its close, with our army in close proximity to Fredericksburg, it indicated peaceable, unopposed possession, or delay of our own forces. But of the delay and its cause, provoking as it was, and costly as it has proved, enough has probably been written. An Investigating Committee has given the public full records. If we do not learn that delinquents have been punished, let us hope that the warning has been sufficient to avoid like difficulties in the future.

Our army quietly turned into camp among the wooded heights of Stafford, opposite the town of Fredericksburg. The Rebels as quietly collected their forces and encamped on the heights upon the opposite side of the river. Day by day we could see them busily at work upon their fortifications. Each morning fresh mounds of earth appeared at different points in the semi-circular range of hills bounding Fredericksburg upon the South and West. This valuable time was made use of by the pontoon train at the rate of four miles per day.

The three Grand Divisions, now that their stately march by the flank was over, had settled comfortably down among the hills of Stafford. Wood and water, essentials for camp comfort, were to be found in abundance. While the little parleying between the Commander of the Right Grand Division[2] and the civil authorities of Fredericksburg continued, matters were somewhat in suspense. But a gradual quiet crept over the army, and in a few short weeks that heavily timbered country was one vast field of stumps, with here and there clusters of pine trees left standing for the comfort of different Head-quarters. As the timber disappeared, the tents and huts of the army before concealed in the forests were disclosed, and the whole country in the vicinity of the railroad was a continuous camp. The few open fields or barrens afforded fine review and drill grounds, and the toils of the march were scarcely over before in all directions could be heard the steady tramp of solid columns engaged in the evolutions of the field.

---

(2)    Maj. Gen. Edwin V. Sumner.

Those who think that duties are light in camp, know nothing of the legions of reports, statements in duplicate and triplicate, required by the too often senseless formalities of red tape. These duties vary greatly in different divisions. With a place-man, mechanical in his movements, and withal not disposed to lighten labor, they multiply to a surprising extent, and subs intrusted with their execution often find that the most laborious part of the service is drudgery at the desk. Night after night would repose at Regimental Head-quarters be interrupted by repetitious and in many cases inconsistent orders, the only purpose of which appeared to be, to remind drowsy Adjutants and swearing Sergeant-Majors that the Commanding General of Division still ruled at Division Head-quarters, and that he was most alive between the hours of nine and twelve at night. Independently of the fact that in most cases in ordinary camp-life there was no reason why these orders should not have issued in business hours, their multiplicity was a nuisance. The pen may be mightier than the sword, but in all conscience when the pen has been through necessity ignored, and the sword is uplifted for rapid and earnest blows, and the heart of a nation hangs in heavy suspense upon its movements, these travelling Bureaux had better be abolished. Superadded to all this, was the labor resulting from the mania for Court-Martialing that raged at Division Head-quarters. Mechanical in its movements, not unfrequently malignant in its designs, officer after officer, earnest in purpose, but in some instances perhaps deficient in detail, had been sacrificed to an absolutism that could order the charges, detail the Court, play the part of principal witness for the prosecution, and confirm the proceedings.

"Our volunteer force will never amount to much, until we attain the exact discipline of the French service," was the frequent remark of a General of Division. Probably not. But how much would its efficiency be increased, had the policy of the great Napoleon, from whose genius the French arms derive their lustre, prevailed, in detailing for desk duty in quiet departments the mechanical minds of paper Generals. His master tact in assigning to commanders legitimate spheres of work, and with it the untiring zeal of a Cromwell that would run like a purifying fire through the army, imparting to it its own impetuosity, and ridding it of jealousy and disaffection, were greatly needed in this Grand Army of the Potomac. Nobler men never stood in ranks! Holier banners never flaunted in the sunlight of Heaven! God grant its directing minds corresponding energy and wisdom.

## CHAPTER XV.

*Red Tape and the Soldier's Widow—Pigeon-holing at Head-Quarters and Weeping at the Family Fireside—A Pigeon-hole General Outwitted—Fishing for a Discharge—The Little Irish Corporal on Topographical Engineers—Guard Duty over a Whiskey Barrel.*

—————————, Penna., Nov. —, 1862.

MY DEAR GEORGE:—This is the first spare time that I have been able to get during the last week for a letter to my dear husband. And now that there is quiet in the house, and our dear little boys are sound asleep, and the covers nicely tucked about them in their little trundle, I feel that I can scarcely write. There is such a heaviness upon my heart. When I saw the crowd at the telegraph office this morning while on my way to church, and heard that they were expecting news of a great battle on the Rappahannock, such a feeling of helplessness, sinking of the heart, and dizziness came over me, that I almost fell upon the pavement. The great battle that all expect so eagerly, may mean our dear little children fatherless and myself a widow. Oh, George, I feel so sad and lonely, and then every footstep I hear at the door I am afraid some one is coming with bad news. Your last letter, too, I do not like. I am afraid that more is the matter with you than you are willing to admit. You promised me, too, that you would apply for a furlough. Lieut. H— has been twice at home since he went out. You know he is in Sickles' Division.

Our precious little boys keep asking continually when papa will come home. Little Georgie says he is a "du-du," you know that is what he calls a soldier, and he gets the old sword you had in the three months' service, and struts up and down at a great rate. They can both say the Lord's prayer now, and every night when they get through with it, they ask God to bless papa and mamma, and all the Union "du-dus." I do wish that you could see them in their little "Gadibaldis," as Harry calls them. When I see Mr. B— and others take their evening walks with their children, just as you used to do with Georgie, it takes all the grace and all the patriotism I can muster to keep from murmuring.

Mr. G— says that we need not trouble about the rent this quarter, that he will wait until you are paid. The neighbors, too, are very kind to me, and I have been kept so busy with work from the shops, that I have made enough to pay all our little expenses. But for all, George, I cannot help wishing every minute of the day that "this cruel war was over" and you safe back. At a little sewing party that we had the other day, Em D— sang that old song "When wild war's deadly blast was blown," that you used to read to me so often, and when I heard of "sweet babes being fatherless," and "widows mourning," I burst into tears. I do not know why it is, but I feel as if expecting bad news continually. Our little boys say "don't cry, mamma," in such a way when I put them to bed at night, and tell them that I kiss them for you too, that it makes me feel all the worse. I know it is wrong. I know our Heavenly Father knows what is best for us. I hope by this time you have learned to put your trust in him. That is the best preparation for the battle-field.

Do not fail to come home if you can. God bless you, George, and protect you, is the prayer of

Your loving wife,
MARY.

On a low cot in the corner of a hospital tent, near Potomac Creek, propped up by some extra blankets kindly loaned him by his comrades, toward the close of a December afternoon, lay a slightly-built, rather handsome man of about thirty, holding with trembling hand the above letter, and hurriedly gathering its contents with an eager but unsteady eye. The Surgeon noticing the growing flush upon his already fevered cheek suggested that he had better have the letter read to him. So intent was the reader, that the suggestion was twice repeated before heeded, and then only drew the remark "Mary and the boys." A sudden fit of coughing that appeared to tear the very life strings came upon him, and at its close he fell back exhausted upon his pillow.

"What luck, Adjutant?" inquired the Surgeon in a low tone, as he went forward, cautiously treading among the sick, to admit that officer into the tent.

The Adjutant with a shake of the head remarked that the application had gone up two weeks previously from Brigade Head-quarters, and that nothing had been heard of it since. "As usual," he added, "pigeon-holed at Division Head-quarters."

"Poor Wilson has been inquiring about it all day, and I very much fear that should it come now, it will be too late. He has failed rapidly today."

"So bad as that? I will send up to Division Head-quarters immediately."

The Lieutenant, a week previously, had been brought into the hospital suffering from a heavy cold and fever in connection with it. For some weeks he had been in delicate health; so much so, in fact, that the Surgeon had urged him to apply for a furlough, and had stated in his certificate to the same, that it was absolutely necessary for the preservation of his life. As the Surgeon stated, a furlough, that might then have been beneficial, promised now to be of little avail. The disease had assumed the form of congestion of the lungs, and the Lieutenant seemed rapidly sinking.

When the Adjutant left the hospital tent he sought out a Captain, an intimate acquaintance of the Lieutenant's, and charged him with a special inquiry at Head-quarters, as to the success of the application for a furlough. Thither the Captain repaired, through the well trodden mud and slush of the camp ground. The party of young officers within the tent of the Adjutant-General appeared to be in a high state of enjoyment, and that functionary himself retained just presence of mind sufficient to assure the Captain, after hearing his statement and urgent inquiry—"that there was no time now to look—that there were so d—n many papers he could not keep the run of them. These things must take their

regular course, Captain,—regular course, you know. That's the difficulty with the volunteer officers," continued he, turning half to the
crowd, "to understand regular military channels,—channels." As he
continued stammering and stuttering, the crowd inside suspended the
pipe to ejaculate assent, while the Captain, understanding red-tape to
his sorrow, and too much disgusted to make further effort to understand
the Captain, retraced his steps. Finding the Adjutant he told him of his
lack of success, and together they repaired to the hospital tent to break
the unwelcome news.

At the time of his entry into the Hospital the Lieutenant was impressed with the belief that the illness would be his last, and he daily
grew more solicitous as to the success of his application for a furlough.
Another coughing fit had, during their absence, intervened, and as the
two cautiously untied the flaps and entered the stifling atmosphere of
the crowded tent, the Surgeon and a friend or two were bending
anxiously about the cot. Their entry attracted the attention of the dying
Lieutenant; for that condition his faint hurried breathing, interrupted by
occasional gasps, and the rolling, fast glazing eye, too plainly denoted.
A look of anxious inquiry,—a faint shake of the head from the Captain
—for strong-voiced as he was, his tongue refused the duty of informing
the dying man of what had become daily, unwelcome news.

"Oh, my God! must I,—must I die without again seeing Mary and
the babies!" with clasped hands he gasped, half rising, and casting at
the same time an imploring look at the Surgeon.

But the effort was too much. His head fell back upon the blankets. A
gurgling sound was heard in his throat. With bowed heads to catch the
latest whisper, his friends raised him up; and muttering indistinctly
amid his efforts to hold the rapidly failing breath, "Mary and the babies.
The babies,—Ma—" the Lieutenant left the Grand Army of the Potomac on an everlasting furlough.[1]

---

(1)    This was probably 2d Lt. Edward Wertley, Company H of the 129th, who
        died on November 30, 1862, of typhoid fever and inflammation of the lungs.

Mary was busily engaged with the duties of her little household a week later, enjoying, as best she might, the lively prattle of the boys, when there was the noise of a wagon at the door, and closely following it a knock. "Papa! papa!" exclaimed the children, as with eager haste they preceded the mother. With scarcely less eagerness, Mary opened the door. Merciful God! "Temper the wind to the shorn lambs." Earthly consolation is of little avail at a time like this. It was "Papa;"—but Mary was a widow, and the babies fatherless.

By some unfortunate accident the telegram had been delayed, and the sight of the black pine coffin was Mary's first intimation of her loss. Her worst anticipations thus roughly realized, she sank at the door, a worthy subject for the kind offices of her neighbors.

A fortnight passed, and the Adjutant was disturbed in his slumbers, almost at the solemn hour of midnight, to receive from an Orderly some papers from Division Head-Quarters. Among them, was the application of the Lieutenant, returned "approved."

Measured by poor Mary's loss, how insignificant the sigh of the monied man over increased taxes! how beggarly the boast of patriotic investments! how contemptibly cruel, in her by no means unusual case, the workings of Red Tape!     *     *     *     *

*     *     *     Occurrences such as these, may sadden for the moment the soldier, but they produce no lasting depression.

> "Don't you think I had oughter
> Be a going down to Washington
> To fight for Abraham's Daughter?"

sang our ex-newsboy Birdy, on one of those cold damp evenings in early December, when the smoke of the fires hung like a pall over the camp ground, and the eyes suffered terribly if their owner made any attempt at standing erect.

"And who is Abraham's Daughter?" queried one of a prostrate group around a camp fire.

"Columbia, the Gem of the Ocean," continued Birdy, to another popular air, until he was joined by a manly swell of voices in the closing line—

"Three cheers for the Red, White, and Blue!"

"Not much life here," continued Birdy, seating himself. "I have just left the 2—th. There is a high old time over there. They have got the dead wood on old Pigey nice."

"In what way?" inquired the crowd.

"You know that long, slim fellow of Co. E, in that Regiment, who is always lounging about the Hospital, and never on duty."

"What! The fellow that has been going along nearly double, with both hands over the pit of his stomach, for a week past?"

"The same," resumed Birdy. "He has been going it on diarrhoea lately; before that he was running on rheumatism. Well, you know he has been figuring for a discharge ever since he heard the cannonading at the second Bull Run, but couldn't make it before yesterday."

"How did he make it?" inquired several, earnestly.

"Fished for it," quietly remarked Birdy.

"Come, Birdy, this is too old a crowd for any jokes of yours. Whose canteen have you been sucking Commissary out of?" broke in one of his hearers.

"Nary time; I'm honest, fellows. He fished for it, and I'll tell you how," resumed Birdy, adjusting the rubber blanket upon which he had seated himself.

"You see old Pigey was riding along the path that winds around the hill to Corps Head-Quarters, when he spied this fellow, Long Tom, as they call him, sitting on a stump, and alongside of the big sink, that some of our mess helped to dig when on police duty last. Tom held in both hands a long pole, over the sink, with a twine string hanging from it—for all the world as if he was fishing. On came old Pigey; but Tom never budged.

" 'What are you doing there, sir?' said the General.

" 'Fishing,' said Tom, without turning his head.

" 'Fishing! h—l and d—n! Must be crazy; no fish there.'

" 'I've caught them in smaller streams than this,' drawled out Tom, turning at the same time his eyes upon the General, with a vacant stare. 'But then I had better bait. The ground about here is too mean for good red worms. Just look,' and Tom lifted up an old sardine box, half full of grubs, for the General to look at.

" 'Crazy, by G—d, sir,' said the General, turning to his Aide, 'Demented! Demented! Might be a dangerous man in camp; must be attended to,' continued the General; striking, as he spoke, vigorous blows across his saddle-bow, with his gauntlet; Tom all the while waiting for a bite, with the patience of an old fisherman.

"It was after three in the afternoon, and the General took the bait.

" 'Must be attended to. Dangerous man! dangerous man!' said he, adjusting his spectacles.

" 'Your name and Regiment, sir?'

"Tom drawled them out, and the General directed his Aide to take them down.

" 'Go to your Quarters, sir,' said the General.

" 'Haven't caught anything yet, and hard tack is played out,' replied Tom.

"At this the General put spurs to his horse, and left. Half an hour afterward, a Corporal's Guard came after Tom. They took him up to the marquee of the Surgeon of the Division. Tom played it just as well there, and yesterday his discharge came down, all O.K., and they've got the Commissary on the strength of it, and are having a high old time generally."[2]

"Bully boy with a glass eye! How are *you*, discharge!" and like slang exclamations broke rapidly and rapturously from the crowd.

"But," said one of the more thoughtful of the crowd, as the condition of a brother then lying hopelessly ill, with no prospect of a discharge,—although it had been promised repeatedly for months past,—pressed itself upon his attention, "how shameful that this able-bodied coward and idler should get off in this way, when so many better men are dying by inches in the hospitals. A General who understood his command and

---

(2)     A similar story, said to be that of Col. Thomas B. Van Buren, 102nd New
        York, appeared some twenty years later in *Camp-Fire Chats of the Civil War*
        by Washington Davis.

had more knowledge of human nature, could not be deceived in that way."

"Tom had lounged about Division Head-Quarters so much, that he knew old Pigey thoroughly, and just when to take him," said a comrade.

"All the greater shame that our Generals can be taken off their guard at any time," retorted the other.

"Oh, well," continued he, "about what might be expected of one educated exclusively as a Topographical Engineer, and having no acquaintance with active field service, and with no talent for command; for it is a talent that West Point may educate, but cannot create."

"And what is a Tippo, Typo, or Toppographical Engineer, Sergeant?" broke in the little Irish Corporal, who chanced to be one of the group, rather seriously. "Isn't it something like a land surveyor; and be Jabers, wasn't the great Washington himself a land surveyor? Eh? Maybe that's the rayson these Tippos, Typos, or Toppographical Engineers ride such high horses."

"Not badly thought of, Corporal," replied the Sergeant, amid laughter at Terence's discovery, and his attempt at pronunciation; "but Washington was a man of earnestness and ability, and not a guzzler of whiskey, and a mouther of indecent profanity. There are good officers in that Corps. There is Meade, the fighter of the noble Pennsylvania Reserves; Warren, a gentleman as well as a soldier. Others might be named. Meritorious men, but kept in the background while the place-men, cumberers of the service, refused by Jeff. Davis when making his selections from among our regular officers, as too cheap an article, are kept in position at such enormous sacrifices of men, money, and time. I have heard it said, upon good authority, that there is a nest of these old place-men in Washington, who keep their heads above water in the service, through the studied intimacy of their families with families of Members of the Cabinet—a toadyism that often elevates them to the depression of more meritorious men, and always at the expense of the country,—but—

"Dark shall be light."

Keep up your spirits, boys."

"Keep up your spirits," echoed Birdy; "that is what they are doing all the time at Division Head-Quarters,—by pouring spirits down. Jim," continued he, turning suddenly to a comrade, who lounged lazily alongside of him, holding, at the same time, at the end of a stick, a tin cup with a wire handle, over the fire, "tell the crowd about that whisky barrel."

Some of the crowd had heard the story, from the manner in which they welcomed the suggestion, and insisted upon its reproduction.

"Can't, till I cook my coffee," retorted Jim, pointing to the black, greasy liquid in the cup, simmering slowly over the half-smothered fire. Jim's cup had evidently been upon duty but a short time previously as a soup-kettle. "But it is about done," said he, lifting it carefully off, "and I might as well tell it while it cools."

"About one week ago I happened to be detailed as a Head-Quarter guard, and about four o'clock in the afternoon was pacing up and down the beat in front of the General's Head-Quarters. It was a pleasant sunshiny spring day,—when gadflies like to try their wings, and the ground seems to smoke in all directions,—and the General sat back composedly in the corner of his tent on a camp stool, with his elbow on his knee and his head hanging rather heavily upon his hand. The flaps were tied aside to the fly-ropes. I had a fair view of him as I walked up and down, and I came to the conclusion from his looks that Pigey had either a good load on, or was in a brown study. While I was thinking about it up comes a fellow of the 2—th, that I used to meet often while we were upon picket. He is usually trim, tidy-looking, and is an intelligent fellow, but on that day everything about him appeared out of gear. His old grey slouch hat had only half a rim, and that hung over his eyes—hair uncombed, face unwashed, hands looking as if he had been scratching gravel with them, his blouse dirty and stuffed out above the belt, making him as full-breasted as a Hottentot woman, pantaloons greasy, torn, and unevenly suspended; and to foot up his appearance shoes innocent of blacking, and out at the toes. When I saw him, I laughed outright. He winked, and asked in an undertone if the General was in, stating at the same time that he was there in obedience to an order detailing one man for special duty at the General's Head Quarters, 'and you know,' said he, 'that the order always is for intelligent soldierly-looking men. Well, all our men that have been sent up of that stripe have been detained as orderlies, to keep his darkies in wood and water, and hold his horses, and we are getting tired of it. *I* don't intend running any risk.'

" 'Don't think you will,' said I, laughing at his make-up.

"Just then I noticed a movement of the General's head, and resumed the step. A moment after, the General's eye caught sight of the Detail. He eyed him a moment in a doubtful way, and then rubbing his eyes, as if to confirm the sight, and straightening up, shouted—

" 'Sergeant of the guard! Sergeant of the guard!'

"The sergeant was forthcoming at something more than a double-quick; and with a salute, and 'Here, sir,' stood before the General.

"Old Pigey's right hand extended slowly, pointing towards the Detail, who stood with his piece at a rest, wondering what was to come next.

" 'Take away that musket, sergeant! and that G— d— looking thing alongside of it. What is it, anyhow?' said the General, with a significant emphasis on the word 'thing.'

"And off the sergeant went, followed by the man, who gave a sly look as he left."

"Pretty well played," said one of the crowd; "but what has that to do with a whisky barrel?"

"Hold on, and you will see; I am not through yet.

"About half an hour afterward another man from the same regiment presented himself, and asked permission to cross my beat, saying that he had been detailed on special duty, and was to report to the General in person. This one looked trim enough to pass muster. He presented himself at the door of the tent and saluted; but the General had taken two or three plugs in the interim, and was slightly oblivious. Anxious to see some sport, I suggested that he should call the General.

" 'General,' said he, lowly, then louder, all the while saluting, until the General awoke with a start.

" 'Who the h—ll are you, sir?'

" 'I was ordered to report to you in person, sir, for special duty.'

" 'Special duty, sir! Has it come to this? Must I assign the duty to be performed by each individual man, sir, in the Division, sir!'

"The disheveled hair, flashing eyes, and fierce look of the General, startled this new Detail, and he commenced explaining. The General broke in abruptly, however, as if suddenly recollecting; and rubbing his hands, while his countenance assumed a bland smile:

" 'Oh, yes; you are right, sir, right; special duty, sir; yes, sir; follow me, sir.'

"And the General arose and with somewhat uncertain strides left his marquee, and, followed by the man, entered a Sibley partly in its rear.

" 'There, sir,' said the General, pointing, with rather a pleased countenance; 'do you see that barrel, sir?'

" 'Yes, sir,' replied the Detail, saluting.

" 'That barrel holds whisky, sir—whisky;'—rising upon his toes and emphasizing the word; 'and I want you to guard it G— d—d well. Don't let a d—n man have a drop, sir. Do you understand, sir?'

" 'Yes, sir,' rejoined the Detail, saluting, and commencing his beat around the barrel.

"The General was about leaving the Sibley, when he turned suddenly;

" 'Do you drink, sir?'

" 'Once and a while, sir,' replied the Detail, saluting.

" 'Have you had any lately?'

" 'No, sir.'

" 'By G—d, sir, I'll give you some, sir;' and he strides into his marquee and returns with a tin cup full of liquor, which he placed upon the barrel, and told the man to help himself. After the General had gone, the Detail did help himself, until his musket lay on one side of the Sibley and himself on the other."

"The General knows how to sympathize with a big dry," said one, as the crowd laughed over the story.

Pen cannot do justice to the stories abounding in wit and humor wherewith soldiers relieve the tedium of the camp. To an old campaigner, their appearance in print must seem like a faded photograph, in the sight of one who has seen the living original. Characters sparkling with humor, such as was never attributed to any storied Joe Miller, abound in every camp. The brave Wolfe, previously to the victory which cost him his life, is reported to have sung, while floating down the St. Lawrence:

> "Why, soldiers, why,
> Should we be melancholy,
> Whose business 'tis to die?"

Whether induced in his case by an effort to bolster up the courage of his comrades or not, the sentiment has at all times been largely practiced upon in the army of the Potomac.

# CHAPTER XVI.

*The Battle of Fredericksburg—Screwing Courage up to the Sticking Point—Consolations of a Flask—Pigeon-Hole Nervousness—Abandonment of Knapsacks—Incidents before, during, and after the Fight.*

IN this wintry weather, striking tents meant stripping the log huts of the bits of canvas that ordinarily served as the shelter-tents of the soldiers. The long rows of huts thus dismantled,—soldiers at rest in ranks, with full knapsacks and haversacks,—groups of horses saddled and bridled, ready for the rider,—on one of these clear, cold December mornings, indicated that the army was again upon the move. Civilians had been sent back freighted with letters from those soon to see the serious struggle of the field; the sick had been gathered to hospitals nearer home; the musicians had reported to the surgeons, and the men were left, to the sharp notes of sixty rounds of ball cartridge carried in their boxes and knapsacks,—in the plight of the Massachusetts regiment that marched through the mobs of Baltimore, to the music of the cartridge-box, in the first April of the Rebellion.

The time intervening between the removal of McClellan and the battle of Fredericksburg, was a period of uneasy suspense to the nation at large and its representatives in the field. Dear as the devoted patriotism, the earnest conduct of the Rhode Island Colonel—the hero of the Carolinas and now the leader of the Grand Army of the Potomac—were to the patriotic masses of the nation, the fact of his being an untried man, gave room for gloom and foreboding. With the army at large, the suspense was accompanied by no lack of confidence. The devotion of the Ninth Army Corps for its old commander appeared to have spread throughout the army; and his open, manly countenance, bald head, and unmistakable whiskers, were always greeted with rounds for "Burny." The jealousy of a few ambitious wearers of stars may have been ill concealed upon that morning, only to be disclosed shortly to his detriment; but the earnest citizen-soldiery were eager, under his guidance, to do battle for their country. Time has shown, how much of the misfortune of the subsequent week was attributable to imperfect weeding of McClellanism at Warrenton.

Like a lion at bay, restless in easy view of the hosts of the Rebellious, the army had remained in its camp upon the heights of Stafford until the arrival of the pontoons. For miles along the Rappahannock, the picket of blue had his counterpart in the picket of grey upon the opposite shore. Unremitting labor upon fortifications and earthworks, had greatly increased the natural strength of the amphitheatre of hills in the rear of Fredericksburg. Countless surmises spread in the ranks as to the character and direction of the attack; though the whims of those who uttered them were variant as the reflections of a kaleidoscope. But the sun, that through the pines that morning, shone upon burnished barrels, polished breast-plates, and countenances of brave men, radiant, as if reflecting their holy purpose, has never, since the shining hosts of Heaven were marshalled for the suppression of the great prototype of this Rebellion, seen more earnest ranks, or a holier cause.

The bugles call "Attention," then "Forward." Horses are rapidly mounted; and speedily coming to the shoulder, and facing to the right, the army is in motion by the flank towards the river. Far as the eye could see, in all directions, there were moving masses of troops. Cowardly beneath contempt is the craven, who in such a cause, and at such a time, would not feel inspirited by the firm tread of the martial columns.

"Hear 'em! Oh, Hear 'em!" exclaimed an earnest-looking country boy, hastily closing a daguerreotype case, into which he had been intently gazing, and replacing it in his pocket, as the booming of a heavy siege gun upon the Washington Farm, followed instantly by the reports of several batteries to the right, broke upon the ear like volleyed thunder. A clap of thunder from a clear sky could not have startled him more, had he been at work upon his father's farm. His earnest simplicity afforded great amusement to his comrades, and for a while made him the butt of a New York Regiment that then chanced to be marching abreast. Raw recruit as he was, cowardice was no part of his nature, and he indignantly repelled the taunts of his comrades. Gloom deep settled was visible upon his countenance, however, although firm his step and compressed his lip.

"Terence," said he, to the little Irish Corporal who marched by his side, as another suggestive artillery fire that appeared to move along the entire front, made itself heard, "may I ask a favor of you?"

"Indade ye may, John, and a thousand ov them if ye plaze, to the last dhrop in my canteen."

One of those jams so constant and annoying in the movements of large masses of men, here gave the opportunity for John to unbosom himself, which he did, while both leaned upon the muzzles of their pieces.

"Terence, I do not believe that I will be alongside of you many days," said John, with an effort.

"Why, what's the matter wid ye, boy? if I didn't know ye iver since you thrashed that bully in the Zouaves, I wud think ye cowardly."

"It is not fear, Corporal," continued John, more determinedly. "I'm looking the danger squarely in the face, and am ready to meet it, and I want to be prepared for it."

"Be jabers, John," retorted Terence, "ye should have prepared for it before you left home. I saw Father Mahan just before I left, and he tould me to do my duty like a thrue Irishman; and that if I was kilt in such a cause I wud go straight through, and be hardly asked to stay over night in Purgatory. There's my poor brother, peace to his soul;—and did ye hear—"

"But, Terence," interrupted John, "I am not afraid of death; and for the judgment after death I have made all the preparation I could in my poor way, and I can trust that to my Maker; but"—and here John clapped his hand over his left breast.

"Oh, I see," said Terence. "It's a case of disease of the heart."

"I want you, in case I fall, to take the daguerreotype that you will find in the inside pocket on the left side of my blouse, and a sealed letter, and see that both are sent to the address upon the letter," continued John.

"Faith, will I, John. But who tould you that you wud be kilt, and meself that's alone and friendless escape? Well, I'll take them, John, if I have to go meself; and it's Terence McCarty that will not see her suffer; and maybe—but it's hard seeing how a girl could take a fancy to a short curly-headed Irishman, like meself, after having loved a sthrapping, straight-haired man like you."

How John relished the winding-up of the corporal's offer could not well be seen, as an order to resume the step interrupted the conversation.

Progress was slow, necessarily, from the caution required in the approach to the river. Over the rolling ground, to an artillery accompaniment unequalled in grandeur, the troops trudged slowly along. Here and there was a countenance of serious determination, but the great mass were gay and reckless, as soldiers proverbially are, of the risks the future might hold in reserve.

After a succession of short marches and halts, the forward movement appeared to cease about four o'clock in the afternoon, and the men quietly rested on their arms, as well as the damp, and in many places muddy ground would allow. Towards evening countless fires, fed by the dry bushes found in abundance upon the old fields of Virginia, showed that amidst war's alarms the men were not unmindful of coffee.

Throughout the day, with but brief cessation, artillery firing had continued. The booming of the siege guns, mingled with the sharp rattle of the light, and the louder roar of the heavy batteries, all causing countless echoes among the neighboring hills, completed the carnival of sound.

Night crept gradually on, the fires were extinguished, the cannonading slackened gradually, then ceased, and the vast army, save those whom duty kept awake, silently slept under frosted blankets.

Cannonading was resumed at early dawn of the next day, and the slow progress of the troops towards the river continued. Before night our advance had crossed upon the pontoon bridges, notwithstanding a galling fire of the Rebel sharpshooters under cover of the buildings along the river, and was firmly established in the town. Late in the day our Division turned into a grove of young pines, a short distance in the rear of the Phillips House.[1] Upon beds of the dead foliage, soft as carpets of velvet, after the fatigues of the day, slumber was sound.

The reveille sounded at early morn of the next day,—Saturday, the memorable thirteenth of December,—by over three hundred pieces of artillery, again aroused the sleeping camps to arms, and in the grey fog, the groves and valleys for some miles along the river appeared alive with moving masses. As soon as the fog lifted sufficiently, a large balloon between us and the river arose, upon a tour of observation.[2] It was a fine mark for a rifled battery of the Rebels, and some shells passed close to it, and exploded in dangerous proximity to our camp.

Under an incessant artillery fire the main movement of the troops across the river commenced. Leaving our camp and passing to the right of the Phillips mansion, we found our Division, one of a number of columns moving in almost parallel lines to the river. On the western slope of the hill or ridge upon which the house stood, we came to another halt, until our turn to cross should come.

Whatever modern armies may have lost in dazzling appearance, when contrasted with the armies of old that moved in glittering armor and under "banner, shield, and spear," they certainly have lost nothing in the enginery of death, and in the sights and sounds of the fight itself. A twelve-pound battery under stern old Cato's control, would have sent Caesar and his legions howling from the gates of Rome, and have saved the dignity of her Senate. The shock of battle was then a medley of human voices, confused with the rattle of the spear upon the shield; now a hell of thunder volumed from successive batteries,—and relieved by screaming and bursting shell and rattling musketry. The proper use of a single shell would have cleared the plains of Marathon. More appropriately can we come down to later times, when

---

(1)    Phillips House was then the headquarters of General Burnside.
(2)    The balloon was the creation of Prof. Thaddeus S. C. Lowe.

"The old Continentals,
    In their ragged regimentals,
    Faltered not,"

for the ground upon which our army stood had repeatedly been used as
a rallying point for troops, and a depot for military stores in Continental
and Revolutionary times. How great the contrast between the armies
now upon either side of the Rappahannock, and the numbers, arms, and
equipage then raised with difficulty from the country at large. Our
forefathers in some measure foresaw our greatness; but they did not
foresee the magnitude of the sin of slavery, tolerated by them against
their better judgment, and now crowding these banks with immense and
hostile armies. Since that day the country has grown, and with it as part
of its growth, the iniquity, but the purposes of the God of battles prevail
nevertheless. The explosion that rends the rock and releases the toad
confined and dormant for centuries, may not have been intended for
that end by the unwitting miner, nor the civil convulsion that shatters a
mighty nation to relieve an oppressed people and bestow upon it the
blessings of civilization, may not have been started with that view by
foul conspirators.

But while we are digressing, a cavalcade of mounted men have left
the area in front of the Phillips mansion, and are approaching us upon
the road at a full gallop. The boys recognize the foremost figure, clad
in a black pilot frock, his head covered with a regulation felt, the brim
of which is over his eyes and the top rounded to its utmost capacity,
and cheer upon cheer for "Burney" run along the column. With a firm
seat, as his horse clears the railroad track and dashes through the small
stream near by, he directs his course to the Lacy House[3] on the bank of
the river.

It was near noon when we passed over the same ground, and taking
a road to the right of the once tasteful grounds of that mansion,
debouched by a narrow pass cut through the bank to the water's edge.
As we did so, some shells thrown at the mounted officers of the Regi-

---

(3)    Lacy House was then the headquarters of Gen. Edwin Sumner.

ment passed close to their heads and exploded with a dull sound in the soft ground of the bank. With a steady tramp the troops crossed, scarcely the slightest motion being perceptible upon the firm double pontoon bridge. Another column was moving across upon the bridge below. Gaining the opposite bank, the column filed to the left, in what appeared to be a principal street of the town. Here knapsacks were unslung and piled in the store rooms upon either side.

The few citizens who remained had sought protection from the shells in the cellars, and not an inhabitant of the place was to be seen. Notwithstanding the heavy concentrated artillery fire,—beyond some few buildings burned down,—nothing like the destruction was visible that would be imagined. Deserted by its proper inhabitants, the place had, however, a heavy population in the troops that crowded the streets parallel with the river. The day previous the Rebels had opened fire upon the town. It was continued at intervals, but with little effect. Z-i-i-s-s! a round shot sings above your head, and with a sharp thud strikes the second story of the brick house opposite, marking its passage by a tolerably neat hole through the wall. P-i-i-n-g! screams a shell, exploding in a room with noise sufficient to justify the total destruction of a block of buildings. The smoke clears away, ceilings may be torn, floors and windows shattered, but the building, to an outside observer, little damaged.

From an early hour in the morning the musketry had been incessant, —now in volleys, and now of the sharp rattling nature that denotes severe skirmishing. On the left, where more open ground permitted extended offensive movements, the firing was particularly heavy. But above it all was the continuous roar of artillery, and the screaming and explosion of shells. To this music the troops in light order and ready for the fray, marched up a cross street, and in the shelter of the buildings of another street on the outer edge of the place and parallel with the river, stood at arms,—passing on their way out hundreds of wounded men of different regiments, on stretchers and on foot, some with ghastly wounds, and a few taking the advantage of the slightest scratch to pass from front to rear. Legs and arms carelessly heaped together alongside of one of the amputating tents in the rear of the Phillips House, and passed in the march of the day before, had prepared the nerves of the

*Union view of the battlefield, looking westward toward Marye's Hill.
(1) Stratton's brick house; (2) stone wall; (3) Brampton mansion on Marye's
Hill; (4) Rowe House; (5) Hanover Street; (6) canal ditch.*

men somewhat for this most terrible ordeal for fresh troops. Many of
the wounded men cheered lustily as the men marched by, and were
loudly cheered in return, while here and there an occasional skulker
would tell how his regiment was cut to pieces, and like Job's servant
he alone left.

From this point a fine view could be had of the encircling hills, with
their crowning earthworks, commanding the narrow plateau in our
immediate front. On the right and center the Rebel line was not to be
assailed, but by advancing over ground that could be swept by hundreds
of pieces of artillery, while to protect an advancing column our batteries
from their position must be powerless for good. A stone wall following
somewhat the shape of the ridge ran along its base. Properly banked in
its rear, it afforded an admirable protection for their troops. As there
was no chance for success in storming these works, the object in making
the attempt was doubtless to divert the Rebel attention from their right.

*Confederate view of the battlefield, looking eastward toward Fredericksburg.*
*(1) stone wall; (2) second line on hill; (3) Hanover Street;*
*(4) Stratton House; (5) artillery emplacement.*

Column after column of the flower of the army, had during the day charged successively in mad desperation upon that wall; but not to reach it. Living men could not stand before that heavy and direct musketry, and the deadly enfilading cannonade from batteries upon the right and left. The thickly strewn plain attested at once the heroic courage of the men, and the hopelessness of the contest.

"Boys, we're in for it," said a Lieutenant on his way from the right. "Old Pigey has just had three staving swigs from his flask, and they are all getting ready. There goes 'Tommy Totten,' " as the bugle call for "forward" is familiarly called in the army.

Our course was continued to the left—two regiments marching abreast—until we neared a main road leading westward from the town.[4]

---

(4) Hanover Street meets Telegraph Road near the stone wall.

In the meantime the movement had attracted the Rebel fire, and at the last cross street a poor fellow of the 2—th Regiment[5] was almost cut in two by a shell which passed through the ranks of our Regiment and exploded upon the other side of the street, but without doing further damage. At the main road we filed to the right, and amid dashing Staff officers and orderlies, wounded men and fragments of regiments broken and disorganized, proceeded on our way to the front. There was a slight depression in the road, enough to save the troops, and shot and shell sang harmlessly above our heads. When the head of the column— really its rear—as we were left in front, was abreast of a swampy strip of meadow land, at the further end of which was a tannery, our Brigade filed again to the right.[6] The occupation of this meadow appeared to be criminally purposeless, as our line of attack was upon the left of the road; while it was in full view and at the easy range of a few hundred yards from a three-gun Rebel battery. The men were ordered to lie down, which they did as best they could from the nature of the ground, while the mounted officers of the Division and Brigade gathered under the shelter of the brick tannery building.

The movement was scarcely over, before one head and then another appeared peering through the embrasures of the earthwork, then a mounted officer upon a lively sorrel cantered as if for observation a short distance to the left of the work. Some sharp-shooters in our front, protected slightly by the ground which rose gently towards the west, tried their breech-loaders upon him. At 450 yards there was certainty enough in the aim to make the music of their bullets unpleasant, and he again sought the cover of the work. An upright puff of smoke,—then a large volumed puff horizontally,—shrill music in its short flight,—a dull, heavy sound as the shell explodes in the soft earth under our ranks, —and one man thrown ten feet into the air, fell upon his back in the ranks behind him, while his two comrades on his left were killed out-

---

(5)    The man almost cut in half belonged to the 134th Pennsylvania.

(6)    The meadow was between Hanover Street and the Plank Road (Williams
       Street). John Hurkamp's tannery was a hundred and fifty yards west of the
       millrace on the south side of the Plank Road.

*Part of the nine-gun battery of the Washington Artillery of Louisiana under Col. J. B. Walton was in the direct line of fire of Federals attacking the stone wall. The affected portion of the battery had been replaced by Col. E. P. Alexander's reserve artillery battalion by the time of the Humphreys division attack.*

right, his Lieutenant near by mortally wounded,[7] a leg of his comrade on the right cut in two, and a dozen in the neighborhood bespattered with the soft ground and severely contused. Shells that exploded in the air above us, or screamed over our heads; rifle balls that whizzed spitefully near, were now out of consideration. The motions of loading and firing, and as we were in the line of direction, the shell itself, could be seen with terrible distinctness. There was the dread certainty of death at every discharge. All eyes were turned toward the battery, and at each puff, the "bravest held his breath" until the smothered explosion announced that the danger was over. From our front ranks, who had gradually crept up the side of the hill, an incessant fire was kept up; but the pieces could be worked with but little exposure, and it was harmless.

_____

(7)    Jacob Parvin Jr. of Company B.

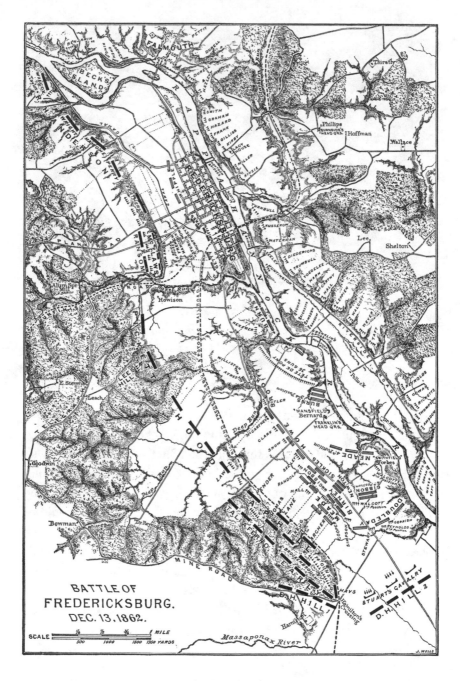

*Battle of Fredericksburg*

Fortunately the shells buried themselves deeply before exploding, and were mainly destructive in their direct passage. Again the horseman cantered gaily to his former place of observation on the left; but our sharp-shooters had the range, and his fine sorrel was turned to the work limping very discreditably. This trifling injury was all that we could inflict in return for the large loss of life and limb.

"Well, Lieutenant, poor John is gone!" said the little Irish Corporal, coming to the side of that officer.

"What, killed?"

"Ivery bit of it. I have just turned him over, and shure he is as dead as he was before he was born. That last shot murthered the boy. It is Terence McCarthy that will do his duty by him, and may be—"

"Corporal! to your post," broke in the Lieutenant. "Old Pigey is taking another pull at the flask, and we will move in a minute."

The surmise of the Lieutenant was correct. "Tommy Totten" again called the men to ranks, and right in front, the head of the column took the pike on another advance. The Rebels seeing the movement, handled their battery with great rapidity and dexterity, and shells in rapid succession were thrown into the closed ranks, but without creating confusion. Among others, a Major of the last Regiment upon the road,[8] an old Mexican campaigner, and a most valuable officer, fell mortally wounded just as he was about leaving the field, and met the fate, that by one of those singular premonitions before noticed in this chapter,—so indicative by their frequency of a connection in life between man's mortal and immortal part,—he had already anticipated.

It was now about four o'clock in the afternoon. The day was somewhat misty, and at this time the field of battle was fast becoming shrouded by the commingled mist and smoke.

On the left of the road the Brigade formed double line of battle along the base and side of a rather steep slope which led to the plateau above. The ground was muddy and well trodden, and littered with dead bodies in spots that marked the localities of exploded shells. Hungry and

---

(8)    George W. Todd of the Ninety-first Pennsylvania.

fatigued with the toil of the day, yet expectant of a conflict which must prove the death scene of many, the men sank upon their arms. From this same spot, successive lines of battle had charged during the day. Brave souls! With rushing memories of home and kindred and friends, they shrank not because the path of duty was one of danger.

We were there as a forlorn hope for the final effort of the field. With great exertion and consummate skill upon the part of its Commander, a battery had been placed in position on the summit of the slope. Officers and men worked nobly, handling the pieces with coolness and rapidity. What they accomplished, could not be seen. What they suffered, was frightfully apparent. Man after man was shot away, until in some instances they were too weak-handed to keep the pieces from following their own recoil down the slope, confusing our ranks and bruising the men. Volunteers sprang forward to assist in working the guns. The gallant Commander,[9] almost unaided, kept order in what would otherwise have been a mingled herd of confused men and frightened horses. No force could withstand the hurricane of hurtling shot and shell that swept the summit.

"Lieutenant, take command of that gun," was the short, sharp, nervous utterance of a General of Division, as in one of his tours of random riding he suddenly stopped his horse in front of a boy of nineteen, a Lieutenant of infantry, who previously to bringing his squad of men into service, a few brief months before, had never seen a full battery.

"Sir!" he replied, in unfeigned astonishment.

"By G—d! sir, I command you as the Commanding General of this Division, sir, to take command of that piece of artillery."

"General, I am entirely unacquainted with—"

"Take command of that piece, sir. You should be ready to enter any arm of the service," replied the General, flourishing his sword in a threatening manner.

"General, I will do my duty; but I can't sight a cannon, sir. I will hand cartridge, turn the screw, steady the wheel, or I'll ram—"

---

(9)    Capt. John G. Hazard, Battery B, First Rhode Island Artillery.

"Ram—ram!"—echoed the General with an oath, and off he started on another of his mad rides.

"Fall in," was passed rapidly along the line, and a moment after our Brigadier, cool as if exercising his command in the evolutions of a peaceful field, rode along the ranks.

"Boys, you are ordered to take that stone wall, and must do it with the bayonet."

Words full of deadly import to men who for long hours had been in full view of the impregnable works, and the field of blood in their front. Ominous as was the command, it was greeted with cheers; and with bayonets at a charge, up that difficult slope,—preserving their line as best they could while breaking to pass the guns, wounded and struggling horses, and bodies thickly strewn over that most perilous of positions for artillery,—the troops passed at a rapid step. The ground upon the summit had been laid out in small lots, as is customary in the suburbs of towns. Many of the partition fences were still remaining, with here and there gaps, or with upper rails lowered for the passage of troops. For a moment, while crossing these fallow fields, there was a lull in the direct musketry. The enfilading fire from batteries right and left still continued; the fierce fitful flashes of the bursting shells becoming more visible with the approach of night. Onward we went, picking our way among the fallen dead and wounded of Brigades who had preceded us in the fight, with feet fettered with mud, struggling to keep place in the line. Several regiments lying upon their arms were passed over in the charge.

"Captain," said a mounted officer when we had just crossed a fence bounding what appeared to be an avenue of the town, "close up on the right." The Captain partly turned, to repeat the command to his men, when the bullets from a sudden flash of waving fire that for the instant lit up the summit of the stone wall for its entire length, prostrated him with a mortal wound,[10] and dismounted his superior. Pity that his eye

---

(10)   The mortally wounded captain was probably George J. Lawrence, Company
A, who died at Georgetown Hospital on January 4, 1863.

should close in what seemed to be the darkest hour of the cause dearest to his soul!

Volley after volley of sheeted lead was poured into our ranks. We were in the proper position on the plain, and a day's full practice gave them exact range and terrible execution. In the increased darkness, the flashes of musketry alone were visible ahead, while to the right and left the gloom was lit up by the lurid flashing of their batteries. This very darkness, in concealing the danger, and the loss, doubtless did its share in permitting the men to cross the lines of dead that marked the halting-place of previous troops. Still onward they advanced,—the thunder of artillery above them,—the groans of the wounded rising from below;—frightful gaps are made in their ranks by exploding shells, and many a brave boy staggers and falls to rise no more, in that storm of spitefully whizzing lead.

Regularity in ranks was simply impossible. Many officers and men gathered about a brick house on the right[11]—a narrow lawn leading directly to the fatal wall was crowded; indeed, caps bearing the regimental numbers were found, as has since been ascertained, close by the wall, and a Lieutenant who was stunned in the fight and fell almost at its base, was taken prisoner.[12] Nearly every officer who had entered the fight mounted, was at this time upon foot. In the tempest of bullets that everywhere prevailed the destruction of the force was but a question of brief time, and to prevent further heroic but vain sacrifices the order to retire was given. With the Brigade, the Regiment fell back, leaving one-third of its number in dead and wounded to hallow the remembrance of that fatal field.

"This way, Pap! This is the way to get out safe," shouted a Captain as he rose, from the rear of a pile of rubbish, amid the laughter of the

---

(11)    The brick house owned by Allen Stratton was also the haven for the previously wounded soldiers from the Second Corps. Their commander, Maj. Gen. Darius N. Couch, found so many men there that he had to seek shelter from Confederate fire elsewhere.

(12)    This was probably 2d Lt. Joseph Oliver of Company B. Seven privates of his company were also captured by the Confederates.

men now on their backward move. The burly form of the exhorting Colonel was seen to follow the no less burly form of the Captain, and father and son were spared for other fields.[13]

An effort was made to reform after the firing had slackened, but the increased darkness prevented the marshalling of the thinned ranks. Out of range of the still not infrequent bullets and occasional shell, and drowsy from fatigue, the men again lay upon their arms at the foot of the slope; and the battle of Fredericksburg was over.

What happened upon the left, where the main battle should have been fought, and why Franklin was upon the left at all, are problems that perhaps the reader can pass upon to better advantage than the writer of these pages. His "corner of the fight" has been described, truthfully at least, whatever the other failings may be.

We had left the field; but the Rebels had not as yet gained it. Pickets were thrown out to within eighty yards of their line, and details scattered over the field to bear off the wounded. No lights were allowed, and the least noise was sure to bring a shell or a shower of bullets. In consequence, their removal was attended with difficulty. The evil of the practice too prevalent among company commanders, of sending skulkers and worthless men in obedience to a detail for the ambulance corps, was now horribly apparent. Large numbers of the dead, and even the dying, were found with their pockets turned inside out, rifled of their contents by these harpies in uniform.

But little rest was to be had that night. At 8 P.M. the troops were marched back into the town, only to be brought out again at midnight and reformed in line of battle about a hundred yards distant from the wall. The moon had now risen, and in its misty light the upturned faces of the dead lost nothing of ghastliness. Horrible, too, beyond description —ringing in the ears of listeners for a lifetime—were the shrieks and groans of the wounded,—principally Rebel,—from a strip of neutral ground lying between the pickets of the two armies. Whatever the object

---

(13)   The "exhorting" colonel's son was Capt. Francis H. Gregory, Company A, Ninety-first Pennsylvania.

of reforming line of battle may have been, it appears to have been abandoned, as after a short stay we were returned to the town and assigned quarters in the street in front of the Planters' House.[14]

Fredericksburg was a town of hospitals. All the churches and public buildings, very many private residences, and even the pavements in their respective fronts, were crowded with wounded. In one of the principal churches on a lower street, throned in a pulpit which served as a dispensary, and surrounded by surgical implements and appliances, flourished our little Dutch Doctor, never more completely in his element. Very nice operations, as he termed them, were abundant.

"How long can I live?" inquired a fine-looking, florid-faced young man of two-and-twenty, with a shattered thigh, who had just been brought in and had learned from the Doctor that amputation could not save his life.

"Shust fifteen minutes," was the reply, as the Doctor opened and closed his watch in a cold, business way.

"Can I see a Chaplain?"

"Shaplain! Shaplain! eh? Shust one tried to cross, and he fell tead on bridge. Not any follow him, I shure you. Too goot a chance to die, for Shaplains. What for you want him? Bray, eh?"

The dying man, folding his hands upon his breast, nodded assent.

"Ver well, I bray," and at the side of the stretcher the Doctor kneeled, and with fervid utterance, and in the solemn gutturals of the German, repeated the Lord's prayer. When he arose to resume his labor, the soldier was beyond the reach of earthly supplication; but a smile was upon his countenance.

The Sabbath,[15] with the main body of our troops, was a day of rest. Chance shots from Rebel sharp-shooters, who had crept to within long range of the cross streets, were from time to time heard, and shell occasionally screamed over the town. To ears accustomed to the uproar of the preceding days, however, they were not in the least annoying.

---

(14)   Planters' House or Hotel building, with its slave auction block out front, still stands at the corner of Williams and Charles streets.

(15)   December 14.

Over one-half of the army were comfortably housed, bringing into requisition for their convenience the belongings and surroundings of the abandoned dwellings. Notwithstanding our slow approach, the evidences of hasty exit on the part of the inhabitants were abundant on all sides. Warehouses filled with flour and tobacco were duly appreciated by the men, while parlors floored in Brussels, and elegantly ornamented, were in many instances wantonly destroyed.

"Tom," said a non-commissioned officer, addressing a private whom we have before met in these pages, "where did you get that box?"

"Get it? Why I confiscated it. Just look at the beauties," and opening a fine mahogany case, Tom disclosed a pair of highly finished duelling pistols.

"What right have you to confiscate it?" retorted the Sergeant.

"It is contraband of war, and Rebel property. Record evidence of that. Just look at this letter found with it," and Tom pulled out of an inside pocket of his blouse a letter written in a most miserable scrawl, assuring some "Dear Capting" of

> "Here's my heart and here's my hand,
> For the man who fit for Dixy land."

Monday[16] passed in much the same manner. About 9 P.M. of that day the Regiment, with others, was employed in throwing up breastworks, and digging rifle-pits on the west of the town. Expecting to hold it on the morrow against what they knew would be a terrible artillery fire, the men worked faithfully, and by midnight, works strong as the ground would admit of, were prepared. It was a perilous work; performed in the very face of the enemy's pickets;—but was only an extensive ruse, as at 1 A.M. we were quietly withdrawn and assigned a position in the left of the town. The sidewalks were muddy, and disengaging shutters from the windows, loose boards from fences,—anything to keep them above the mud,—the men composed themselves for slumber. Before 2

---

(16)   December 15.

o'clock an excited Staff officer had the Brigade again in line, and after moving and halting until 4 A.M., we crossed the lower bridge in much lighter order than when we entered the place; for notwithstanding urgent solicitations of officers, from Brigadier down, permission was refused the men to obtain their knapsacks. Besides the loss of several thousand dollars to the Government in blankets and overcoats, hundreds of valuable knapsacks, and even money in considerable sums, were lost to the men.[17] The matter is all the more disgraceful when we consider the abundance of time, and the fact, that details had been sent by the Colonels to arrange the knapsacks upon the sidewalk, in order that they could be taken up while the command would pass. It was marched by another route, however, and in the cold, pelting rain, the men, while marching up the opposite slopes of the Rappahannock, had ample reason to reflect upon the cold forethought that could crowd a Head-quarters' train, and deprive them of their proper allowance of clothing. Six hours later, our Division had the credit of furnishing about the only booty left by the army that the Rebels found upon their reoccupation of the town.

Sadly and quietly, the troops retrod the familiar mud of their old camp grounds. The movement had been a failure—a costly one in private and national sacrifices,—and no one felt it more keenly than the broad-shouldered, independent, and much injured Burnside. Strange that this costly sacrifice should have been offered up on ground hallowed in our early struggle for freedom—that the bodies of our brave volunteers, stripped by traitor hands, should lie naked on the plain that bears a monument to that woman of many virtues, "Mary, the mother of Washington"—that ground familiar to the early boyhood of the Great Patriot, should have been the scene of one of the noblest, although unsuccessful, contests of the war. Fit altar for such a sacrifice! A shrine for all time of devout patriots, who will here renew their vows,—of eternal enmity to traitors,—and thus consecrate to posterity the heavy population we have left in the Valley.

---

(17)   The loss of knapsacks would become the subject of future courts-martial.

# CHAPTER XVII.

*The Sorrows of the Sutler—The Sutler's Tent—Generals manufactured by the Dailies—Fighting and Writing—A Glandered Horse—Courts-martial— Mania of a Pigeon-hole General on the Subject—Colonel and Lieutenant-Colonel in Strait-Jackets.*

IF the reader can imagine the contents of his nearest corner grocery thrown confusedly together under a canvas covering, he will have a tolerably correct idea of the interior of a Sutler's tent. Probably, to make the likeness more truthful, sardines, red herring, and cheese, should be more largely represented than is customary in a corner grocery.

Our Sutler, although upon his first campaign, was no novice in the craft. He could be hail-fellow-well-met with the roughest of crowds thronging the outside of his rude counter, and at the same time keep an eye upon the cash drawer. And he was behind no one in "casting his bread upon the waters," in the shape of trifling presents and hospitable welcomes, in order that it might return at the next pay-day. Notwithstanding all his tact, however, Tom Green was in many respects an awkward, haphazard fellow, continually in difficulty, although as continually fortunate in overcoming it. His troubles were known to the Regiment, as the Sutler's interests were individualized to a great extent, and while all might be amused, he was never beyond the pale of sympathy. During the long winter evenings, the barrels and boxes in his tent seated a jovial crowd of officers, who in games and with thrice-told stories, would while away what would otherwise be tedious hours. Not unfre-

*The Gallant Charge of Humphreys's Division at the Battle of Fredericksburg,
a sketch by A. R. Waud published in* Harper's Weekly, *lacked reality but
provided good press for the division.*

quently was the Chaplain, who quartered close by, disturbed with a
"sound of revelry by night," to have his good-humor restored in the
morning by a can of pickled lobster or brandied cherries.

On one of the merriest of the merry nights of the holidays, our
Western Virginia Captain was the center of a group of officers engaged
in gazing intently upon a double page wood-cut, in one of the prominent
illustrated weeklies, that at one time might have represented the storming of Fort Donelson, but then did duty by way of illustrating a "Gallant
Charge at Fredericksburg."

"There it is again," said the Captain. "Not one half of our Generals
are made by honest efforts. Their fighting is nothing like the writing
that is done for them. They don't rely so much upon their own genius
as upon that of the reporter who rides with their Staffs. By George, if
old Rosey in Western Virginia—"

"Dry up on that, Captain," interrupted a brother officer. "Old Pigey
is the hero of the day. He understands himself. Didn't you notice how

*The Sutler's Tent (sketch by Arthur Lumley)*

concertedly all the dailies after the fight talked about the cool, courageous man of science; and just look at this how it backs it all up. Old
Rosey, as you call him, never had half as many horses shot under him
at one time. Just see them kicking and floundering about him, and the
General way ahead on foot, between our fire and the Rebels, as cool as
when he took the long pull at his flask in the hollow."

"And half the men will testify that that was the only cool moment he
saw during the whole fight."

"No matter," continued the other, "he has the inside track of the
reporters, and he is all right with all who 'smell the battle from afar.' "

"Well, there's no denying old Pigey was brave, but he was as crazy
as a boy with a bee in his breeches," said the Captain, holding up the

caricature to the admiration of the crowded tent. "Our Division gets the credit of it at any rate. Bully for our Division!"

"Not one word," breaks in the Poetical Lieutenant, "of Butterfield, with his cool, Napoleonic look, as he rode along our line preparatory to the charge; or of Fighting Old Joe, unwilling to give up the field; or of our difficulty in clambering up the slope, getting by the artillery, which made ranks confused, and so forth, but

> 'On we move, though to self-slaughter,
> Regular as rolling water.'

Never mind criticizing, boys, It will sound well at home. We did our duty, at any rate, if we did not do it exactly as represented in the picture. The reporter was not there to see for himself, and he must take somebody's word, and it is a feather in our cap that he has taken Pigey's."

The conversation was at this stage interrupted by the sudden entry of the Adjutant, with a loud call for the Sutler. That individual, notwithstanding the unusual excitement of the night, had been singularly quiet. Rising from his buffalo in the corner, he approached the Adjutant with a countenance so full of apprehension and alarm as to elicit the inquiry from the crowd of "What's the matter with the Sutler?"

"He hasn't felt well since I told him a few hours ago," said a Lieutenant, a lawyer by profession, "that Sutlers were liable to be court-martialed."

"And he'll feel worse," adds the Adjutant, "when he hears this letter read."

Amid urgent calls for the letter, the Adjutant mounted a box, and by the light of a dip held by the Captain, proceeded to read a letter signed by the Commanding General of the Division, and considerably blurred, which ran somewhat in this wise:

"COLONEL:—

"Is your Sutler sagacious?

"Has he ordinary honesty?

"Has he the foresight common among business men? Is he likely to be imposed upon?"

The letter was greeted with roars of laughter that were not diminished by the dismay of the Sutler. The Adjutant was forthwith requested by one of the crowd to suggest to the Colonel to reply—

"That our Sutler was a sagacious animal. That he had the honesty ordinary among Sutlers. That if the General was disposed to deal with him, he would find out that he had the foresight common among business men, especially in the way of calculating his profits; and that as far as making change was concerned, he was not at all likely to be imposed upon."

Loud calls were now made upon the Sutler for an explanation, and with look and tones that indicated that with him at least it was no laughing matter, he commenced—

"On the forenoon of the day that we crossed into Fredericksburg—"

"We crossed!" roared the Captain. "Well, that's cool for a man who suddenly recollected when that Quarter-Master was killed by a shell near the Lacy House, just before our brigade crossed, that he had business in Washington."

"Well, then, that *you* crossed," continued the Sutler, correcting himself hastily, to allow the crowd to make as little capital as possible out of his blunder, "the General sent for me, and said that he had been informed that I thought of going to Washington, and wanted to know whether I would take a horse with me;—pointing to one that was blanketed, and that one of his orderlies was leading. I looked upon it as an order to take the horse, and thought that I might as well put a good face on the matter. So I told him that I would take it with pleasure. Well, I mounted the horse, thinking that I might as well ride, and took the road for Aquia. But I found out after half an hour's travel, that the horse was very weak,—in fact hardly able to bear me, and so I took the halter strap in hand and trudged along by his side. Presently I noticed a very bad smell. Carrion is so common here along the road that I didn't pay much attention to it at first, but the smell continued, and got worse, and I thought it strange that the carrion should keep with me. By and by I noticed his nostrils, and then found out to my rage that I, a Regimental Sutler, accustomed to drive good nags, was leading a glandered horse in a country where horse flesh was cheap as dirt. Well, at Aquia we had a great time getting the horse on the boat,—indeed, he fell off the gangway, and we had to fish him out of the water. The passengers crowded me, with the horse, into a little corner in the stern of the boat, and looked at me as if I deserved lynching for bringing him on board. But that was nothing to the trouble I had with him in Washington. After the boat landed, I led that horse around from one stable to another in Washington for four mortal hours, but couldn't get him in anywhere; and besides they threatened to prosecute me if I did not have him shot.[1] Finding that I could do nothing else, I gave a man three dollars to have him taken away and shot. The thing bothered me mightily. I did not want to write to old Pigey, for fear that he might take some course to prevent me from collecting the greenbacks due me in the Regiment, and I did not like to tell him in person. Well, I have been putting it off and off for nearly a week past since my return—my mind made up to tell him all about it, but delaying as long as possible, until this afternoon he happened to see me, and in about half an hour afterward sent for me. It was after three o'clock, an unsafe time with the General, and I expected there would be the d—l to pay. From the way in which he asked me to be seated, shook hands with me, and went on inquiring about my stock and business, and so forth, I saw at once that he knew nothing of it. All the while I was fairly trembling in my boots. At last says he:

" 'Well, how did you leave the horse?' and without waiting for an answer, went on to say that he was a favorite animal, highly recommended by the Ohio Captain he had purchased him from, and wound up by repeating the inquiry.

"There was no chance to back out now, and gathering my breath for the effort, said I—

" 'General, I regret to say, that your horse is dead.'

---

(1)    Glanders is an ancient disease that caused major respiratory distress and death in horses. It spread where horses were crowded in stables and around watering troughs. The "great glanders epozootic" caused immense problems for both sides during the war. For instance, of the 6,875 Confederate horses stabled at Lynchburg over a fifteen-month period, only 1,000 were sent to the field. Almost 3,000 died, 449 were shot, and the rest were deemed unfit for service. The disease was finally eradicated in 1934.

" 'Dead! did you say?' echoed the General, rising.

" 'Yes, sir; I was compelled to have him shot.'

" 'Shot! did you say, sir?' advancing; 'shot! compelled to have him shot, sir! By G—d, sir, I would like to know, sir, who would *compel* you to have a horse of mine shot, sir.'

" 'He was glandered,' said I timidly.

" 'Sir! sir!! sir!!! D—d lie, sir,—mouth as sweet as sugar. D—d lie, sir,' retorted the General.

"The General was furiously mad, his eyes flashing, and all the while he took quick and long steps up and down his marquee.

"I attempted an explanation, but he would listen to none; and kept on repeating 'glandered!' 'shot!' and scowling at times at me;— saying, too, 'By G—d, sir, this matter must be investigated.'

" 'General,' said I, at length, 'in justice to myself, I would like'—

" 'Justice to yourself!' shouted the General, looking at me as if he believed me mean enough to murder my grandmother. 'Who the h—l ever heard of a sutler being entitled to any justice? —you, sir, I'll teach you justice. Get out of my tent, sir.'

"I thought it best not to wait for another opportunity to get away, and as I sloped I heard the General swearing at me until I had passed the Surgeon's tent. You see what makes the matter worse with the General is, that he has been told several times that the horse was unsound, but would not admit that as much of a horseman as he professed to be, had been taken in by the 'Buckeye Officer.' "

The recital of the story appeared to have lightened the load upon the breast of the sutler, and he wound up somewhat humorously, by telling the crowd that there was another on the list to be court-martialed, and that they must give him all possible aid and comfort.

"Be easy, sutler! there are too many ahead of you on that list," observed an officer. "Your case can't be reached for some time yet. It is admitted on all sides that our material, officers and men, are as good as any in the army; and, for all that, although one of the smallest divisions, we have more courts-martial than any other division. Why, just look at it. A day or two before the battle of Fredericksburg, twenty-three officers were released from arrest. Thirteen of them, Lieutenants under charges for lying, as old Pigey termed it, when, in fact, it was nothing more than a simple misunderstanding of one of his night orders, such as any men might make. Poor fellows! over one-half of them are out of his power now; but I wouldn't wonder if the General would be presumptuous and malignant enough to respectfully refer their cases to the Chancery of Heaven, with endorsements to suit himself!"

"Well, that brave Lieutenant," said the Captain, "who asked permission of the Colonel to charge with our regiment when himself and squad had become separated from his own, has been reinstated. You know that at the time old Pigey gave permission to the Colonels to send Volunteer Officers before the board for examination, the Lieutenant-Colonel of his regiment, instead of sending him a written order, as was customary, sought him out when engaged in conversation with some non-commissioned officers of his command, and in an insulting manner gave him a verbal order to report. They had some hot talk about it, and in the course of it the Lieutenant said that 'he'd be d—d if he came into the army to study tactics; he came to fight,'[2] and on the strength of that, the General had him tried and dismissed. Our Colonel and Lieutenant-Colonel sent up a statement to 'Burney,' giving a glowing account of his gallant conduct in the fight; and the General seeing how dead in earnest he was when he said he came to fight, restored him to his position."

"I am very much afraid," said the Lieutenant, slowly, interrupted by frequent whiffs at a well colored meerschaum, "that the Colonel and Lieutenant-Colonel will have difficulty to save themselves."

"Save themselves!" echoed several, from different parts of the tent, their faces hardly visible through the increasing smoke. "Why, what's in the wind now?"

"A good deal more than a great many of you think," continued the Adjutant. "I think I see the dawning of considerable difficulty. The Colonel, you recollect, was compelled to correct our Division-General in some of his commands, to prevent confusion; and the General, although clearly in the wrong, submitted with a bad grace; and then at the last

---

(2)    The lieutenant who came to fight and not to take examinations was William
        H. Wolfe, Company E, 131st Pennsylvania.

review you all remember how a whiffet chanced to yelp at the heels of the Staff horses, and how the General—it was after three, you recollect, —d—d the puppy and its ancestry, particularly its mother, until his Staff tittered behind him, and the Regiments of his command, officers and men, particularly ours, fairly roared. And then, too, when General Burnside saluted the colors, and requested Pigey to ride along, how he started off with his Staff, leaving us all at a 'Present Arms'; and how the quick eye of Old Joe saw the blunder; and how he called the General's attention to it, without effect, until 'Burney' sharply yelled out, 'General, you had better bring your men to a shoulder, sir'; and then, how the General, amid increased tittering and laughter, rode back, and with a face like scarlet squeaked out—'Division! Shoulder arms!' Now I have heard that the General blames the Field Officers of our Regiment with a good deal of that laughter; and that and this Sutler matter will make him provide a pretext for another Court-martial at an early day."

"Double, double, toil and trouble,"

said the poetical Lieutenant. "Why, the Adjutant talks as if he could see the witches over the pot; certainly—

' No lateness of life gives him mystical lore.' "

"No, but—

' Coming events cast their shadows before,' "

continued the Adjutant, finishing the couplet. "I do not know that any gift of prophecy is given unto me, but I will venture to predict that the pretext will be that very order,—outrageous and unreasonable as it is,— that our Brigadier not only flatly and positively refused to obey before he left, but told his command that it was unlawful and unreasonable, and should not be obeyed."

"What! that dress-coat order," cried the Western Virginia Captain, springing to his feet; "compel a man who has two new blouses, and who belongs to a regiment that came out with blouses and never had dress-coats, to put a dress-coat in his knapsack besides, when his clothing account is almost exhausted, and the campaign only half through. Is that the order you mean? By George, you must think that old Pigey is only going to live and do business after three o'clock in the afternoon, if you think that he will insist upon that order. Our Brigadier did right to disobey it. Old Rosey would have put any officer in irons, who—"

"But, Captain," resumed the Adjutant, "unfortunately we are not in Western Virginia, and not under old Rosey, as you call him, but in the Army of the Potomac, where Red Tape clogs progress more than Virginia mud ever did, and where position is attained, not so much by the merit of the officer, as by the hold he may be able to get upon the favoritism of the War Department."

"Is it possible," continued the Captain, thrusting his hands into the lowest depths of his breeches pockets, and casting upon the Adjutant a half inquiring, half reflecting look, "that this Regiment, which the General himself admits is one of the best disciplined in his Division, and which has been one of the most harmonious and orderly, is to be imposed upon in this way by a whimsical superior officer, who, whatever his reputation for science may be, has shown himself over and over again to have no sense! I tell you, our men can't stand it. Just look at my own Company, for instance, nearly all married men, families dependent upon them for support, and now when they have each two lined blouses, as good as new, and their clothing account about square, they are to take seven dollars and a half of their hard earned pay—more than half a month's wages—and buy a coat that can be of no service, and that must be thrown away the first march. I do not believe that the Government designs that our Volunteer Regiments should be compelled to take both blouses and dress coats. The General had better enter into partnership with some shoddy contractor, if he intends giving orders of this kind. I tell you, the men will not take them."

"Come, Captain, no 'murmuring or muttering' against the powers that be," said the Adjutant. "The men will either take them, in case the order is made, or go to the Rip-raps. I am inclined to think that the Field Officers will not see the men imposed upon. And at the same time they will not bear the brunt of disobeying the order themselves, and not let the men run any risk. It is hard to tell," continued the Adjutant, in a measured tone, refilling his pipe as he spoke, "what it will result in; but

Pigey is in power, and like all in authority, has his toadies about him, and you may make up your minds that he will not be sparing in his charges, or in the testimony to support them. Our Colonel and Lieut.-Colonel, I know, feel outraged at the bare idea of being subjected to such an order. They are both earnest men, have both made heavy sacrifices to enter the service, and have never failed in duty, although, like most volunteer officers of spirit, they are somewhat restiff under authority. The Colonel, being an old soldier, and thoroughly acquainted with his work, is especially restiff under the authority of an officer so poorly fitted for his position as our Division General. But our turn must come. Every Regiment in the Division has suffered from his Court-martialling and studied interference, and so far we have been fortunate enough to escape. And with the insight I now have, I believe the glandered horse and the little whiffet that yelped and disturbed the General's ideas of a proper Review, will prove to be at the bottom of the whole matter."

"Tom," interrupted the Captain, "you will have to put your record in better shape."

"How can I do it?" said the Sutler.

"By sending Pigey a bill for the three dollars you paid to have the horse shot."

The crowd boisterously applauded the proposition, and insisted upon its execution. Desultory conversation followed until "Taps" dispersed them to their quarters.

Grumbling is claimed as a soldier's privilege, and the Sutler's tent being a lounging place when off duty, becomes a place of grumbling, much like the place of wailing that the Jews have on the outskirts of Jerusalem.

A fortnight later saw the crowd in their old position, but with countenances in which it was difficult to say whether anxiety or anger predominated.

"Fellows, it is terminating just as the Adjutant prophesied a short time ago in this very place," said a Captain slightly past the prime of life, but of vigorous build. "In trying to keep the men out of dress coats, the Colonel and Lieutenant-Colonel have got themselves into all manner of trouble, and there is no let-up with old Pigey. I saw them this morning both as cheerful as crickets, and determined to have the matter thoroughly investigated."

"Did they intimate any opinion as to what we ought to do?" inquired the Adjutant.

"Not a word. In that respect they say just as they did before they were placed in close confinement, that it is a case in which each man must act for himself. They are willing to shoulder the responsibility of their own acts, and were very indignant when they heard that Pigey had ordered the other Brigade under arms, and two pieces of artillery to be trained upon our camp, as if the whole Regiment was guilty of mutiny, when there was not at the same time a more quiet or orderly Regiment in camp."

"They understand," remarked the Adjutant, "however, why that was done. The General must have something to justify this unusually harsh treatment. A charge of simple disobedience of orders would not do it, so he charges them with mutiny, and trumps up this apprehension and parade to appear consistent. The Lieutenant-Colonel anticipated it, I know. I heard him say, while under simple arrest, that he believed that after three o'clock they would be placed in close confinement, and on the strength of it some letters were sent by a civilian giving full details. Well, I am glad that they are in good spirits."

"In the very best," replied the Captain, "although the General starts as if he intended giving them a tough through. The Sibley that they were turned into late last night, was put up over ground so wet that you couldn't make a track upon it without it would fill with water, and the Lieutenant-Colonel had to sleep upon this ground with a single blanket, as it was late when his servant Charlie came to the guard with his roll of blankets, and the General would not permit him to pass. In consequence he awoke this morning chilled, wet through, and with a fair start for a high fever. And then they are denied writing material, books, even a copy of the Regulations. The General relented sufficiently, to tell an aide to inform them, that they might correspond with their families if they would submit the correspondence first to inspection at Division Head-quarters; to which they replied—that 'the General might insult them, but could not compel them to humiliate their families.' No one is permitted to see them unless by special permission of the General."

"And when I saw those three guards today pacing about that Sibley," excitedly spoke the Virginia Captain, "I felt like mounting a cracker-box in camp and asking the men to follow me, and find out on what grounds, this puss-in-boots outraged in this way men more well-meaning and determined than himself in the suppression of this rebellion. But it will all come right. They are not to be crowded clear out of sight in a single day. One of my men told me that he was present on duty when that wharf-rat of an Adjutant,[3] that the exhorting Colonel is trying to make an Adjutant-General of, came into the General's tent with the Lieutenant-Colonel, and he said that the General asked the Colonel whether he was still determined to disobey the lawful order of his superior officer, the Commanding General of the Division?

" 'The legality of the order is what I question,' said the Colonel. 'An order to be lawful should at least be reasonable. That order is unreasonable, unjust to the men, and I cannot conscientiously obey it.'

" 'This money for the coats does not come out of your pocket,' said the General, blandly. 'Why need you concern yourself about it?'

" 'It comes out of the pockets of my men, General,' said the Colonel, 'and I consider it my duty to concern myself sufficiently to prevent imposition upon them.'

" 'Tut,' said the General. 'You wouldn't hear a Regular officer say that.'

" 'The greater shame for them,' said the Colonel. 'My men are my neighbors and friends. They look to me to protect their interests. As a general thing the Regulars are recruited from the purlieus of great cities, and are men of no character.'

" 'Colonel,' said the General, sternly, 'listen to this definition of 'Mutiny,' and then, as you are a lawyer, think of your present position.'

"The Colonel heard it read and replied that 'it had nothing whatever to do with the case, as there was no mutiny, nor even an approach to it.' Considering the time of day, the General, so far, had been unusually cool, but he could keep in no longer.

---

(3)    Lt. B. J. Tayman of the Ninety-first Pennsylvania, Colonel Gregory's adjutant.

" 'Colonel,' said he, in a loud, angry tone, as he advanced towards him, 'by G—d, sir, you are mutinous, sir!'

" 'General,' replied the Colonel, coolly, and looking him full in the eye, 'with all due deference to your superior rank, permit me to say, that if you say I am guilty of mutiny you overstep the bounds of truth.'

"The Colonel's confident manner rather staggered the General, and he turned to the Adjutant, who has been his runner throughout this matter, and called upon him to substantiate his assertion; which he did.

"With the remark that he would not dare to make such false assertions away from the General's head-quarters, the Colonel turned upon him indignantly, and the General called for the Provost Guard to conduct him to the Sibley. Now I tell you, fellows," said the Captain, "the General will make nothing out of this matter."

"He has his malice gratified by the present punishment he is subjecting them to, as if fearful that they might come unharmed from a Court-martial. But I don't believe that he will be able to get the Regiment into dress coats," remarked the Adjutant.

The Adjutant was right. The Regiment did not get into dress coats; although its Colonel and Lieutenant-Colonel slipped into strait-jackets.

# CHAPTER XVIII.

*Dress Coats versus Blouses—Military Law—Bill the Cook—Courts Martial—
Important Decision in Military Law—'A Man with Two Blouses on' can be
compelled to put a Dress Coat on top—A Colored French Cook and a Beefy-
browed Judge-Advocate—The Mud March—No Pigeon-holing on a Whiskey
Scent—Old Joe in Command—Dissolution of Partnership between the Dutch
Doctor and Chaplain.*

NECESSITY knows no law. Military law springs from the necessity of the case, and may be said, therefore, to be equivalent to no
law. However plausible the principles embodied in the compact periods
of Benet and De Hart[1] may appear, in actual practice they dwindle to
little else than the will of the officer who details the court. General Officers, tried at easy intervals, before pains-taking courts, in large cities,
may have opportunity for equal and exact justice; but Heaven help their
inferiors who have their cases put through at lightning speed, before a
court under marching orders, and expecting momentarily to move.

The Act of Congress, with a wise prescience of the jealousies and
bickerings always arising between Regulars and Volunteers, provides
that Regulars shall be tried by Regular, and Volunteers by Volunteer
Officers. In practice, the spirit of the law is evaded by the subterfuge,

---

(1)    Steven Benet and William De Hart were the authorities on military law in
       Civil War courts-martial.

that a Regular Officer, temporarily in command of Volunteers, is *pro tempore* a Volunteer Officer. In the Mexican War, where the number of Volunteer Officers was comparatively small, there may have been a necessity for this. With our present immense Volunteer force there can be none whatever; and the practice is the more inexcusable, when we consider the great amount of legal as well as military ability among the officers of this force. The gross injustice of this violation of the act, must be apparent to any one upon a moment's reflection. Officers, whose only offense may be their belonging to the Volunteer Service, are too frequently subjected to the tender mercy of a Board of Martinets; —men of long service and tried ability, degraded by the fiat of a court composed of officers as tender in intellect as in years, and whose only recommendation to be members of the court, is their recent transfer from lessons in gunnery and drills,—with patent leather knapsacks, to field or higher positions in the Volunteer Service. Thus, the officer whose earnestness in the cause and heavy sacrifice of family ties and business affairs, first raised the command,—who grew with its growth during months, perhaps years, of hard service,—saw through his untiring efforts the awkwardness of his men change gradually for the precision of the veteran,—not unfrequently by the snap judgment of men whose only service has been in Pay, Quartermaster, Commissary Departments,—anywhere but in a Fighting Department,—finds himself dishonored, his service thrown aside for naught, and his worst enemy the misuse of the laws he had taken arms to vindicate.

Not an officer or soldier but must recollect a case in point. Now, this mainly arises from the undue and unjust deference paid by the War Department to Regular Officers, and the curse that attends them and upholds them—Red Tape. *Undue and unjust deference.* Does not the history of the Army of the Potomac prove it? Its heroic fighting, but ill-starred generalship!      *      *      *      *      *

"Halloa, Bill! what news from the Sibley?" shouted one of a group of officers who sat and lay upon the ground, cheerfully discussing hard tack and coffee in the camp of a grand picket reserve, near the Rappahannock. The man addressed would, in build, have made a good recruit for the armies of New Amsterdam in their warfare against the Swedes,

so graphically described by Irving. Short and thickly set, with a face
radiant as a brass kettle in a preserving season, trousers thrust in a pair
of cast-away top boots, the legs of which fell in ungainly folds about
his ankles, a greasy blouse, tucked in at the waist-band, and a cap ripped
behind in the vain effort to accommodate it to a head of Websterian
dimensions. With all his shortcomings, and they were legion, Bill's
education, unfailing humor and kindness of heart made him a favorite
at regimental Head-quarters, where he had long been employed as an
attendant. When the sickness of the Lieutenant-Colonel grew serious
in the Sibley, Bill took his post by the side of his blankets, and in well-
meaning attention made up what he lacked in tenderness as a nurse.

"Nothing new since the trial," drawled out Bill, seating himself
meanwhile, and mopping with his coat sleeve the perspiration that stood
in beads upon his forehead.

"Since the trial!" echoed the officer. "Why, they have not had notice
yet, and the General said he would give them ample opportunity for
preparation for trial."

"So he did," continued Bill. "They were put into the Sibley on Monday night, and on Thursday night following, about half-past ten, when
it was raining in torrents, and storming so that the guards and myself
could scarcely keep the old tent up, that sucker-mouthed Aide of old
Pigey's popped his head inside the flaps and handed the Colonel and
Lieut.-Colonel each a letter. Both letters went on to say, that their trial
would take place the next day, at ten o'clock, at Pigey's Head-quarters,
and that each letter contained a copy of the charges and specifications,
and that, in the meanwhile, they could prepare for trial, provide counsel,
and so forth. The best part of two sheets of large-sized letter paper was
filled with the charges against each, all in Pigey's hand-writing.

" 'Disrespectful language towards the General Commanding Division;' 'Conduct tending to Mutiny;' 'Disobedience of Orders,' and
'Violation of at least half a dozen different articles of war.'

"The ink was green yet, as if it had all been done after three o'clock.
The Lieutenant-Colonel, you know, told that wharf rat of an Adjutant
before the General, that he would not dare to make such mis-statements
away from Division Head-quarters. Well, on the strength of that, he had
him charged with sending a challenge to fight a duel, and telling his

superior officer that he lied. Lord! when I heard them read, I thought they ought to be thankful that one of the darkies about Division Head-quarters hadn't died in the meanwhile, or there would have been a charge of murder. It might just as well, at any rate, have been murder as mutiny, that we all know. Time for trial!—lots of time! Just the time to hunt a lawyer, consult law books, and drum up testimony."

"Timed purposely, of course," broke in the officer, indignantly, "and the Court, no doubt, packed to suit. But," his face brightening, "there is an appeal to Father Abraham."

"It is all very well to talk about Father Abraham," continued Bill, in the same drawling tone; "but if you have to hunt up Honest Old Abe through the regular military channels, as they say you have to, he'll seem about as far off as the first old Father Abraham did to that rich old Cockey that had a big dry on in a hot place."

"Bill," said the officer, as he saw the crowd inclined to laugh at the remark, "this is by far too serious a matter to jest about. Here are two men of character and position, devoted to the cause body and soul, com-pletely at the mercy of an officer whose conduct is a reproach to his command, and who is malicious alike in deeds and words."

"Especially the latter," interrupted Bill, more hurriedly than before. "The Colonel says he was chief witness, and swore the charges right straight through, without wincing. The Judge Advocate,[2] they said, was a right clever gentlemanly fellow, but ignorant of law, and completely at the disposal of the General. I saw him several times when I was passing backwards and forwards, and he looked to me as if the beef was a little too thick on the outside of his forehead, for the brains to be active inside. Still, the Colonels have no fault to find with him, except that between times he would talk about drinking to Little Mac, and brag about the prospect, as the papers seem to say, of Fitz John Porter's being cleared. But then most of the Court did as much at that as he did. He did his duty in the trial, I guess, as well as his knowledge and old Pigey's will would allow."

---

(2)    The judge advocate was Lt. Col. Alexander Webb.

"Well, Bill, give us some particulars of the trials, if you know them," suggested an officer of a neighboring regiment—the party during the conversation being increased by additions of officers and privates.

"I only know what I saw passing back and forth, and what I heard from the Colonels themselves. They wouldn't allow any one to go within three yards of the tent in which they held Court; but I'll give you what I have, although to do it I must go back a little:—Before it was light on the day of trial the Major posted off to our Corps Commander[3] with an application for a continuance, on the ground of want of time for preparation. About daylight the General came out, rubbing his eyes, wanting to know who that early bird was?

" 'Playing Orderly, sir,' said he, as his eye lit upon the letter in the Major's hand. 'Fine occupation for a man of six feet two, with a Major's straps upon his shoulders.'

"The Major wilted till he felt about two feet six, but mustered presence of mind sufficient to tell the General his errand, and how his personal solicitude had prompted him to perform it himself. The General heard him kindly; stated that he had no doubt but that the Court would act favorably upon the application, and that it should be referred to them. The Court, when it met, acted favorably, so far as to give the Colonel, who was tried first, fifteen minutes to hunt a lawyer. But they wouldn't let the Lieut.-Colonel act, as he was a party, and several others were excluded on the ground of being witnesses, although they took good care not to call them. Both pleaded guilty to the 'simple disobedience of orders,' and the Court was ashamed to try them upon anything besides but the 'disrespectful conduct;' in regard to which old Pigey's assertions were taken, instead of the circumstances being proved. The Colonel was too indignant at the treatment to set up any defense, but the Lieutenant-Colonel cross-examined old Pigey until his testimony looked like a box of fish-bait. The General swore that he had given him 'the lie,' but upon being questioned by the Colonel, stated that 'he did not believe the Colonel intended to call his personal veracity into

_____

(3)     Maj. Gen. George G. Meade was now commander of the Fifth Corps.

question.' In the same manner he had to explain away that duelling
charge. At last he got so confused that he would ram wood into the stove
to gain time, bite the ends of his moustache, play with the rim of his
hat, and when cornered as to the Lieutenant-Colonel's character as an
officer, to relieve himself, stated;—that he must say that the Colonel
had hitherto obeyed every order with cheerfulness, promptitude, great
zeal and intelligence, and that his intercourse with the Commanding
General had been marked by great courtesy at all times.

"The Colonel also stated further, that he had testimony to contradict
that Adjutant, or Wharf-Rat, as you know him best by. He had told me
before the trial to tell that young law student, Tom, a private of Co. C,[4]
who heard the conversation that the Adjutant had testified to, to be
within calling distance during the trial, with his belt on, hair combed,
and looking as neat as possible. Well, in Tom came, his face and eyes
swelled up from a bad cold, a stocking that had been a stranger to soap
and water for one long march at least, tied about his neck to cure a sore
throat, his belt on properly, but his blouse pockets stuffed out beyond
it with six months' correspondence, and his matted and bleached head
of hair, through the vain effort to comb it, resembling the heads of Fee-
jee Islanders, in Sunday-school books. A smile played around the lips
of the gentlemanly old Massachusetts Colonel,[5] who presided over the
Court, as he surveyed him upon entering, and a titter ran around the
Board, especially among some of the young West-Pointers. The Colonel's face colored, and the Judge Advocate's eyes glowed as if he had
a soft block. But Tom was a singed cat; he always was a slovenly fellow,
you know, and he turned out to be a file for the viper.

" 'Colonel,' said the Judge Advocate haughtily, 'have you any
officers who are prepared to vouch for the character and credibility of
this witness, as I see he is but a private?'

" 'Yes, sir, if the Court please,' retorted the Colonel indignantly,
—then remembering how this same Judge Advocate had upon former

---

(4)     The private who contradicted Tayman was Howard R. Hetrick, Company D.
(5)     Brig. Gen. James Barnes, Eighteenth Massachusetts.

occasions affected to despise privates, he added: 'His character and credibility are quite as good as those of half the shoulder-strapped gentry of the Corps.'

" 'Colonel,' said the President, blandly, 'there is an old rule requiring privates to be vouched for, rarely insisted upon, at this day, however,' casting, as he said this, a half reproachful look upon the Judge Advocate; 'but we desire you to understand that your word is as good as that of any officer before this Court.'

"The Colonel vouched for him, and Tom was examined, and contradicted still further than his own cross-examination had done, the statement of the Adjutant, besides snubbing the Judge Advocate handsomely. A string of witnesses, from our Brigadier down to all the line officers of the command, was then offered to prove character, but the Court very formally told the Colonel that a superior officer, the Commanding General of the Division, had already testified to this, and that this rendered the testimony of officers inferior in rank quite superfluous. So you see from this and Tom's case, Justice don't go it blind in Courts-Martial, but keeps one eye open to see whether the witness has shoulder-straps on or not."

"But, Bill," inquired a lawyer in the crowd, "did not the Colonel offer to prove that the Regiment was amply supplied with clothing, and that the order was unreasonable, and that it was not therefore a lawful order, as the law is supposed to be founded upon reason?"

"Oh, yes, both did; but the Lieutenant-Colonel was told by the President, that if General Burnside were to order the President to make a requisition in dog-days for old Spartan metal helmets for his Regiment, he would make the requisition.

"Said the Colonel, 'the President of the United States is by the Regulations empowered to prescribe the uniform.'

" 'That,' said the President, 'General Burnside must judge of. I must execute the order, however unreasonable it may seem, first, and question it afterwards.'

" 'Suppose the General would order you to black his boots; or' said the Colonel, thinking that a little too strongly put; 'suppose that you were second in command of a battery lying near a peaceful and loyal town, and your superior, drunk or otherwise, would order you to shell

it, would you obey the order, and question it after having murdered half
the women and children of the place?' To which questions, however,
the Court gave the go-by, remarking simply, that they did not suppose
that the Colonel had any criminal intentions in disobeying the order.
So, really, it is narrowed down to the disobedience of, to say the least,
a most uncalled for order."

"And faithful, well intentioned officers are, for what is at most but
an honest blunder, treated like felons," said one.

"From their lively and confident manner," said Bill, "I believe that
they have assurances from Washington that all will be right. There is
no telling how long the Lieutenant-Colonel will last under this confinement, however. He has failed greatly, and although so weak as to be
unable to walk alone, the General insists upon the guards being upon
either side whenever he has occasion to leave the tent. Even the sinks
were dug at over one hundred yards distance from the Sibley. And the
tent itself is located in such a manner that old Pigey can at all times
have his vengeance gratified by a full view of it, the three guards about
it, and my assisting the Lieutenant-Colonel from time to time. But the
guards esteem, and we all esteem the officers inside the Sibley more
than the General, who abuses his power in his marquee. Letters and
newspapers come crawling under the canvas. Roast partridges, squir-
rels, apples, and delicacies that officers and men deny themselves of,
find their way inside, and while my name is Bill Gladdon they shan't
suffer through any lack upon my part, and I know that this is the opinion
of all of us."

"You all recollect the Sibley," said a Lieutenant, "that stands in the
rear of old Pigey's marquee, in which he gave the collation after the
last corps review, and welcomed our officers as he steadied himself at
the table, with 'Here comes my gallant 210th.' The Court met in that."

"Yes," resumed Bill, "the same. It stands near his cook tent, and while
his darkies were serving up French cookery, the Judge Advocate did
the work allotted him in endeavoring to justify by the trial, in some
slight manner, the General's outrageous conduct. I heard that Tom said,
that after the Judge Advocate had asked that he be vouched for, and the
Colonel became indignant, the Judge Advocate said somewhat blandly,

" 'You must remember, Colonel, that this is not one of your ordinary Courts of Justice.'

" 'That it is not a Court of Justice,' retorted the Colonel, 'is very apparent.'

"Both were put through in a hurry, at any rate. The different members of the Court said that they all had marching orders, and they had no sooner left the Sibley than they were upon horseback and on the gallop towards their different commands. Our Doctor had detailed an ambulance to take the Colonels in the rear of the Division. Old Pigey, in his usual morning survey of the premises, saw it in front of the Sibley, and sent an Orderly to take the rather lively, good-looking bays that were in it and exchange them for the old rips that haul the ambulance his cooks ride in. But we did not move then, although they say we will certainly tomorrow."

That inevitable "they say," the common prefix to rumors in camp as well as civil life, had given Bill correct information. For next morning, in spite of the lowering sky, the camps were all astir with busy life, and during the course of the forenoon column after column trudged along over the already soft roads in a south-westerly direction. The movement was the mad desperation of a Commander of undaunted energy. A vain effort to appease that most capricious of masters, popular clamor. The rains descended, and that grand army of the Potomac literally floundered in the mud.[6]

In an old field, thickly grown with young pines, very near the farthest point reached in the march, our Regiment rested towards the close of the last day of the advance, or to speak more truly, attempted advance. Fatigued with the double duty of struggling with the mud and corduroying the roads, the repose was heartily welcome.

"It does a fellow good to feel a little frisky,"

---

(6)    The infamous Mud March began around January 20, 1863.

sang, or rather shouted, a little Corporal, whom we have met before in these pages, as he made ridiculous efforts to infuse life into heels clodded with mud.

"Talk as you please about old Pigey, boys, he's a regular trump on the whiskey question. He'll cut red-tape any day on that. Don't you see the boys?" continued the Corporal, addressing a crowd reposing at full length upon the freshly cut pine boughs, conspicuous among whom was the Adjutant;—pointing as he spoke to several men in uniform, but boys in years, who were being forced and dragged along by successive groups of their comrades.

"Couldn't stand the Commissary—stomachs too tender. Ha! ha! Pigey and myself are in on that."

"What is up now, Corporal?" queried the Adjutant.

"Nothing is up; it's all down," retorted the Corporal, in a half serious air, as he saluted the Colonel respectfully. "You see, Adjutant, they are bits of boys at any rate, just from school, and the Commissary was too much for their empty stomachs. I was sent back to hurry up the stragglers, and while we were catching up as rapidly as possible, old Pigey came ploughing up the mud alongside of us, followed by that sucker-mouthed Aide. I saw at once that Division Head-quarters had a good load on. With a patronizing grin, said the General stopping short alongside of a wagon belonging to another corps, and that was fast almost up to the wagon-bed, while the mules were fairly floating, 'What's in that wagon?' and without waiting for answer, 'whiskey, by G—d,' he broke out, snuffing at the same time towards the wagon. 'Boys, unload a couple of barrels,' he continued, good-humoredly, as if trying to make up for the outrage he has just committed upon the Regiment. The driver protested, and the wagon guards said that it could not be taken without an order; but it was after three, and old Pigey ripped and swore that his order was as good as anybody's, and the guards were frightened enough to let our boys roll out two barrels. No pigeon-holing on a whiskey scent! One barrel he ordered up to his head-quarters, and the head of the other was knocked in, and he told us to drink our fill, and at it the boys went. Tin cups, canteens, cap-covers, anything that would hold the article, were made use of, and they are a blue old crowd, from the General down. The boys had had nothing but a few hardtack during the day, and it was about the first drink to some, and from the way it tastes it must have been made out of rotten corn and not two months old, and altogether straggling increased considerably."

"Straggling! why they are wallowing like hogs in the mud, Adjutant! It is a shame, and if some one of my superiors will not prefer charges against the General and his Adjutant, I will. Men of mine are drunk that I never knew to taste a drop before," indignantly exclaimed the Western Virginia Captain, as, with hat off, face aglow with perspiration, eyes flashing, and boots that indicated service in taking the soundings of the mud on the march, he came panting up with rapid strides. "Now, sir, fourteen of my best men are drunk—the first drunken man I have had during the campaign—and I'll be shot to death with musketry sooner than punish a single man of them."

"But discipline must be kept up," said the Adjutant.

"Discipline! do you say, Adjutant?" retorted the Captain. "If you want to see discipline go to Division Head-quarters. Why old Pigey is prancing around like a steed at a muster,—crazy! absolutely crazy! His cocked hat is more crooked than ever, and the knot of his muffler is at the back of his neck, and the ends flying like wings. Just a few minutes ago he stopped suddenly while on a canter, right by one of my men, lying along the roadside, that he had made drunk, and chuckled and laughed, and lolled from side to side in his saddle, and then at a canter again rode to another one and went through the same performance. And his Adjutant-General—why one of my men not ten minutes ago led his horse to Head-quarters. He was so drunk, actually, that his eyes looked like those of a shad out of water a day,—his feet out of the stirrups, the reins loose about his horse's neck, his hands hanging listlessly down, and the liquor oozing out of the corners of his sucker mouth. And there he was, his horse carrying him about at random among the stumps, and officers and men laughing at him, expecting to see him go over on the one side or the other every moment. Now, it is a burning shame. And I, for one, will expose them, if it takes the hide off. Here are our Colonels confined just for no offense at all,—for doing their duty, in fact,—and this man, after having Court-martialed all that he could of his command, trying to demoralize the rest by whiskey. Now, sir, the higher the rank the more severe the punishment should be. Just before we started Burney had an order read that we were about to meet the enemy, and that every man must do his duty. And here is a General of Division, in command of nine thousand men, as drunk as a fool."

"Let Pigey alone on the whiskey question, Captain," interrupted the Corporal, who had in the meantime been refreshing his inner man by a pull at his canteen. "He's a regular trump—yes," slapping his canteen as he spoke, "a full hand of trumps any time on that topic. Like other men, he drinks to drown his grief at our poor prospect of a fight."

"A fine condition he is in to lead men into a fight;—but not much worse than at Fredericksburg," slowly observed the Preacher Lieutenant, who, as one of the crowd, had been a listener to the story of the Captain. "Drunkenness has cursed our army too much. But we cannot consistently be silent in sight of conduct like this on the part of Commanders. The interests of our men"—

"Have a care, Lieutenant," quietly observed the Adjutant, "how you talk. 'The interests of the men' have not placed our Colonels under guard in the Sibley."

"Not bolts, nor bars a prison make," resumed the Preacher more spiritedly, "and I would sooner have a quiet conscience in confinement, than the reproach of disgraceful conduct and command a Division."

Corduroying the entire route had not been proposed, when the army commenced its movement; but it became apparent to all that progress was only tolerable with it, and without it, impossible. On the day after the above conversation, the army commenced to retrace its steps. Some days, however, intervened before the smoke ascended from their old huts, and the men in lazy circles about the camp fires rehashed their recollections of the "mud march."

Like our repulse at Fredericksburg, it was, as far as our Commander-in-Chief was concerned, a misfortune and not a fault. A change in command was evident, however, and the substitution of the whole-hearted, dashing Hooker for the equally earnest but more steady Burnside, that took place in the latter part of January, occasioned no surprise in the army. The new Commander went much farther, than old attachments had probably permitted his predecessor in going, in removing McClellanism. Grand Divisions were abolished; rigid inquiries into the comforts and conveniences of the men were frequent, and senseless reviews less frequent. Bakeries were established in every Brigade, and fresh bread and hot rolls furnished in wholesome abundance, to the great benefit of the Government, for hospital rolls were thereby depleted, and reports for duty increased. Rigid discipline and daily drills too were kept up, as "Old Joe" was a frequent visitor, when least expected. His constant solicitude for the welfare of the men, manifested by close personal attention, which the men themselves were witness to, rather than by concocted newspaper reports, by which the friends of the soldier in their loyal homes might be imposed upon, and the soldier himself not benefited, endeared him to his entire command.

One clear, cold morning, during these palmy days of the army, the men of the regiment nearest the Surgeon's Quarters were greatly surprised by the sudden exit of a small-sized sheet iron stove from the tent occupied by the Surgeon and Chaplain, closely followed up by the little Dutch Doctor in his shirt sleeves, sputtering hurriedly—

"Tam schmoke pox!" and at every ejaculation bestowing a vigorous kick. At a reasonably safe distance in his rear was the Chaplain, in half undress also, remonstrating as coolly as possible,—considering that the stove was his property. The Doctor did not refrain, however, until its badly battered fragments lay at intervals upon the ground.

"Efry morn, and efry morn, schmoke shust as the Tuyfel. I no need prepare for next world py that tam schmoke pox. Eh?" continued the Doctor, facing the Chaplain.

"Come, Doctor," said the Chaplain, soothingly, "we ought to get along better than this in our department."

"Shaplain's department! Eh! By G—t! One Horse-Doctor and one Shaplain enough for a whole Division!"

The sudden appearance of Bill, the attendant upon the Colonels in the Sibley, at the Adjutant's quarters, had the effect of transferring hither the crowd, who were enjoying what proved to be a final dissolution of partnership between the Chaplain and the Doctor.

"I know your errand, Bill," remarked the Adjutant, looking him full in the face. "An orderly has just handed me the General Order. But what is to become of the Lieutenant-Colonel?"

"You only have the order dismissing the Colonel, then. There was a message sent about ten o'clock last night, a little after the General Order was received at the Sibley, stating that at day-break this morning the Colonel should be escorted to Aquia under guard, and that before leaving he should have no intercourse whatever with any of his command. Old Pigey also tried further to add insult to injury, by stating that the Lieutenant-Colonel, who cannot, from weakness, walk twenty steps, even though it would save his life, would be released from close confinement, and might have the benefit of Brigade limits in our new camp ground for exercise. You know that is so full of stumps and undergrowth that a well man can hardly get along in it."

"So an officer of the Colonel's merit and services," remarked the Adjutant, "was dragged off before daylight, and disgraced for what was in its very worst light but a simple blunder, made under the most extenuating of circumstances. Boys, if there be faith in Stanton's pledged word, matters will be set right as soon as the record of the case reaches the War Department. I am informed that he denounced the whole proceeding as an outrage, and telegraphed the General; and we all know that the General has been spending a good portion of the time since the trial in Washington."

"And he came back," observed Bill, "yesterday morning, in a mood unusual with him before three o'clock in the afternoon. He had his whole staff, all his orderlies and the Provost Guard out to stop a Maine Regiment from walking by the side of the road, when the mud was over shoe top in the road itself,—and he flourished that thin sword of his, and raved and swore and danced about until one of the Maine boys wanted to know who 'that little old Cockey was with a ramrod in his hand,—' and that set the laugh so much against him that his Aides returned their pistols and he his sword, and he sneaked back to his marquee, and issued an order requiring his whole command to stand at arms along the road side upon the approach of troops from either direction."

"Which," remarked the Adjutant, "if obeyed, would keep them under arms well nigh all the time, and would provoke a collision, as it would be an insult to the troops of other commands, to whom the road should be equally free. But it is a fair sample of the judgment of Pigey."

# CHAPTER XIX.

*The Presentation Mania—The Western Virginia Captain in the War Depart-
ment—Politeness and Mr. Secretary Stanton—Capture of the Dutch Doctor—
A Genuine Newspaper Sell.*

PRESENTATIONS by men to officers should be prevented by
positive orders; not that the recipients are not usually meritorious,
but the practice by its prevalency is an unjust tax upon a class little able
to bear it. A costly sword must be presented to our Captain,—intimates
a man perhaps warmly in the Captain's confidence. Forthwith the list
is started, and with extra guard and fatigue duty before the eyes of the
men, it makes a unanimous circuit of the command. Active newspaper
reporters, from the sheer merit of the officer, may be, and may be from
the additional inducement of a little compensation, give an account of
the presentation in one of the dailies that fills the breasts of the officer's
friends with pride, while the decreased remittance of the private may
keep back some creature comfort from his wife and little ones. Statistics
showing how far these presentations are spontaneous offerings, and to
what extent results of wire-working at Head-quarters, would prove
more curious than creditable.

Our Brigade did not escape the Presentation Mania. Never did it
develop itself in a command, however, more spontaneously. The plain,
practical sense of our Brigadier was the more noticeable to the men, on
account of its marked contrast to the quibbles and conceit of the General
of Division. The officers and men of the Brigade had with great care

and cost selected a noble horse of celebrated stock upon which to mount their Brigadier, and, on a pleasant evening in March, a crowd informally assembled was busied in arranging for the morrow the programme of presentation. The General of Division, so far in the cold in the matter, was just then making himself sensibly felt.

"Colonel," said an officer, who from the direction of Brigade Head-quarters neared the crowd, addressing a central figure, "you might as well take the General's horse out to grass awhile."

"Explain yourself," say several.

"Pigey has his foot in the whole matter nicely. The General, you know, just returned this evening from sick leave. Well, he and his friends, who came with him to see the presentation ceremonies, had not been at Head-quarters an hour before that sucker-mouthed Aide made his appearance, and said that he was directed by the General Command-ing the Division to place him under arrest. The fellow was drunk, and the General hardly deigned to notice him. As he staggered away, he muttered that there were fifteen charges against him, and that he would find the General's grip a tight one."

Amid exclamations, indicating that the perplexity of the matter could not prevent a sly smile at the ludicrous position in which the Brigadier and his friends from abroad were placed, the officer continued—

"But the General brings good news from Washington. The Colonel and Lieutenant-Colonel of the 210th return at an early day."

"Yes, sir, that is so," broke in our Western Virginia Captain, who had just returned from enjoying one of the furloughs at that time so freely distributed. "At last the War Department, or rather Mr. Secretary Stan-ton, for all the balance of the department, as far as I could learn, thought the delay outrageous, fulfils its promise. After the Lieutenant-Colonel had been at home on a sick leave for some time, and we all thought the matter about dropped; what should I see one day but his name, with thirty-two others, in a daily, under the head of 'Dismissals from the Army.' There it was, dismissed for doing his duty, and published right among the names of scoundrels who had skulked five times from the battle-field; men charged with drunkenness, and every offense known to the Military Decalogue. My furlough had just come, and I started for Washington by the next boat, bound to see how the matter stood. The morning after I got there, I posted up bright and early to the War Department, but a sergeant near the door, with more polish on his boots than in his manners, told me that I had better keep shady until ten o'clock, as business hours commenced then. I sat down on a pile of old lumber near by, and passed very nearly three hours in wondering why so many broad-shouldered fellows, who could make a sabre fall as heavy as the blow of a broad-axe, were lounging about or going backward and forward upon errands that sickly boys might do as well. As it grew nearer ten, able-bodied, bright-looking officers, Regulars, as I was told, educated at Uncle Sam's expense to fight, elegantly shoulder-strapped, passed in to drive quills in a quiet department, 'remote from death's alarms,' and I wondered if some spirited clerks and schoolmasters that I knew, who would have been willing to have gone bent double under knapsacks, if the Surgeon would have accepted them, would not have performed the duty better, and have permitted the country to have the benefit of the military education of these gentlemen."

"I see, Captain, that you don't understand it," interrupted an officer. "Our Regular Officers are not all alike patriotic up to the fighting point; and it is a charitable provision that permits one, say,—who is married to a plantation of niggers, or who has other Southern sympathies or affinities, or who may have conscientious scruples about fighting against our 'Southern brethren,'—to take a snug salary in some peaceful department, or to go on recruiting service in quiet towns, where grasshoppers can be heard singing for squares, and where he is under the necessity of killing nothing but time, and wounding nothing but his country's honor and his own, if a man of that description can be said to possess any. In their offices, these half-hearted Lieutenants, Captains, and Colonels, are like satraps in their halls, unapproachable, except by passing bayonets that should be turned towards Richmond."

"Well, if I don't understand it," resumed the Captain, "it is high time that Uncle Sam understood it. If these men are half-hearted, they will write no better than they fight, and I guess if the truth could be got at, they are responsible for most of the clogging in the Commissary and Quarter-master Departments. But you've got me off my story. At ten o'clock I staved in, just as I was, my uniform shabby, and my boots with a tolerably fair representation of Aquia mud upon them. Passing from one orderly to another, I brought up at the Adjutant-General's office, and there I was referred to the head clerk's office, and there a pleasant-looking, gentlemanly Major told me that the matter would be certainly set straight as soon as the court-martial records were forwarded; that they had telegraphed for them again and again; and that at one time they were reported lost, and at another carried off by one of General Burnside's Staff Officers. As I had heard of records of the kind being delayed before, I intimated rather plainly what I thought of the matter, and told him that I wanted to see the Secretary himself. He smiled, and told me to take my place in the rear of an odd-looking mixed assemblage of persons in the hall, who were crowding towards an open door. It was after two o'clock and after I had stood until I felt devotional about the knees, when my turn brought me before the door, and showed me Mr. Secretary himself, standing behind a desk, tossing his head, now on this side and now on that, with quick jerks, like a short-horned bull in fly time, despatching business and the hopes of the parties who had it from their looks, about the same time. Right manfully did he stand up to his work; better than to his word perhaps, if reports that I have heard be true.

"A pretty-faced, middle-aged lady approached his desk, and I thought that I could see a rather awkward effort at a smile hang around the upper corners of his huge, black beard, as his eye caught her features through his spectacles, and he received her papers. But the gruff manner in which he told her the next moment that he would not grant it, showed I was mistaken.

" 'But I was told, Mr. Secretary,' said the woman, in tremulous tones, 'that my papers were all right, and that your assent was a mere formality. I have three other sons in the service, and this boy is not'—

" 'I don't care what you have been told,' retorted the Secretary, in a manner that made me so far forget my reverence that my toes suddenly felt as if disposed to propel something that, strange to say, had the semblance of humanity, and was not distant at the time. 'You had better leave the room, madam!' continued the same voice, somewhat gruffer and sterner, as the poor woman burst into tears at the sudden disappointment. 'You only interrupt and annoy. We are accustomed to this sort of thing here.'

"I looked at him as he took the papers of another for examination, and wondered whether we were really American citizens—sovereigns as our politicians tell us when on the stump, and whether he was really a public servant. But I couldn't see it.

"Now, civility is a cheap commodity, and, in my humble opinion, the least that can be expected of men filling public positions is that they should possess it in an ordinary degree.

"Three o'clock came, but it was not my turn yet. In fact, the treatment of the lady had so disgusted me, that I was quite ready to leave when a servant announced that business hours were over. That evening, I found out to my great satisfaction that men considerably more influential than myself had held the Secretary to the promises he had made them, and that notwithstanding all his backing and filling the order for their return would be issued."

The disappointment of the morrow was a standing topic in camp and on the picket line for the ensuing three weeks. The only doubt that existed with the Court convened for the trial of the Brigadier appeared to be whether the numerous charges excelled most in frivolity or malice, as a slight reprimand for writing an unofficial account of an engagement,—an offense of which several members of the Court had, by their own confession, repeatedly been guilty,—was the sole result of its labor. His restoration to command, the presentation, and the return of the Colonels followed in rapid succession amid the rejoicings of officers and men.

—Amid the waste of meadow and woodland that characterized the face of that country, the houses of the farmers, or rather, to use the grandiloquent language of the inhabitants, "the mansions of the planters," were objects of peculiar interest. In their quaint appearance and general air of dilapidation, they stood as relics of the civilization of another age. Centuries, seemingly, of important events in the law of progress are crowded into years of our campaigning. The social status of a large country semi-civilized—whether you regard the intelligence of its people or the condition of its society—is being suddenly altered. The war accomplishes what well-designing men lacked nerve and ability to execute—emancipation. The blessings of a purer civilization will follow as naturally as sunshine follows storm.

And yet here and there these old buildings would be varied by one evidently framed upon a Yankee model. Such was what was widely known in the army as "the Moncure House."[1] On a commanding site at the edge of a meadow several miles in length, and that seemed from the abrupt bluffs that bordered it to have been once the bottom of a lake, this two-story weather-board frame was readily discernible. Its location made it a prominent point, too, upon the picket line, and it was favored above its fellows by daily and nightly occupancy by officers of the command. At this period the Regiment almost lived upon the picket line. An old wench, with several chalky complexioned children, whose paternal ancestor was understood to be under a musket of English manufacture perhaps, somewhere on the south side of the Rappahannock, occupied the kitchen of the premises. She was unceasing in reminding her military co-lodgers that the room used by them as head-quarters,—from the window of which you could take in at a glance the fine expanse of valley, threaded by a sparkling tributary of the Potomac,— was massa's study, and that massa was a preacher and had written a "right smart" lot of sermons in that very place. In the eyes of Dinah the room was invested with a peculiar sanctity. Not so with its present occupants, who could not learn that the minister, who was a large slave-holder, had remembered "those in bonds as bound with them," and who were quite content that artillery proclaiming "liberty throughout the land" in tones of thunder had driven away this vender of the divinity of the institution of slavery.

In this room, on seats rudely improvised, for its proper furniture had long since disappeared, some officers not on duty were passing a pleasant April afternoon, when their reveries of other days and rehashes of old camp yarns were interrupted by the sudden advent of an officer who a week previously had been detailed in charge of a number of men to

---

(1)   From the description given here, this is possibly Glencairne, which was occupied by Richard Cassius Lee Moncure at this time. He does not appear to have been a minister. According to Jerrilyn Eby, an expert on Stafford County houses, the only houses that survived in the county were those used as hospitals or headquarters for officers.

form part of an outer picket station some distance up the river. His face indicated news, and he was at once the center of attraction.

"Colonel!" exclaimed he, without waiting to be questioned, "two of our best men have been taken prisoners, and the little Dutch Doctor—"

"What has happened to him?" from several at once.

"Was taken prisoner and released, but had his horse stolen."

His hearers breathed freer when they heard of the personal safety of the Doctor, and the officer continued—

"And the loss of our men and his horse has all happened through the carelessness,—to treat it mildly,—of the exhorting Colonel. He is in command of the station, and yesterday afternoon the Doctor was on duty at his head-quarters. In came one of the black-eyed beauties that live in a house near the ford, about half a mile from the station, boo-hooing at a terrible rate—that the youngest rebel of her family was dying with the croup—and that no doctor was near—and all that old story. The Colonel was fool enough to order the Doctor to mount his horse and go with the woman. Well, the Doctor had got near the house, when out sprang two Mississippi Riflemen from the pines on either side of the road and levelled their pieces at him. The Doctor had to dismount, and they sent him back on foot. Luckily the Colonel, who, as black Charley says, has been praying for a star for some time past, had borrowed the Doctor's dress sword on the pretence that it was lighter to carry, but on the ground, really, that it looked more Brigadier-like, or he would have lost that too. I was on duty down by the river hardly two hours after it happened, and as there is no firing now along the picket line the soldiers were free-and-easy on both sides. All at once I heard laughter on the other side, and looking over, I saw a short, thick-set Grey-back riding the stolen horse near the water's edge. Presently two other Grey-backs sprang on either side of the horse's head, and with pieces levelled, in tones loud enough for us to hear, demanded his surrender.

" 'Why, shentlemen Rebels, mein Gott, you no take non compatants, me surgeon,' said the Grey-back on the horse, in equally loud voice.

" 'No, d—n you! Dismount! We don't want you. You can be of more service to the Confederate cause where you are. But we must have the nag.'

" 'Mine private property,' he replied, as he dismounted.

" 'In a horn,' said one of the Grey-backs, pointing to the U.S. on the shoulder of the beast. 'That your private mark, eh?'

" 'You no shentlemen. By G—t, no honor,' retorted the Grey-back who personated the Doctor, as he swelled himself and strutted about on the sand in such a high style of indignation as to draw roars of laughter from both sides of the river.

"That rather paid us with interest for the way we sold them the day before. You know they have been crazy after our dailies ever since the strict general order preventing the exchange of the daily papers between pickets. Well, that dare-devil of a law student, Tom, determined to have some fun with them. So when they again, as they often had before, came to the river with hands full of Richmond papers, proposing exchange, Tom flourished a paper also. That was the old signal, and forthwith a raw-boned Alabamian stripped and commenced wading toward a rock that jutted up in the middle of the river. Tom stripped also, and met him at the rock. Mum was the word between them, and each turned for his own shore, the Grey-back with Tom's paper, and Tom with several of the latest Richmond prints. A crowd of Rebel officers met their messenger at the water's edge and received the paper. The one who opened it, bent nearly double with laughter, and the rest rapidly followed as their eyes lit on the stars and stripes printed in glowing colors on the first page of the little religious paper that our Chaplains distribute so freely in camp, called 'The Christian Banner.' One old officer, apparently of higher rank than the rest, cursed it as he went up the bank as a 'd—d Yankee sell,—' which did not in the least lessen our enjoyment of Tom's success.

"But with our two men and the Doctor's horse they have squared accounts with us since, and all through the fault of the Colonel."

In response to inquiries as to how, when, and where, the officer continued—

"There was a narrow strip of open land between a belt of woods and the river. The Colonel posted our two men on the inside of the woods, where they had no open view towards the enemy at all. That rainy night this week the Rebs came over in boats and gobbled them up.[2] The Colonel attributed their loss to their own neglect, and next morning their place was supplied by four old soldiers, as he called them, from his own Regiment. That same day at noon, in broad day-light, they were taken."

"And if he were not a firm friend at Division Head-quarters there would be a dismissal from the service for cause," said an officer of the crowd.

"Our Corps Commander is too much of a soldier to let it go by," resumed the officer, "if our Brigadier can force it through Division Head-quarters, and bring it to his notice."

The order that introduced into the service the novelty of carrying eight days' rations on a march, had been discussed for some time in the Regiment. That night the Regiment was withdrawn from the picket line, and preparations were forthwith made for a practical illustration of the order on the morrow.

---

(2)    The two captured privates, Amos E. Ehler and James Weaver, were taken at either Kelly's or the U.S. Mine Ford.

# CHAPTER XX.

*The Army again on the Move—Pack Mules and Wagon Trains—A Negro Prophetess—The Wilderness—Hooped Skirts and Black Jack—The Five Days' Fight at Chancellorsville—Terrible Death of an Aged Slave—A Pigeon-hole General's "Power in Reserve."*

IT was some weeks after a Rebel Picket, opposite Falmouth, had surprised one of our own, who had not as yet heard of the change in the usual three days' provender for a march, by asking him across the river "whether his eight days' rations were mouldy yet?" that the army actually commenced its movement. While awaiting the word to fall in, this mass of humanity literally loaded with army bread and ammunition resembled, save in uniformity, those unfortunate beings burdened with bundles of woe, so strikingly portrayed in the Vision of Mirza. To the credit of the men, it must be stated, however, that the greatest good-humor prevailed in this effort to render the army self-sustaining in a country that could not sustain itself.

Another novel feature in the movement was the long strings of pack mules, heavily freighted with ammunition, which were led in the rear of the different Brigades. Wagon trains were thereby dispensed with, and the mobility of the army greatly increased. Stringent orders were issued also as to the reduction of baggage, and dispensing with camp equipage and cooking utensils.

In lively ranks, although each man was freighted with the prescribed eight days' provender and sixty rounds of ball cartridge, our Division, of almost 9,000 men,[1] moved, followed by two ambulances to pick up those who might fall by the way, in the rear of which were five additional ambulances for the especial use of Division Head-quarters. For a General of whom reporters had said that "he was most at home in the field," the supply of ambulances, full of creature comforts, was unusually heavy. On we moved over the familiar ground of the Warrenton Pike, in common with several other Army Corps in a grand march; our Division, with its two ambulances; our General with his five,—and our proportionate number of pack horses and mules. The obstinacy of the latter animal was sorely punished by the apparent effort during that march to teach it perpetual motion. Halt the Division did statedly, but there was no rest for the poor mule. Experience had taught its driver that the beast would take advantage of the halt to lie down, and when once down no amount of tugging and swearing and clubbing could induce it to rise. Hence, while the command would enjoy their stated halts by the wayside, these strings of mules would be led or driven in continuous circles of steady toil. Despite the vigilance of their drivers, a mule would occasionally drop, and his companions speedily follow, to stand a siege of kicks, cuffs, and bayonet pricks, and to be reduced, or what would be more appropriate in their case, raised at length by the application of a mud plaster to the nostrils, which would bring the beast up in an effort to breathe freely; from which may arise the slang phrase of "bringing it up a snorting."

Onward they marched, those wearers of the cross, the square, the circle, the crescent, the star, the lozenge, and the tripod;[2] emblemed representatives of the interest of a common humanity in the triumphal march that the world is witness to, of the progress of Universal Emancipation. Landed aristocracies of the Old World may avow their affinity to the aristocracy of human flesh and blood that has so long cursed the

---

(1)   The division had fewer than thirty-seven hundred men in its two brigades (against seven thousand at formation) when it began its move toward Kelly's Ford on April 27.

(2)   General Hooker had authorized insignia for his various corps. The Fifth Corps wore the Maltese cross.

New; but now that the suicidal hand of the latter has caused the forfeit of its existence, we are the center of the hopes, fears, and prayers of the universal brotherhood of man in the effort to blot out for ever the only foul spot upon our national escutcheon.

"De Lor bress ye. I know yez all. Yez, Uncle Samuel's children. Long looked for come at las," said an old wench on the second day of our march, enthusiastically to the advanced ranks of our Division, as they wound around the hill in sight of Mt. Holly Church, on the main road to Kelly's Ford, curtseying and gesturing all the while with her right hand, as if offering welcome, while with her left she steadied on her head the cast-away cover of a Dutch oven. A pair of half-worn army shoes covered her feet, and the folds of her tow gown were compressed about the waist, beneath a black leathern belt, the brass plate of which bearing the letters "U.S.," wore a conspicuous polish.

"Massa over yonder," continued she, in response to a query from the ranks, pointing as she spoke across the river. "Hope you cotch him. Golly he'um slyer than a possum in a hen-roost."

The anxiety of the wench for the capture of her master, and her statement of a pre-knowledge of the visit of the troops, were by no means exceptional. Rarely indeed, in the history of the Rebellion, has devotion on the part of the slave to the interest of the master been discovered. The vaunted fealty that would make his cause their own, lacks practical illustration. An attempt to arm them will save recruits and arms to Uncle Sam. Nat Turner's insurrection developed their strong faith in a day of freedom. Their wildest dreams of fancy could not have pictured a more auspicious prelude to the realization of that faith than the outbreak of the Rebellion. Well might

> "Massa tink it day ob doom,
> But we ob Jubilee."

The face of the country at this point was adorned by the most beautiful variety of hill and dale. Compared with the region about Aquia, it had been but little touched by the ravages of war. When it shall have been wholly reclaimed under a banner, then to be emphatically "the Banner of the Free," an inviting door will open to enterprising business.

A few miles further on we rested on our arms upon the summit of a ridge overlooking that portion of the Upper Rappahannock known as Kelly's Ford. The brilliant cavalry engagement of a few weeks previously, that occurred upon the level ground in full view above the Ford, invested it with peculiar interest.[3] Who ever saw a dead cavalryman? was a question that had been for a long time uttered as a standing joke. Hooker's advent to command was attended by a sharp and stirring order that speedily brought this arm of the service to a proper sense of duty. Among the first fruits of the order was this creditable fight. While no excuse can be given for the slovenly and ungainly riding, rusty sabres, and dirty accoutrements, raw-boned and uncurried horses that had too often made many of our cavalry regiments appear like a body of Sancho Panzas[4] thrown loosely together; it would still be exceedingly unfair to have required as much of them as of the educated horsemen and superior horse-flesh that gave the Rebel cavalry their efficiency in the early stages of the war. Since then the scales have turned. Frequent successful raids and resistless charges have given the courage, skill, and dash of our Gregg, Buford, Kilpatrick, Grierson, and others that might be named, honorable mention at every loyal fireside.

While on the top of this ridge, Rush's regiment of lancers, with lances in rest and pennons gaily fluttering beneath the spear heads, cantered past the regiment.[5] Their strange equipment gave an oriental appearance to the columns moving toward the ford. With straining eyes we followed their movement up the river and junction with the cavalry then crossing at a ford above the pontoons.[6] The Regiment had been almost continually broken up for detached service, at different head-quarters,

---

(3)    The engagement at Kelly's Ford had been fought on March 17, 1863.

(4)    Sancho Panza was Don Quixote's sidekick, an unimpressive cavalryman who rode a mule.

(5)    The Fifth Pennsylvania Cavalry. General Meade called the lances "turkey driving implements."

(6)    Kelly's Ford on the Rappahannock.

or for the purpose of halting stragglers. With many of the men, their service appeared like their equipment, ornamental rather than useful, and in connection with their foraging reputation, won for them the expressive designation of "Pig Stickers."

Darkness was just setting in when our turn came upon the pontoon bridge, and it was quite dark when we prepared ourselves, in a pelting rain, for rest for the night, as we thought, in a meadow half a mile distant from the road. At midnight, in mud and rain, we resumed the march, in convoy of a pontoon train, and over a by-road which from the manner its primitive rock was revealed, must have been unused for years. The streams forded during that night of sleepless toil, the enjoined silence, broken only by the sloppy shuffle of shoes half filled with water, and the creaking wagons, the provoking halts that would tempt the eyes to a slumber that would be broken immediately by the resumption of the forward movement, have left ineffaceable memories. A somewhat pedantic order of "Accelerate the speed of your command, Colonel," given by our General of Division, as the head of the Regiment neared his presence towards morning, reminded us of the "long and rapid march" that the Commander-in-Chief intended the army to make.

On the last day of April we crossed the Rapidan, fording its breast-deep current,[7] considered too strong for the pontoons, and wondering, especially as the cannonading of the evening previous indicated resistance ahead, that our advance was not at this point impeded. Artillery planted upon the circling hills of the opposite shore would have made the passage, if even practicable, perilous to the last degree. As it was, however, *in puris naturalibus*, with cartridge-box on the musket barrel, and the musket on the shoulder, clothing in many instances bundled upon the head, the troops made the passage. The whys and the wherefores of no opposition—the confidence of Old Joe having stolen a march upon Johnny Reb—and the usual surmises of the morrow—increased in this instance by our having surprised and captured some Rebel

---

(7)    Ely's Ford on the Rapidan.

pickets when just about halting, constituted ample capital for conversation during our night's rest in a pine grove two miles south of the ford.

With the Army of the Potomac the merry month of May had a lively opening. After a march from early dawn, we found our Division, about the middle of the forenoon, massed in a thick wood in the rear of a large and imposing brick building, which, with one or two buildings of minor importance, constituted what was designated upon our pocket maps as the town of Chancellorsville. The region of country was most appropriately styled "The Wilderness." A wilderness indeed, of tall oaks, and a dense undergrowth known as "black-jack." There were but few open places or improved spots. In one of the largest of these, at a point where two prominent roads forked,[8] stood the large building above mentioned. The day previous General Lee and his staff had been hospitably entertained within its walls. Now our fine-looking Commander and his gay and gallant staff were busily engaged in its lower rooms, while the ladies of the house of Secesh sympathies kept themselves closely in the upper story,—their curiosity tempting them however, to occasional peeps from half-opened shutters at the blue coats below.

At twelve, precisely, just as we had taken a position in the open ground abreast of the house, the sharp report of a rifled piece, followed quickly by the fainter explosion of a shell, was heard upon our left. Another and another succeeded,—indicating that the wood was being shelled preparatory to an advance in that direction. Slowly we filed to the left, proceeding by a narrow winding wood-road until the head of our column had almost reached the river.[9] A sudden order at this stage for the right about created considerable surprise, which ceased shortly after, as the sharp rattle of musketry, now as if picket firing, and now swelling into a volleyed roar, told us of a Rebel movement upon our flank. That our advance upon them in that direction had been quite unexpected, was apparent from their hastily abandoned camp grounds; rows of tents left standing, but slit from ridge-pole to pins; abandoned

---

(8)    The Orange-Fredericksburg Turnpike and Plank Road.

(9)    River Road toward Banks's Ford.

caissons and ammunition; and the tubs in which their rations of flour were kneaded, with undried dough in the corners. That they had rallied to regain their lost ground, was also apparent.

"What's the matter, Dinah?" shouted one of our boys to an active young wench, who was wending her way from the direction of the firing as rapidly as the frequent contact of an extensive hooped skirt with the undergrowth would allow.

"Dunno zackly, massa! Don't like de racket at all down yonder," she replied, making at the same time vigorous efforts to release the hold some bushes appeared to have upon her, upon either side. A sudden roar of artillery, apparently nearer by, brought matters to a crisis, and screaming "Oh, Lor," she loosened her clothing, and sprang out of the skirt with a celerity that showed the perfection of muscular development, and won shouts of applause from the ranks.

A sharp engagement was in progress upon a lower and almost parallel road.[10] The roar of cannon, the explosion of shells, the rattle of musketry,—now ragged as if from detached squads,—and now volleyed as from full ranks, mingled with the shrill cheers or rather demoniac yells of the Rebels, pealing their banner cry of "Hell," in their successive charges, and the gruff hoarse shouts of our troops, as they duly repulsed them, formed a most martial accompaniment to our march. The unity of sound of well executed volleys, told us how Sykes's Regulars attacked, whilst marching by the flank, halted at the word, faced to the left with the precision of an ordinary drill, and delivered their fire with murderous exactness.

A few stray bullets flying in the direction of a temporized corral of pack-horses in a corner of the wood in the rear of the brick house, frightened their cowardly drivers, who commenced a stampede to the rear; and as we emerged from the road to our old position, the beasts were rapidly divesting themselves of their packs, in their progress through the undergrowth. In conjunction with this the frequent and

---

(10)    Orange Plank Road.

fierce charges of the Rebel massed columns, favored by the smoke of the burning woods, made a panic imminent among the troops upon the lower road. The quick eye of old Joe saw the danger in a moment, and rushing from the house and springing upon his horse, he dashed down that road unattended, his manly form the mark of many a rebel rifle. Shouts of applause greeted him, and the continuous rattle of our musketry told us of the regained confidence of the men, and the renewed steadiness of our line.

It was now four in the afternoon—the usual time with the Rebels for the execution of their favorite movement—charging in massed columns. On they came in their successive charges, howling like fiends, and with a courage that would have adorned an honorable cause. The steady musketry, but above all the terrific showers of canister from cannon that thundered in doublets from right to left along the line of our batteries, could not be withstood, and they fell back in confusion. The nature of the ground did not permit an advance of our forces, and we were compelled to rest content with their repulse. An hour later our Division moved by still another road to the left, to a ridge in the neighborhood of Banks's Ford.[11] Upon its wooded summit, with no sound to break in upon us save the screaming of whip-poor-wills, which the boys with ready augury construed to mean "whip-'em-well," and picket firing, that would occasionally appear to run along the line, we passed a comfortable night.

Breastworks were the order of the day following, and at noon we were enjoying our coffee in a cleared space, behind a ridge of logs and limbs that fronted our entire Division, and which we would have been content to hold against any attacking force. Cannonading continued at intervals, with occasional musketry firing. As it was considerably to our right, we were not disturbed in our enjoyment of supplies of provisions obtained from vacated Rebel houses in the neighborhood. Our amusement was greatly contributed to, by the sight of some of the

---

(11)   Humphreys's division moved up Mineral Springs Road toward the U.S. Mine (not Banks's) Ford.

men dressed in odd clothing of a by-gone fashionable age. But perhaps the most interesting object was a Text-book upon the Divinity of Slavery, written by a Reverend Doctor Smith, for the use of schools; its marked lessons and dirty dog-ears shewing that it had troubled the brains and thumbs of youthful Rebels. Instilled into infant minds, and preached from their pulpits, we need not wonder that they, with the heartless metaphysics of northern sympathy; should consider slavery "an incalculable blessing," and should now be in arms to vindicate their treason, its legitimate offspring.

Cannonading had been frequent during the day; its heavy booming at times varied by the light rattle of the rifle. From four until eleven P.M. it was a continuous roar, save about an hour's intermission between five and six. At first sounding sullenly away to the right, then gradually nearing, until at nightfall musketry and artillery appeared to volley spitefully almost upon our Division limits. It was apparent that our line had been broken, and apprehending the worst we anxiously stood at arms and awaited the onward.[12] Nearer and nearer the howling devils came; louder and louder grew the sounds of conflict. The fiercest of fights was raging evidently in the very center of the ground chosen as our stronghold. If ever the Army of the Potomac was to be demoralized by the shock of battle, that was the time. But the feeling was not one of fear with our citizen soldiery—the noblest type of manhood—rather of eagerness for the troops in reserve to be called into the contest. Just before six we heard an honest shout, as the boys would call the cheers of their comrades. It grew fainter; the firing became more distant— slackened and ceased at six, to be resumed again at seven, upon another and more remote line of attack.

The terrible distinctness of this alternate howling and cheering—as perceptible to the ear during the thunders of the fight, as the silver lining that not unfrequently fringes the heavily-charged cloud is to the eye,— is a striking illustration of the power of the human voice. We were to

---

(12)    Stonewall Jackson had marched around the Union army and routed the
        Eleventh Corps in the late afternoon of May 2.

have another, however, and that of but a single voice, which from the agony of soul thrown into it, and its almost supernatural surroundings, must eternally echo in memory.

About three hundred yards distant from the left of our Brigade line, in an open field, on elevated ground, stood a large and comfortable looking farmhouse. In the morning it had been occupied; but as its inmates saw our skirmishers prostrating themselves on the one side in double lines that ran parallel to our breastworks, and the Rebel advance at the same time attain the edge of the wood upon the opposite side,—and the skirmishing that occasionally occurred along the lines giving promise of a fight that might center upon their premises,—they packed up a few valuables and left for a place of safety. But not all. We read of noble Romans offering their lives in defense of faithful slaves. That species of self-sacrifice is a stranger to our Southern chivalry. In the garret of the building, upon some rags, lay an old woman, who had been crippled from injuries received by being scalded some months before, and had thus closed a term of faithful service which ran over fifty years, of the life of her present master and of that of his father before him. Worn out, and useless for further toil, she had been placed in the garret with other household rubbish. Her poor body crippled,—but a casket, nevertheless, of an immortal soul,—was not one of the valuables taken by the family upon their departure. As the thunders of the thickening fight broke in upon her loneliness, her cries upon the God of battles, alone powerful to save, could be heard with great distinctness. Isolated and under the fire of either line, there was no room for human relief. Her strength of voice appeared to grow with the increasing darkness, and above the continuous thunder of the cannon were the cries—"God Almighty, help me!" "Lord, save me!" "Have mercy on me!" shrieked and groaned in all the varied tones of mortal agony. Long after the firing had ceased, in fact until we moved at early dawn, our men behind the works and in the rifle pits in front could hear with greater or less distinctness, as if a death wail coming up from the carnage of the field, the piteous plaints of that terror-stricken soul. Rumor has it, that before the building was fired by a shell in the middle of the following forenoon, her spirit had taken its flight; but whether or not, it could not mitigate the retributive justice to be measured out by that God over us all to whom vengeance belongs, upon the heads of the ingrates who had left her to her fate.

We moved, as we have before mentioned, at early dawn on one of those fair, bright Sabbath days[13] so happily spoken of by "good old George Herbert"; marching by the right flank along our works, with a hurried step. It was between five and six when we neared the front,— passing on our way out, hosts of stragglers and disorganized regiments of the Eleventh Corps. They had suffered badly—some said, behaved badly—and some said, posted in such a way that they could not but behave badly. The merits of the case must remain for decisive history. Conceding equally good generalship to both, it is not amiss to say, that what happened under Howard might not have happened under Sigel.[14] The desultory firing along our changed front showed too plainly the ground we had lost the day before. In the wood, alongside of the road fronting the right center of our line, our Regiment lay at arms,—listening to awfully exaggerated stories from stragglers,—watching the posting of artillery in our immediate front, the entry of Brigades into the wood upon our left, and their exit under skilful artillery practice,— and now and then dodging at the sound of the stray shells sent as return compliments from Rebel batteries.

"Good-bye, Colonel; these brass-bull pups will roar bloody murder at Johnny Reb today," said a fine looking, whole-souled Lieutenant, in command of an Ohio battery, pointing to his pieces with pride, as he hurried by at a trot, to relieve a battery on our left center.

Poor fellow! How blind we are to futurity! His pieces were scarcely in position before a shell struck the caisson at which he was adjusting fuses, and his head, picked up at the distance of a hundred yards, was all that remained unshattered of his manly figure, after the explosion.

Files of wounded upon foot, full ambulances, and stretchers laden with the more serious cases, passed us here.

---

(13)    May 3, 1863.

(14)    The predominantly German-American Eleventh Corps was led by Maj. Gen. O. O. Howard, who had replaced German-born Maj. Gen. Franz Sigel.

"I am done for, fellows," said a slightly built, pale-faced sergeant, resting upon his elbow, and pointing to his shattered side, as he was carried by on a stretcher; "but stick to the old flag; it is bound to win."

His passage along the line was greeted with cheers, that must have sounded gratefully to ears fast closing to earthly sounds.

But why individualize? The heroism that may be told of such a day, is but a drop compared with the thousands untold currents of unselfish patriotism and high resolve that well up in the bosoms of our Union soldiers. Not that daring deeds are not performed by Rebel ranks, but—

> "True fortitude is seen in great exploits,
>   That justice warrants, and that wisdom guides;
>   All else is towering frenzy and distraction."

About nine in the forenoon, to the sound of lively musketry on our left, our Brigade left in front, crossed the open space in front of the wood, and in the rear of a white plastered farm-house. A narrow wood-road led us into the wood, and filing to the left we connected with troops already in line of battle.[15] The position was hardly taken before the zip! zip!! zip!!! of Minié balls informed us that we were objects of especial interest to Rebel sharp-shooters. In another minute flashes of flame and puffs of smoke, that appeared to rise from among the dead foliage of the wood—so closely did their Butternut clothing resemble leaves— revealed a strong, well-formed, but prostrate Rebel line. The firing now became general upon both sides. Fortunately our position was such that they overshot us. Our men continued to aim low, and delivered an effective fire. Three times they tried to rise preparatory to the charge, and were as often thrown into confusion, and forced again upon the ground. For nearly two long hours the rattling of musketry was incessant. Finally, the Rebels made the discovery that the supply of ammunition was exhausted upon the right, and the right itself unsupported. It, of course,

---

(15)   The Tyler brigade was ordered to support the Second Corps division of Maj. Gen. William H. French just north of the Bullock Road.

was the point to mass upon, and on they came in solid columns to the charge, completely outflanking our right.

To hold the ground with our formation was simply impossible. The order to retire was given; and facing by the rear rank—the Regiments preserving their ranks as best they could in that thicket of black jack, and carrying their wounded,—among them our Major, shot through the chest—made their way to the open space in rear of the wood. The colors of our regiment were seized,—but the first Rebel hand upon them relaxed from a death shot,—another was taken with the Regiment,—and the flag brought off in triumph. So completely had they gained our flank that our ranks became mixed with theirs, and nothing but the opportune fire of our batteries prevented their taking away a Field Officer, who twice escaped from their hands.[16]

As our Brigade re-formed in the rear of the batteries, treble charges of canister swept the woods of the Rebel ranks. We had suffered heavily, but nothing in comparison to the destruction now visited upon the Rebels. To complete the horrors of the day, the wood was suddenly fired, evidently to cover their retreat, and the fire swept to the open space, enveloping in flame and smoke the dead and wounded of both sides; and all this at the very time when throughout the length and breadth of this Christian land, thousands of churches were resonant with the words of the Gospel of Peace. But "Woe be unto those by whom offenses come." "They have taken the sword, and must perish by the sword."

So completely were the Rebels masters of the only available fighting ground that no further effort was made to advance our lines, and the army stood strictly upon the defensive. The open space, in which stood the Chancellorsville mansion, at this time a mass of smoking ruins, was in their possession. At arms behind the breastworks we awaited the onset; but although there was occasional firing, no general attack was made during the remainder of the day. With the thanks of our Corps Commander publicly given for services during the fight, our Brigade

---

(16)    This field officer was the author, Lieutenant Colonel Armstrong.

rested at night, speculating upon which side the heavy firing told then heard in the vicinity of Fredericksburg.

During the next day we were stationed as a Reserve upon the right, and called to arms frequently during the day and night, when the Rebels with their unearthly yells would tempt our artillery by charging upon the works. On the day after we were moved to support the center, and kept continually at arms. In the afternoon a violent thunderstorm raged —the dread artillery of Heaven teaching us humility by its striking contrast to the counterfeit thunder of our cannon. Rain generally follows heavy cannonading. All that afternoon and the greater part of the night it fell in torrents. Cannonading in the direction of Fredericksburg had ceased during the day. Sedgwick's disastrous movement was not generally known,—but our wounded had all been sent off;—our few wagon trains and our pack-horses had crossed,—and notwithstanding the show of fight kept up in front, enough was seen to indicate that the army was about to recross the Rappahannock.[17]

Favored by the darkness, battery after battery was quietly withdrawn, their respective Army Corps accompanying in Regiments of two abreast.

The movement was in painful contrast to the spirited order that gave such a merry May-day to our hope upon the first of the month. In blouses that smoked that wet night around camp fires kept up for the purpose of misleading the enemy, our men stood discussing the orders, and the counter-orders, and what had happened, and what might happen, from the step. Hooker had credit for the successful execution of his part of the programme. What was wrong below was conjecture then, and does not yet appear to be certainly understood.

"Where is Old Pigey?" said one of a group of officers, suddenly turning to a comrade, as they stood about one of their camp fires. "He has not been near our Brigade during the day."

---

(17)    The Sixth Corps under Maj. Gen. John Sedgwick had carried Marye's Heights, attacked up the Orange Plank Road from Fredericksburg, and been defeated at Salem Church.

"No! nor near the other, except to damn it in such a style as to draw down the rebuke of a superior officer," replied the man addressed. "Follow me, if you desire to see how a 'cool, courageous man of science,' one, whose face, as the Reporters say of him, 'indicates tremendous power in reserve,' meets this crisis."

The two retired, and on a camp stool, with cloak wrapped closely about him, in front of a fire whose bright blaze gave him enormous proportions upon the dark background of pines, surrounded by his Staff, his hat more pinched up and askew than usual, and receiving frequent consolation from a long, black bottle, evidently his power in reserve upon this occasion, the General was discovered in a pensive mood.

"Do you know," continued the officer, "that he reports, as a reason for his absence today, that he did not consider it prudent to be near our Brigade during the loading and firing exercise."

"The torturing of a guilty conscience," was the reply. "Our men, as true soldiers, know but one enemy in the field."

At length, at two in the morning of the 6th of May, we cautiously commenced our movement to the river. The dawn of a rainy day saw us formed in line of battle, supporting artillery planted to protect the crossing. About eight our turn came upon the swollen stream. The rain pelted piteously as we ascended the steep slope of the opposite bank, and after a day's march over roads resembling rivers of mud, we slept away our sorrows under wet blankets, in the comfortable huts of our old camp ground.

## CHAPTER XXI.

*The Pigeon-Hole General and his Adjutant under Charges—The Exhorting Colonel's Adieu to the Sunday Fight at Chancellorsville; Reasons thereof— Speech of the Dutch Doctor in Reply to a Peace-Offering from the Chaplain— The Irish Corporal stumping for Freedom—Black Charlie's Compliments to his Master—Western Virginia at the Head of a Black Regiment.*

"HEAD-QUARTERS, —— DIVISION.
"—— ARMY CORPS, *7th May*, 1863.[1]

"GENERAL ORDERS, NO. 22.

THE term of service of six of the eight Regiments forming my Division is about to expire. In the midst of the pressing duties of an active Campaign there is but little time for leave-taking, yet I cannot part from the brave officers and men of my command without expressing to them the satisfaction and pride I have felt at their conduct, from the time when I assumed command, as they marched through Washington, in September last, to join the Army of the Potomac, then about to meet the Enemy, up to the present eventful period.

---

(1)    The blanks in general order twenty-two should read "Third Division, Fifth Army Corps." The order was signed by Andrew A. Humphreys.

"The cheerfulness with which they have borne the unaccustomed fatigues and hardships which it is the lot of the soldier to endure; their zealous efforts to learn the multifarious duties of the soldier; the high spirit they have exhibited when called on to make long and painful marches to meet the enemy, and their bravery in the field of battle have won my regard and affection. I shall part from them with deep regret, and wish them, as the time of each regiment expires, a happy return to their families and friends.

"_____,

"Brig. Gen'l Com'g Division."

However profound the *regret* of the General at parting, he must, from the phraseology of the above Order, have been conscious, that in his own conduct was to be found the reason that such regret was not in the least reciprocated by his command. So completely had he aliened the affections of officers and men that the ordinary salute in recognition of his rank was given grudgingly, if at all. When there is no gold in the character, men are not backward in proclaiming that they consider

"The rank is but the guinea's stamp."

As their campaign approached its close, he added studied insult to long continued injury. His inconsistency, and willingness to make use of a quibble for the accomplishment of tyrannical purposes were shown by his non-approval of the requisition for dress coats, when it was handed in by the officer in command of the Regiment, a short time after the removal of the Colonel and Lieutenant-Colonel for refusing to obey the order requiring it. Charges had been preferred against his Adjutant-General for repeated instances of "Drunkenness upon Duty," "Disgraceful Conduct," and "Conduct unbecoming an Officer and a Gentleman."[2] They were returned to the Brigadier, through whom they had been submitted, with an insulting note, in which the General took occa-

---

(2)    The charges against Capt. Carswell McClellan were probably filed by the
       West Virginia captain, David Eckar.

sion to state, by way of pre-judgment, that the charges were malicious and false, notwithstanding the scores of names appended as witnesses; —and that no *Volunteer Captain* had a right to prefer charges against one of his Staff; and that it was the duty of the Brigadier to discountenance any charges of the kind. They were again forwarded, with the statement of the Brigadier, that he himself would prefer them, should objection be taken to the rank of the officer whose signature was attached. But pigeon-holing was a favorite smothering process at Division Head Quarters, and the drunken and disgraceful conduct of the Adjutant-General remains unpunished.

Charges supported by a large array of reputable witnesses, ranking from Brigadier to Privates, were preferred against the General himself, for "Drunkenness," "Un-officerlike conduct," "Conduct tending to mutiny," and the utterance of the following treasonable and disloyal sentiments:[3]—

"That he wished some one would ask the army to follow General McClellan to Washington, and hurl the whole d—d pack into the Potomac, and place General McClellan at the head of the Government, —that the removal of the said General McClellan was a political move to kill the said General; and that the army had better be taken to Washington, and turned over to Lincoln."

The charges and specifications, of one of the latter of which the above is an extract, alleged that the offense was committed at Camp near Warrenton, about the time of McClellan's removal. Whether they too have been pigeon-holed at Division Head-Quarters is not known. Attention to their merit was promised by superior officers. The patriotic sacrifices of our citizen soldiery are surely worthy of an unceasing and unsparing effort to procure loyal, temperate, and capable commanders. A timely trial, besides affording a salutary example, might have done much in

---

(3)     The charges against General Humphreys were filed by Colonel Frick. When they were brought to the attention of higher authority, Judge Advocate General Holt recommended to Secretary of War Stanton that they be forwarded to General Hooker for possible court-martial.

preventing the disgraceful Rebel escape at Williamsport, which alone dims the glory of Gettysburg.  *   *   *   *   *   *   *

The last that was seen of the exhorting Colonel and his Adjutant, was their sudden exit from the wood at Chancellorsville, in an early stage of Sunday's fight,—the one with a slight wound, and the other with a headache caused by the cannonading, as alleged.[4] A performance which has not, thus far, brought the coveted star.[5]  *   *   *   *   *   *

"I propose the health of the Assistant Surgeon," said the Chaplain, at a supper given by the Sutler on the day of our muster out, and the occasion of the presentation of a costly sword to our worthy Colonel,— proposing thereby to make an advance towards healing their differ- ences. The Doctor could not escape; and winking, as usual with him during excitement, he rose to his feet.

"My ver goot kind friend, the English language he am a shtranger to me. No shpeak so goot as Shaplain, but py tam," and the Doctor struck the table until the plates rattled—"was py the Shaplain over six month, and my opinion is, Shaplains, women, and whiskey not goot for soldiers."

The Doctor's look and tones were irresistibly ludicrous, and a roar of laughter at the expense of the Chaplain ran round the board.   *   *

The Regiment returned with ranks sadly thinned. Many of the survi- vors; among them, most of the Field and Staff, the poetical and the preacher Lieutenants, and privates Tom and Harry,—have re-entered service. The two latter now carry swords.  *   *   *   *   *   *   *

---

(4)    In General Tyler's view, Adjutant Tayman did not return in a timely manner after having escorted Colonel Gregory from the field. When a court-martial found Tayman not guilty, he retaliated by bringing charges against General Tyler for calling him an "impudent puppy" and other terms of endearment.

(5)    Colonel Gregory did get his "coveted star." In July 1864 he became commander of the Second Brigade, First Division, Fifth Corps, and was brevetted a brigadier on September 30, 1864.

Bill the cook is the presiding genius of a restaurant; his face, in the way of reminding one of hot stews and pepper-pot, his best sign. Charlie, his assistant, was last noticed in a photographic establishment in Philadelphia, inclosing a full length card portrait of himself in uniform, as a Corporal in a Black Regiment, for the benefit of his master's family in Dixie. *   *   *   *   *   *   *   *   *   *   *   *

The little Irish Corporal was heard to tell a brawling peace man,—as he menaced with the stump of an arm,—lost at Chancellorsville—in a saloon a short time after his return, to "hould his tongue; that the boys who had lost limbs in defense of the country were the chappies to stump for freedom, and that they would keep down all fires in the rear, while our brave boys are fighting in front." *   *   *   *

A late mail brings the news that our Western Virginia Captain is soon to take the field at the head of a Black Regiment, and that the happiest results are anticipated from his enforcement of military law and tactics, as learned by him under "Old Rosey," in Western Virginia.   *   *   *

Thus we go on. Necessity hastens the progress of civilization and freedom. Desolating war—protracted by mistaken leniency—has educated the nation to a proper sense of the treason, and nerved it to the determination to crush it by all possible means and at every hazard. The man who has heretofore objected to Negro enlistments, acquiesces when his own name appears upon the list of the Enrolling Officer. The day that saw the change in the miserable, not to say treasonable, policy of alienating the only real friends we have had in the South, and their successful employment as soldiers, stands first in the decline of the Rebellion. Its suppression is fixed, and is to be measured by the vigor with which we press the war.

> "Vengeance is secure to him
> Who doth arm himself with right."

Commentary on
*Red-Tape and Pigeon-Hole Generals*

The following editorial comment provides further insight into and
documentation of William Armstrong's exposé, which was written less
than a year after he left the army in 1863. He did a highly competent
job, irrespective of the veil of fiction employed, in relating an account
of his regiment, brigade, and division from the limited sources available
to him. The passage of time allows the incorporation of material from
official government records, the works of historians of other regiments
of the Humphreys division, and the diaries and letters of fellow members
of the 129th. In contrast to Armstrong's contemporaneous and sometimes heated narrative, some of these accounts were prepared years after
the events described. The weight to be given to each in determining
the most objective version of the events is the most challenging task of
the historian.

The "History of the 129th" (pp. 255-290) also contains some background information on the First Pennsylvania, particularly as it is
relevant to the text of *Red-Tape*. A look at "Short-Term Regiments,
Manpower Policy, and Political Feuds" (pp. 291-293) explains the
circumstances that resulted in Pennsylvania's raising of several different
types of regiments and describes the intense and long-enduring feud
between the two major political players in the state during the war:
Simon Cameron and Andrew Curtin.

A recurring theme in Armstrong's book is the conflict between the
volunteers and the regulars. This is examined in "Friction between

Regular Officers and Volunteers" (pp. 294-302) to determine whether such friction pervaded the army or was more pronounced in the Fifth Corps, where it may have been linked to the personalities of Generals Humphreys and Fitz-John Porter.

The section entitled "Discipline by Courts-Martial," including "The Frock Coat Mutiny" (pp. 303-322), examines Humphreys's impressive contribution to the volume of military jurisprudence using the original trial transcripts, which verify to a remarkable degree the accounts that appear in Red-Tape. "The Many Faces of Andrew A. Humphreys" (pp. 323-351) pulls together a plethora of comments on one of the most enigmatic Union generals. Accounts from the ranks such as Red-Tape have largely been ignored in the traditional portrayals of the general. His scientific credentials are also briefly examined here. Armstrong, who was only vaguely aware of this aspect of Humphreys's background, probably would not have gotten past the hundred-word title of the general's report on the physics and hydraulics of the Mississippi River. The results of Humphreys's post-war assignment as head of the Corps of Engineers and his influence on the corps and a flawed government flood control policy are also examined.

In "Final Reckoning" (pp. 352-361), the post-Red-Tape careers of the major characters in the book are related, with emphasis on the military exploits of Colonel Frick on the Susquehanna and General Tyler on the Monocacy.

## History of the 129th Pennsylvania Volunteer Infantry and the Tyler Brigade

The fictional 210th Pennsylvania in *Red-Tape* is based on the 129th Pennsylvania Volunteer Infantry, a nine-month regiment that was organized and mustered on August 15, 1862, at Camp Curtin in Harrisburg. Five of the companies (A, B, E, G, and H) were from Schuykill County. Four companies (C, D, F, and K) were recruited from Northampton County (Easton), and one company (I) from Montgomery County. Armstrong as author apparently believed he was safe in assigning a fictional regimental designation substantially beyond those in existence at the time he wrote the book, but he underestimated the ability of Pennsylvania to raise regiments. The real 210th Pennsylvania was recruited in August 1864 and fought in the final campaign of the war.

The colonel of the 129th was thirty-nine-year-old Jacob G. Frick, a businessman from Pottsville, Schuykill County, who had served as a lieutenant in the Third Ohio Volunteers in the Mexican War. As a lieutenant colonel of the Ninety-sixth Pennsylvania, Sixth Corps, he had already seen action at West Point, Gaines's Mill, Charles City Cross Roads, and Malvern Hill in the Peninsula Campaign. He was an imposing figure, described as "of Saul-like stature, being six feet two inches in height and well proportioned."[1]

---

(1)    Samuel P. Bates. *Martial Deeds of Pennsylvania.* (Philadelphia: T.H. Davis &

Frick's departure from the Ninety-sixth in July 1862 might also be termed an escape. The colonel of the regiment—Henry L. Cake, also from Pottsville—was in a constant and bizarre conflict with his officers until he retired from military service in March 1863. One of his most controversial actions was a sweetheart deal with the regimental sutler to force hats and leggings on his troops at an inflated price. While Lieutenant Colonel Frick attempted to mold the Ninety-sixth into an effective fighting force in the fall of 1861, Colonel Cake was frequently absent campaigning for a seat in the state senate. Although unsuccessful in this election, he eventually served two terms in the U.S. House of Representatives.[2]

The lieutenant colonel of the 129th was thirty-year-old William H. Armstrong, the author of *Red-Tape*, a lawyer from Easton. (He should not be confused with another William H. Armstrong, of Lycoming County and a close associate of Simon Cameron, who was not in the military but served in the U.S. Congress just after the Civil War.[3])

Colonel Armstrong, like many of the soldiers from Easton, had served in the First Pennsylvania Volunteer Infantry, a three-month regiment whose colonel was Samuel Yohe, a judge from Easton, who in *Red-Tape* is described as "too old for service." Armstrong was a captain of Company C.

The major of the 129th was Joseph Anthony, an Irish innkeeper from Pottsville who had served previously with Frick and Cake as a company commander in the Ninety-sixth Pennsylvania during the Peninsula Campaign and in the three-month Sixteenth Pennsylvania in 1861. The adjutant of the 129th was a thirty-year-old lieutenant, David B. Green, a Yale graduate who was an attorney in Pottsville. The "West Virginia Captain" can be identified as David Eckar, the thirty-three-year-old

Co., 1876), 833-844. (Hereafter *Martial Deeds*)

(2)   David A. Ward. "Of Battlefields and Bitter Feuds: The Ninety-sixth Pennsylvania Volunteers." *Civil War Regiments: A Journal of the American Civil War.* (Vol. 3, Number 3, 1993), 4-8, 18-21.

(3)   Alexander K. McClure. *Abraham Lincoln and Men of War Times.* (Philadelphia: Times Publishing Co., 1892), 106. (Hereafter *Men of War Times*)

commander of Company F of the 129th, who had served as an enlisted man in the First U.S. Artillery in the Mexican War and in the Second (West) Virginia Infantry in 1861 and 1862.

The history of the Second (West) Virginia Regiment (which became the Fifth West Virginia Cavalry) says of David Eckar:

> [He] was a native of Easton, Pa., his parents being what is known as Pennsylvania Dutch. He was a private in a battery during the Mexican War, and an excellent drillmaster; and to him was due the credit of the efficiency that [D] company attained in skirmish drill and in the bayonet exercise. He resigned early in 1862, just when the company began to show the training he had given them.[4]

The "little Dutch Doctor" was in reality Otto Schittler, a physician from Philadelphia and the assistant surgeon of the 129th; his Tyrolean background and education is outlined in *Red-Tape* (pp. 35-36). The surgeon, Joseph Rossiter, is mentioned only in passing. The chaplain of the 129th was twenty-two-year-old William H. Rice of Bethlehem, Pennsylvania, a pastor of the Moravian church.

The 129th was hastily organized, rushed to Washington, and encamped near Alexandria, Virginia. On August 30, 1862, eight of its companies were detailed to guard an ammunition train being sent to Centreville to supply the retreating Union army in the late stages of the battle of Second Bull Run. Toward evening the regiment came under fire from Confederate artillery (pp. 26-27). On September 3 the 129th was placed in a brigade with the 91st, 126th, and 134th Pennsylvania under the command of Brig. Gen. Erastus B. Tyler—the axe-wielding and red-tape-cutting brigadier described on pages 12-13. Tyler helped raise the Seventh Ohio Infantry at the outset of the war and was elected its colonel in a hotly contested race against James A. Garfield, the future president of the United States. The forty-four-year-old general had been

---

(4)    Frank S. Reader. *History of the Fifth West Virginia Cavalry formerly the Second Virginia Infantry.* (New Brighton, Pa.: Daily News, 1890), 69.

in the fur-trapping business before the war, and that experience helped in his first assignment, fighting with Generals George McClellan and William Rosecrans in West Virginia. In June 1861 he spent eight days consulting with McClellan, giving him "information as to the mountain passes, roads, streams, fords, and general topography of the entire section."[5]

Tyler also learned from early misadventures. In August 1861 the Seventh Ohio was surprised by Confederates while eating breakfast at Cross Lanes and routed. Earlier that month Rosecrans had written to Washington suggesting that promoting Tyler to brigadier general would be premature.[6] The following spring Tyler commanded a brigade of Gen. James Shields's division and was made a brigadier general for conduct in the battle of Kernstown in March 1862, where "seven balls passed through his clothes."[7] His brigade fought successfully against Jackson's Stonewall Brigade, then commanded by Gen. Richard Garnett. In June 1862 at Port Republic, Tyler's brigade again engaged in a seesaw battle with the Stonewall Brigade, then commanded by Gen. Charles S. Winder. "For four hours it [Tyler's brigade] had waged a masterful struggle"; the Union troops finally broke when Richard Taylor's Mississippi brigade was introduced.[8] Lt. Col. David Rowe, commander and historian of the 126th Pennsylvania, wrote of his brigade commander:

> General Tyler . . . was not an educated soldier, but full of military spirit and aptitude, and admirably suited to have charge of a brigade of men fresh from the people. He was heartily liked by all under him, and was as much respected as liked.[9]

---

(5)    Whitelaw Reid. *Ohio in the War, Vol. 1.* (New York: Moore, Wilstach & Baldwin, 1868), 831. (Hereafter *Ohio in the War*)

(6)    Tyler Military File, National Archives.

(7)    *Ohio in the War*, 833.

(8)    James I. Robertson Jr. *The Stonewall Brigade.* (Baton Rouge: Louisiana State University Press, 1963), 112. See a more critical account in Robert K. Krick, *Conquering the Valley: Stonewall Jackson at Port Republic.* (New York: William Morrow & Co., 1996), 414-416.

(9)    David W. Rowe. *A Sketch of the 126th Regiment Pennsylvania Volunteers Prepared by an Officer.* (Chambersburg, Pa.: Cook and Hays, 1869), 12.

Brig. Gen. Andrew A. Humphreys, the new commander of the two-brigade Third Division of the Fifth Corps, had served as the chief topographical officer of the Army of the Potomac under Maj. Gen. George B. McClellan in the Peninsula Campaign and approximated Little Mac in stature. Humphreys, age fifty-one in 1862, had graduated from West Point thirteenth in a class of thirty-three in 1831 and had spent the first thirty-one years of his military career on topographical and engineering assignments.

When the 129th Pennsylvania was ordered to join Humphreys on September 13, 1862, the Humphreys division was at Camp Whipple on the heights of Arlington, at what is now Fort Myer and the national cemetery. The camp was named after their "former and favorite" division commander, Brig. Gen. Amiel W. Whipple.

On September 14 the division began its march to join McClellan's army, and late on the 15th it established a camp on the Monocacy River near the junction of the Baltimore & Ohio Railroad. The unit's proximity to Frederick brought to mind stories of the old First Pennsylvania, which had been stationed there in late June 1861, and in which Armstrong and others in the 129th had served (pp. 5-7). The Humphreys division stayed in the Monocacy camp on September 16 and 17. Here it encountered paroled Union troops on their way to Camp Parole near Annapolis. The parolees were a portion of those captured at Harper's Ferry on September 15, 1862, when about 12,700 men surrendered and forty-seven artillery pieces fell into Confederate hands; it was the largest federal loss of soldiers to capture during the Civil War.

On the afternoon of the 17th the division was ordered to the western outskirts of Frederick. As it passed through Frederick, the author was again reminded of his experiences there in the First Pennsylvania (pp. 9-10). At that time Armstrong was associated with loyalist society and not considered to be of "Bradley T. Johnson's race." Johnson, an attorney and captain of the Frederick Mounted Guards, was one of the town's leading secessionists. During the session of the Maryland legislature in Frederick in May 1861, Johnson led a group of men to join the

---

(Hereafter *History of 126th*)

Confederates at Harper's Ferry and ultimately formed the First Maryland Cavalry Regiment, C.S.A. He later returned to Frederick as commander of a brigade of Confederate cavalry at the battle of Monocacy.

About sunset on September 17 the division arrived at its proposed campsite outside of Frederick. There the men received an order from McClellan to join the other two divisions of the Fifth Corps at Antietam. They marched all night, over Braddock Heights and South Mountain and through Fox's Gap, where Maj. Gen. Jesse Reno, the Ninth Corps commander, had been killed on September 14. In the early morning of September 18 they moved through Boonsboro and Keedysville, arriving at the Antietam battlefield about 9:30 (pp. 11-13).

With the rest of the army, the Humphreys division remained idle throughout the day of the 18th. In partial explanation of the army's inactivity, McClellan wrote in his report on the battle, "And Humphreys's division of new troops, fatigued with forced marches, were arriving throughout the day, and were not available near its close."[10]

In March 1863 Humphreys saw this excerpt in a newspaper and fired off a letter to Secretary of War Edwin Stanton complaining that "this statement is irreconcilable with the facts, and I am at a loss to understand how such a misapprehension on his [McClellan's] part could have occurred." Humphreys stated that he had arrived at McClellan's headquarters at 7 A.M. on September 18 and that by about 9:30 A.M. six thousand of his troops and eight pieces of artillery were in place and ready for action. He noted that McClellan had ridden "through or past my division" and concluded that:

> Notwithstanding the long night march they had made of over 23 miles (our only forced march), the men were in good heart, and, refreshed by their rest and coffee, would have fought well. Had they been wanting in spirit, a large portion of them might have remained behind, for the night was very dark. When I saw the long lines of the regiments as they filed into their

---

(10)    OR, Vol. XIX, Part 1, 31.

position, in the rear of Morell [Maj. Gen. George Morell was commander of the First Division of the Fifth Corps], I knew the kind of men I commanded, and their conduct on the field since that time has justified my confidence in them.[11]

On September 19 the soldiers of the 129th viewed the horrific Antietam battlefield and then marched through Sharpsburg (pp. 22-23). That night they camped near Gen. Fitz-John Porter's Fifth Corps headquarters at the Steven Grove Homestead, about a mile and a half from the Potomac River. On the morning of the 20th they moved up the Shepherdstown Road behind Morell's First Division and Brig. Gen. George Sykes's Second Division of the Fifth Corps. The "new and most promising" regiment noted on page 24 was the 118th Pennsylvania 'Corn Exchange' regiment in Col. James Barnes's brigade of Morell's division. It and elements of Sykes's division had crossed the Potomac and were attacked by Confederate general A. P. Hill just downstream from Shepherdstown, West Virginia. The 118th was slow to be withdrawn and suffered severe losses scrambling back across the Potomac.

The 129th then settled into camp for the next six weeks. From the description given in Red-Tape, examination of maps, and discussion with individuals familiar with the area and its history, the camp of the 129th appears to have been in the valley that runs almost due south from the Steven Grove Homestead to the Boteler or Blackford Ford. In his diary, Pvt. Luther Horn of Company K called it 'Camp Tower,' as did other soldiers.[12] A few hundred yards up the Potomac from the ford, toward Shepherdstown, was an old cement mill and decaying dam, the site of the disastrous retreat of the 118th Pennsylvania.[13]

In early October 1862 President Lincoln waited impatiently for McClellan to move. On October 10 Confederate general J. E. B. Stuart began a two-day ride that took him around the Union army camped at Antietam; his audacity apparently energized McClellan to make a coun-

---

(11)   OR, Vol. XIX, Part 1, 373-374.

(12)   Diary of Pvt. Luther Horn, First and 129th Pennsylvania Volunteer Infantry, Easton (Pa.) Area Public Library. (Hereafter Horn Diary)

(13)   John W. Schildt. Mount Airy: The Grove Homestead. (self-published), 23-24.

ter move across the Potomac. Humphreys, with various elements of the Fifth Corps, was ordered to make a reconnaissance from Shepherdstown to the vicinity of Bunker Hill, near Martinsburg, West Virginia, with a force of five hundred cavalry, six pieces of artillery, and six thousand infantry. The infantry included Erastus Tyler's brigade, Robert C. Buchanan's brigade from Sykes's Second Division, and Charles Griffin's brigade from Morell's First Division. The force moved through Shep-herdstown to Kearneysville, some seven miles, and fought a small engagement in which the Union lost three killed, seven wounded, and three missing.

Colonel Frick wrote of the engagement in the *Miners Journal* of Pottsville on November 1:

> Occasionally the fire from their batteries was pretty brisk and they seemed to give special attention to the 129th which was on the extreme left. While the shells exploded and fell in great numbers in uncomfortable proximity to the regiment but not one man was injured. The men behaved well and received after their return, the thanks of generals Porter and Humph-reys.

The Confederate losses from three regiments of the Stonewall Bri-gade, the Fourth, Fifth, and Twenty-seventh Virginia, were three killed and twenty-one wounded.

On October 17 Humphreys, who greatly overestimated his opposi-tion, notified Porter that "we have a very large force of the enemy in front and on our right flank, and are moving cautiously." Porter ordered Humphreys to retire and endorsed Humphreys's report, declaring that he "had accomplished in a most satisfactory manner the object of the expedition."[14]

Apparently Lincoln was as unimpressed with the tenor of these operations as were the officers of the 129th (p. 79), as both McClellan and Porter were removed from their commands early in November.

---

(14)   OR, Vol. XIX, Part 2, 85-89.

\* \* \* \*

When they neared Martinsburg on reconnaissance, the members of the fictional 210th discussed the inadequacies of Gen. Robert Patterson, who had opposed Gen. Joseph E. Johnston here a year earlier (pp. 73-76). Their real counterparts in the 129th had also served in the First Pennsylvania in this theater of operations. In early July of 1861 Patterson had been instructed by General-in-Chief Winfield Scott to exert pressure on Johnston's forces at Winchester so that those troops could not be diverted to Manassas to oppose Gen. Irvin McDowell's offensive operation. The initial role of the First Pennsylvania in Patterson's campaign was to guard the supply base at Martinsburg. On July 16, 1861, the First was ordered to Charles Town, where it joined Patterson's Second Division.

On the same day Patterson made a weak 'demonstration' in the direction of Winchester, which he believed was heavily defended. Patterson greatly overestimated Johnston's strength through this whole period. At one time he thought there were as many as 42,000 Confederates around Winchester. In fact, on June 30, 1861, Johnston's Army of the Shenandoah had 10,654 present for duty.[15] In any event, Patterson spent a few days following the July 16 demonstration debating with his staff (which included Fitz-John Porter) as to whether he should take further action.

On July 18 Johnston began to withdraw from Winchester for the march and train ride to Manassas.

On July 21, as the battle of Bull Run reached its climax, the First Pennsylvania and the rest of Patterson's army moved back to Harper's Ferry. The First Pennsylvania marched to Sandy Hook on the Potomac River on July 23 and took the train to Harrisburg as its term of enlistment expired.

---

(15)   OR, Vol. II, 167-199, especially 187. See also William C. Davis. *Battle at Bull Run*. (Baton Rouge: Louisiana State University Press, 1977), 148-151; Samuel P. Bates. *History of the Pennsylvania Volunteers, 1861-1865*, Vol. 1. (Harrisburg: B. Singerly, State Printer, 1870), 15. (Hereafter Bates)

*Gen. Robert Patterson, a veteran of the War of 1812, was supposed to keep Joe Johnston's army from supporting the Confederates at Manassas, the first battle of Bull Run.*

In many of his communications with General Scott, Patterson emphasized the problem of the expiring enlistments of the three-month regiments and their rejections of his pleas to stay on. He wrote on July 19, "Almost all the three-months' volunteers refuse to serve an hour over their term, and except three regiments which will stay ten days and most of them are without shoes and without pants." But this "beggarly" and "false" excuse was rejected in *Red-Tape* (p. 100):

The great mass volunteered to remain as it was, with no prospect of service ahead. All would have stayed had the General shown any disposition for active work, or made them promise of a fight.

On July 19 General Scott ordered Patterson honorably discharged and replaced in command. Patterson asked for an official inquiry, but his request was rejected. The friendship of the sixty-nine-year-old Patterson and the seventy-five-year-old Scott, which dated back to the War of 1812, was terminated. [16]

\* \* \* \*

---

(16)   OR, Vol. II, 174-179.

Although they had had a relatively pleasant experience there, the soldiers of the 129th were happy to break their camp on the Potomac at noon on October 30, 1862.

Not all was roses, however. Colonel Frick wrote in the *Miners Journal* of November 1, 1862, after the "reconnaissance":

I regret to say . . . that the sick list of the regiment is awfully large. The morning report shows 181 in quarters, regimental, and general hospitals. The people of North-

*Gen. Winfield Scott, a hero of the Mexican War and commander-in-chief at the outbreak of the Civil War, would be replaced by McClellan in the fall of 1861.*

ampton and Montgomery Counties are untiring in their efforts to alleviate the suffering of the sick and supply the wants of the well men in the regiment from their counties. I wish I could say as much of the people of our county [Schuykill].

They marched from Sharpsburg through a valley to Sandy Hook on the Potomac, and then to Harper's Ferry, where the regiment crossed the Potomac on a pontoon bridge on October 31 (pp. 90-92).

The Fifth Corps marched southward along the east side of the Shenandoah Valley. To protect his army from a flanking movement, McClellan plugged the gaps in the Blue Ridge. In the first days of November the Fifth Corps was assigned to Snickers's Gap (pp. 105-106, 108-113). Joshua L. Chamberlain of the Twentieth Maine (First Division, Fifth Corps) was there. On November 3 he wrote to his wife:

What names they have in the land of Rebeldom! *Snickers* Gap! what an undignified name for a battlefield. Yet here we are expecting a battle with the Rebels who are just over the mountain at the other end of the Gap.[17]

Perhaps Chamberlain would have been more impressed had he known that the gap was named for Capt. Edward Snickers, who served with George Washington in the Braddock expedition in the French and Indian War and was a recruiting officer in the Revolutionary War. The town, called Bluemont since the turn of the century, had once been called Pumpkin Town because "the back end of the wagon fell down and the pumpkins all rolled down the market through the town."[18] As the 129th marched through the town they passed the 1846 Snickersville General Store, which still stands today.

In a letter written the next day, Chamberlain also noted that it was difficult to get food, for the "Rebels who live here will neither sell nor give" and an "amiable lady" from whom they tried to buy milk "said she would like to kill the whole lot." He observed that "it is quite possible however that she indirectly contributed to our good *living*, for I am afraid our naughty boys helped themselves to a few pigs & turkeys & other delicious articles of diet, which must be *had* even if they cannot be bought or accepted as presents."[19]

Pvt. Luther Horn of the 129th wrote of his experience:

We spent a very cold and windy night on the stony ground [on picket duty]. Here we remained up till the fourth of November, shivering with the cold and short of rashions. Rashions however was obtained by some who went on a forage expedition, appropriating to their benefit whatever they

---

(17)   *Joshua L. Chamberlain Papers*, Manuscripts Division, Library of Congress. (Hereafter *Chamberlain Papers*)

(18)   Research memo by Elizabeth Morgan; Jean Herron Smith, *Snickersville*, unpublished pamphlet; both at Thomas Balch Library, Leesburg, Virginia.

(19)   *Chamberlain Papers*.

could—on in the eating line in the shape of poltry, pork, beef, veal etc.[20]

The 129th marched from Snickers's Gap to Middleburg on November 5, then on to White Plains the following day.

Armstrong wrote in *Red-Tape* that the region previously had an "almost total exemption from the despoiling hand of war" (p. 124). That this was altered to some degree by the men on the march did not escape the notice of one correspondent of a Philadelphia newspaper, to the apparent consternation of Humphreys and Tyler. Private Horn wrote in his diary that on November 25 "we were formed into a line and Brigadeare General Tyler read an article from the Philadelphia Press reflecting on his and Olleback's brigade, the substance of said article was that when these brigades returned from Snickers Gap, they plundered everything they came across." The article, written by a "special correspondent," ran on the front page of the November 13 issue. It referred specifically to the Third Division's brigades and regiments and noted that "the kitchen gardens were over-run with soldiers, while cabbages flew through the air in myriad," and poultry was seized without "objection" by the officers. Horn also noted, as had Armstrong, that in the requisitioning of about thirty horses, the owners received "a draft on the government for their value."[21]

The 129th camped two miles north of Warrenton, arriving just after the removal of McClellan as head of the Army of the Potomac and Porter as commander of the Fifth Corps (pp. 138-146). It participated in McClellan's farewell review on November 10 and another review on November 16 for Maj. Gen. Joseph Hooker, who had been appointed commander of the new Center Grand Division comprising the Third and Fifth Corps. The grand divisions in the Army of the Potomac (Right, Left, and Center) were the creation of Maj. Gen. Ambrose Burnside, who assumed command on November 9; they lasted only as long as he was in command.

---

(20)  *Horn Diary*, 16.
(21)  *Ibid.*

On November 18 the 129th marched to the railroad junction, where it camped for the night. At dawn the next day the division started its march to Falmouth. By November 22 the regiment was at Potomac Creek, near Henry House, and a few days later was encamped on the heights of Stafford, near the town of Falmouth, across the Rappahannock River from Fredericksburg.

### The Battle of Fredericksburg (Red-Tape, pp. 175-195)

General Burnside's proposed campaign over the Rappahannock was delayed for two weeks due to the failure of the pontoon bridges to arrive. The Humphreys division finally left its camp on the heights of Stafford on the morning of December 11, 1862, and on that day moved toward the river until 4 P.M. and camped for the night. A letter written by one of the regimental officers and published in the *Miners Journal* fills in some details as to why the army was not on schedule:

We broke camp early on the morning of the 11th, and were to have been at the river, ready to cross by 9 A.M. The cannonading commenced long before the break of day, principally from our side, for the purpose of clearing the opposite bank of the enemy's sharpshooters, so as to enable us to throw the bridges across the river. The attempt was fruitless for a long time, until several boats, filled with volunteers from different regiments pushed themselves across right in the face of the enemy, and soon had the bank of the river and houses nearby cleared of the rebels. It was nearly dark, however, by the time it was effected, and in the meantime the air was filled with the roar of artillery.

We encamped about one and a half miles from the river, on hard frozen ground, with nothing over us but the clear, blue sky, and by the time morning came we were all pretty well chilled. We started early in the morning again (the 12th) and moved forward a mile when we halted. The large number of troops in advance of us, and the resistance met on the other side, made our movements very slow. We bivouacked for the night in a pine woods, where we were suffocated and blinded by the smoke.

During the whole of the day the cannonading was continuous, and every now and then we could distinguish the sharp rattle of musketry. Dense clouds of smoke hung over the town and about the batteries of the enemy and our own. The town itself had been fired in a dozen different places and was burning furiously. The sight from the hill where we were encamped was magnificent. We could see from right to left of the whole line of batteries, where the contest raged most furiously.[22]

There is some disagreement among students of the 129th as to which regimental officer is the author of this letter. At one point the account refers to Colonel Frick in the third person; both Major Anthony and Lieutenant Green came from Pottsville. Green is designated herein as the probable author on the basis of his educational background and the statement that he was slow in writing because of the report and returns on the battle that he had to finish.

On the night of December 12 the 129th camped a short distance from the Phillips House, the headquarters of Maj. Gen. Edwin Sumner, commander of the Right Grand Division. Sumner, on orders from Burnside, vacated the premises before noon on the 13th and moved to the Lacy House, about a mile closer to Fredericksburg. Burnside occupied the Phillips House for the duration of the day, with Sumner returning there later in the evening.[23] The regiment marched to the right of the Phillips House, past the launching site for the observation balloon, the creation of Prof. Thaddeus S. C. Lowe that had also been

---

(22)  *Miners Journal*, Pottsville, Pennsylvania. January 3, 1863. (Hereafter Green Letter)

(23)  Teall, "Ringside Seat at Fredericksburg," *Civil War Times Illustrated*, May 1965, 27.

used in the Peninsula Campaign. Private Horn identified the balloon as 'the Eagle.' He had previously noted its presence and use at Camp Tower on September 25, after the Antietam campaign.[24]

Lieutenant Green wrote that, about noon on December 13, the 129th crossed the middle pontoon bridge. As the regiment entered the town,

> the rebels commenced to pepper us with ball and shell from the batteries beyond the town, though without doing us much damage, than giving us lessons in the art of dodging. . . . As we got into the streets of the town, where we marched and countermarched for an hour and more, the shell fast and furiously about us, shattering the buildings and creating havoc all around. Here I saw the first man killed. He belonged to the One Hundred and Thirty-fourth Pennsylvania Volunteers, and was not more than thirty feet from me when he was struck. He was almost cut in two. He threw up his hands, exclaiming, "Oh, my God!, take me," and expired immediately. I have no doubt the sight of this made some of the boys feel a little queer —a little qualmish—as though playing with such balls was not exactly such harmless sport as many of them had imagined.[25]

The passage through the intersections and the streets that ran to the river were the most dangerous, as there were no buildings to provide shelter. As they moved forward toward the staging area for their attack on the Confederate left, the 129th and the other regiments of the Humphreys division left their knapsacks in the town with a few men to guard them. Their eventual loss would become an issue of much contention.

According to Humphreys's report, the division moved up Hanover Street, which became Telegraph Road as it left the town of Fredericksburg and wound around the base of Marye's Heights. Along here the road was bordered by a stone wall. The Humphreys and Allabach

---

(24)   *Horn Diary*, 14, 18; see also Teall, *Ibid.*
(25)   Green Letter.

brigades went to the left of the road while the Tyler brigade, after a slight pause on the left, was sent to the right.[26]

General Tyler reported that "the position first assigned to us on right of the Plank Road subjected us to an enfilading fire from the enemy's batteries on the crest of the hill beyond."[27] Tyler appears to be wrong about being on the right of the Plank Road since all the evidence indicates that his brigade was in the meadow between the Hanover and Plank roads. The heavy enfilading fire was very real, however. The tannery referred to in Red-Tape (p. 184) was owned by John G. Hurkamp. It was situated on the left side of the Plank Road.[28]

Between Tyler's brigade in the meadow and the Confederate rifle pits, which extended to the left of the Confederate line beyond the stone wall, were regiments from Col. Norman J. Hall's and Gen. Alfred Sully's Second Corps brigades of Maj. Gen. O. O. Howard's division. Hall's regiments had unsuccessfully stormed the rifle pits while Sully's were in reserve.[29] The latter were in sheltered positions in a line running roughly from the Rowe House on Hanover Street to the tannery on Plank Road.

The conspicuous arrival of the Pennsylvanians sparked unwelcome shelling by the Confederate artillery on Sully's men. Lt. Col. James Huston of the Eighty-second New York complained that his troops had been shelled because "a brigade came on the ground in our rear in a rather noisey manner . . . making a good deal of display before they were in a position to do any service."[30] Col. James A. Suiter, Thirty-fourth New York, also complained that at about 5 P.M., "Gen. Tyler's brigade came upon the field with loud cheers," which brought on shelling that killed and wounded men of his command.[31]

Adjutant Green wrote:

---

(26)   OR, Vol. XXI, 430.

(27)   OR, Vol. XXI, 437.

(28)   Noel G. Harrison. Fredericksburg Civil War Sites. (Lynchburg, Va.: H.E. Howard, Inc., 1995), 57-59.

(29)   Colonel Hall's map in Mark De Wolf Howe, ed. Touched with Fire: Civil War Letters and Diary of Oliver Wendell Holmes, Jr. (Cambridge, Mass.: Harvard University Press, 1947), 88.

(30)   OR, Vol. XXI, 276.

(31)   OR, Vol. XXI, 275.

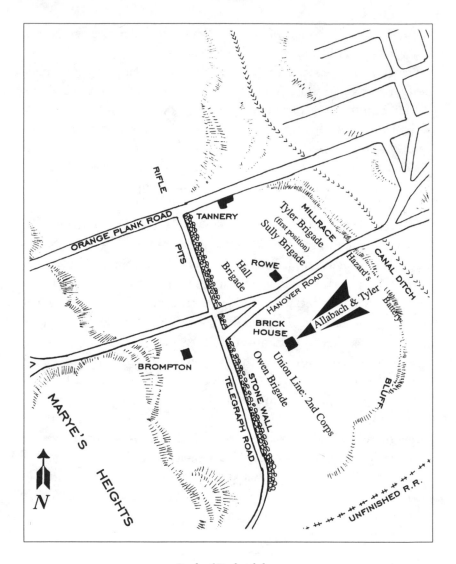

*Battle of Fredericksburg*
*Last Attack at Marye's Hill*
*December 13, 1862*

We were not here more than a minute, when from the position where I stood (on my horse) I could see the shell come whizzing right down into our ranks, where it exploded, killing several and wounding others. I could see them drawing the cannon back, reloading it, and firing again. . . . [I]t required more cool courage to witness this without flinching, than afterward to go into the charge where everything was excitement and uproar. Lieutenant [Jacob] Parvin, Company B, was mortally wounded here.[32]

The rebel artillery was on the right of the Plank Road (Confederate left) behind protected emplacements. In his report, Confederate general Robert Ransom Jr. called attention to Lt. R. P. Landry of the Donaldsonville (Louisiana) Artillery, who "took his piece from behind the epaulement in order to dislodge a body of the enemy upon whom the battery could not play. Most effectually he performed this service, but in doing so lost several of his men and had his piece disabled. His conduct was admirable, for during the times he was exposed to a direct fire of six and an enfilade fire of four guns."[33]

Humphreys ordered the Tyler brigade moved from the meadow on the right to the left of the Hanover Road. The "forlorn hope" assaults on Marye's Heights had been going on all afternoon, one brigade at a time. William Marvel wrote about the lack of effectiveness of bayonet charges against troops behind stone walls:

[B]ut such brutal tricks still worked now and then: a different brigade led by the same man who commanded this one, Erastus B. Tyler, had successfully charged another stone wall at Kernstown the previous March, giving Stonewall Jackson his only defeat.[34]

---

(32)   Green Letter.

(33)   OR, Vol. XXI, 628.

(34)   William Marvel. *The Battle of Fredericksburg.* (Conshohocken, Pa.: Eastern National Parks and Monuments Association, 1993), 16.

The Allabach brigade had just been repulsed as the Tyler brigade, summoned by Humphreys, formed behind an artillery battery—Battery B, First Rhode Island Artillery, commanded by Capt. John G. Hazard (p. 188). The battery was attached to Howard's division. Hazard wrote in his official report that he was ordered to take his battery

> on the double-quick and place them in position on an emi-
> nence some 150 or 200 yards in front of the enemy's rifle-pits.
> I placed the center and left sections on the brow of the hill,
> and the right section in the road, about 30 yards in advance
> of other sections, and opened on the enemy with solid shot
> from the center and left sections and shells from the right. I
> continued firing with rapidity for forty-five minutes, when
> Gen. Humphreys requested me to cease firing, that he might
> charge through my battery with his brigade on the enemy's
> work. . . . I sustained a loss of 16 men and 12 battery horses;
> also the horses of Lts. Bloodgood, Milne, and my own were
> shot.[35]

The Tyler brigade formed a double line of battle with the 134th on the right and the 129th on the left in the front line and the 126th behind the 134th and the 91st behind the 129th. After the war Frick declared that the 129th "was specially assigned on the field, just before the forward movement to take the place of the 91st Pennsylvania Regiment, by Generals Tyler, Humphreys, and [Daniel] Butterfield, to lead the final charge of the day on the Stone wall." [36]

According to General Hooker's testimony before the Joint Commit-tee on the Conduct of the War, when the order to charge was given to Tyler's men they "moved forward with great impetuosity. They ran and hurrahed, and I was encouraged by the great good feeling that pervaded them."[37]

---

(35)   OR, Vol. XXI, 267-268.
(36)   Frick Medal of Honor file, National Archives.
(37)   *Report of the Committee on the Conduct of the War*, Part I. (Washington: General Printing Office, 1863), 668.

Adjutant Green, in the detailed account of the 129th's charge and repulse, reported:

> When the order to charge was given, we moved forward with a loud hurrah, and charged at a run, with bayonets fixed, over the gently rising plain towards the enemy. Our line was well preserved, even though we were obliged to pass over two other regiments lying down, and cross a fence that stood in our way. Immediately the batteries began to play upon us from every side, and there was a continuous line of fire upon from the top of the stone wall right into our ranks. How the bullets whistled and hissed about our head, and the shell exploded right in our midst. Nothing could withstand that withering line of fire. Men fell around me on all sides, and it seemed almost a miracle I was untouched. The line was kept in as good order as was possible under the circumstances. We advanced to within a short distance of the wall—perhaps fifty or seventy-five yards —and then flesh and blood could stand it no longer. The line began to waiver and part—our advance was checked. We could not keep the gaps in the ranks filled up. The officers did their best to urge the men forward, but it was worse than use-less, as nothing but death stared them in the face. We began to retire, and the enemy seeing this, poured in a more destruc-tive fire than ever. Still there was no panic among the men, and although some confusion occurred in the ranks, we retired slowly and deliberately to our first position, where we formed once more, ready to meet an attack from the enemy.
>
> The charge our brigade had made was the most spirited of the whole day, and we advanced nearer the enemy's position than any other troops. From the time we first started on the charge to the time we returned, was scarcely more than fifteen or twenty minutes; . . .
>
> Our Colonel [Frick] exposed himself fearlessly, keeping the line in good order, and cheering the men forward in the fearful advance; and, afterwards, when we were compelled to retire,

restored the line once more, so as to be prepared for any movement of the enemy.[38]

Colonel Frick, in his brief official report, wrote that the killed and wounded were 131 (increased to 143 in later counts) and praised the regiment, saying, "I believe every officer and every soldier was in his proper place and did his whole duty." He specifically recognized Lieutenant Colonel Armstrong, Major Anthony, and Adjutant Green for their courage and coolness.[39] After the war he offered a more complete picture of his own participation:

> In our progress my Color Bearer was shot down. Seizing the colors myself, on my horse, continued the movement forward; the flag staff being shot off in uncomfortable proximity to my head. The movement was somewhat obstructed by the troops lying down in advance of us; over whom I leaped my horse, followed by the brave men of the Brigade. We reached a point within a few feet of the wall; losing 143 of my men of the 129th.[40]

It should be noted that the attacks of the Allabach and Tyler brigades were somewhat different. When Allabach's troops encountered the prone troops of Maj. Gen. Darius N. Couch of the Second Corps, they too lay down on the ground and joined them in firing on the Confederates behind the stone wall. The men they encountered were probably from Col. Joshua Owen's brigade of Howard's division, which was on the left of the Hanover Road, and Colonel Hall's men, who were on the right side.

General Humphreys wrote that he finally realized "that our fire could have little effect on him [the enemy] and that the only mode of attacking him successfully was with the bayonet."[41] He and his staff offi-

---

(38)  Green Letter.
(39)  OR, Vol. XXI, 442.
(40)  Frick Medal of Honor file, National Archives.
(41)  OR, Vol. XXI, 431.

cers, Allabach and his staff, and the various regimental officers organized the bayonet charge, which made an advance of about fifty yards.
Some of Allabach's men then fell back to the line where the bayonet
charge had originated, while others fell back to the millrace ravine or
even to the town. Some of the regiments that stayed in the forward
position made a second attack; whether this was done at the time of the
Tyler brigade attack is not altogether clear. Tyler's attack was with the
bayonet from the start. When the attack was repulsed the brigade, with
minor exceptions, retreated as a body back to the ravine. (Martin
Werkheiser, Company K, wrote in his diary that part of his company
remained on the advance line and was not reunited with the body of
the 129th until the following day.) Thus the regiments of the Tyler
brigade had to pass over the other regiments lying on the field, including
some of Allabach's regiments, both going up and coming back.

General Tyler pointed out that as his troops passed over the prone
regiments they encountered soldiers who were "crying out that we
would be slaughtered" but "we marched over them." He also reported
some firing from the rear:

> When we were within a very short distance of the enemy's line,
> a fire was opened on our rear, wounding a few of my most
> valuable officers, and, I regret to say, killing some of our men.
> Instantaneously the cry ran along our lines that we were being
> fired upon from the rear. The column halted, receiving at the
> same time a terrible fire from the enemy. Orders for the mo-
> ment were forgotten, and a fire from our line was immediately
> returned. Another cry passed along the line that we were being
> fired upon from the rear, when our brave men, after giving the
> enemy several volleys, fell back.[42]

Humphreys did not mention a 'friendly fire' problem in his own
report.

---

(42)   OR, Vol. XXI, 437.

### Who Was Closest to the Wall?

The battle of Fredericksburg spawned another of those classic Civil War disputes that went on interminably after the war. General Humphreys wrote in his report that his division approached "nearer to the wall than any other troops had reached." Francis Walker, in his history of the Second Corps, questioned this strongly, insisting that elements of the Second Corps brigades of Samuel K. Zook, Thomas Meagher, and John C. Caldwell of Gen. Winfield Scott Hancock's division and Brig. Gen. Nathan Kimball's brigade of Gen. William French's division got closest to the wall, as attested to by a Union burial detail that was ordered to inter the dead in front of Marye's Heights three days after the battle. Walker also objected to Humphreys's claim that the reason he did not capture the wall was because his troops were impeded by the Second Corps men lying prone on the field, yet the reports of both of Humphreys's brigade commanders and their regimental commanders all mention the problem of troops remaining on the field from previous attacks.[43]

Capt. Joseph Orwig, in his history of the 131st Pennsylvania,[44] countered Walker's claim that Second Corps soldiers advanced farther than did Humphreys's men with a letter from a Confederate artillery officer, Robert J. Fleming of the Richmond Fayette Artillery, which was attached to Maj. Gen. Lafayette McLaws's division. Fleming witnessed Humphreys's attack and went out on the field after the battle under a flag of truce to discuss arrangements for burying the federal dead. The Confederate officer wrote that "the dead bodies I saw closest to our works belonged to General Humphreys's division." In their writings on

---

(43)   OR, Vol. XXI, 437 et seq.
(44)   Joseph R. Orwig. *The History of the 131st Pennsylvania Volunteers.* (Williamsport, Pa.: Sun Book Printing House, 1902), 121-123. (Hereafter Orwig)

the matter, Henry Humphreys, the general's son, and Carswell McClellan also relied heavily on the Fleming letter in disputing Walker's account; the three exchanged voluminous correspondence on the subject after the general's death.[45] The most recent exposition of the dispute is contained in the essay *Humphreys' Pennsylvania Division*, by Carol Reardon, who gives a more detailed account of the charges of the regiments other than the 129th.[46]

### After Fredericksburg

The reference on page 193 of *Red-Tape* to one half of the army being "comfortably housed, bringing into requisition for their convenience the belongings and surroundings of the abandoned dwellings" does not quite do justice to the bleak conditions the 129th faced on the Sunday following the battle. Adjutant Green wrote,

> Late at night [Saturday the 13th] we moved back to town and rested for a time on the sidewalk of one of the streets, tired, weary, and dirty. We were called into line again after midnight, and once again moved out to the field. It presented a terrible sight. The dead lay all around us, in every conceivable position, the groans of the wounded and dying filled the air—one poor fellow, who had a terrible wound in the side, begged to

(45) Francis A. Walker. *History of the Second Army Corps*. (New York: Charles Scribner's Sons, 1887), 185-187(Hereafter *History of Second Corps*). See also William H. Powell. *The Fifth Army Corps: A Record of Army Operations During the Civil War, 1861-1865*. (New York: G.P. Putnam's Sons, 1896), 385-387; Henry H. Humphreys. *General Andrew A. Humphreys at Fredericksburg and Farmville*. (Chicago: R.R. McCabe & Co., 1896), 7-25 (Hereafter *Humphreys Biography*); Carswell McClellan. *General Andrew A. Humphreys at Malvern Hill and Fredericksburg*. (St. Paul, Minn.: privately printed, 1888), 15-24.

(46) Gary Gallagher, ed. *The Fredericksburg Campaign*. (Chapel Hill: University of North Carolina Press, 1995), 104-107.

be shot so as to put him out of his misery—another young soldier was talking incoherently of his mother and home, while another still was uttering fearful imprecations.

You could also hear the groans of the rebel wounded, as they lay behind the stone wall. Broken muskets were strewn over the ground—some of the dead held their guns firmly in their hands, as though unwilling to give them up, though the power to use them had long since departed, and they have been summoned to another land, far away. It was a sight never to be forgotten. We lay in our old position until morning, wet, cold, and hungry, and then moved back again to the town, having been relieved by other troops.

We found shelter in some of the deserted houses. The field and staff of the regiment procured ample accommodation in the "Planters' Hotel"—a fine three story brick—we occupied the "ladies' parlor," and had fine mattresses to sleep on, an old fashioned piano to discourse sweet music, plenty of flour in the larder, out of which we baked "flap-jacks," an abundance of cooking utensils, enough to supply several regiments. The accommodations were extensive and the food very good for soldiers accustomed to nothing but hard bread and salt pork. The place had evidently been left very hastily, just before breakfast time, for the table was set, the spoons in the sugar-bowls, the cups and saucers ready to be filled, with rye coffee, I presume, and the table-cloth spread. I did not get there in time to see what kind of meats or preserves the proprietor had intended to regale his guests with that morning, probably, however, the usual beefsteak was on the table, with corncakes, "hog and hominy."[47]

In the enlisted-man-friendly 129th, Private Horn also got a sample of the good life at the Planters' Hotel. He wrote simply, without the erudition and the proper spelling of his Yale-educated adjutant:

---

(47)   Green Letter.

The night was very cold, and we were obliged to lay down on the ground amongst the dead and wounded without blankets and overcoats, as we had as already stated left them in a building in town. After remaining here for what seemed a very long time . . . we then again returned to the town and quartered in the Planters Hotel, where some of us managed to get a bed to sleep in but was soon routed out of this by the noise of heavy musketry. . . . The boys from the regiment threw out of the hotel plenty of bed quilts and ticks, which they spread on the pavement in front of the building, upon which they layed to prepare them selves for action in case of being called upon.

On Sunday . . . there was little firing going on, and the boys had a grand feast, baking pancakes in the hotel, where they manage to get plenty of indian meal, besides other eatables such as meat, fish, etc., if any one in civil life would have seen us now, they would have thought that there was no fighting going within twenty miles of us instead of a few yards off. In fact we ransacked the town and found all we wanted in the eating line, as no citizens were in the town to clame these goods.[48]

The building that housed the Planters' House or Hotel still stands at the northeast corner of Williams and Charles streets, less than a half mile from the scene of the charge. After the war its name was changed to the more politically correct Farmers' Hotel, but the stone slave auction block remains at its door as a reminder of the clientele it once served.

The feast-or-famine, and probably freezing, character of the 129th's experience at Fredericksburg repeated itself on Monday night, when its men became part of an "extensive ruse" to convince the Confederates that the Army of the Potomac intended to remain on the Fredericksburg side of the Rappahannock. Early Tuesday morning, in a cold rain, they

---

(48)  *Horn Diary*, 19-20.

crossed the pontoon bridge opposite the town—some of the last troops to leave Fredericksburg—many without their knapsacks and tents. Private Werkheiser of Company K wrote that they recovered their belongings, while Private Horn wrote that Company D did not. Horn's diary reflects the dire situation, although his chronology appears to be one day off, since the 129th actually got back to camp on the 16th:

> We arrived at our old camping ground on Monday 15th and looked like lost sheep, as the day was cold, and without shelter tents, which as already stated was left at Fredericksburg, made things rather gloomy. We however managed to start a fire, with great trouble, as everything was wet from the rains that set in on starting, and continued part of the time up to our return. With this we managed to keep from freezing. On the 16th the day was a clear one and we took advantage of it by cleaning our muskets, and fixing up the camping grounds. On the 17th and 18th without rashions. On the 19th inspection, but nothing to eat. Saturday, Dec. 20 and Sunday 21st but little to eat. On Monday 22nd, received blankets in the place of those lost at Fredericksburg and on Tuesday 23d we received tents and clothing, besides having visitors from Easton, and members of other regiments who came to see how their friends were getting along. Wednesday Dec. 24th and Thursday 25 (Christmas Day) short of rashions, Friday 26 the same, dress parade and company drill.[49]

In early January 1863 Colonel Frick and Lieutenant Colonel Armstrong were court-martialed and convicted for refusing to obey Humphreys's order to requisition frock coats for the Fifth Corps dress reviews (*Red-Tape* pp. 203-217, 221-223; commentary pp. 307-312), and Major Anthony became interim commander of the 129th. Burnside's abortive offensive, the infamous Mud March, began for the Humphreys division on January 21 and ended on the 23d with a return to its camps at

---

(49)  *Horn Diary*, 20-21.

Falmouth. Frick and Armstrong accompanied the troops in an ambu-lance wagon. In late February General Tyler was charged by Humphreys with various offenses, and on March 10 he was convicted of the unauthorized release of an official report; but after a published repri-mand by General Hooker he was returned to duty as commander of the First Brigade.

On April 11, 1863, Secretary Stanton returned Frick and Armstrong to command of the 129th. A letter to the *Miners Journal* of that date reported:

> [T]heir return to the Regiment yesterday, was the occasion of a sense of enthusiasm and rejoicing not often witnessed even in the army. The regiment was drawn up in line with open ranks, and as Frick and Armstrong rode into camp, the cheers which broke forth gave abundant evidence of the esteem and affection which the officers and men have for those com-manders.[50]

Upon his return, Colonel Frick almost immediately filed extensive charges against General Humphreys, and Captain Eckar filed charges against Captain McClellan for drunkenness (pp. 249-250).

### Chancellorsville

The Chancellorsville campaign began on April 27, 1863, and the Humphreys division was the last division in General Hooker's pincer movement to cross the Rappahannock at Kelly's Ford, some twenty-one miles north and west Falmouth. The Fifth Corps had been preceded to the ford by the Eleventh and Twelfth Corps.

---

(50)   *Miners Journal*, Pottsville, Pennsylvania. May 9, 1863.

The Humphreys division crossed the Rappahannock on the night of April 29, having had to wait for Gen. George Stoneman's late-arriving cavalry corps to cross first. Originally Stoneman was to have been two weeks ahead of the infantry to cut Lee's supply lines and communications with Richmond. Hooker's failure to retain an adequate cavalry force adversely affected him at Chancellorsville.

After crossing the Rappahannock, the Eleventh and Twelfth Corps headed for the crossing of the Rapidan at Germanna Ford, while the Fifth Corps was directed to Ely's Ford. On April 30 the Humphreys division, *in puris naturalibus,* waded the Rapidan and camped near Big Huntington Creek. It caught up with the rest of the Fifth Corps on the morning of May 1 at the Chancellor House, at the intersection of the Ely's Ford Road and the Orange-Fredericksburg Turnpike. The mansion served as General Hooker's headquarters. Humphreys was ordered to follow General Griffin's First Division of the Fifth Corps down the River Road toward Banks's Ford, yet later in the afternoon the divisions were recalled. Sykes's Second Division of the Fifth Corps had been ordered down the turnpike and was attacked as it fell back on Hooker's order. Humphreys was then ordered to proceed with his division a number of miles up the Mineral Springs Road and take a position covering the U. S. Mine Ford. By noon of May 2 the position was entrenched and the division listened from afar to the sounds of Stonewall Jackson's famous march around the Union army and the rout of the Eleventh Corps.

Early in the morning of May 3 the Humphreys division was ordered to march back down the Mineral Springs Road and join the fighting around the Ely's Ford and Bullock roads, where the Second Corps was hard pressed by the Confederates.

General Tyler reported on the May 3 battle:

> About 9 A.M. I received an order from Major-General [George G.] Meade to put my command in motion, and go to the support of General [William H.] French [Third Division, Second Corps], Lieutenant Colonel Webb to indicate the position we were to occupy. That officer in person pointed out the line we were to take possession of, directly in the face of

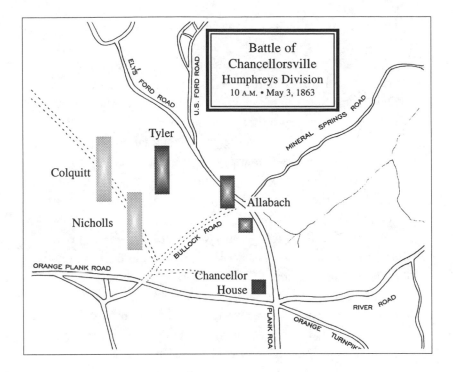

the enemy, and on the right of Gen. French's command, in the woods.

The regiments were scarcely in position before the enemy opened fire upon us, which was promptly and effectively returned by our men. I at once saw the enemy outnumbered us, as they were in double line, and extended beyond our right. . . . The rapid and incessant fire of our men prevented the enemy from advancing, although they made several efforts to do so.

After holding our position for nearly or perhaps quite an hour, reports reached me that our ammunition was being exhausted, many of the men supplying themselves from the dead and wounded. . . . [General French] replied that he could not furnish me with ammunition, and that we should retire in as good order as we could when we exhausted what we had. The moment our fire slackened the enemy pushed forward with at least twice our number.

As near as I can tell, we were in position from an hour to an hour and three-quarters before we were forced to retire. During this time the whole line was under my eye, and I have to say that I never saw officers and men behave with more bravery and coolness than did the entire command. The officers were very active, I saw many of them aiding the men by preparing their cartridges for the guns. The field officers were passing up and down the lines, encouraging their men with great spirit and coolness. . . .

The 129th Regiment Pennsylvania Volunteers was on our left, and no man ever saw cooler work on field drill than was done by this regiment. Their firing was grand—by rank, by company, and by wings, in perfect order. Colonel Frick's stentorian voice was heard above the roar of the musketry, and, with the aid of his lieutenant colonel and major, his regiment was spendidly handled, doing its duty well.[51]

Major Anthony was severely wounded—shot through the chest and lungs—but, surprisingly, he survived. The field officer who twice escaped from the Confederates in *Red-Tape* (p. 244) was its author, William Armstrong.[52]

There is a vivid account of the battle in a letter printed in the *Miners Journal* from someone in Company E (who was recruited in Tamaqua, Pennsylvania, by Capt. E. G. Rehrer) of the 129th:

Three different times they charged on us and each time they were driven back, with great slaughter. I am proud to say that the boys behaved with the coolness of veterans,—firing by company, by wing and by volley, as Colonel gave command. The Colonel took his position on the left of our company,

---

(51)   OR, Vol. XXV, Part 1, 551-552.
(52)   Bates, Vol. 4, 186.

directly by the colors, and his cool bravery inspired the whole command, It made the boys "feel good" as they expressed it, to see him occasionally take a rifle and try his hand. Adjutant Green at length came down from his position on the right, and told the Colonel that the Rebs had outflanked us on the right, and that the right of the line was falling back. (Our position was on the extreme left of the Brigade.) Colonel Frick replied that he had no order to fall back, and that he would hold his ground;—but looking up, and seeing that the whole line was in retreat, that we were far outflanked, and must be cut off, he found it necessary to retire, and accordingly gave an order to that effect. We had some hard hand-to-hand fighting in the woods, for our colors, the Rebs making a desperate effort to capture them. But the boys defended them bravely, and brought them out, with some of their would-be captors. Lieut. Colonel Armstrong came near being taken. He was surrounded by about twenty gray-backs, but he broke away and ran, and although his pursuers poured a volley after him he made his escape. . . . The soldiers are in the very best of spirits and swear that "Fighting Joe" is worth a dozen "Young Little Mac Napoleons."

Colonel Frick described the flag-recovering incident long after the war:

Capt. John Stoneback, of Co. K, rushed to the rescue of the colors. He was a tall, powerfully-built man of dark complexion. The sword-thrust aimed by him at the foremost rebel was turned aside by the Colonel, who desired to take him prisoner, but was followed by a blow from the Captain's fist, which staggered the audacious Johnny, and in the rush then made by other brave men of the guard (the names of whom have escaped me) the colors were retaken, and the prisoners captured marched to the rear.[53]

---

(53) *National Tribune,* January 5, 1893.

After May 3 the principal action switched to Fredericksburg, where Maj. Gen. John Sedgwick had made a successful bayonet charge on Marye's Heights and driven up the turnpike toward Chancellorsville. On May 4, while Hooker's forces remained in place, Lee attacked Sedgwick at Salem Church and forced him to withdraw across the Rappahannock at Banks's and Scot's fords early in the morning of May 5. After a midnight council of war on May 4-5, Hooker decided to withdraw the Army of the Potomac across the river. Private Horn wrote about the thunderstorm of May 5 "which drenched us to the skin" but became "very acceptable as it put out all the fires in the woods, thus making it more acceptable for the wounded who had not yet been picked up by the stretcher-bearers."[54]

The Fifth Corps served as the rear guard as the other five corps crossed the swollen Rappahannock at U. S. Mine Ford and was last over on the early morning of May 6.

For a good description of the May 3 fight, see E. B. Furgurson's *Chancellorsville, 1863.* It includes a graphic account by Lt. Clay Mac-Cauley of the 126th Pennsylvania, which was the regiment next to the 129th in the line. MacCauley was captured by the Confederates and barely survived the subsequent hail of federal cannister, the shelling that apparently facilitated Armstrong's escape. The Confederates facing the Tyler brigade were the Louisiana Tigers from R. E. Colston's division, and the Confederates flanking the right of the 129th were Georgians from Alfred H. Colquitt's brigade, R. E. Rodes's division.

For a description of the action from the Confederate perspective, see Terry L. Jones, *Lee's Tigers,* pp. 147-149, which describes the severe nature of the fighting between Tyler's brigade and the Louisianians before Colquitt's brigade was introduced decisively into the engagement. On page 148 Jones writes: "The Pennsylvanians put up a staunch defense, killing one Tiger when he grabbed a Federal battle flag and shooting off Colonel [Edmund] Pendleton's finger." Pendleton was with the Fifteenth Louisiana.

---

(54)  *Horn Diary,* 29.

The Tyler brigade took by far the greatest number of casualties of any brigade in the lightly engaged Fifth Corps: twenty-one killed, one hundred sixty-six wounded, and fifty-three missing.

The service time of some of the Humphreys division's nine-month regiments had already expired by the time they returned to their Falmouth camp. Only the three-year Ninety-first Pennsylvania in the Tyler brigade and the 155th Pennsylvania in the Allabach brigade remained, and they were transferred to the Second Division of the Fifth Corps. Humphreys gave a farewell testimonial to his short-term volunteers; the story of their not-so-polite farewell "salute" to him appears on pages 329-330 in this commentary.

The men of the 129th boarded the train on May 12, 1863, and were mustered out at Harrisburg on May 18, little realizing that in just over a month some of them would be back in service defending the bridges over the Susquehanna.

On May 20 the companies from Schuykill County returned to their homes. Captain Rehrer's Company E marched to Tamaqua, while Capt. William W. Clemens's Company A returned home to Minersville. Companies B, H, and G arrived at Pottsville at 2 P.M. and were welcomed home by the Pottsville Cornet Band and the Point Carbon Band.[55] The three Northampton County companies appear to have enjoyed the most elaborate welcome when the train pulled into Easton. The program was described in the *Easton Argus* of May 28:

> The firing of guns from Mount Jefferson at 1 o'clock [May 20] announced the arrival of the train. The scene at the Depot and on this side of the river cannot be described. Third street was densely packed with human beings, and amid the booming of cannon, the ringing of bells and patriotic martial music, a procession was formed under the direction of Colonel Yohe which marched . . . in the following order:

---

(55)   Richard Hostetter. *Draft History of the 129th.* (Unpublished)

Committee on Arrangements
Carriages containing wounded and sick soldiers
Orator of the day and invited guests
Guard of Honor commanded by Lieut. Joe Oliver
Company D, Commanded by Capt. Fried
Company F, Commanded by Capt. Eckar
Company K, Commanded by Capt. Stoneback
Citizens of Easton and vicinity.

After going over the route the procession halted in Centre Square, when they were welcomed in a neat speech by Edgar F. Randolph, Esq., which was responded to by Lieut. Col. W. H. Armstrong. From here they were taken to Masonic Hall and treated to a splendid repast. . . . It affords us pleasure to state that the deportment of all of the returned volunteers since their return home, has been gentlemanly and correct. They do not seem to have forgotten that the citizen soldiers can be a true gentleman as well as a brave hero.

## Short-Term Regiments, Manpower Policy, and Political Feuds

The once-colonel and now again judge Samuel Yohe, who organized the welcome home for the 129th, was the former commander of the First Pennsylvania Volunteer Infantry, the three-month unit formed in 1861. Pennsylvania presented a confusing array of three-month, nine-month, and three-year regiments which reflected the Union's ad hoc manpower policy early in the war. In his history of Pennsylvania volunteers Samuel Bates includes one-year regiments, such as the real 210th; whether these were enlisted for a set period or until the end of the war is not clear. There were also some sixty emergency militia regiments raised as a result of the Confederate invasions of Maryland and Pennsylvania in 1862 and 1863 respectively.

Under the Militia Act of 1795, the president in 1861 could call up the militia for only three months; the result was that the terms of some of those who answered Lincoln's first call, in April 1861, such as the First Pennsylvania, were expiring just as the first large battles of the war were getting under way. The president then relied on three-year enlistments until the Army of the Potomac got into its next manpower crisis, in the middle of the Peninsula Campaign.

In late June 1862 Lincoln called for an additional 300,000 troops, and the governors were consulted as to how this could be best accomplished. They cited the difficulty of getting three-year enlistees but maintained that they could get shorter-term enlistees fairly expeditiously. Gov. Andrew G. Curtin of Pennsylvania wrote that speedy enlistments would result if they were "made for a shorter time, say six months." A few three-year regiments were, in fact, formed at this time; one, the 155th Pennsylvania, was mustered a month or so after the 129th. Congress acted and modified the law so that the President could call out the militia for a period not to exceed nine months.

Jefferson Davis was having similar problems at this time; the terms of enlistment of his twelve-month regiments were expiring. His final solution, after a number of creative failures, resulted in the Conscription Acts of April 1862, which declared that the men whose enlistments had run out, and who did not reenlist, would be drafted. The terms were three years or the duration of the war, whichever was shorter. The wisdom of the Confederate approach was apparent when the two-year enlistments of federal regiments from New York and Maine expired in the spring of 1863 and the nine-month regiments of August 1862 expired on the eve of the Gettysburg campaign.[56]

Easton had another nine-month regiment, the 153rd, which was mustered a month and a half after the 129th. Its enlistment expired on July 5, and it was heavily engaged at both Chancellorsville and Gettysburg. The Confederate invasion of Pennsylvania would also see the formation on June 21, 1863, of the Twenty-seventh Emergency Militia Regiment which, at the request of Governor Curtin, was organized by Colonel Frick and contained other members of the 129th. These units served only until the Confederate invasion had been repelled in July.

### Cameron-Curtin Feud

Both the 'War Governor of Pennsylvania,' Andrew Curtin, and 'The Chieftain,' Simon Cameron, are mentioned in Red-Tape (pp. 31-34). What is not stated is that they had been intense political rivals for years. Both, however, were needed by President Lincoln to assure the success of his presidential campaigns of 1860 and 1864. Simon Cameron was a

---

(56)    Fred A. Shannon. The Organization and Administration of the Union Army, 1861-1865. (Cleveland: Arthur H. Clark Co., 1928), 272-276; Douglas Southall Freeman. Lee's Lieutenants. (New York: Charles Scribner's Sons, 1942), 171-172.

power in Pennsylvania politics for almost fifty years. Originally a Democrat, he was elected to the United States Senate in 1845 but fell out with the party and was not reelected. In 1856 he regained his senate seat as a Republican, thus becoming a political enemy of his former Democratic ally from Pennsylvania, then-president James Buchanan. Cameron was a candidate for the Republican nomination for president in 1860, but subsequently helped obtain the nomination for Abraham Lincoln. Cameron's support at the party's convention was a major factor in his appointment to the cabinet as Lincoln's first secretary of war.

The Republican party in Pennsylvania was badly split in 1860-1861. A feud had begun between the Curtin and Cameron factions with Cameron's run for the Senate in 1855, and Lincoln spent a considerable amount of time mediating.[57] William Armstrong was clearly affiliated with Curtin, while Frick was on record in support of Cameron's appointment as secretary of war.

Many charges of corruption in procurement matters were made early in Cameron's administration of the War Department. To get more support from the Radical Republicans in late 1861, he issued a report that urged the immediate emancipation and utilization of blacks as soldiers—without first clearing it with the White House. A month later the president appointed Cameron ambassador to Russia. In Lincoln's renomination and reelection in 1864, Cameron again played a prominent role. And again the president had to mediate between the forces of Cameron and Curtin, whose support for him appeared to be all they had in common. The feud hurt Lincoln in the Pennsylvania vote in both the state and federal elections, but the soldiers, who voted overwhelmingly for the president, saved the day.[58]

---

(57)  David H. Donald. *Lincoln*. (New York: Simon & Schuster, 1995), 253 (Hereafter *Lincoln*); Edwin Stanley Bradley. *Simon Cameron, Lincoln's Secretary of War*. (Philadelphia: University of Pennsylvania Press, 1967), 101.

(58)  Roy P. Basler, ed. *Collected Works of Abraham Lincoln, Vol. 4*. (New Brunswick, N.J.: Rutgers Univ. Press, 1953), 103-104, 112-113; U.S. Congress, *Biographical Directory of the American Congress 1774-1949*. (House Doc. No. 607, 1950); Allen Johnston and Dumas Malone. *Dictionary of American Biography Vol. 2*. (N.Y.: Scribner's Sons, 1944), 437-439; *Lincoln*, 495, 502, 538, 543.

### Friction between Regular Officers and Volunteers

A recurring theme in *Red-Tape* is the conflict between the regular army officers and the volunteer officers who carried out the policy and philosophy of Gen. George McClellan. The major general of the Fifth Corps and one of McClellan's favorite commanders, Fitz-John Porter, exemplifies the regular army position. He and his immediate staff were Democrats who did not endorse a 'total war.' The irony of the situation was that the 129th, led by Republican volunteer officers, was placed in the Fifth Corps, whose leaders supported a strict policy of protecting Southern property, which they saw as part of a campaign designed to lure their wayward brothers back into the Union. The volunteer officers, who were of a semi-abolitionist stripe, considered this policy to be at odds with the well-being of their troops. The volunteers also shared both Lincoln's unhappiness with McClellan's maddeningly slow style of prosecuting the war and his doubts as to McClellan's and Porter's loyalty to the war aims of the Republican administration.

The Fifth Corps comprised a strange conglomeration at Fredericksburg and Chancellorsville. The new Third Division was all volunteer and, other than Humphreys, was staffed by non–West Point officers. The first and second brigades of the Second Division were the only regular units of any size in the Army of the Potomac. (Regular batteries of artillery were, unlike the infantry, dispersed throughout the army.) The regular brigades had been led since the first battle of Bull Run by Brigadier General Sykes, who became head of the Fifth Corps at Gettysburg. The First Division was led by Brigadier General Griffin, who had just replaced a relatively silent McClellan man, Maj. Gen. George W. Morell. His division had all-volunteer regiments but included a number of West Pointers as regimental and brigade commanders.

Although Armstrong speaks disparagingly of the regular army, West Point, and the fighting qualities of engineers, he excludes from his condemnation a number of West Point graduates, such as Generals Rosecrans, Hooker, Hancock, Samuel P. Heintzelman, and, more surprisingly, Meade and Gouveneur K. Warren, each of whom had an engineering and topographical background very similar to that of Humphreys.

Gen. David B. Birney, who came up as a volunteer officer, was not so forgiving of Meade. He wrote in a letter on October 23, 1863:

> Meade, while commanding Brigade and Division, . . . was always badly beaten, troops flying in disorder & has no confidence in soldiers of the volunteers. He regards the entire salvation of the army depending on the Engineer Corps and places men without regard to their power over troops in command, believing in their skill, and erudition in ditches. His only salvation is that he is occasionally led by Warren, otherwise he is a vacillating clever man, who has good defensive qualities but is not aggressive and his campaigns will be voted a failure.[1]

Neither does Armstrong criticize the Second Division's brigades of regulars led by General Sykes other than to say that they are too often held in reserve, a result of McClellan's general predisposition not to commit all available troops. Sykes himself appears not to have been a great believer in regulars as perpetual reserves, for at a crucial time in the battle of Antietam on September 17, he proposed sending his Second Division of the Fifth Corps into action. The cautious McClellan,

---

(1)    Letter to George Gross. David B. Birney papers, U.S. Army Military History Institute, Carlisle, Pa. It should be noted that Birney was a loyal member of the more volunteer-friendly Third Corps. He was an admirer of Hooker, Daniel Sickles, and the late Philip Kearny, whom he succeeded.

according to the account, seemed inclined to approve the attack, but he decided otherwise when Fitz-John Porter slowly shook his head and reportedly stated, "Remember, General, I command the last reserve of the last army of the republic."[2]

The reaction of some members of the 155th Pennsylvania to their transfer to Sykes's division when the Humphreys division broke up seems to indicate that Humphreys himself was more of a problem for the volunteers than their interaction with Sykes's regulars. An officer wrote:

> We did not like the thought of being too near the Regulars, lest the law of strict military discipline might be enforced with us as it was with them, but in our association with them we found them good and reliable neighbors, especially in battle. But we were rejoiced at getting from under Gen. Humphreys's command.[3]

Between Humphreys and his troops there appears to have been little feeling of comradeship, and many of the volunteers doubted that taking care of his men was one of his highest priorities. The general's dour attitude, explosive temper, and profanity were not appreciated, and he made little attempt to enhance his popularity with the troops. Lt. Col. David Rowe, the historian and commander of the 126th Pennsylvania, wrote that Humphreys "knew little of human nature in civilians, and when he first assumed command of this division he was not well fitted to handle citizen volunteers. Nevertheless, he was greatly relied upon."[4]

The volunteer officers believed that the conduct of the Fifth Corps's gold-braided regular staff officers was often at odds with the well-being

---

(2)    Thomas M. Anderson. *Battles and Leaders of the Civil War* (New York: Thomas Yoseloff, 1952), 656n. For a fuller exposition of this incident see Timothy J. Reese, *Sykes' Regular Infantry Division, 1861-1864.* (Jefferson, N.C.: McFarland & Co., 1989).

(3)    D. P. Marshall. *Company K, 155th Pennsylvania Volunteer Zouaves* (privately printed, 1887), 99.

(4)    *History of the 126th*, 19.

of their troops when it came down to prosaic subjects, such as the use of fence rails for firewood and the commandeering of chickens, pigs, and even persimmons for hungry soldiers. Through the character of the West Virginia Captain, Armstrong points out that General Rosecrans, in looking out for his men, applied the hands-off Confederate property and Secesh woman rule very loosely (pp. 57-63).

The strict prohibition of fraternization between officers and enlisted men that Armstrong speaks of in *Red-Tape* has bothered volunteers in all wars in which short and long termers—so-called thirty-year-men— have been brought together. This is particularly true in units from specific geographic areas. Armstrong ridiculed the nonfraternization order in recounting a conversation between Frick and a junior Fifth Corps staff officer who declared that he would have Frick arrested if he continued to allow one of his lieutenants to talk to two privates (p. 143).

The 129th's soft fraternization policy had particular relevance to the background of the West Virginia Captain, David Eckar, who had apparently found a home in the regiment. In late October 1861, while a first lieutenant in the Second West Virginia, Eckar had been convicted of "conduct unbecoming an Officer and a Gentleman." One of the charges was playing cards with enlisted men. The other charge, which probably carried more weight in his conviction, was that when asked the nature of his company commander's illness by a newspaper correspondent, he stated that it was the clap. His case remained in limbo for several months, and he wrote to Rosecrans for relief in January 1862. The outcome was an honorable discharge resignation on the basis of disability on March 22, 1862. The following July a newspaper in Easton announced that Captain Eckar was raising a company. While citing his extensive military background, it did not mention his court-martial and concluded by saying that "those disposed to serve their country could not find a better officer." Thus, the West Virginia Captain launched his third military career.[5]

---

(5)    Files of the Judge Advocate General (II 634), National Archives; *Easton* (Pa.) *Argus*. July 17, 1862.

In addition to the usual friction found in such circumstances, an element in Humphreys's background may have played a significant role in shaping how he felt about the volunteers and how some of them, particularly the Mexican War veterans, felt about him. During the 1840s Humphreys's military engineering assignments were primarily of a civilian nature. In those very limited instances when he had to carry out the routine duties of an officer in the field, he appears to have been eager to return to his studies.[6] Trying to harness the Tiber Creek (which has impeded construction at the base of Capitol Hill for more than one hundred years), supervising the paving of the streets of Washington, and planning the construction of the House side of the capitol building were among his projects. These were not unusual assignments for a Corps of Engineers officer.

In March 1844 Humphreys reported for duty to Prof. A. D. Bache, superintendent of the United States Coast Survey. Humphreys's son described his father's approach to the coast survey assignment: "He possessed method, order, and administrative ability of a higher order, and with it the faculty of getting to the bottom of all things. 'I cannot understand how any man can be willing to assume charge of a work without making it his business to know everything about it from A to Izzard.' "[7] On October 30, 1846, Humphreys was notified that he should prepare for duty with the army in Mexico. His son noted that the order was revoked November 15, 1846, upon the urgent representations of Professor Bache, who wrote of "the serious inconveniences which would result from his removal from the duties on the survey of the coast upon which he was engaged."[8] There is no indication that Humphreys disagreed with Professor Bache's assessment, and he continued his work on the coast survey until 1850.

Neither is there any indication that Humphreys was opposed to the Mexican War on philosophical or political grounds, unlike Ulysses S. Grant, who served with distinction in Mexico yet was "bitterly opposed"

---

(6)    Henry H. Humphreys. *Andrew Atkinson Humphreys: A Biography.*
       (Philadelphia: John C. Winston, 1924), 35. (Hereafter *Humphreys Biography*)
(7)    *Ibid.*, 52.
(8)    *Ibid.*, 35.

to the war "as one of the most unjust ever waged by a stronger against a weaker nation." Grant even went so far as to say that "for myself, a young second-lieutenant who had never heard a hostile gun before, I felt sorry I had enlisted."[9] While most of his fellow junior regular officers experienced field or staff commands in the Mexican War and led volunteers in action, Humphreys did not; the consequences of this deficiency became evident some fifteen years later. Humphreys boasted of his success at training and disciplining raw troops, but he failed to mention that when it came to leading troops in action he was pretty raw himself.

Finally, Humphreys's reputation as a strict adherent to the scientific method and a lover of bureaucratic red tape did not increase his stature in the eyes of a substantial number of officers in his division, especially veterans such as the restive Colonel Frick.

Other regular officers, particularly those with more extensive field experience, appreciated some of the positive attributes of the volunteers. For instance, Gen. John Gibbon, a severe disciplinarian, noted that the volunteer soldiers were fast learners compared to the regular enlisted men to whom he had been accustomed. Of his first command of a volunteer artillery battery, he wrote:

> The first marked feature I noted with these men was their quick intelligence. It was only necessary to explain a thing but once or twice to enable them to catch the idea and then with a little practice they became perfect. I think my non-commissioned officers, some of them soldiers nearly all their lives, and sensible of the hard struggle through which they had gone to gain their information, were astonished to see what little trouble they had in instructing these men.[10]

---

(9)     Ulysses S. Grant. *Personal Memoirs, Vol. 2.* (New York: Charles Webster Co., 1886; reprint 1994), 18, 36. (Hereafter *Grant Memoirs*)

(10)    John Gibbon. *Personal Recollections of the Civil War.* (New York: G. P. Putnam & Sons, 1928), 13-14. (Hereafter Gibbon)

Of the training of the Wisconsin and Indiana troops who eventually came to be called the Iron Brigade, Gibbon wrote:

> School teaching of any kind is at best a laborious business but when the scholars number several thousand and the head teacher has to assist him but a few who know even the A. B. C. of the subject to be taught, the task becomes Herculean. In this case, however, the quick intelligence of the scholars [the volunteers] smoothed over many of the rough places and served to nullify even the strong opposition exhibited to a Regular officer being in command.[11]

But in regard to rail fences, even Gibbon struck out with the volunteers:

> One great difficulty I experienced was in regard to the destruction of fences. Many of the farmers had growing crops on which they depended to prevent starvation. Stringent orders had been published against tearing down the fences around these, or burning the rails. But dry fence rails were a sore temptation to soldiers who wanted fuel, or who did not fancy having to protect the property of "the miserable Secessionists" who were the cause of their being down here away from their families and comfortable homes. It was a waste of time to discuss with them the propriety of the order, hence I could only say: "It is an *order* and must be obeyed." Where a fence was torn down, therefore, the command camped near it was required to rebuild it and this being done on one occasion was the cause of considerable excitement, and I have reason to believe, resulted in my being reported to the Washington authorities by some of the malcontents as not being as "loyal" as an officer fighting rebels ought to be.[12]

---

(11)  *Ibid.*, 31.
(12)  *Ibid.*, 31-32.

COMMENTARY 301

General Grant also wrote of the comparative merits of the regulars and volunteers based upon his experiences in Mexico:

> At the battles of Palo Alto and Resaca-de-la-Palma General [Zachary] Taylor had a small army, but it was composed exclusively of regular troops, under the best drill and discipline. Every officer, from the highest to the lowest, was educated in his profession, not at West Point necessarily, but in the camp, in garrison, and many of them in the Indian war. The rank and file were probably inferior, as material out of which to make an army, to the volunteers that participated in all the later battles of the war; but they were brave men, and then drill and discipline brought out all there was in them.[13]

Meade was more critical of volunteers in the early stages of the Mexican and Civil wars. His opinions may have had an effect on Humphreys, however, since the two became closely associated when Meade became commander of the Fifth Corps of the Army of the Potomac.[14]

The volunteers in *Red-Tape* heaped their contumely primarily on regular staff officers rather than regular line officers, and they associated Humphreys with Porter and McClellan and their immediate staffs of West Pointers. Humphreys epitomized the hauteur of the Fifth Corps West Pointers with his dancing-master manners and his quick and constant reliance on the court-martial as the principal tool to enforce his concept of discipline. In some quarters comparison to a dancing master was considered humorous, if not downright insulting. Henry Blake pointed out that Humphreys's favorite Third Corps brigade commander and good friend, Gen. Joseph B. Carr, really had been a dancing master. His troops made fun of him by calling out "all promenade to the bar" while on the march. Lt. Col. Theodore Lyman of Meade's staff also

---

(13)  *Grant Memoirs*, 71.
(14)  George Meade. *The Life and Letters of General George Gordon Meade, Vol 1.* (Baltimore: Butternut & Blue, reprint 1994), 231, 237-238, 312.

wrote of the dancing-master backgrounds of Carr (Irish) and Gen.
Edward Ferrero (Italian).[15]

---

(15)   Frederick B. Arner. *The Mutiny at Brandy Station, the Last Battle of the Hooker
       Brigade: a Controversial Army Reorganization, Courts Martial, and the Bloody
       Days that Followed.* (Kensington, Md.: Bates & Blood Press, 1993), 14.
       (Hereafter *Mutiny at Brandy Station*) George R. Agassiz, ed. *Meade's
       Headquarters, 1864-1865: Letters of Colonel Theodore Lyman.* (Boston: Atlantic
       Monthly Press, 1922), 180.

## Discipline by Courts-Martial

It was in the military courts and the political and administrative review forums that the volunteers and General Humphreys fought their battles. As noted in Red-Tape (pp. 209-210), Congress recognized the tension between regulars and volunteers by passing legislation that prevented regulars from serving on court-martial boards trying volunteers. Armstrong maintained that the spirit of the legislation was violated by allowing the participation of regular officers who had received their commissions in volunteer service. The contest between Humphreys and the dissident volunteer officers was perhaps closer than traditional historical accounts have acknowledged. Humphreys had the regular army establishment generally on his side, while the volunteers were backed by Governor Curtin of Pennsylvania and a judge advocate general and secretary of war who would consider the possibility that a McClellan man might be involved.

**The Trial of Private Stevens:** The event that precipitated the first major incident between Humphreys and the volunteer officers was the court-martial of Pvt. Robert Stevens of the 155th Pennsylvania (pp. 49-53). The basic facts in Armstrong's account in Red-Tape have been validated by independent sources. When he was officer-of-the-guard, Capt. Joseph Orwig, the historian of the 131st Pennsylvania, found a young camp guard sleeping. The captain did not intend to pursue the case because there were mitigating circumstances, but Humphreys

learned of the incident and forced him to file charges. In his history
Orwig wrote:

> General Humphreys was greatly displeased with [the acquit-
> tal] and roundly berated all concerned, in language more for-
> cible than polite, as he was wont to do on occasions, and there-
> by gave rise to resentments which played a very important part
> in the history of the division. . . . It was stated that reporters
> and a large number of army officers confidently expected a
> public execution at division headquarters, and the failure to
> convict Stevens was therefore a great disappointment. The
> prisoner's life was doubtless spared by the friendly interest of
> the officer who found that the identity of the boy was not
> clearly shown, and had secured a recall of the witnesses, and
> his guilt had seemingly been clearly established. It is probable
> that the distinguished lawyer, who was also an officer in the
> division, keenly enjoyed the finding of the court, and that all
> the rights of that gallant young soldier who had innocently
> subjected himself to a fearful penalty, were properly secured
> to him in the case. He had not friends at his hand, but he was
> nevertheless "somebody's darling," and was deserving of a
> better fate.[16]

The official transcripts of the court-martial of Private Stevens, October 3 and 10, 1862, substantiate both the account in *Red-Tape* and
that related by Captain Orwig. The "Detail for the Court"—at least that
terminology was correct according to Humphreys's requirements—included almost every regimental commander in the division, with Col.
Edgar M. Gregory of the Ninety-first Pennsylvania as the presiding
officer and Armstrong as the judge advocate. When the second trial
also resulted in acquittal, Humphreys fired some final shots. He wrote
on the transcript that the use of an enlisted man as clerk "may vitiate

---

(16)   Orwig, 57-58.

the whole proceedings" and that the unexplained absence of some members of the court was another "irregularity."[17]

The judge advocate general in *Red-Tape* to whom Armstrong would defer (p. 50) was Joseph Holt, a famous lawyer from Kentucky and a War Democrat. He became President Buchanan's last secretary of war early in 1861 when the attorney general, Edwin Stanton, recommended him as a replacement for John B. Floyd, who was considered treasonous because he wanted to withdraw the Union troops from Fort Sumter. A strong Unionist, Holt was again considered seriously for the office of secretary of war, this time as a replacement for Cameron. He was appointed by President Lincoln as the first judge advocate of the army, a position created by Congress in July 1862. Later in the war he was offered the position of attorney general, but he elected to continue as judge advocate. Judge Holt played a role in resolving most of Lincoln's delicate legal problems of a military nature, such as the court-martial of Fitz-John Porter.[18]

**The Trial of William Wolfe, "The Lieutenant Who Came to Fight":** Humphreys's attempt to teach tactics to his volunteer junior officers resulted in a plethora of courts-martial and a dearth of lieutenants to storm Marye's Heights at Fredericksburg. The lieutenant who came to fight, not to take examinations, was 2nd Lt. William H. Wolfe, Company E, 131st Pennsylvania, and he was indeed court-martialed.[19] Captain Orwig related the circumstances of the court-martial:

> One of the unpleasant events which so sadly marred social life in the regiment, occurred here a short time previous to the battle of Fredericksburg. Nearly all the lieutenants of the [131st] regiment were cited before a board of examiners. Under a clause in the Army Regulations provision is made for the

---

(17)  Files of the Judge Advocate General (KK 270), National Archives.

(18)  Ezra J. Warner. *Generals in Blue.* (Baton Rouge: Louisiana State Univ. Press, 1964), 232; George C. Gorham. *Edwin M. Stanton, Life and Public Services,* Vol. I. (New York: Houghton Mifflin & Co., 1899), 162; *Lincoln,* 325, 550.

(19)  Files of the Judge Advocate General (KK756), National Archives.

dismissal of incompetent, or otherwise objectionable officers, and it is a wholesome and necessary provision. . . . It was susceptible of great injustice in the hands of incompetent officers, who resorted to this means sometimes out of other motives than for the good of the service. Lt. Wolf was among those who had been cited for examination, who resented the matter as an insult, and regarded it as a vindictive measure, aimed at one or two officers in his regiment, by the lieutenant colonel who was temporarily in command of the regiment. [The 131st's regular colonel was Peter Allabach, who was at that time the acting commander of the Second Brigade.] At a casual meeting of Lt. Col. [William B.] Shaut and Lt. Wolf, the former made some irritating remark, when Lt. Wolf, with his open hand, struck Lt. Col. Shaut squarely in the face, as his reply, accompanied with remarks extravagantly expressive of his contempt.[20]

The court-martial was held just before the battle of Fredericksburg, with Armstrong as the judge advocate, but the transcript reflects no charge against Wolfe for striking Shaut. Orwig noted that because of some error in the finding of the court, the finding was subject to revision. In the meantime Wolfe distinguished himself in the battle of Fredericksburg by leading Company E after his captain was wounded and the first lieutenant was killed. After the battle Shaut "followed up his action against the Lts. by an order placing ten of them under arrest upon charges of conduct unbecoming officers, on account of alleged criticisms made of the Lt. Col." Shaut relented on the charges against the officers, but the examinations by the officers' board were undertaken. Orwig wrote that the board became suspicious because of the number of cases from the 131st and abandoned the exercise after hearing only two. "The unfortunate incident left resentments that never healed,"[21] Orwig

---

(20)   Orwig, 87-89.
(21)   *Ibid.*

concluded. At Chancellorsville Colonel Shaut was in the hospital, and Maj. Robert W. Patton commanded the 131st.

## The Frock Coat Mutiny

The courts-martial of Frick and Armstrong, held on January 16, 1863, were remarkably consistent with the account in *Red-Tape* (pp. 210-217). The primary charge was "conduct subversive of good order and military discipline, tending to mutiny" in that the officers failed to forward a requisition for "frock coats" to enable their regiment "to appear on dress parade . . . in the uniform prescribed by Army Regulations."[22]

**Trial of Jacob G. Frick:** Colonel Frick saw the charges the night before the trial. He requested a postponement in order to obtain counsel but was unable to do so within the fifteen minutes he was allotted. Humphreys testified about a meeting in his tent on January 12 and noted that Frick had attempted then to explain why the men did not need or want frock coats. Humphreys said he had told him to answer yes or no to the question of whether he would obey the requisition order. Frick answered in the negative, and Humphreys characterized the answer as "insubordinate, it was defiant."

Lt. Benjamin J. Tayman, the "wharf-rat of an adjutant" of the Ninety-first Pennsylvania in *Red-Tape* and Frick's arresting officer, testified that during the arrest, when Frick was told to leave his sword in his tent, he threatened Tayman. Frick was alleged to have said, "there is something more that you can have or will have."

Colonel Frick, in examining Armstrong (who was called as a defense witness), tried to elicit an explanation of why the troops did not need

---

(22)    Files of the Judge Advocate General (KK572, Frick; KK641, Armstrong), National Archives.

frock coats and the financial burden it would place on them. The judge advocate, Lt. Col. Alexander Webb, objected, and the court ruled that the line of questioning was irrelevant. Frick also asked Armstrong, "Was it not a suggestion of Lt. Tayman that the order could not be enforced and that the officers should all stand together, and that he would see Colonel Rowe [of the 126th Pennsylvania] and call again and let us know what Colonel Rowe had to say?" Armstrong answered in the affirmative.

Rowe testified that, "I told [Frick] that the company officers of my regiment had refused to make requisitions, under the impression that they, the company officers, could not compel the men to take clothing and they alleged Gen. Tyler for their authority for supposing that they were not bound to make such a requisition."

Although Rowe, a future judge, was also arrested, he was more politic than Frick or Armstrong, whom he later characterized as "contumacious." Rowe wrote, "[Humphreys] clung to his caprice, and the men refused to take the coats. The regimental and company commanders were placed in an awkward position. The order was arbitrary, but it was imperative. They finally refused to compel their men, and were placed in arrest." Rowe deemed it unwise to further resist Humphreys when confronted in his tent and signed the requisition order for the frock coats, but he noted that the men "threw them away."[23]

Colonel Frick was found guilty of "conduct subversive of good order and military discipline tending toward mutiny" but innocent of the fourth specification to the charge: in the presence of Armstrong, Rowe, and other officers, he did "murmur and mutter against the lawful authority" of General Humphreys and "combine or attempt to combine with said officers to resist such lawful order." He was also convicted of a second charge of "positive and willful disobedience of orders and insubordination" and conducting himself "in an insubordinate and threatening manner."

---

(23)  *History of the 126th*, 25-26.

**The Trial of William H. Armstrong** (pp. 207-217): General Humphreys testified that he had read the following to Armstrong in the tent:

> Mutiny is resistance either action or passive. It implies not only extreme insubordination and individually resisting by force or collectively rising against or opposing military authority but murmuring or muttering against the exercise of authority, tending to create disgust or dissatisfaction in the army. It may originate and conclude with a single person.

The general then asked if Armstrong still refused to obey the order to requisition frock coats. Armstrong replied affirmatively, and Humphreys announced that his conduct amounted to mutiny.

Humphreys went on to say that Armstrong "replied that this was false. I understood him to apply this term to my charging him with 'mutiny' as well as to the fact that he had communicated with others. I suppose that the passion of the moment had made him forget what had occurred, and I pointed to Lt. Tayman saying in substance 'the testimony of this officer established it.' Whereupon he addressed some hasty and hot remarks to this officer, ending with passing what I understood to be a challenge [to a duel] to him. His manner at first was perfectly courteous and respectful, at the latter part of the interview he, upon fixing the charge of Mutiny upon him, it was disrespectful to insubordinate."

Armstrong then cross-examined Humphreys, asking, "Did you understand me to call in question your personal veracity during this interview?" The general answered, "Not so far as related to any facts. But so far as related to the designation of his offense. I consider his use of the term 'false' as an insubordinate and disrespectful manner of referring to my charge, but not as calling in question my personal veracity."

Armstrong then asked the general to characterize the nature of his previous conduct. Humphreys replied, "I should state to the court that [Armstrong] has complied with every order and performed a duty with promptitude, cheerfulness and great intelligence previous to this occurrence, that his intercourse with me had always been of the most courteous kind." Ironically, the court used this statement to justify the exclusion of a host of character witnesses for Armstrong.

Lieutenant Tayman also testified for the prosecution, declaring that Armstrong told him, "Adjutant, you might as well make [an arrest order] out for the Major [Anthony], too, for we will all go together." On cross-examination Armstrong asked if at the time of his alleged statement he was not talking to a private. Tayman answered in the affirmative. The defense then called Howard R. Hetrick, Company D, the private in question, who testified that he had heard no such statement as alleged by Tayman. In *Red-Tape* the private is portrayed as a disheveled law student, which gives further credence to the proposition that the names used by Armstrong are pseudonyms.

The charges against Armstrong were almost identical to those against Frick, and the court found him guilty on both counts. He was found not guilty on the specification based on Tayman's allegation that Armstrong had said he should get a charge ready for Major Anthony.

In *Red-Tape* Armstrong complains that the courts-martial of volunteers were dominated by regulars and West Pointers (p. 210). It is true that none of the judges came from the all-volunteer Third Division; however, the implication that the court was completely dominated by West Point graduates appears ill-founded. The only U. S. Military Academy graduates on the board were Gen. Gouveneur K. Warren, U.S. Volunteers (who was initially designated presiding officer but did not serve); Col. James Barnes, Eighteenth Massachusetts, presiding officer; Col. Patrick H. O'Rorke, 140th New York; and the judge advocate, Lt. Col. Alexander Webb. None of the officers came from Sykes's brigade of regulars.

Attached to the court-martial file is a paper signed by General Barnes and the ranking colonels on the board, Henry A. Weeks, Twelfth New York; J. B. Sweitzer, Sixty-second Pennsylvania; O'Rorke; and Lt. Cols. W. B. Bartram of the Seventeenth New York and George Varney of the Second Maine, which stated: "The undersigned members of the Court in consideration of his previous good character as testified by his Commanding General; and in view of his statement in writing found in the proceeding of the Court, recommend Lt. Col. Armstrong to such degree of clemency as the Commanding General may think proper to extend to him." No clemency was forthcoming, however, and the two officers were cashiered. Both General Meade and General Hooker endorsed the convictions and the sentence.

**Reaction on the Home Front:** The arrests and courts-martial of Armstrong and Frick were reported in some detail in the Easton newspapers. An article in the *Easton Express* of January 17, 1863, declared:

> From what we can learn, these officers have always had the welfare of their troops at the heart, and in this case did not think it was in accordance with the wishes of the men to have more clothing, which they would be compelled to pay for out of their hard earned wages to help some government contractor out of a scrape, in getting rid of his supply. The time of the men is nearly out, and as they had sufficient clothing to last them, we think the officers did right, and the community here will uphold them for it, no matter how the matter may terminate. If all the officers in the army would defend the men under their respective command, we would not have to hear of so much discontent in the army. The price of the coat, which they wanted them to take, was $6.71—a half month's pay!

Two days later the newspaper noted the continued incarceration of the officers, who were "not even permitted to write, or receive letters." The paper hoped that ". . . they will stand up to the last. The whole community here accord them praise. We glory in the spunk of these officers and the soldiers we are pleased to know, look upon the matter in the right light." The paper also reported that a soldier had written that ". . . the Regiment showed a disposition to have the officers released, and were about carrying out their design, when another Regiment was ordered out, with two pieces of cannon loaded with grape and pointed in the direction of the camp of the 129th. The 153rd Regiment also showed a disposition to help the 129th boys in releasing their officers, Jan. 19, 1863."[24]

Even the Democratic paper in Easton, the *Argus*, from which Humphreys might have expected some support, reported the affair with some humor on January 29, 1863. It stated that "good soldiers can't be imposed upon" and reported that "they told the General they intended to purchase at Pyle's Hall of Fashion, when they wanted coats, where they could get good ones for less money. Soldiers and Citizens, remember the place, opposite the old Bank."

Governor Curtin asked the War Department to reinstate the two colonels. On March 24, 1863, the judge advocate general, Joseph Holt, made a favorable recommendation regarding Armstrong to Secretary Stanton; he cited his past record, attested to by Humphreys, and the recommendation for clemency by the court-martial board. Holt wrote, "In a moment of misguided devotion to the supposed interest of his regiment, he lost sight of the severe and wise discipline of the service, but from the tone of his character, no doubt is entertained but that he has been sufficiently rebuked and admonished to prevent a recurrence of the offense. At a period like this, the Government can ill afford to lose from its Army, so zealous, faithful, and capable an officer as Lt. Col. Armstrong is shown to have been."[25]

On April 11, 1863, Frick and Armstrong were reinstated as the commanders of the 129th.

**The Trial of Gen. Erastus B. Tyler:** When General Humphreys returned to camp from Washington in early February 1863, he was informed that General Tyler had, in effect, stolen his thunder by sending a report of the battle of Fredericksburg to Governor Curtin and that it had been printed in a Harrisburg newspaper. The fact that Tyler at this very time was being presented with a sword, sash, and horse by an admiring brigade did not improve Humphreys's disposition. He reacted in typical Humphreys fashion: another court-martial was ordered.

The order convening the court was dated March 2, 1863, and specified as judges Maj. Gen. William H. French, presiding officer; Brig.

---

(24)    The 153rd was an Eleventh Corps nine-month regiment from Easton and Northampton County. Rather than a single regiment, the entire Allabach brigade turned out.

(25)    Office of the Judge Advocate General (Record Book No. 2, 107-108), National Archives.

Gens. David B. Birney, Joseph J. Bartlett, Joseph B. Carr, Gershom Mott, and J. H. Hobart Ward; and Col. Strong Vincent.[26]

Of the seven charges, only two involved the report on the battle that had been sent to Governor Curtin. The remaining five had an everything-but-the-kitchen-sink quality and included falsehood (not mentioning in his official report that Humphreys was present and had issued commands at various times during the battle of Fredericksburg); misbehavior in the face of the enemy (not moving his brigade quickly enough from the right to the left prior to the charge of Marye's Heights); neglect of duty (not recovering a portion of his brigade's knapsacks after the battle); and conduct subversive of good order and military discipline, tending to mutiny (advising Frick and Armstrong not to obey Humphreys's frock coat requisition orders).

The court, rather significantly, questioned Humphreys as to whether he had intended to file charges against Tyler for misconduct in the presence of the enemy at Fredericksburg prior to learning of his report to Curtin. Humphreys responded that he "had not and for the reason that I did not understand nor did I suppose that the delay [in Tyler moving to the left] was intentional until my return [in February]." Humphreys testified at length to support the many charges, and Tyler himself conducted the cross-examination on much of the testimony.

The following is a typical exchange and indicates that Tyler was trying to show that Humphreys was not completely on top of the situation:

*Tyler:* When ordered to change their position to the left of the road, how did the Brigade come into line?

*Humphreys:* It appeared to be forming in succession. I did not give it my particular attention.

*Tyler:* Was or was not General Tyler's Brigade ready to move as soon as the firing of the Battery formed on its front ceased?

*Humphreys:* Very soon after but the firing might have stopped at any moment.

(26) Files of the Judge Advocate General, (LL608), National Archives.

*Tyler:* Did or did not General Tyler aid in arresting the fire of the Battery formed on the front of his Brigade?

*Humphreys:* I do not recollect that he did, he may have done so before I was there. . . .

*Tyler:* Was or was not General Tyler in command of his Brigade when Colonel Frick and Lieutenant Colonel Armstrong refused to obey the order in regard to the estimates and requisition for frock coats?

*Humphreys:* He was not in command when they refused to obey the second order I issued. He was in Washington. I believe he was in command when I issued the first directive.

*Tyler:* Did they refuse to obey the order when it was first issued?

*Humphreys:* I do not understand that they did, my recollection is that there was something reported to me which induced me to dispense with an exact compliance of that order.

The court found Tyler guilty of the first two charges of conduct prejudicial to good order and military discipline and violation of the general orders which related to the confidentiality of official reports and military events. He was found not guilty of "conniving" to have them printed in the Harrisburg papers. More significantly, Tyler was found not guilty of the charges of misbehavior in the face of the enemy and neglect of duty.

Tyler was sentenced "to be reprimanded in General Orders." The reprimand stated in part:

Brigadier General E. B. Tyler, convicted of having violated this well known and most proper regulation, thus lending the sanction of his rank to a practice which cannot be too severely reprobated. It is, to be sure, alleged in the defense that the facts relating to the operation in question had been given to the world in the report of the Investigating Committee of Congress. It is not seen how this fact applied to the case under consideration. The orders and regulations of the Army are made for the government of soldiers; the action of Congressional

Committees is not subjected to such rules, and can in no way affect the question of a soldier's amenability.

The Major General Commanding [Hooker], carrying out the sentence of the Court, reminds Brigadier General E. B. Tyler that high rank brings with it duties, as well as privileges. One of the most important of these duties is the setting of an example of exact obedience of orders and regulations to subordinates; and no amount of zeal and bravery in discharge of other duties is a sufficient excuse for a neglect of this one. Brigadier General E. B. Tyler will be released from arrest, and will return to duty.

**Col. Matthew Quay:** In his arguments to the court-martial board, Tyler stated that he had given his account of the battle of Fredericksburg to Governor Curtin to call his attention to the action of Colonel Quay, who had conducted himself "with a gallantry and spirit worthy of the highest commendation." The fact that Tyler was from Ohio, not Pennsylvania, adds some credence to his argument. Quay had commanded the 134th Pennsylvania in the Tyler brigade and was discharged for poor health after developing malarial fever. Although he had left the army, he was serving as a volunteer aide to Tyler during the battle of Fredericksburg.

Governor Curtin subsequently appointed Quay his military agent for the state of Pennsylvania and later his military secretary.[27] As such, Quay probably played a role in the efforts of the governor to return Frick and Armstrong to duty.

Quay himself had narrowly avoided becoming one of Humphreys's court-martial statistics when he was commander of the 134th. In November 1862 Humphreys charged him with possession of a government horse, which Quay had 'borrowed' when his private horse was stolen. His orderly had been wise enough to leave a receipt, which Humphreys, in a good humor at the preliminary hearing, considered sufficient to avoid a court-martial.

---

(27)  *Martial Deeds*, 684.

After the war Quay went into politics. He served as a United States senator for many years and was the chairman of the Republican National Committee. In 1867 Quay endorsed Simon Cameron for the Senate rather than Curtin and later in the century formed a political dynasty in Pennsylvania with Cameron's son, James Donald Cameron, which lasted into the twentieth century.[28] The younger Cameron succeeded his father to the Senate in 1877 and served for twenty years. He, like Quay, also served as chairman of the Republican National Committee.[29]

In 1888, some fifty-five surviving members of the 134th successfully nominated Quay for a Medal of Honor. One of the interesting details in Quay's file on the award is the assertion that he had been entrusted to carry some $20,000 of his troops' pay to relatives in Pennsylvania. Capt. J. M. Clark wrote, "Seeing the carnage ahead of us and what seemed our inevitable doom, [Quay] said, 'My hope is that every man will know that I have his money, then my bones won't be left on the field.' "

General Tyler also penned an endorsement for the honor, stating that "duty impelled [Quay] to go into the fight with his regiment, insisting if he could go no other way he would carry a musket. . . . In the charge on Marye's Heights on the afternoon of Dec. 13th, his coolness, gallantry, and marked bravery was of a most conspicuous character, such indeed as few men in sound health could have equaled."[30]

Incidentally, Quay's medal was one of many awarded to politicians long after the war. Pursuant to legislation in 1916, the records of all medals thus bestowed were examined by a board of officers to see if the recipients met the standard of having been in "action involving actual conflict with an enemy distinguished conspicuously by gallantry or intrepidity, at the risk of . . . life, above and beyond the call of duty."

(28)   Cameron, 301.
(29)   *Under the Maltese Cross: Antietam to Appomattox, the Loyal Uprising in Western Pennsylvania, 1861-1865, Campaign of 155th Pennsylvania Regiment Narrated by the Rank and File.* (Pittsburgh: Regimental Association, 1910), 537. (Hereafter *Maltese Cross*); *Dictionary of American Biography*, Vol. 7, 296-298.
(30)   Medal of Honor files, National Archives.

Quay and Frick passed the test, but the entire Twenty-seventh Maine flunked. Its members had been given the medal for agreeing to extend their two-year enlistments in June 1863, although 309 of them went home anyway. In all, 911 persons lost their medals, including William "Buffalo Bill" Cody and Mary Walker, a Civil War contract surgeon and the only woman to receive the award.[31]

**Charges Against Humphreys and Capt. Carswell McClellan:** On April 14, 1863, Humphreys found himself the target of a court-martial action. Immediately upon his reinstatement and return to camp, Colonel Frick preferred charges. Like Humphreys's charges against Tyler, Frick's litany covered a multitude of alleged sins. The printed document that contains the accusations states:

> At the time the commanding General [Hooker] was informed that proof was POSITIVE but notwithstanding this fact the charges were suppressed, but by whom it is not known to the officer who preferred them. They necessarily had to be sent through General Humphreys' Head Quarters. Copies, however, of these charges and specifications with all the facts connected with them were subsequently sent to the President, Gen. [Henry W.] Halleck and Col. Joseph Holt, Judge Advocate General, U. S. Army.[32]

The charges also matched those lodged by Humphreys against Frick in their intensity. The first, "uttering disloyal and treasonable sentiments," was based on the allegation that Humphreys had stated at Warrenton at the time of General McClellan's dismissal, "By God I wish some one would ask the Army to follow [General McClellan] to Washington and hurl the whole d—d pack into the Potomac, and place

(31)   Frederick B. Arner. *The Congressional Medal of Honor: Statutory and Administrative History* (Legislative Reference Service, Library of Congress, monograph: 1954), 4-5.

(32)   *John L. Nicholson Papers*, Huntington Library, Pasadena, California.

General McClellan at the head of affairs. I believe the army would willingly go."

The incident in question is alluded to briefly by his son in Humphreys's biography: "Some expressions of Humphreys showing regret at the relief of General McClellan were enlarged upon by his enemies in the division. At a later period, when discipline was enforced with an iron hand, his harmless expression was made to militate against him in promotion to higher rank."[33] He is referring to Humphreys's long-delayed confirmation by the Senate. Apparently General Tyler raised some questions with the congressional committees in March-April of 1864.

In the postscript of the draft of a letter to a Mr. Odell (probably Moses Odell, a member of congress from New York), which was heavily edited by Humphreys himself and is difficult to decipher, the general wrote, "Probably I cannot furnish a copy of [Tyler's] testimony; I would like to hear its character from you if you are at liberty to mention it. . . . All the charges of Col. Frick have grown out of some careless, petulant words used by me to him at a social gathering in a moment of warmth . . . at the clique after McClellan."[34]

Apparently Frick's action against Humphreys also figured in the congressional deliberation on Humphreys's confirmation. On April 5, 1864, in one of two letters that touch on this subject, General Birney wrote to a friend in Pennsylvania, "Humphreys is violently opposed for his strong and bitter McClellan speeches after his hero was decapitated. Frick of a Pennsylvania regiment has filed regular charges against him and substantiates them."[35]

Similar charges by Frick stemming from the same alleged statement cited "conduct subversive of good order and military discipline, tending to mutiny and sedition" and a "violation of the Fifth Article of War."

The fourth charge against Humphreys was for "tyrannical conduct and conduct unbecoming an officer and a gentleman" in that he called

---

(33)   *Humphreys Biography*, 173.
(34)   *Andrew A. Humphreys Papers*, Historical Society of Pennsylvania, Philadelphia.
(35)   David B. Birney letter to George Gross, U.S. Army Military History Institute, Carlisle, Pa.

a number of officers into his tent "to show them how a G–d d—d coward looked." (The coward in question was Major Danver of the 123rd Pennsylvania Volunteers.) The final charge was for "drunkenness" and cited an incident on January 8, 1863, in which Humphreys "was grossly intoxicated in the presence of Privates of his command."

The charges made an impression on Joseph Holt, the judge advocate general, who wrote in his recommendation to Secretary Stanton that they be forwarded to General Hooker "with directions to have General Humphreys tried upon them by a General Courts Martial." Holt wrote,

> [T]he charges formally made by Colonel Frick against Gen. Humphreys are of the gravest character, and should be thoroughly investigated. The sentiments which he is alleged to have uttered are not only disloyal, but express the most atrocious form of military treason. Col. Frick avers that positive proof of these charges can be produced and it seems to me that under these circumstances, it is the duty of the Government to put this officer on trial, and that duty cannot be declined with safety to the interests of the service. A General capable of entertaining, or uttering such a sentiment, is not only unfit for command, but his presence in the army cannot be otherwise than fraught with extreme peril to the Government.[36]

The Major Danver to whom the charges referred was himself the subject of a Humphreys court-martial in early March 1863. Colonel Rowe was president of the court; Capt. Adolfo Cavada, an aide to Humphreys, was the judge advocate; and Colonel Sweitzer was the defense attorney. The testimony showed that during the charge at Marye's Heights, as the 123rd of Allabach's brigade approached the stone wall, Danver began "to bleed from the lungs" and went to the rear. His commanding officer, Col. John Clark, testified that he had not given him permission to leave the field but that an officer had told him

---

(36)   Letters of the Judge Advocate General (May 23, 1863, Book 2, 417), National Archives.

that Danvers was spitting blood. On cross-examination, Colonel Clark testified that it might have been difficult and dangerous to get to him to secure permission and further allowed that none of the six officers who had been wounded had gotten his permission to leave the field. Many witnesses attested to Danver's bleeding, which appeared to have been a chronic condition, and to his incapacity as he lay on a bed in a cellar in Fredericksburg for the next two or three days. Eventually Danver was assisted over the pontoon bridge when the city was evacuated. The assistant surgeon of the 123rd, Thomas E. Stathem, testified that when he finally saw the major on December 18 he was a very sick man and not fit for duty. His right lung was "very much congested."

Danver was found not guilty of the charge of "misbehavior before the enemy." As to the specification of leaving the field without permission, the court found him "guilty, but the accused was justified in leaving." On March 24 General Humphreys approved the findings of the court yet appended this curious comment: "A simple verdict of not guilty of a charge of misbehavior before the enemy, is in itself a sufficiently severe condemnation of an officer who without orders leaves his regiment on the field of battle when he has strength sufficient to stand, walk, or ride."[37] The major was dishonorably discharged on March 31, 1863.

The charges of drunkenness against Capt. Carswell McClellan (p. 248) were most likely brought by the West Virginia captain, David Eckar. Chaplain Hartsock of the 133rd Pennsylvania in Allabach's brigade recorded the following version of the drunken scene on the Mud March, which can be compared with the account on pages 218-220:

Add to this the appearance of now & then a drunken Brigadier & tons of privates on a drunk. The secret is this. The Gen. ordered whiskey for the men and had a negro drive the team. Some soldiers called out to the darkey asking what he had in the barrel. "Whiskey," cried the old man. No sooner said than the men pitched into the wagon, ordered the negro to halt and broke in the head and at whiskey. The Gen. ordered the negro

(37)   Files of the Judge Advocate General (LL191), National Archives.

on and the boys decently unloaded the barrel and took the whiskey. Some amusing scenes occurred, such as fellows tumbling into the mud, etc. etc.[38]

The Irish Corporal in *Red-Tape* might have declared it Humphreys's finest hour.

**General Tyler and Lieutenant Tayman Exchange Charges:** The sudden exit at Chancellorsville of the wounded "exhorting Colonel," Edgar Gregory, accompanied by Tayman, the "wharf-rat of an Adjutant," resulted in still another court-martial in the brigade. This time Tyler charged Tayman with "misbehavior before the enemy" because he, after accompanying Colonel Gregory off the field, remained out of action until "the regiment was forced to retire." At the trial the lieutenant colonel and major of the Ninety-first testified that they had not seen Lieutenant Tayman during the engagement and had not been notified by him of Colonel Gregory's wounding.

A lieutenant of the Ninety-first testified for the defense that he had seen Tayman a half hour before the regiment retired. Ironically, lost knapsacks were also the subject of "neglect of duty" charges against Tayman, who had relieved the officer in charge of knapsacks but had not seen to a replacement. The trial was held on May 25, 1863. General Tyler, with the breakup of the Humphreys division, had left the Fifth Corps and taken with him the "staff officer" who was to have been the principal prosecution witness. Tayman presented a written argument that stated, "I do not hesitate to declare that this entire prosecution had its origin in Malice, which my accuser has for some time entertained toward me." He asked for a verdict of "honorable acquittal" but must have been satisfied with the one handed down: not guilty on all counts.[39]

---

(38)   James C. and Eleanor A. Duram, eds. *Soldier of the Cross: The Civil War Diary and Correspondence of Rev. Andrew Jackson Hartsock.* (Manhattan, Kans.: Military Affairs/Aerospace Historian Publishing, 1979), 51.

(39)   Files of the Judge Advocate General (NN52), National Archives.

Later that year Tayman may have tried to balance the scale when he preferred charges against Tyler, stating that Tyler had called him an "impudent pup" and threatened to "have him strung up [and] put in irons." Judge Advocate General Holt, who had to decide whether the charges should go forward, declared that it was for Secretary Stanton "to determine whether in time of war, the interests of the service will permit its officers to be occupied with the investigation of offenses importing no higher degree of culpability than this."[40] Apparently they did not.

The mutual admiration between Humphreys and Tayman continued to flourish and is described in Humphreys's biography. In late 1864, as Tayman was leaving the service, Humphreys "wrote him a very brief note expressing my opinion of his faithful performance of duty under every circumstance. . . . Knowing the good opinion I had of him and his great regard for me, General Tyler endeavored to damage him by preferring false accusation against him in connection with the battle of Chancellorsville, of which the Court *honorably* acquitted him."

Tayman's reply to Humphreys may have lived up to Armstrong's expectations of a "sucker-mouthed aide." It stated in part: "A desire to answer your kind and valued favor of the 8th inst., so flatteringly complimentary to myself, I now offer as my excuse for thus trespassing upon your valuable time. I beg of you to believe me, General, your friendly letter and honorary testimonial will be treasured and cherished by me during my entire life; and will be transmitted to my children with a history of its origins that the name of its author may have a place in their memories along with the name of their father as one who held no second place in the galaxy of patriots during the Great Rebellion."[41]

---

(40)   Letters of the Judge Advocate General (September 22, 1863, Record Book 3), National Archives, 622.

(41)   *Humphreys Biography*, 266-267.

# The Many Faces of Andrew A. Humphreys

In the never-ending process of grading Civil War generals, historians and other commentators have generally accorded Andrew Humphreys very high marks as a scholar and scientist-turned-combat-soldier who, despite his limited military experience, exhibited great courage and competency when exposed to some of the most difficult and dangerous assignments of the war. When he burst onto the national scene on December 13, 1862, at the battle of Fredericksburg, he was an engineer and topographical officer whose primary claim to fame was a study entitled *The Physics and Hydraulics of the Mississippi River*, which had earned him a charter membership in the National Academy of Sciences and an international reputation in the engineering community. Author and historian John M. Barry goes so far as to say that the report would "become the single most influential ever written about the Mississippi River . . . [and] one of the most influential single engineering reports ever written on any subject. It would have influence both because of the position Humphreys would soon attain and because of its quality."[1]

---

(1)    John M. Barry. *Rising Tide: The Great Mississippi Flood of 1927 and How It Changed America.* (New York: Simon & Schuster, 1997), pp. 50-51. (Hereafter Barry) Barry explains the effect of Humphreys's report and his subsequent actions as head of the Corps of Engineers, which were sometimes at odds with the science of the report. The "levees only" flood control policy that was adopted at the corps during Humphreys's tenure ultimately resulted in the 1927 catastrophe.

With the final, futile charge on the stone wall at Marye's Heights, Humphreys's reputation attained another dimension. General Hooker testified before a congressional committee that "no campaign ever saw a more gallant advance than Humphreys's division."

*Harper's Weekly* published a full page woodcut of the "raw" division's charge led by the "brave man of science" (p. 196). Whether the result of competence, providence, accident, or design, the accolades that stemmed from the battles of Fredericksburg and Gettysburg color the high reputation that Humphreys enjoys today.

The positive commentaries on Humphreys's career, the basis for the prevailing view of Humphreys as a great general, range from very favorable to downright euphoric. After the war Assistant Secretary of War Charles A. Dana, who was Secretary of War Edwin Stanton's eyes in

*Andrew A. Humphreys wearing a "frock coat" dress uniform.*

the field in late 1863 and 1864, noted Humphreys's fifteen months of service as chief of staff to Meade (a role that was the prototype for that position as it exists in modern military organizations) as he lauded the general:

In my opinion, the great soldier of the Army of the Potomac
at this time was General Humphreys. He was chief of staff to
General Meade, and was a strategist, a tactician, and an engineer. He was a fighter, too, and in this an exception to most
engineers. He was a very interesting figure. He used to ride
about in a black felt hat, the brim of which was down all round,
making him look like a Quaker. He was very pleasant to deal
with, unless you were fighting against him, he was not so pleasant. He was one of the loudest swearers that I ever knew.[2]

   Some of the more flamboyant of Humphreys's accolades were penned
by New York militia general J. Watts DePeyster, who wrote in a
memorial:

   A great and at the same time a good man, who attained the
   ripest age with undiminished faculties, a magnificent soldier
   who combined the calmest intrepidity with executive ability
   in battle, a mind capable of working with the nicest precision
   amid the wildest churn of conflict under exceptional circumstances of peril . . . Physically and morally it is true of him what
   is narrated of Nelson, when asked if on one occasion Fear had
   not influenced his conduct, he said, "I have never met Fear."
   In one of his letters to the writer [Humphreys] suddenly breaks
   out, filled with fond memories of the joys of the battle (*guardia
   certamini*), and portrays his sensations with vivid forces of language which present living pictures (*tableaux vivant*) of scenes
   which he held, constituted the superlatives of the sublime.[3]

   Humphreys penned one of his "superlatives of the sublime" in a letter
to his wife written immediately after the battle of Fredericksburg:

---

(2)   Charles A. Dana. *Recollections of the Civil War*. (New York: Collier Civil War
      Classics, 1899, reprint), 173-174.
(3)   J. Watts DePeyster. *Andrew Atkinson Humphreys of Pennsylvania*. (Lancaster,
      Pa.: Intelligencer Print, 1886), 14-15.

The charge of my division is described by those who witnessed it as sublime, and H[enry, his son and aide] tells me, that he heard some general officers (who did not know him) discussing it, and saying that it was the grandest sight they ever saw, and that as I led the charge and bared my head, raising my right arm to heaven, the setting sun full upon my face gave me the aspect of an inspired being.

This is quite egotistical, is it not? I felt gloriously, and as the storm of bullets whistled around me, and as the shells and shrapnel burst close to me in every direction scattering with a hissing sound their fragments and bullets, the excitement grew more glorious still.

Oh, it was sublime! As we neared the enemy's works their lines became a sheet of flame that enveloped us in front and flank.[4]

Equally laudatory yet less flowery than those of DePeyster and Humphreys himself were the assessments of the general by his personal staff—his son Henry and Carswell McClellan, whose books and articles were written in the 1880s.

Relying to a large degree on the materials of Henry Humphreys and McClellan, Gen. James H. Wilson put together a lengthy and highly laudatory sketch of the general in 1893. Wilson, an 1860 West Point graduate, was a topographical-engineer-turned-successful-cavalry-general under Grant and Gen. William T. Sherman in the West; at Antietam he was an aide-de-camp to McClellan. His sketch contains the following passage, which is typical of its tone and content:

The appearance of Humphreys on the bloody but doubtful field of Antietam was timely and reassuring. Although travel-stained, he presented at the head of his enthusiastic Pennsylvanians a cheerful and confident figure. He was a gentleman of perfect manners and habits, who always used the regulation

(4)    *Humphreys Biography*, 179.

equipments and wore the regulation uniform. His gloves and footgear were faultless; his fine intelligent face was clean-shaven, except as to the mustache; his eyes were gray and full of kindliness, except when aroused by anger. He was about five feet, seven inches high, erect and graceful in carriage, and weighed at that time not far from one hundred and fifty pounds. There was nothing rough or harsh about him. Calmness, composure, without the slightest trace of assumption or bravado, were apparent in every feature. Altogether he was as prepossessing a figure in whatever aspect he was viewed as could be found in that or any other army. Like Caesar at a corresponding age, his military career was all before him; but unlike Caesar he had led only a virtuous and studious life, for without thirst for power, and with no ambition, except to serve his country and to assist in the maintenance of its unity, under the Constitution and the laws.[5]

Lyman, on the other hand, is more equivocal. Of Humphreys's period as Meade's chief of staff, Lyman wrote: "[He] is most easy to get on with, for everybody; but, practically, he is just as hard as the Commander [Meade], for he had a tremendous temper, a great idea of military duty, and is very particular. When he does get wrathy, he sets his teeth and lets go to a torrent of adjectives that must rather astonish those not used to little outbursts." Later in 1864 he wrote: "The good General is fond of sitting awhile and talking after meals. He discourses sometimes on the art military and said it was 'a godlike occupation!' 'Ah,' he said, 'war is a very bad thing in the sequel, but before and during a battle it is a very fine thing!' " Having said this, Lyman then commented, "I don't see it."[6]

---

(5)  Papers of the Military Historical Society of Massachusetts, Vol. X, 81-82.

(6)  George R. Agassiz, ed. *Meade's Headquarters, 1863-1865: Letters of Col. Theodore Lyman from the Wilderness to Appomattox.* (Boston: Atlantic Monthly Press, 1922), 73, 243.

Despite the tributes and laurels bestowed upon him, there were those among the ranks of his first command who saw his actions and abilities in quite a different light. The most extreme view was expressed by William Armstrong in *Red-Tape*. He wrote the Humphreys character, Old Pigey, as an eccentric, hyperactive, profane, and whiskey-loving martinet "who has no judgment" and styled him as a micromanaging military bureaucrat who, in the name of controlling his nine-month volunteers, developed the use of the court-martial as discipline into an art form. This assessment arose from Armstrong's close observation, in his role as judge advocate, of the general. Armstrong's opinions of Humphreys were so strong that he risked a libel action to publish *Red-Tape*, a thinly veiled fictionalization of his own experiences and observations, while the war still raged.

Andrew Humphreys had neither the military bearing nor the voice of a Hancock or a Hooker; nor did he have their down-to-earth rapport with troops, which helped to establish authority and respect. The general seemed to gloss over this deficiency, perhaps even make it a step on the path to martyrdom, as he wrote somewhat plaintively of his experience with the Pennsylvania volunteers:

> The life of a Division Commander is solitary, the chief satisfaction is in having your troops in good order, feeling that the officers know their duty, and will perform it without incessant overlooking and being reminded of it. It is acknowledged throughout this army that no officer did as much with troops of short term of service as I have done with these, and it is acknowledged at the same time that no one else would or could have done as much.[7]

Armstrong apparently disagreed with that assessment. In *Red-Tape* he plays on the irony of Humphreys's antipathy to the 129th, one of his better-disciplined regiments. Armstrong saw the root of the animosity in the snickering of the men after the yelping dog incident (pp. 153-

---

(7)    *Humphreys Biography*, 184.

154), Burnside's rebuke to the general for abandoning his men at attention (p. 203), and Humphreys's fussy management style and general inability to get along with his volunteer officers. He points out that Colonel Frick, a volunteer officer who had greater experience leading men in the field than Humphreys, was "restiff under the authority of an officer so poorly fitted for his position" (p. 205). This seems to be at odds with Humphreys's claim that "no one else would or could have done as much [with short-term volunteer troops]."

That Humphreys's attitude toward his troops was often considered more of an insult than an inspiration is pointed out by Maj. D. P. Marshall of the 155th in his report of Humphreys's speech prior to the battle of Chancellorsville:

> He had, we fancied, insulted us before going into the Chancellorsville battle. He had us drawn up in line so he could make us a speech. He began it by swearing, he ended it with swearing and he had oaths mixed all through it. He said: "You have come out to fight (we knew that), you must fight, and if you won't fight I'll make you fight." With the oaths mixed this was about all of his speech. We did not like to be branded cowards before we had met the enemy or shown any signs of cowardice. If the boys did forgive that speech, they never forgot it. He was like some wagon drivers, who stall before the team does, and the first intimation the team has of any danger of stalling is from the shouting and frothing of the driver.[8]

Armstrong indicated that by the end of his tenure Humphreys had so alienated his soldiers that "the ordinary salute in recognition of his rank was given grudgingly, if at all" (p. 248). Humphreys did receive a special kind of final salute on May 7, 1863, the night before the Allabach brigade left for home. The historian of the 155th Pennsylvania wrote:

---

(8)    D. P. Marshall. *Company K, 155th Pennsylvania Volunteer Zouaves.* (privately printed, 1887), 99-100.

[S]ome mischievous devils of the nine-month troops . . . the night before disbandment of the Division . . . gathered up their cartridges, and with the powder from the same laid a mine leading to General Humphreys' tent. This they ignited by a slow match, thus giving them time to escape before its explosion. The detonation caused a great excitement and a scattering of tin cans and bottles in the vicinity of the distinguished General's headquarters. The irascible General, thus aroused from his slumbers, called the provost guard and made an awful commotion in the camp, almost as much so as if the enemy had broken through. It was generally supposed that if the General had possessed the power, instead of deploying the peaceful One Hundred and Fifty-Fifth—a three-years regiment—to escort the nine-months troops to the station next morning, he would have enjoyed assigning that Regiment to the duty of shooting a couple of battalions of the nine-months' regiments of his late command for their terrible act of insubordination and violation of rules and regulations and articles of war so dear to one so rigid in the enforcement of the same.[9]

Some history recent to the soldiers may have inspired the selection of this particular parting celebration. Armstrong questioned Humphreys's military expertise and experience in *Red-Tape* when the general insisted that "friendly" explosions were enemy artillery (pp. 81-82). The "ground blasts" became something of an institution with the 131st Pennsylvania. Captain Orwig wrote in his history:

Of course an explosion was a most offensive noise to the order-loving commanders, as it is a signal for alarm, and they were justly indignant. But the severe discipline in the division had given offense which was shared largely throughout the division, and when this means of mischief was found to worry, and

---

(9)     *Maltese Cross*, 145.

offered protection through its secrecy, the setting of bombs became epidemic.

At first Humphreys threatened the commanders and officers-of-guard of the 131st, but their arrests were "so much fuel to the flame and [were] only enjoyed by the perpetrators of the offense." Work details for all members of the 131st were suggested, and this, Orwig reported, "worked like a charm." Of the final expression of displeasure, which presumably was the same as the one described by the 155th's historian, Orwig wrote, "a bomb had been placed under the very fly of the general's tent, the explosion of which covered him and his headquarters with a cloud of earth and dust, as a parting salute."[10]

In describing what he called a "troubled history," Orwig also recounted two incidents discussed previously in this commentary: the proposed execution of the mentally deficient private of the 155th (when Humphreys countered almost all of the senior volunteer line officers of his division and threatened to court-martial the "whole d—d establishment"); and the examination incident and the courts-martial of the lieutenants prior to the battle of Fredericksburg. Orwig concluded that "General Humphreys was an able and an accomplished soldier, but he had yet to learn, and did learn, many necessary but valuable lessons in his command of Pennsylvania Volunteers."[11]

With only two regiments of his Fifth Corps division left after the expiration of the nine-month regiments in May 1863, Humphreys needed a new command. Upon the death of Gen. Hiram Berry at Chancellorsville, General Hooker assigned Humphreys to the Second Division of the Third Corps (formerly the Hooker division). Humphreys seems to have expected a far different experience with the seasoned volunteers than what he had been through with the raw recruits when he wrote:

I understand General Hooker himself has done this, complimentary certainly, and to tell you the truth, the command of

---

(10)　Orwig, 183-185.
(11)　*Ibid.*, 57-58.

an old troop promises much less labor than I have had for the past eight months.[12]

The veteran volunteers, however, proved themselves to be just as difficult and critical as some of the short termers. Humphreys's stay with the old Hooker division was just fifty days, but it included a heavy engagement at Gettysburg and was certainly long enough for him to make an impression on his troops. Most of the complaints about him centered on the march to Pennsylvania to counter the Confederate invasion. As reflected in the regimental histories (and even in Humphreys's official reports), he kept the division marching for extremely long periods of time with few rests, and those brief stops were often taken in sun-baked fields. The debilitating marches, made primarily during the Virginia stage of the operation, produced many stragglers and victims of sunstroke. Units arrived piecemeal and required a lot of time for reorganization and resuscitation. The caustic Captain Blake of the Eleventh Massachusetts, which had been taking long, hard marches since first battle of Bull Run, wrote that "Caligula and other monsters of antiquity never displayed a more diabolical spirit than certain generals in the corps. . . . There is not more than one in ten officers of high rank that understands the proper mode of moving a division."[13] Blake did not include Humphreys or his own brigade commander, Joseph B. Carr, among the one in ten.

During one eighteen-hour march, Humphreys sent his men along the C & O Canal towpath instead of a paved road with the expectation that this would prevent straggling. The result, however, was just the opposite. In darkness and a driving rain the troops stumbled, slipped, and slid, often into the canal. The majority finally just lay down in the mud to await daylight, and the general, when he "had arrived at his goal [the mouth of the Monocacy River], had hardly enough men to form a respectable headquarters guard." This commentator, a captain in the

---

(12)  *Humphreys Biography*, 183-184.

(13)  Henry N. Blake. *Three Years in the Army of the Potomac*. (Boston: Lee & Shepard, 1865), 191-192. (Hereafter Blake)

Second New Hampshire, wrote that General Humphreys "can have full credit for the affair since no other general would contest for the 'honors' of this night's work."[14]

The comments of *Red-Tape*'s little Irish corporal about Old Pigey's meandering marches and Topographical Corps background (p. 2) may have related to Humphreys's somewhat humorous entry into Gettysburg on the night and morning of July 1 and 2, respectively. He led his troops along the wrong road, ignored the warnings of a local black man that they were marching into "heaps of rebels," and stumbled onto the edge of a Confederate camp near the Black Horse Tavern on the Fairfield-Hagerstown Road. The division had to backtrack very quietly "three long miles," and instead of joining the Third Corps on Cemetery Ridge in the early hours of the evening of July 1, it arrived at about 2 A.M. on July 2, a day that would prove to be a very long one.[15] General Humphreys blamed the near fiasco on Lt. Col. Julius Hayden of Daniel Sickles's Third Corps staff, who had been sent to guide them in.[16]

Later in the day, Humphreys led his division off Cemetery Ridge to a forward position on the Emmitsburg Road. The wisdom of and authority for Sickles's controversial realignment of the Third Corps would be argued for years. At the end of the day, Humphreys led his troops back to where they had started. In a fighting retreat, his division suffered casualties even greater than those of his Fifth Corps division at Fredericksburg.

Humphreys described the July 2 action:

> [T]he fire we went through was hotter in artillery and as destructive as at Fredericksburg. It was for a time positively terrific; the troops on my left retired, leaving me to catch it, my left flank being turned all the time; I had to retire, withdrawing my left flank and falling back on open ground under a precise and heavy artillery fire and infantry fire; twenty times

(14) Martin A. Haynes, *A History of the Second Regiment, New Hampshire Volunteer Infantry.* (Manchester, N. H.: C. F. Livingston, Printer, 1896), 134-135.

(15) Blake, 203.

(16) *Humphreys Biography*, 190.

did I bring my men to a halt and face about, myself and H[enry] and others forcing the men to it; . . .

The troops that were to support me were sent to others. As the last demands were made upon me to help others I remonstrated, but it was useless. Finally having driven back others, the enemy in my front advanced upon me, while those on my left having forced off our troops also gave their attention to me. I have lost very heavily.

When I reached the line of another corps my men advanced with them; the enemy were driven back and hundreds of prisoners taken and our troops got back close to the line I had occupied.[17]

Captain Blake, however, wrote that the First Brigade's participation in the Second Corps–led counterattack and capture of its old ground and artillery occurred despite Humphreys's orders to remain in place:

At this critical time, in obedience to a universal cry among the soldiers, "Charge on them!" "Take our old ground!" the fragment of the brigade, with the colors of five regiments unfurled within the distance of one hundred feet, in the absence of its general [Carr], and against the orders of General Humphreys, the division commander, who vainly shouted, "Halt, halt!— stop those men!" pursued the enemy half of a mile, captured several hundred prisoners, retook cannon that had been left upon the field, and assisted to achieve a conclusive success.[18]

Despite a lack of evidence that the generals had been in each other's company during the battle on July 2 except after the retreat to Cemetery Ridge, General Carr's report contained the following statement, which must have been greatly appreciated by Humphreys:

---

(17)   *Humphreys Biography*, 198.
(18)   Blake, 210-211. This version is also at odds with General Carr's report.

I may be pardoned, perhaps, for referring in my report to the conspicuous courage and remarkable coolness of the brigadier-general commanding the division during this terrific struggle. His presence was felt by the officers and men, as the enthusiastic manner in which he was greeted will testify.[19]

The general's wisdom in praising his commander may have paid off the following year when Carr's Senate confirmation was in doubt. There were a number of allegations of cowardice entered against Carr, yet he elicited a strong endorsement from his old commander.[20]

### Brave Warrior

So far as Humphreys's bravery is concerned, Armstrong wrote that it contained a manic element, which he uncharitably attributed in part to the general's liberal swigs at his canteen. Lieutenant Colonel Rowe of the 126th seems to have supported the manic diagnosis, as he observed that Humphreys was "brave to a fault," and "raving in front of the lines—urging the men on whilst pulling his holsters from under his dead horse."[21]

---

(19)  OR, Vol. XXVII, Part 1, 544. Humphreys's report is on pp. 529-537.

(20)  *Andrew A. Humphreys Papers, Vol. 18*, 93. Humphreys's response is contained in an article entitled "Sketch of General Carr," which ran in the Troy, New York, *Daily Times* on June 15, 1865. For a comprehensive description of Humphreys's and Carr's performances at Gettysburg on July 2 see Kevin O'Brien, "To Unflinchingly Face Danger and Death: Carr's Brigade Defends Emmitsburg Road," *The Gettysburg Magazine*, January 1, 1995. This article contains much material from Henry Blake, along with a more sympathetic treatment of Humphreys from the diary of Capt. Adolfo F. Cavada of Humphreys's staff.

(21)  *History of 126th*, 18.

Two members of the 155th attested to Humphreys's bravery in writings long after the fact. In 1908 S. W. Hills wrote that after the first charge of the Allabach brigade:

> The air was full of cannister and minies, cannon shot were sweeping close overhead. . . . Grim old General Humphreys was sitting on his horse in rear of the men, looking cross and savage. Col. [Edward J.] Allen was walking up and down the line.[22]

Albert L. Pearson, a major at Fredericksburg and a future general and brigade commander in the Fifth Corps, made this comment at a reunion in the 1890s:

> You thought, at the beginning, he was austere, and disposed to be tyrannical, but when you saw him in action, at Fredericksburg and at Chancellorsville, and discussed his many good qualities, dislike turned to admiration; for in him you found one who knew how to command, and whose bravery no one could for a moment question.[23]

Later in the war, in the spring of 1864, Lieutenant Colonel Lyman remarked on Humphreys's propensity to seek gunfire:

> You never saw such an old bird as General Humphreys! I do like to see a brave man; but when a man goes out for the express purpose of getting shot at, he seems to me in the way of a maniac![24]

(22)   *National Tribune*, April 16, 1908.
(23)   A. L. Pearson. Speech at Fourth Reunion of 155th Pennsylvania, in *Report of Fifth Reunion at Clarion, Pa.* (Pittsburgh: Rawshorne Engraving & Printing, 1896), 28.
(24)   Lyman Letters, 108.

Thomas L. Livermore, a member of Humphreys's Second Corps staff in late 1864, who described him as "a most determined fighter, a military savant, and as modest as, and more courteous, if possible, than a lady," noted that some of the more intimidated of his staff avoided his presence when he got too close to the action.[25]

John Barry observed that Humphreys's thirst for recognition as an exemplary soldier grew:

> And in combat Humphreys showed the iciness of a man who saw others as a means to his end. He displayed his temperament chiefly in letters to his wife, where a portrait emerges of a man enormously prideful and enormously sensitive to position, while his desire for glory showed itself in war.[26]

In *Red-Tape*, Armstrong has the "West Virginia Captain" (David Eckar of the 129th) sum up the issue of bravery by putting these words in his mouth: "There's no denying old Pigey was brave, but he was as crazy as a boy with a bee in his breeches" (p. 197).

### Court-Martial Mania

In a non-threatening, one-on-one social relationship Humphreys could be, as Armstrong readily acknowledged, a charming companion. When crossed, however, he was capable of great "malignity," a fact that Armstrong learned when he and Colonel Frick were brought up on charges for refusing to order their men, who had only a few months left to serve, to obtain expensive frock coats that would be worn only at dress parade. The fact that Humphreys went after one of his best officered and disciplined regiments and then after his most experienced

---

(25)   Thomas L. Livermore. *Days and Events, 1860-1865*. (Boston: Houghton Mifflin Co., 1920), 414.

(26)   Barry, 49.

and effective brigade commander gives substance to Armstrong's questioning of his judgment at this stage of his career. His actions endangered and adversely affected the military careers of all involved.

At his trial Armstrong declared in writing that his actions and those of Colonel Frick's were ill advised, but he argued that their cashiering was not justified "for what in its very worst light [was] but a simple blunder, made under extenuating circumstances." During the course of the trial Humphreys proved to be a strong character witness for the man he had brought up on charges when he testified that Armstrong had on previous occasions performed his duties "with promptitude, cheerfulness and great intelligence," and that "his intercourse with me had always been of the most courteous kind."

The court seized on this admission of error and regret and Humphreys's statement of Armstrong's previous good conduct to support a recommendation for "such degree of clemency as the Commanding General may think proper to extend to him." This gave Humphreys an opportunity to back off from the confrontation with the regimental officers with some grace, yet his reaction was to file charges against General Tyler. With this move he exacerbated the disruption in his command instead of quieting it. Moreover, the action brought Humphreys's name before the congress, Judge Advocate General Holt, Secretary Stanton, and even the president at a time when supporters of generals McClellan and the court-martialed Fitz-John Porter were a suspect commodity in official Washington.[27]

There were others in the division who questioned their commander's actions. For example, the men of the 131st Pennsylvania, in the Allabach brigade, although not immediately involved in the frock coat affair other than to surround the unhappy 129th with their cannister-loaded cannon, registered some sympathy for their compatriots. Captain Or-

---

(27)    *Humphreys Biography*, 166. See *Humphreys Biography*, 184, for Stanton's
        charge that Humphreys was a McClellan man and Humphreys's denial of the
        allegation, despite his August 1862 visit with McClellan at Alexandria.
        Humphreys was relatively silent on the major political issues of the day. He
        did lobby extensively in regard to his scientific projects, his career, and
        promotions.

wig, historian of the 131st, wrote that there was "no more gallant regiment in the service than the 129th in the recent battle of Fredericksburg and the subsequent courts-martial of some of its officers was generally condemned as a most inconsiderate act."[28]

Since Humphreys's career to that point had been almost exclusively that of a staff topographical engineer with minimal command responsibility, the concept of the court-martial was quite new to him. Had he commanded men in the field before the war, he might have been more acquainted (and perhaps even bored) with such affairs and not so concerned with strict adherence to regulations and the interpretations of "[his] French authorities" (p. 47).

## A Sublime Ego

General Humphreys's ego seemed to expand rapidly during the post-Fredericksburg period, perhaps bolstered by the attention he received from the press after the battle and the euphoria that resulted from his successful introduction to command in combat. While he was court-martialing the officers of the 129th and General Tyler for reasons which might appear to be primarily reflections of his personal pique, he was also demanding a promotion to major general, even going so far as to declare to General Meade that he would quit the service if it were not forthcoming.

Evidence of growing tension was revealed in a letter from Humphreys to Joseph Hooker, the new commanding general of the Army of the Potomac, in early March 1863:

A letter that I received last night from Washington makes it certain that the two persons who visited me under pretense of a friendly regard for me as well as for General Tyler—went

(28) Orwig, 178.

immediately to the President of the United States taking some
Penna politicians with them and, regardless of the truth, made
some secret allegations respecting my loyalty. This I know from
a conversation Senator [Solomon] Foot of Vermont had with
the President the day following, when he found him strongly
prejudiced by these statements.[29]

In 1860 Humphreys, then a captain, had served with Senator Foot
on a board of officers charged with "revis[ing] the program of instruction
at the Military Academy." Also on this board was Jefferson Davis, with
whom Humphreys had been friendly since Davis, as secretary of war,
had assigned him to work on the Pacific railroad route project in 1854.
Humphreys's son wrote that "from his well-known friendship for Mr.
Davis, [Humphreys] was suspected of sympathizing with the South."[30]
This no doubt added to the tension.

Abundant evidence supports the idea that Humphreys, throughout
his career, was particularly—even obsessively—concerned that he get
the credit and/or promotions that he believed were his due. When, after
the battle of Fredericksburg, he learned that General Tyler had sent his
own report to Governor Curtin, Humphreys sent a letter to the governor
requesting that the report be returned. The letter makes it clear what
Humphreys considered to be "pernicious" in Tyler's report. He noted
that Tyler "omits all mention of the three successive orders he received
from me" and that "I desire now to state explicitly . . . that I was present
with those troops throughout the whole of the time they were in action,
and commanded them throughout in person."[31]

The battle of Chancellorsville was hardly over before Humphreys and
Tyler were again sniping at each other, in part because Tyler had
studiously avoided mentioning his commanding officer in his reports.
Humphreys fired the first shot by stating in his official report that his
division had been delayed one hour in reaching Chancellorsville "by the

(29)　*Humphreys Papers*, March 7, 1863 (Vol. 36), 24.
(30)　*Humphreys Biography*, 147.
(31)　General Correspondence, Office of the Adjutant General, Department of
　　　 Military Affairs, Pennsylvania State Archives, Harrisburg.

tardiness of the First Brigade, a tardiness General Tyler attributed to the fatigue of the men."[32]

Humphreys returned Tyler's report with instruction to correct his "statement to accord with the fact that he received the order to support Major-General French from Brigadier-General Humphreys, through his assistant adjutant general, Captain McClellan." Tyler responded, "Respectfully reforwarded with the remark that the order was received from Major-General Meade in the very language used in this report, and upon that order my command was put in motion." McClellan then returned the report with instruction to "state whether he did or did not receive from Brigadier-General Humphreys (through Capt. McClellan) . . . an order to support Major-General French." The report was again forwarded by Tyler, who noted,

> I am informed by one of my staff that while on the march, in execution of the order received from Major-General Meade, Captain McClellan rode up to me. He may have repeated the order received from Major-General Meade, but I have no recollection of hearing it from him, and have but a very faint idea of seeing him, the order from General Meade being of such an urgent character that my attention was given entirely to its prompt execution.

In the sixth and final endorsement, Humphreys himself gave his version of the facts, having received no amended report from the equally stubborn Tyler.[33]

Humphreys's propensity to protest lack of credit or acknowledgment also surfaced in his protest after the battle of Malvern Hill, when he maintained that he, not Gen. J. G. Barnard, was the officer who established the Union defensive line. He also objected to the Gettysburg reports of Hancock and Birney; he engaged in substantial correspon-

---

(32)   OR, Vol. XXV, Part 1, 546.
(33)   *Ibid.*, 551-553.

dence with them in October 1863 in which they usually yielded to his persistent pleas of injustice to him and his division.[34]

After his death, Humphreys's "correction of the record" effort was carried on by his son Henry, Carswell McClellan, and others. Humphreys's friend, General Warren, who was coordinating the effort to gain vindication for his own treatment by Gen. Philip H. Sheridan and Grant at Five Forks, wrote to Joshua Chamberlain regarding one of Chamberlain's lectures on Appomattox, saying, "In any allusion to the surrender I would be careful not to slight Genl. H by claiming too much for the Fifth Corps, for Genl. H is ready to fight on our side any time."[35]

## Military and Scientific Micromanager

In his farewell appraisal of his division General Humphreys noted that his greatest satisfaction was "feeling [that] the officers know their duty, and will perform it without incessant overlooking," yet it appears that throughout his career he was, as Armstrong suggested, slow to delegate and a believer in the use of hands-on supervision that might today be termed micromanagement. Armstrong noted that Humphreys's intensive review of courts-martial records was taking him away from more important work, pointing out that "T's must be crossed when we ought to be crossing the Potomac; I's dotted when we ought to be dotting Virginia fields with our tents" (p. 48).

General Birney wrote, "Humphreys, the chief of staff, is what we call an old granny, a charming, clever, gentleman, fussy and unused to troops."[36] Humphreys's perceived fussiness and other strange characteristics bothered line officers such as Armstrong and Birney, both of

---

(34)  *Birney Letters.* Brake Collection. U.S. Army Military History Institute, Carlisle, Pa.
(35)  *Chamberlain Papers,* Letter of November 12, 1879.
(36)  Letter to George Gross, October 1863. U.S. Army Military History Institute.

whom were unhappy with the clique of engineer officers running the Army of the Potomac.

In one instance, Humphreys's proclivity for supervising every detail produced an unintended and very unhappy result at Fredericksburg, according to the historian of the 155th:

> Colonel [Edward J.] Allen, with that solicitude for his men which marked his whole service, made a detail of the very youngest and least sturdy looking boys of the Regiment to guard the knapsacks, which had been unslung and piled up just preparatory to the advance and charge on Marye's Heights. General Humphreys, who seemed ubiquitous in making his final preparations for the "forlorn hope," soon after discovered half a dozen boys hanging round the piled-up knapsacks, a short distance from the troops, and in his excitement, ignorant that the boys had been detailed there by Colonel Allen, indignantly and profanely ordered the knapsack guards to report at once to their companies, insinuating most unjustly that they were a lot of skulkers. Two of the boys thus ordered to their companies in less than half an hour later were killed in the charge ordered.[37]

In one rather significant deviation from his usual practice, the "ubiquitous" general was not in attendance during the Tyler brigade engagement on Sunday, May 3, at Chancellorsville. Armstrong wrote in *Red-Tape* that Humphreys "reports as a reason for his absence today, that he did not consider it prudent to be near our Brigade during the loading and firing exercise," but then added that "our men, as true soldiers, know but one enemy in the field" (p. 246).

Humphreys was with the Allabach brigade, which supported the artillery during the May 3 fighting. Most of its casualties occurred in the 133rd and the 155th regiments, which were ordered to support the

---

(37)   *Maltese Cross*, 97.

Second and Third Corps, which were then withdrawing from the Chancellorsville area. According to Humphreys's report:

> [The two regiments] advanced their skirmishers, engaging those of the enemy, to the ground they were directed to occupy. Upon their near approach to it, the enemy opened upon them with shell and cannister. The new position of the two corps having been taken up, the two regiments retired slowly through the woods . . . losing 1 officer and 3 enlisted men killed and 1 officer and 30 enlisted men wounded.[38]

The historian of the 155th describes the operation in a more graphic fashion:

> The military term for the duty of these two regiments is called "feeling the enemy" but, in point of fact, it proved to be the enemy feeling them. . . . At the first advance into the woods, the enemy evidently did not know of the approach of the two regiments and no shots were fired. A rather humorous incident took place at this time, Major Pearson, deeming it a proper occasion to imitate General Humphreys' inspiring address to the 155th, made a speech demanding that each man stand up to his work; that no hiding behind trees or holding back should take place, etc. He had scarcely finished his impassioned oratory when the enemy, discovering the presence of the two regiments in the woods, opened out as brisk a grape and cannister and musketry fire as they did on Marye's Heights; so that without express orders every man in the 155th fell flat on the ground, including the redoubtable Pearson, who, his men afterwards claimed, got a little nearer down, and hugged mother Earth a little closer than his men. The range, however, of the Confederate artillery and musketry was all above the heads of the prostrate men. Soon the enemy ceased firing and

---

(38)   OR, Vol. XXV, Part 1, 548.

jumping over their breastworks advanced to capture the deployed troops. General Humphreys, however, who was present
and on the alert to the situation, ordered the men . . . to arise
instantly and retreat as promptly and rapidly as they could, so
that the fifty-four pieces of artillery under Captain Steven H.
Weed could let loose their fire on the pursuing foe.[39]

Humphreys's dedication to detail, which the volunteers saw as un-
productive, bureaucratic red tape, could be viewed as a continuation of
his prewar scientific management style, which is revealed by a description of how he carried out his study of the Mississippi Delta:

> Captain Humphreys gave the closest personal attention to the
> work . . . passing from one to the other [of the three work
> parties] continuously and correcting all omissions or misappre-
> hensions. His written instructions, which have never appeared
> in print, are most minute, and might well serve as models in
> conducting similar work. They cannot fail to impress the
> reader with his firm grasp of the subject and his care to include
> every element which might enter into the ultimate discussion
> of the results. These arduous labors performed under a burning
> sun, for which his sedentary life in Washington had ill pre-
> pared him, were suddenly terminated by a *coup de soleil* in the
> summer of 1851. . . . After the loss of the master spirit, the
> operations soon fell into confusion.[40]

Toward the end of the summer of 1851 Humphreys became more and
more intense and obsessive as it was rumored that Charles Ellet, a civilian engineer and rival who had a grant from Congress to do a similar
study, had finished his report. Humphreys "stopped writing to his wife
because it distracted him. . . . He tongue-lashed his assistants for

---

(39)  *Maltese Cross*, 137-138.
(40)  Henry Larcom Abbot. "Memorial to Andrew A. Humphreys." Address before
the National Academy of Sciences, April 24, 1885. Monograph.

speaking with outsiders, even though they had simply been trying to glean information about Ellet. [However], he himself talked to reporters. He basked in their attention, basked in their portrayal of him as a major figure so much that his superiors reprimanded him for talking so much to the press."[41]

His superior officer, Lt. Col. Stephen Long, wrote in a letter, "With poor Humphreys, mental labor produces agitation, bordering on distraction."[42] Humphreys finally collapsed and was confined to bed in Philadelphia when Ellet submitted his report. His recovery took years, during which he took a restful tour of Europe studying river deltas and performing other engineering assignments.[43]

At his private expense Humphreys attacked Ellet's report, and he swore that he would complete his own work. "He had become not merely Ellet's rival now, but his enemy."[44] He did not, however, return to the Delta Survey until 1857. In March of 1861 he requested relief from his other assignments to give his time "exclusively to the work of his life, 'The Physics and Hydraulics of the Mississippi River.' " He finished it just after the first battle of Bull Run. Once again, as in the Mexican War, it appeared that Humphreys's highest priority was his scientific work and reputation. While First Bull Run was raging, he was in a Washington office building finishing his report and attacking Charles Ellet. When the report was submitted to the secretary of war shortly after the battle, Humphreys had a thousand copies printed privately so that it would not be lost in the chaos of Washington.[45]

With the report filed and copies distributed to the "learned Societies of this country and those of Europe," Humphreys emerged from his Washington office building opposite the War Department and announced his availability for more active military service. His son explained that "bad health at this period of the year, May and June, prevented his entrance upon military duty in the field," and after a "system

---

(41)   Barry, 44.
(42)   Delta Survey, Record Group 77, National Archives.
(43)   *Humphreys Biography*, 141-153.
(44)   Barry, 45. Barry concluded that the act reflected a "nervous breakdown," 44.
(45)   *Humphreys Biography*, 154; Barry, 47.

of training to fit himself for the field," he sought such duty in October 1861. "Officers of the Army were assigned to the care of public buildings ... to which they are to repair in times of danger. Humphreys, probably through a request of Professor Joseph Henry, was placed in charge of the Smithsonian Institution."[46]

Humphreys had been made a major in August 1861 and rose to colonel when he was appointed to McClellan's staff as his chief topographical officer in March 1862. He became a general of volunteers in April 1862.

Interestingly, it could be argued that the civilian Ellet also beat Humphreys in the race to combat and glory. Ellet convinced the army of the feasibility of using rams in the fighting on the Mississippi early in 1862, and he, as a nautical colonel, successfully led four of his rams and six gunboats against a Confederate fleet off Memphis on June 6. The unit wiped out the Confederate boats, and Ellet's son raised the Stars and Stripes over Memphis. Ellet was the only Union casualty, dying from injuries two weeks later. His son subsequently took command of the ram fleet, but he, too, was dead within a year.[47]

### Chief of Staff of the Army of the Potomac and Commander, Second Corps

During the march to Gettysburg Meade asked Humphreys to become chief of staff of the Army of the Potomac, but it was agreed that the transfer would not take place until after the battle. Humphreys was made a major general when he entered into his new assignment on July 8, 1863, yet his promotion was not confirmed by the Senate for almost

---

(46)   Ibid., 155-156.
(47)   James M. McPherson. Battle Cry of Freedom. (New York: Oxford University Press, 1988), 417-418.

a year. Apparently General Tyler and some of the Pennsylvania volunteers fought it with vigor and some effectiveness.

Humphreys wrote of his appointment to his wife on July 16, 1863:

> I prefer infinitely the command of troops. . . . at the first opportunity I shall leave it, and if necessary to do will send my Major General's Commission, and take the Brigadier general. I cannot bear to be without command.[48]

Meade appreciated Humphreys's ability to plan campaigns and to execute the important job of receiving and sending dispatches under the pressures of battle. As it turned out, Humphreys served as Meade's chief of staff for the next fifteen months and would never again command a division. Within a few months of taking the position, his attitude had changed:

> When I think how much depends upon this Army of the Potomac, I recognized that the command of it is the most important command in the country, and the position of Chief of Staff is no mean place in that army; . . . I prefer command of course, but hardly the command of a division.[49]

Humphreys continued in this staff capacity until November 1864, when he was given command of the Second Corps, which he led with distinction through the Appomattox campaign. He remained in command until the corps was disbanded on July 12, 1865. He had been sounded out earlier by Grant for command of the Tenth Corps, of which almost half were black troops, but Humphreys wrote "that I could not have such a feeling for any other than my own race and my own people and that therefore I preferred not to command the corps he mentioned."[50]

---

(48)  *Humphreys Biography*, 201.
(49)  *Ibid.*, 205.
(50)  *Humphreys Biography*, 241. See also *Mutiny at Brandy Station*, 177-178, for a fuller discussion of this incident.

### Back to the Corps of Engineers

In 1865 Humphreys briefly commanded the Department of Pennsylvania, with headquarters in his hometown of Philadelphia, but late that year he returned to his prewar army career to conduct a study of the levees on the Ohio and Mississippi rivers. On August 8, 1866, he was placed in charge of the Corps of Engineers as a brigadier general in the regular army.

At this point in his life, in a somewhat strange way, Humphreys's Mississippi Delta Survey played a major role in his future and that of the Corps of Engineers. Some of the negative personality traits that Armstrong noted in *Red-Tape* apparently accompanied Humphreys to his postwar assignment. Martin Reuss, historian of the Corps of Engineers, wrote:

> With a worldwide reputation, largely resulting from the widespread dissemination of the Mississippi Delta report, Humphreys was unquestionably in the perfect position to enhance both his reputation and that of the corps. Ironically, events took a different course. Humphreys oversaw and partly caused a decline, not an increase, in the corps' influence. He defended his report before both the political and engineering communities and came to identify attacks on the report as attacks on the corps itself. . . . Conservative by nature, possessing an ego largely untouched by failure, and convinced of the soundness of his position, Humphreys became increasingly frustrated and defensive in the face of changing political and engineering concepts. The more he was attacked, the less willing he

seemed to modify his position. Tragically for the corps, it was this inflexibility that became his main legacy, rather than the scientific dedication to truth that had characterized his report on the Mississippi. An examination of his career and its effect on the Army Corps of Engineers shows how a bureaucracy can be crippled when it elevates theory to dogma and forgets that scientific research is, by definition, innovative and not stagnant.[51]

Barry describes the new chief of engineers:

Ironically, by then there was no scientist left within him. Only the soldier remained. He cared now only about obedience, power, and rank. Rank in particular obsessed him. . . . He began lobbying congressmen to make the chief of engineers a major general. . . .

Inside the Corps his rule was absolute. He sought to have all engineering officers formally "detached" from the Army, thus making them answerable only to him. . . . Humphreys tolerated no criticism. And even less would he tolerate a rival. But a rival far more formidable than anyone he had ever encountered was emerging.[52]

The rival was James Buchanan Eads, a self-made engineer who had been able to deliver gunboats and ships of quality in quantity to the Union cause. He was Humphreys's equal in determination and intelligence and, probably, his superior in charm. Both were always immaculately dressed. Eads pursued his ends with disciplined ferocity, which to many seemed rigid and unreasonable, but the trait helped him "succeed

---

(51)   Martin Reuss. "Andrew A. Humphreys and the Development of Hydraulic Engineering: Politics and Technology in the Army Corps of Engineers, 1850-1950," *Technology and Culture: Quarterly of the Society for the History of Technology.* (Chicago: University of Chicago Press, January 1985), 4. (Hereafter Reuss)

(52)   Barry, 55-56.

in any mechanical proposition suggested. . . . [At] plan[ning] and execut[ion], no man was his equal."[53] He and Humphreys would fight over Eads's proposed bridge over the Mississippi at St. Louis and whether the Mississippi River Commission should be created. In the main, Eads was the winner.

In 1878 Humphreys resigned from the National Academy of Sciences because one of its boards had recommended the establishment of a Geological Survey Office, which Congress implemented. The following year, over his strenuous objection, Congress also created the Mississippi River Commission, which reduced the corps's influence on river and flood control policy. This spurred his retirement from service.[54]

Humphreys retired from the army on June 30, 1879, having served as head of the Corps of Engineers for thirteen years. He spent his last years writing his two histories of the Army of the Potomac—*From Gettysburg to the Rapidan* and *The Virginia Campaign of '64 and '65*. The latter was published just before his death in Washington on December 27, 1883.

Statues of the general stand on both the Fredericksburg and Gettysburg battlefields. The monument at Marye's Heights was dedicated on November 11, 1908; the keynote speech was delivered by Col. Alexander K. McClure, a Pennsylvania politician who was a close associate of both Governor Curtin and President Lincoln during the war. Somewhat appropriately, an extinct volcanic mountain near Flagstaff, Arizona, was named in honor of the volatile general.

---

(53)   Statement of Emerson Gould quoted in Barry, 29.
(54)   Reuss, 14-15.

## Final Reckoning

### *Jacob G. Frick*

Colonel Frick returned home to Pottsville, Pennsylvania, when the 129th was mustered out, yet his military career was not quite concluded. He had been a civilian for less than a month when Governor Curtin asked him to raise a militia regiment to help repel Lee's invasion of Pennsylvania. Frick was mustered in as the colonel of the Twenty-seventh Emergency Militia on June 22, 1863, accompanied by many of his old staff and men. Former adjutant David Green was the lieutenant colonel, Captain Fried of Company D was the major, and the "little Dutch Doctor," Otto Schittler, was the regimental surgeon.

The unit was assigned to guard the crossings of the Susquehanna River from Columbia to the Connawingo Bridge. On June 24 Frick arrived at Columbia and set up a defensive line on the south side of the river, on both sides of the York Turnpike near Wrightsville. Three days later York surrendered to Gen. Jubal Early's forces. Four days later the Confederates' lead brigade, under Gen. John B. Gordon, was facing Frick's troops. The colonel's command was a hodgepodge of militia regiments, some convalescent soldiers from York, the Patapsco Guards, and a "negro company, the other [three white] companies from Columbia having left for their homes." Frick wrote in his official report:

[The Confederates] depended exclusively upon their artillery to drive us from our position here. Having no artillery, ourselves on that side of the river with which to reply, and after retaining our position for about one and a quarter hours, and discovering that our remaining longer would enable the enemy to reach the river on both my flanks, which I was unable to prevent because of the small number of men under my command, and thus get possession of the bridge, cut off our retreat, and secure a crossing of the Susquehanna. . . . I retired in good order, and crossed the bridge to the Lancaster side.

Before the enemy had left York for the river here, I made, as I supposed, every necessary arrangement to blow up one span of the Columbia Bridge. . . . [A]fter I supposed every man of my command was over the river, and when the enemy had entered the town with his artillery, and reached the barricade at the bridge-head, I gave the order to light the fuse, but our object in blowing up the bridge failed. It was then that I felt it to be my duty, in order to prevent the enemy from crossing the river and marching on to Harrisburg in the rear, destroying on his route railroads and bridges, to order the bridge to be set on fire. The bridge was completely destroyed, though a vigorous attempt was made to save a part by the soldiers.[1]

The destruction of the bridge was also described in a letter published in the October 24, 1863, edition of the *Miners Journal*:

The bridge burned for several hours, presenting a grand spectacle as span after span was consumed, the burning embers falling hissing into the water. Thousands of citizens witnessed the fire with a sense of relief, for the passage of the river could now be contested by our small force.

---

(1)　OR, Vol. XXIX, Part 2, 278-279.

INVASION OF PENNSYLVANIA—ACTION AT WRIGHTSVILLE AND DESTRUCTION OF THE COLUMBIA RAILROAD BRIDGE, JUNE 28.—FROM A SKETCH BY OUR SPECIAL ARTIST, A. BERGHAUS.

*Invasion of Pennsylvania—action at Wrightsville*
*and destruction of the Columbia railroad bridge.*

Colonel Frick considered that of all his military acts, "I esteem that at Columbia the greatest because of the results flowing from it." Jubal Early's original orders were to burn the Columbia Bridge, but he had broadened his plan by the time he reached York and realized there would be only a feeble defense by the militia. He reported that he

> determined to cross the Susquehanna, levy a contribution on the rich town of Lancaster, cut the Central Railroad, and then move up in rear of Harrisburg while General [Richard S.] Ewell was advancing against that city from the other side. This scheme, in which I think I could have been successful, was, however, thwarted by the destruction of the bridge, as there was no other means of crossing the river.[2]

---

(2)    Jubal A. Early. *War Memoirs: Autobiographical Sketch and Narrative of the War between the States.* (Baltimore: Nautical & Aviation Publishing Co., reprint 1989), 259.

Gordon wrote that while passing through York he was given a bouquet of roses with a note describing Frick's defenses at Wrightsville. It pointed to a ravine on the left flank of the defenses. "Not an inaccurate detail in that note could be discovered," he reported. "I did not hesitate, therefore, to adopt its suggestion of moving down the gorge."

He described the bridge fire and the Confederates' attempt to control it with a call on the citizens for "buckets and pails." None were found, "but when the burning bridge fired the lumber-yards on the river's banks, and the burning lumber fired the town, buckets and tubs and pails and pans innumerable came from their hiding-place, until it seemed that, had the whole of Lee's army been present, I could have armed them with these implements to fight the rapidly spreading flames."[3]

Frick was mustered out a month later. After the war he was engaged in the manufacture of wire screens in Pottsville.[4] In 1892 Frick was awarded the congressional medal of honor for gallantry in action at Fredericksburg and Chancellorsville. The citation declared:

> At Fredericksburg he seized the colors and led the command through a terrible fire of cannon and musketry. In a hand-to-hand fight at Chancellorsville, he recaptured the colors.[5]

Jacob Frick died in Pottsville on March 5, 1902, and is buried in the Presbyterian cemetery. His gravesite is kept up by the Schuykill County Civil War Discussion Group.

(3)     John B. Gordon. *Reminiscences of the Civil War*. (New York: Charles Scribner's Sons, 1905), 134-144, 147-148. Gordon, as a U.S. senator from Georgia, visited Frick in Pottsville on November 23, 1895. They recounted the Wrightsville Campaign and bridge burning to an overflow audience.

(4)     Bates, 178-180, 833-844. Frick's military career, including the Susquehanna action, is described.

(5)     *Medal of Honor Recipients, 1863-1978*. (U.S. Senate Committee on Veterans Affairs), 91.

### Erastus B. Tyler

After his brigade in the Fifth Corps was dissolved, General Tyler, probably not viewed with any particular favor by the current leadership of the Army of the Potomac, was put in charge of the defenses of Baltimore. He was soon joined in this quasi-military exile by Maj. Gen. Lew Wallace, who had lost favor with Grant at Shiloh. Tyler and Wallace took part in one more significant military event before the war ended—the battle of Monocacy in July 1864. Like Colonel Frick's last battle, Tyler also faced the forces of Jubal Early in defense of a crucial bridge.

General Wallace, commander of the Eighth Corps, ordered Tyler's command to Monocacy Junction on the outskirts of Frederick. Tyler's First Separate Brigade was made up of the First and Third Potomac Home Brigades, the Ohio National Guard (one-hundred-day men mustered to guard the railroads), and the Eleventh Maryland Infantry Brigade, newly recruited in Baltimore. The Third Division of the Sixth Corps, commanded by Maj. Gen. James B. Ricketts, was ordered by Grant to leave the Petersburg front to reinforce the troops at the Monocacy. The Confederates and Ricketts's division arrived at about the same time, on July 8-9. Ricketts was assigned to the left and center of the defensive line, to guard the road to Washington, and Tyler was given the right wing, to protect the road to Baltimore. Tyler's troops were centered at the Jug Bridge, a stone bridge built early in the century. Wallace burned the covered bridge on the road to Washington, but the Confederates found a ford and attacked Ricketts's division. By the end of the day they had broken through the Union forces. Wallace told Tyler that he must continue to hold the Jug Bridge until the retreating Union army passed behind him and reorganized on the Baltimore Turnpike. In his autobiography Lew Wallace relates his conversation with Tyler using his postwar, *Ben Hur* literary style, far different from his official report:

*The stone demijohn is all that remains of the Jug Bridge, constructed in 1808 over the Monocacy on the Baltimore Turnpike. Legend has it that there is a keg of whiskey inside the ten-ton, ten-foot monument. The demijohn was moved to a little park on Route 40, two miles south of Frederick, in 1965.*

"That work, general, you must do. In other words, upon you more than any other man I can think of now depends whether we are not all enclosed in the woods and killed or taken like a herd of sheep."

"You want me to hold the bridge?"

"Yes, until Ricketts and his men gain the pike and are advanced well towards New Market; in fact, I want it until the enemy following Ricketts through the woods show themselves in your rear."

"And then?" he asked.

"Let your men cut their way out, all who can—not a difficult thing to a regiment like [Col. Charles P.] Gilpin's and [Capt. Charles J.] Brown's [commanders of the First and Third Potomac Home Brigades], since the pursuers will be in disorder and few in numbers when they reach the pike. Should there be any who cannot cut their way out, order them to disperse, every man for himself, with New Market or Monrovia for rendezvous. It will be desperate work. What do you say?"

I watched General Tyler closely; and there was revelation of the man in his answer, simple, without bravado, unmelodramatic: "I will go to the bridge now, picking up my men on the way. They will not be needed except at the bridge."

General Wallace concluded that Tyler's "gallantry and self-sacrificing devotion are above all commendation of words."[6]

The Jug Bridge force held out until the army passed behind it toward New Market. Tyler then pulled his troops back to the east side of the bridge, and a portion of them were able to rejoin the main retreating Union forces on the Baltimore Turnpike. Tyler and his staff were cut off and hotly pursued by Confederate cavalry along the east bank of the Monocacy to Liberty Road, where they turned toward Baltimore. At the village of Mount Pleasant they encountered more Confederate cavalry, and another wild chase ensued. Tyler and two of his staff escaped by releasing their riderless horses and hiding in a forest with the help of a black civilian. The following Monday they were rescued by Union cavalry, who recaptured Frederick as Jubal Early moved on to Fort Stevens on the outskirts of Washington.[7]

General Tyler remained in command of the First Separate Brigade stationed around Baltimore until June 1865 and was mustered out in August. He was one of the brigadiers who was brevetted a major general of volunteers "for gallant and meritorious service during the war."

Tyler, who was married to a Baltimore woman, remained in that city after the war. He was in private business for a time but was then appointed postmaster of Baltimore by Rutherford B. Hayes. When President Garfield was elected, Tyler was replaced; perhaps Garfield was still unhappy about Tyler's successful campaign for colonel of the Seventh

(6)     Lew Wallace. *An Autobiography.* (New York: Harper & Brothers, 1906), 787-800; OR, Vol. XXXVII, Part 2, 215.

(7)     E. Y. Goldsborough. *Early's Great Raid.* (Frederick Historical Society, undated), 26-27.

Ohio. Erastus Tyler died on January 9, 1891, in a suburb of Baltimore and was buried in Green Mount Cemetery in Baltimore, as were seven Union generals and eight Confederate generals, led in rank by Joseph E. Johnston.[8]

## Other Officers of the 129th Pennsylvania

**William H. Armstrong** returned to his law practice in Easton and wrote *Red-Tape* in the last six months of 1863. He was appointed deputy secretary of the commonwealth under Governor Curtin during the later phases of the war. The balance of his life was spent as a practicing attorney in Easton, except for a brief period of practice in Philadelphia in the 1870s. He continued his writing, and in addition to *Red-Tape*, he wrote a number of sketches and stories that appeared in newspapers under the pen name William Henry. He was active in politics, and, according to his obituary, his "voice was often heard on the stump in behalf of Republican candidates." He suffered from chronic rheumatism which dated from the 'camp fever' he picked up during his incarceration at Falmouth in 1863, and he became totally blind a number of years before his death in 1896.[9]

**Joseph Anthony's** chest and lung wound suffered at Chancellorsville was quite debilitating; "he was not able to perform the lightest manual labor and not able to keep accounts or write a letter" and needed a constant attendant. He went on disability compensation in 1882. The

---

(8)    Obituary, *Baltimore Sun*, January 10, 1891 (Supplement), 4; Ezra J. Warner. *Generals in Blue*. (Baton Rouge: Louisiana State University Press, 1964), 515; Susan C. Sonderberg. *Lest We Forget: A Guide to Civil War Monuments in Maryland*. (Shippensburg, Pa.: White Mane Publishing Co., 1995), 15-21.

(9)    Obituary, *Easton Semi-Weekly Free Press*, April 19, 1896; Military and Pension Records, National Archives.

records show that he was receiving compensation in 1888 and that his widow died in 1910.

**David B. Green,** as noted earlier, joined Colonel Frick and served as the lieutenant colonel of the Twenty-seventh Emergency Militia. When the Twenty-seventh was mustered out he returned to his practice of law in Pottsville. In 1867 Gov. John Geary appointed him the presiding judge of the new criminal court of Schuykill, Dauphin, and Lebanon counties. In 1874 he was transferred to the Court of Common Pleas of Schuykill County; he was reelected twice to that position before his death in 1893.

**Otto Schittler,** the "little Dutch Doctor," also served in the Twenty-seventh Emergency Militia. After the war he practiced medicine in Philadelphia and then moved to Fremont, Nebraska, perhaps in the hope that his no-nonsense bedside manner would be more appreciated there. When Armstrong wrote in *Red-Tape* about the Dutch doctor's ride on his new horse (pp. 125-126), he could not have known that Schittler's inability to stay on a horse would become contentious long after the war.

Schittler eventually returned to Philadelphia and in 1885 applied for disability compensation for a hernia. He alleged that the injury had occurred in November 1862 at Warrenton and involved a horse he had borrowed from the chaplain and used to pick up some medical supplies. His primary corroborating witness should have been surgeon Joseph Rossiter, but he had died soon after the war. The examination of the claim for compensation by a skeptical government was extensive, and the depositions of many of the leading characters in *Red-Tape* appear in the file. The sworn statements of Armstrong and Frick, who testified that the doctor had complained about the injury very soon after the end of the war, were probably the most persuasive. They also testified with great certainty that Schittler was a lousy horseman. The Board of Re-Review, as it was formally named, finally awarded Schittler a pension in 1888.[10]

In the 1890s Schittler returned to his beloved Tyrol.

**William H. Rice,** the chaplain, returned initially to his church in Bethlehem. At the time of his deposition in Schittler's pension case in 1886 he was the pastor of a Moravian church in New York City.

**David Eckar,** the West Virginia captain, returned to Easton after the war. He too applied for a disability pension in the 1880s, on the basis of chronic rheumatism resulting from the malarial fever he had contracted immediately after the battle of Fredericksburg, when the tents, blankets, and knapsacks were abandoned in the town.

**Edgar Gregory** and his Ninety-first Pennsylvania continued in the Fifth Corps, in Sykes's division. In July of 1864 he was given command of the Second Brigade, First Division of the Fifth Corps. He was promoted to brigadier general in September 1864 on the basis of his performance at Poplar Spring Church. He served until November 1865 and was brevetted a major general for his conduct at Five Forks. After the war Gregory served in the Freedmen Bureau and as a U.S. marshal. He died in Philadelphia on November 7, 1871, and was buried in Laurel Hill Cemetery. His grave was recently marked with a new headstone.[11]

**Peter Allabach's** primary occupation after the war was as a captain in the U. S. Capitol Hill Police. He was appointed to this position in 1878 and served until his death on February 11, 1892.[12]

---

(10)   Pension Records, National Archives.
(11)   Roger D. Hunt and Jack R. Brown. *Brevet Brigadier Generals in Blue.* (Gaithersburg, Md.: Olde Soldier Books, 1990), 241; *Civil War News,* February/March 1995, 77.
(12)   Orwig, 239.

# Select Bibliography

Agassiz, George R., ed. *Meade's Headquarters, 1864-1865: Letters of Col. Theodore Lyman from the Wilderness to Appomattox.* Boston: Atlantic Monthly Press, 1922.

Alexander, Ted. *The 126th Pennsylvania.* Shippensburg, Pa.: Beidel Printing House, 1984.

Arner, Frederick B. *The Mutiny at Brandy Station, The Last Battle of the Hooker Brigade: a Controversial Army Reorganization, Courts Martial, and the Bloody Days that Followed.* Kensington, Md.: Bates & Blood Press, 1993.

Badeau, Adam. *Military History of U. S. Grant.* New York: D. Appleton & Co., 1888.

Barry, John M. *Rising Tide: The Great Mississippi Flood of 1927 and How It Changed America.* New York: Simon & Schuster, 1997.

Basler, Roy P., ed. *Collected Works of Abraham Lincoln.* New Brunswick, N.J.: Rutgers University Press, 1953.

Bates, Samuel P. *History of the Pennsylvania Volunteers, 1861-1865.* Harrisburg, Pa.: B. Singerly, State Printer, 1870.

_____. *Martial Deeds of Pennsylvania.* Philadelphia: T. H. Davis & Co., 1876.

*Battles and Leaders of the Civil War.* New York: Thomas Yoseloff, 1952.

Billings, John D. *Hardtack and Coffee.* Boston: George M. Smith & Co., 1887.

Blake, Henry N. *Three Years in the Army of the Potomac.* Boston: Lee & Shepard, 1865.

Botkin, B. A., ed. *A Civil War Treasury of Tales, Legends and Folklore.* New York: Random House, 1960.

Bradley, Edwin Stanley. *Simon Cameron, Lincoln's Secretary of War.* Philadelphia: University of Pennsylvania Press, 1967.

Caldwell, Robert G. *James A. Garfield.* New York: Dodd, Mead & Co., 1931.

Catton, Bruce. *Glory Road: The Bloody Route from Fredericksburg to Gettysburg.* Garden City, N.Y.: Doubleday & Co., 1952.

Collins, Darrell L. *The Battles of Cross Keys and Port Republic.* Lynchburg, Va.: H. E. Howard, Inc., 1993.

Condit, Uzal W. *The History of Easton, Pennsylvania, 1739-1885.* Easton, Pa.: George W. West, 1886.

D'Arcy, William. *The Fenian Movement in the United States: 1858-1886.* Washington, D.C.: Catholic University Press, 1947.

Dana, Charles A. *Recollections of the Civil War.* New York: Collier Civil War Classics, 1899.

David, Donald H. *Lincoln.* New York: Simon & Schuster, 1995.

Davis, O. W. *Life of David Bell Birney.* Philadelphia: King & Baird, 1867.

Davis, Washington. *Camp-Fire Chats of the Civil War.* Boston: B. B. Russell, 1887.

Denney, Robert E. *Civil War Prisons & Escapes.* New York: Sterling Publishing Co., 1993.

DePeyster, J. Watts. *Andrew Atkinson Humphreys of Pennsylvania.* Lancaster, Pa.: Intelligencer Print, 1886.

De Trobriand, Regis. *Four Years in the Army of the Potomac.* Boston: Tichnor & Co., 1889.

Duram, James C., and Eleanor A. Duram, eds. *Soldier of the Cross: Civil War Diary and Correspondence of Rev. Andrew Jackson Hartsock.* Manhattan, Kans.: Military Affairs/Aerospace Historian Publishing, 1979.

Early, Jubal A. *War Memoirs: Autobiographical Sketch and Narrative of the War between the States.* Baltimore: Nautical & Aviation Publishing Co., reprint 1989.

Freeman, Douglas Southall. *Lee's Lieutenants.* New York: Charles Scribner's Sons, 1942.

Furgurson, Ernest B. *Ashes of Glory.* New York: Alfred A. Knopf, 1996.

_____. *Chancellorsville, 1863.* New York: Alfred A. Knopf, 1992.

Gibbon, John. *Personal Recollections of the Civil War.* New York: G. P. Putnam & Sons, 1928.

Golay, Michael. *To Gettysburg and Beyond.* New York: Crown Publishers, Inc., 1994.

Gordon, John B. *Reminiscences of the Civil War.* New York: Charles Scribner's Sons, 1905.

Gorham, George C. *Edwin M. Stanton: Life and Public Services.* New York: Houghton Mifflin & Co., 1899.

Gramm, Kent. *Gettysburg: A Meditation on War and Values.* Bloomington, Ind.: Indiana University Press, 1994.

Grant, U. S. *Personal Memoirs, Vol. 2.* New York: Charles Webster Co., 1885.

Hanchett, William. *The Lincoln Murder Conspiracies*. Urbana, Ill.: University of
    Illinois Press, 1983.

Harrison, Noel G. *Fredericksburg Civil War Sites*. Lynchburg, Va.: H. E. Howard, Inc.,
    1995.

Haynes, Martin A. *A History of the Second Regiment, New Hampshire Volunteer
    Infantry*. Manchester, N.H.: C. F. Livingston, Printer, 1896.

*History of the Fifth Massachusetts Battery*. Boston: Luther E. Cowles Publishers, 1902.

Howe, Mark De Wolf, ed. *Touched with Fire: Civil War Letters and Diary of Oliver
    Wendell Holmes, Jr.* Cambridge, Mass.: Harvard University Press, 1947.

Humphreys, Andrew A. *From Gettysburg to the Rapidan*. New York: Charles
    Scribner's Sons, 1883.

_____. *The Virginia Campaign of '64 and '65*. New York: Charles Scribner's Sons,
    1883.

Humphreys, Henry H. *Andrew Atkinson Humphreys: A Biography*. Philadelphia: John
    C. Winston, 1924.

_____. *General Andrew A. Humphreys at Fredericksburg and Farmville*. Chicago:
    R. R. McCabe & Co., 1896.

Hunt, Roger D., and Jack R. Brown. *Brevet Brigadier Generals in Blue*. Gaithersburg,
    Md.: Olde Soldier Books, 1990.

Johnston, Allen, and Dumas Malone. *Dictionary of American Biography*. New York:
    Charles Scribner's Sons, 1944.

Jones, Terry L. *Lee's Tigers*. Baton Rouge, La.: Louisiana State University Press, 1987.

Keller, S. Roger. *Civil War in Washington County, Maryland*. Shippensburg, Pa.:
    Beidel Printing House, Inc., 1995.

Kiefer, W. R. *History of the One Hundred and Fifty-third Regiment, Pennsylvania
    Volunteer Infantry*. Easton, Pa.: Chemical Publishing Co., 1909.

Krick, Robert K. *Conquering the Valley: Stonewall Jackson at Port Republic*. New York:
    William Morrow & Co., 1996.

Lord, Francis A. *They Fought for the Union*. Harrisburg, Pa.: Stackpole Co., 1960.

Livermore, Thomas L. *Days and Events*. Boston: Houghton Mifflin & Co., 1920.

MacCall, Seamus. *Irish Mitchel: A Biography*. London: Thomas Nelson & Son, 1938.

Marshall, D. P. *Company K, 155th Pennsylvania Volunteer Zouaves*. Privately printed,
    1887.

Marvel, William. *The Battle of Fredericksburg*. Conshohocken, Pa.: Eastern National
    Parks and Monuments Association, 1993.

McClellan, Carswell. *General Andrew A. Humphreys at Malvern Hill and
    Fredericksburg*. St. Paul, Minn.: privately printed, 1888.

_____. *The Personal Memoirs and Military History of U. S. Grant vs. the Record of the Army of the Potomac*. Boston: Houghton Mifflin & Co., 1887.

McClellan, George B. *McClellan's Own Story*. New York: C. L. Webster & Co., 1887.

McClure, Alexander K. *Abraham Lincoln and Men of War Times*. Philadelphia: Times Publishing Co., 1892.

McKinney, Folger. *History of Frederick County, Maryland*. L. R. Titworth & Co., 1910.

Meade, George. *The Life and Letters of General George Gordon Meade*. New York: Charles Scribner's Sons, 1913; Baltimore: Butternut & Blue, reprint 1994.

Orwig, Joseph R. *The History of the 131st Pennsylvania Volunteers*. Williamsport, Pa.: Sun Book Printing House, 1902.

Pearson, A. L. Speech at Fourth Reunion of 155th Pennsylvania. In *Report of Fifth Reunion at Clarion, Pa*. Pittsburgh: Rawshorne Engraving & Printing, 1896.

Pfanz, Henry W. *Gettysburg: The Second Day*. Chapel Hill, N.C.: University of North Carolina Press, 1987.

Porter, Horace. *Campaigning with Grant*. Bloomington, Ind.: Indiana University Press, 1961.

Powell, William H. *The Fifth Army Corps: A Record of Army Operations During the Civil War, 1861-1865*. New York: G. P. Putnam's Sons, 1896.

Reader, Frank S. *History of the Fifth West Virginia Cavalry Formerly the Second Virginia Infantry*. New Brighton, Pa.: Daily News, 1890.

Reardon, Carol. "The Forlorn Hope: Gen. Andrew A. Humphreys' Pennsylvania Division at Fredericksburg." In *The Fredericksburg Campaign*, edited by Gary Gallagher. Chapel Hill, N.C.: University of North Carolina Press, 1995.

Reese, Timothy J. *Sykes' Regular Infantry Division, 1861-1864*. Jefferson, N.C.: McFarland & Co., 1989.

Reid, Whitelaw. *Ohio in the War, Vol. 1*. New York: Moore, Wilstach, & Baldwin, 1868.

Robertson, James I. Jr., ed. *The Civil War Letters of General Robert M. McAllister*. New Brunswick, N.J.: Rutgers University Press, 1965.

_____. *The Stonewall Brigade*. Baton Rouge, La.: Louisiana State University Press, 1963.

Rowe, David W. *A Sketch of the 126th Regiment Pennsylvania Volunteers Prepared by an Officer, and Sold for the Benefit of Franklin County Soldiers' Monumental Association*. Chambersburg, Pa.: Cook & Hayes, 1869.

Sauers, Richard A. *Advance the Colors: Pennsylvania Civil War Battle Flags, Vol. 2*. Harrisburg: Capitol Preservation Commission, 1991.

Schaff, Morris. *The Battle of the Wilderness*. New York: Houghton Mifflin & Co., 1910.

Schildt, John W. *Four Days in October.* Self-published, 1978.

_____. *Mount Airy: The Grove Homestead.* Self-published.

Sears, Stephen W. *Chancellorsville.* Boston: Houghton Mifflin & Co., 1996.

Shannon, Fred A. *The Organization and Administration of the Union Army, 1861-1865.* Cleveland: Arthur H. Clark Co., 1928.

Simon, John Y., ed. *Papers of Ulysses S. Grant.* Carbondale, Ill.: Southern Illinois University Press, 1967.

Sonderberg, Susan C. *Lest We Forget: A Guide to Civil War Monuments in Maryland.* Shippensburg, Pa.: White Mane Publishing Co., 1995.

Taylor, John M. *Garfield of Ohio.* New York: W. W. Norton & Co., 1970.

*Under the Maltese Cross: Antietam to Appomattox, the Loyal Uprising in Western Pennsylvania, 1861-1865, Campaign of 155th Pennsylvania Regiment Narrated by the Rank and File.* Pittsburgh: Regimental Association, 1910.

Wallace, Lew. *An Autobiography.* New York: Harper & Brothers, 1906.

Walker, Francis A. *History of the Second Army Corps.* New York: Charles Scribner's Sons, 1887.

Warner, Ezra J. *Generals in Blue.* Baton Rouge, La.: Louisiana State University Press, 1964.

Weaver, Ethan Allen. *Easton and Vicinity in the Civil War.* Easton, Pa.: Easton Area Public Library, 1936.

Wentz, Abdel Ross. *History of the Evangelical Lutheran Church of Frederick, Maryland, 1738-1938.* Harrisburg, Pa.: Evangelical Press, 1938.

Whan, Voren E., Jr. *Fiasco at Fredericksburg.* Gaithersburg, Md.: Olde Soldier Books, 1961; reprint 1994.

Wilson, James H. *Sketch of General Humphreys.* Mass.: Military Historical Society of Massachusetts, 1895; Wilmington, N.C.: Broadfoot Publishing Co., reprint 1989.

## Government Publications and Files

United States Army. Office of Judge Advocate General Files, Record Group 153, Courts-Martial transcripts; Record Book 2, National Archives, Washington, D.C.

United States Congress. *Biographical Directory of the American Congress 1774-1949.* House Doc. No. 607, 1950.

United States War Department. *The War of the Rebellion: A Compilation of the Official Records of the Union and Confederate Armies.* Washington, D.C.: Government Printing Office, 1880-1991.

## Monographs

Abbot, Henry Larcom. "Memorial to Andrew A. Humphreys." Address before the National Academy of Sciences, April 24, 1885.

"Dedication of Monument to Commemorate the Charge of General Humphreys' Division." Philadelphia: J. B. Lippincott Co., November 11, 1908.

"Schuykill County in the Civil War." Pottsville, Pa.: Historical Society of Schuykill County, 1961.

## Articles

O'Brien, Kevin. "To Unflinchingly Face Danger and Death: Carr's Brigade Defends Emmitsburg Road." *The Gettysburg Magazine*, January 1, 1995.

Reuss, Martin. "Andrew A. Humphreys and the Development of Hydraulic Engineering: Politics and Technology in the Army Corps of Engineers, 1850-1950." *Technology and Culture: Quarterly of the Society for the History of Technology.* University of Chicago Press, January 1985.

Round, Harold F. "A. A. Humphreys: A Personality Profile." *Civil War Times Illustrated,* February 1966.

Ward, David A. "Of Battlefields and Bitter Feuds: The 96th Pennsylvania Volunteers." *Civil War Regiments: Journal of the American Civil War,* Vol. 3, No. 3, 1993.

## Periodicals

*Baltimore* (Md.) *Sun.* January 10, 1891.

*Easton* (Pa.) *Argus.* July 1862–May 1863.

*Easton* (Pa.) *Free Press.* January–April 1863.

*Easton* (Pa.) *Semi-Weekly Free Press.* April 19, 1896.

*Easton* (Pa.) *Express.* December 1862.

*Harrisburg* (Pa.) *Daily Telegraph.* February 10, 1862.

*Miners Journal,* Pottsville, Pa. November 1862–May 1863.

*National Tribune.* 1892–1893.

*Philadelphia Press.* November 13, 1862.

## Manuscript Collections

Birney, David B. Letters. Brake Collection. United States Army Military History Institute, Carlisle, Pa.

Cavada, Adolfo. Diary. Historical Society of Pennsylvania, Philadelphia.

Chamberlain, Joshua L. Papers. Manuscripts Division, Library of Congress.

Christiancy, Henry Clay. Diary. United States Army Military History Institute, Carlisle, Pa.

Horn, Luther. Diary. Easton Area Public Library, Easton, Pa.

Hass, Jacob. Letters. Northampton County Historical Society, Pa.

Hostetter, Richard. Manuscript: "History of the 129th Pennsylvania Volunteer Infantry." Unpublished manuscript, property of the author.

Humphreys, Andrew A. Papers. Historical Society of Pennsylvania, Philadelphia.

Meade, George G. Papers. Historical Society of Pennsylvania, Philadelphia.

Nicholson, John L. Papers. Huntington Library, Pasadena, Calif.

Quay, Matthew. Papers. Manuscripts Division, Library of Congress.

Werkheiser, Martin K. Manuscript. Fredericksburg National Park Library, Fredericksburg, Va.

## Acknowledgments

In my efforts to unmask the characters in *Red-Tape* and match the happenings related in the book with the real activities of the 129th Pennsylvania Volunteer Regiment, I was extremely fortunate to meet Charles Joyce, who has done considerable research on the 129th's role in the battle of Fredericksburg. His help has been invaluable. It's always good to have a Philadelphia lawyer on your team.

The two Mikes at the National Archives were essential to this undertaking. Michael Musick called *Red-Tape* to my attention initially, and Michael Meier pointed out provocative information on General Humphreys as head of the Corps of Engineers.

In Pennsylvania, the local experts on the 129th have my thanks. Rev. Richard A. Purnell and Rich Hostetter helped identify some of the players and provided valuable materials necessary to tell the full story of the regiment. Mr. Hostetter generously suppled a preliminary draft of his history of the 129th for my enlightenment.

Frank A. O'Reilly, a talented U.S. Park Service historian, provided additional insight into Humphreys's relationship with his soldiers. He is writing the history of the battle of Fredericksburg and working on editorial notes for *Under the Maltese Cross*, the history of the 155th Pennsylvania.

The illustrations come from the Library of Congress, the National Archives, and the U.S. Army Military History Institute at Carlisle, Pennsylvania. The staffs at each of these places were, as usual, very cooperative and patient. Rosemary Hall was my capable photographic assistant.

The drawing on the dust jacket is from the Ann S. K. Brown Military Collection, John Hay Library, Brown University. My thanks to Peter Harrington.

The historical societies of Northampton and Schuykill counties in Pennsylvania and Frederick, Maryland, were of great assistance, as was the Historical Society of Pennsylvania, which houses the Andrew Humphreys Collection. The Thomas Balch Library in Leesburg, Virginia, was a source of Loudoun County lore, as was the ultimate expert on Loudoun, the late John Devine.

Clark B. "Bud" Hall helped identify people and houses in the Rappahannock area, and John Schildt, through personal contact and his writings, provided valuable information on the Shepherdstown/Sharpsburg area. Jerrilyn Eby supplied background on houses in Stafford County, Virginia.

Finally, my thanks to Katherine Tennery of Rockbridge Publishing for her decision to publish this unusual book and to tolerate, edit, and arrange my accompanying lengthy explanatory materials. Tracey Barger, assistant to the publisher, provided both skill and patience in helping to bring this book into being.

# Index